Michael C. McIntyre

Emory Symposia in Cognition 1

Concepts and conceptual development:
Ecological and intellectual factors in
categorization

Concepts and conceptual development: Ecological and intellectual factors in categorization

Edited by
ULRIC NEISSER

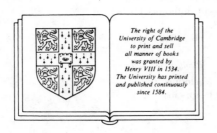

The right of the
University of Cambridge
to print and sell
all manner of books
was granted by
Henry VIII in 1534.
The University has printed
and published continuously
since 1584.

CAMBRIDGE UNIVERSITY PRESS
Cambridge
London   New York   New Rochelle
Melbourne   Sydney

Published by the Press Syndicate of the University of Cambridge
The Pitt Building, Trumpington Street, Cambridge CB2 1RP
32 East 57th Street, New York, NY 10022, USA
10 Stamford Road, Oakleigh, Melbourne 3166, Australia

First published 1987

Printed in the United States of America

Library of Congress Cataloging-in-Publication Data
Concepts and conceptual development.
(Emory symposia in cognition ; 1)
Papers from the First Emory Cognition Project
Conference, held Oct. 11–12, 1984.
Includes index.
1. Categorization (Psychology) – Congresses.
2. Environmental psychology – Congresses.
3. Cognition – Congresses.   I. Neisser, Ulric.
II. Emory Cognition Project Conference (1st : 1984 :
Emory University)   III. Series.
BF445.C66   1987   153   86-30740

British Library Cataloguing in Publication Data
Concepts and conceptual development :
ecological and intellectual factors in
categorization
1. Concepts
I. Neisser, Ulric
153.2′3   BF311

ISBN 0 521 32219 7

Contents

Preface

This is the first of a projected series of volumes to appear under the sponsorship of the Emory Cognition Project. Because the work of the Project is especially focused on the ecological approach to cognitive psychology, we hope that each volume will serve a dual purpose: not only to present a state-of-the-art summary of research and theory on a particular issue, but to show what an ecological approach can contribute to that state and that art. I believe that this collection of papers on *Concepts and Conceptual Development* achieves both of those aims.

Something close to a consensus seems to be emerging in the study of concepts – a set of assumptions broad enough to make sense to cognitive scientists of many different theoretical orientations, and still so new that it has not yet appeared in textbooks. I do not mean that there are no more disagreements. Many serious differences were aired at the conference that gave rise to this volume, and they remain apparent in the chapters ahead. Nevertheless, those differences seem to lie within an accepted overall framework – a framework that (in my view) includes at least the following propositions:

- categories are never defined by objective similarity alone, but always in relation to what are – in some sense – theories or models;
- nevertheless, perceptual similarity plays a critical role in categorization, especially early in development and especially for "basic-level" categories;
- it is essential to distinguish among (a) the processes by which individual objects are categorized, (b) the gradients of "typicality" that appear so regularly in modern studies of category structure, and (c) the meaning of the category itself;
- language plays a key role in establishing categories, both developmentally and culturally.

All these points are elaborated in subsequent chapters.

This new consensus has arisen in the aftermath of what I like to call the "Roschian revolution" – the radical reformulation of the study of categories that was brought about by the work of Eleanor Rosch in the 1970s. It seems to me that the spirit of Rosch's work was essentially ecological. She and her collaborators – especially Carolyn Mervis – were interested in culturally existing rather than experimentally designed categories; moreover, they were more concerned with describing the actual structure of those categories than with modeling the cognitive processes of category users. Their discoveries – particularly the discovery that natural categories always have a graded structure (i.e., include more and less typical exemplars) – left the "classical" theory of concepts in a shambles. To say that an object is a *chair* (or a *bird,* or any such category term) is evidently not a matter of claiming that the object has just exactly a certain set of defining features. But – as we shall see – neither is it just a matter of the object's overall similarity to a certain prototype. What is it, then, to be a chair? A new – and still at least partially ecological – way of thinking about such questions has gradually taken shape since the Roschian revolution. By now, it seems to have crystallized into the framework of assumptions described above.

This book is the final product of a process that began in my first year at Emory University, when Larry Barsalou and I decided to offer a graduate seminar entitled "Concepts and Conceptual Development." By a fortunate coincidence Douglas Medin was at Emory in that spring of 1984, and agreed to join us in leading the seminar. A lively group of faculty, graduate students, and regular visitors soon formed; among the most stimulating was Bob McCauley, who had just arrived to join the Emory Philosophy Department. From the first, we were determined to examine the *development* of categorization as well as the structure of adult or expert categories; the Emory Cognition Project is committed to the principle that the study of cognitive development is an integral part of the study of cognition itself. We were also determined not to let traditional disciplinary boundaries interfere with our pursuit of the issues: psychologists, philosophers, linguists, and anthropologists have all made important contributions to the study of categorization.

Although the primary purpose of the seminar was to gain the best possible understanding of categorization, we soon developed a secondary goal as well: to identify individuals who were doing interesting and important work in the area, so that we could invite them to come and talk with us. Our discussions eventually resulted in the first Emory Cognition Project Conference, held on October 11–12, 1984: *The Ecological and Intellectual Bases of Categorization.* The Conference was an extraordinary intellectual experience for all of us: collegial, stimulating, and – somewhat to our own surprise – ultimately coherent.

After a meeting, a book: each chapter of the present volume is an expanded version of a talk given at the 1984 conference. I believe the contributors have largely succeeded in preserving the force of their ideas through the transition from speech to print, and hope that through this book their readers may experience some of the same intellectual excitement that characterized the Conference itself. For me the entire experience, from the first plans for our seminar to the final preparation of the manuscript, has been a very rewarding one.

I am deeply grateful to all the contributors to this book, not just for their hard work and their cheerful compliance with my demands but even more for having such good ideas and being willing to share them with us. It has been a pleasure to work with Susan Milmoe and the Cambridge University Press in what I hope is the beginning of a continuing relationship. The graduate students in the concept seminar deserve a special note of appreciation, especially those who helped out with so many concrete details of the conference: Robert Soloway, Jody Usher, Dan Sewell, Juliana Lancaster. Most of all I am grateful to Emory University for its consistent support of me and my work, for making the Emory Cognition Project possible, and generally for making me feel so welcome here. Thanks!

Ulric Neisser

Contributors

LAWRENCE W. BARSALOU is Assistant Professor of Psychology at Emory University.

LEE R. BROOKS is Professor of Psychology at McMaster University.

ROBYN FIVUSH is Assistant Professor of Psychology at Emory University.

FRANK C. KEIL is Professor of Psychology at Cornell University.

GEORGE LAKOFF is Professor of Linguistics at the University of California, Berkeley.

ELLEN M. MARKMAN is Professor of Psychology at Stanford University.

ROBERT N. MCCAULEY is Assistant Professor of Psychology at Emory University.

DOUGLAS L. MEDIN is Professor of Psychology at the University of Illinois, Champaign-Urbana.

CAROLYN B. MERVIS is Associate Professor of Psychology at the University of Massachusetts, Amherst.

ULRIC NEISSER is Robert W. Woodruff Professor of Psychology at Emory University.

WILLIAM D. WATTENMAKER is a Research Associate in Psychology at the University of Illinois, Champaign-Urbana.

1

Introduction: The ecological and intellectual bases of categorization

ULRIC NEISSER

To categorize is to treat a set of things as somehow equivalent: to put them in the same pile, or call them by the same name, or respond to them in the same way. Psychologists have been studying categorization for over sixty years. (See Woodworth, 1938, and Bourne, 1966, for useful reviews.) During most of that time – until the mid-1970s – they showed little interest in the linguistic and cultural categories that people use every day – in *chair* or *dog* or *tool* or *star*. Their research was concerned instead with so-called "concept formation": the process by which individuals acquire new category terms. It was implicitly assumed that all categories, regardless of their origin and structure, are acquired in much the same way. Given this assumption, concept formation could be studied in whatever domain and with whatever methods were most convenient. In the upshot it was usually studied by presenting artificial and meaningless stimuli, trial by trial, to college-age laboratory subjects.

Concept formation was not the only area of psychological research dominated by the use of artificial materials and contrived tasks. The classical theories of "learning," for example, were rarely applied to learning as it occurs in fields or forests or homes or schools. They were concerned instead with "basic mechanisms" – mechanisms assumed to be so basic that they could be studied in virtually any species and with virtually any task. The predictable result was a focus on conveniently available species (rats, pigeons, homo sapiens) and contrived tasks (maze running, lever pressing). A similar line of reasoning prompted students of human memory to ignore almost everything that people ordinarily remember. Their research did not deal with places or stories or friends or life experiences, but with lists of syllables or words. Given the tacit assumption that all forms of memory are basically the same, the attractive possibilities of experimental control led to a preference for meaningless materials and unnatural learning tasks from the first.

A preference for artificial and decontextualized stimulus materials was long apparent even in the study of perception, a field otherwise less influenced by positivistic assumptions. This preference was supported

1

both by prevailing philosophical assumptions about sense-data (if the visual system operates by assembling meaningless fragments anyway, why not present it with such fragments in our experiments?) and by apparently incontrovertible facts from sensory physiology. The structure of the visual system was well known: the lens of the eye focuses an image on the retina, where it impinges on millions of receptors that are connected to the optic nerve and thus to the brain. When such a receptor is stimulated by a ray of light, a neural signal is dispatched to higher centers. What could be more scientifically sound than to present such receptors with points of light or single lines, preferably while the eye itself was motionless? If more complex processes had to be studied, the stimulus materials should be kept as simple and convenient as possible: outline drawings were popular for this purpose. Almost no one studied the kinds of looking involved in routine human activities like walking or driving, reaching, catching thrown balls, or examining the nearby environment.

These "artificialist" views are now everywhere in retreat. The change came first in the field of animal behavior, where the study of species-specific behavior patterns – initially in the animal's own habitat and then often in laboratory studies designed with natural behavior in mind – now takes firm precedence over the use of standardized boxes and mazes. It is also well under way in the study of memory, where stories, scripts, and general knowledge became acceptable memory materials in the 1970s; school learning and autobiographical experience are achieving that status in the 1980s. Moreover, in perception, where the old views had been longest and most deeply entrenched, they have been challenged in the most fundamental possible way. In *The Senses Considered as Perceptual Systems* (1966), James J. Gibson insisted that the visual system had not evolved to deal with fixed punctate stimuli: it is tuned instead to the complex optical structures that are created as animals move through their environments in the presence of ambient light. The study of perception should then begin with an analysis of those environments, and of the information they make available – information that is much more specific than has usually been supposed. Gibson's analysis led him to a reformulation of perceptual theory that has become widely influential, though it is far from being universally accepted.

Meanwhile, the study of concepts and categories has not stood still. Here too, the first step was an essentially ecological one: to examine and describe the categories that are used in everyday experience. That step was taken in a series of brilliant studies by Eleanor Rosch and her collaborators (Rosch 1973; Rosch & Mervis 1975; Rosch et al. 1976). Their work demonstrated the existence of two distinct kinds of structure. *Within* a given category, some members are usually regarded as especially good or typical examples; the very best are called "prototypes." Other members of the category are relatively more marginal, and the category boundary is often poorly defined. The prototypical *chair,* for example, is the four-legged straightbacked kind often seen in dining rooms. Modernistic single-pedestal armchairs are much less typical of the category, while beanbags and barstools hardly count as chairs at all. We now know that this "graded structure" appears in every kind of category, although, as Barsalou shows in Chapter 5 of this book, it is appreciably less stable than Rosch originally supposed.

Across categories there is often a hierarchical structure with several levels: *animal, dog, collie,* for example. Most such hierarchies include an objectively identifiable "basic level," at which the categories (*dog, cow, mouse, . . .* or *chair, table, bed, . . .*) are most distinct from one another by perceptual and functional criteria. We learn basic-level categories first: almost all the nouns used by young children are at the basic level. Later, we acquire the superordinate (*animal, furniture, . . .*) and subordinate (*armchair, high chair, . . .*) categories that our particular culture has established. Within each category, we learn the prototypes long before we can correctly classify the marginal cases. In this way, the development of effective category use ("concept formation"?) is partly driven by the ecological distribution and characteristics of the to-be-categorized domain itself.

Rosch's work may be regarded as a first step toward a theory of categorization consistent with the ecological approach: it established basic facts about the structure of cultural and linguistic categories. Since that time, a new interdisciplinary grouping of scholars interested in those facts has begun to take shape. These scholars include not only psychologists but also philosophers and anthropologists and linguists: representatives of other fields that have long been concerned with understanding the meanings of category terms. The resulting discussions have made it clear, however, that no adequate theory of categorization can be based only on characteristics of the categorized objects themselves. The claim that something is a *dog* does more than assert some degree of similarity to a prototype; it also appeals to our underlying intuitions and beliefs about the nature of animals. The effect of these beliefs is to make some similarities between objects decisive and others simply irrelevant. Categorization has an intellectual as well as an ecological basis.

This book is an attempt to take the next step. It is the product of a symposium held at Emory University in October 1984, the first symposium sponsored by the Emory Cognition Project.[1] A principal goal of the Cognition Project is to explore the implications of the ecological approach for issues in cognitive psychology: categorization was an obvious place to start. The participants were not selected for their commitment to an ecological point of view, however; far from it. They were selected because their work is at the forefront of the modern study of concepts and categories, and they were encouraged to address the most fundamental issues. I think this book will show that they succeeded in doing so.

Of the ten essays that follow, my own Chapter 2 is the most explicitly ecological in orientation. This does not mean, however, that I believe categories are defined by the environment alone or that categorizing can be treated as just another form of perceiving. On the contrary, Chapter 2 distinguishes sharply between perception and categorization. The former is based on the direct pickup of objectively existing information, while the latter goes beyond that information on the basis of beliefs about the world. This distinction is hardly new – language and common sense have both long insisted that seeing and thinking are different – but I have not stressed it in earlier theoretical ventures.[2] Now, however, the charms of parsimony no longer outweigh what seem to be elementary facts. Seeing is one thing, thinking another.

Though separate in principle, perception and conceptualization are often tightly intertwined. This is especially true at the basic level, where we *both* see directly what things are *and* have theories that tell us how they should be classified. My chapter explores these relations, drawing heavily on the work of Gibson, Rosch, Frank Keil, and George Lakoff. It ends by proposing a definition of "category" that is formally similar to Gibson's concept of "affordance," though very different in its terms. To categorize an object, I believe, is to assert that it bears a particular relation to a particular set of ideas.

Although Douglas Medin and William Wattenmaker also stress the importance of ecological factors in Chapter 3, their treatment of the mental models or "theories" on which categories depend is more thorough and systematic than mine. Medin and Wattenmaker's argument is very much in the tradition of the modern ("post-Roschian") experimental study of categories,[3] but they are concerned to demonstrate the inadequacy of the theoretical proposals that have dominated that field up to now. They insist that notions like "correlated attributes" and "similarity" can never be adequate to explain the structure of categories because attributes can only be defined – and similarity can only be scaled – with reference to particular theories. If theories are really fundamental to categorization, however, we will need some basis for preferring one theory to another. Medin and Wattenmaker conclude their chapter with a thoughtful discussion of this difficult issue.

George Lakoff, too, underscores the importance of theories in categorization; he calls them "idealized cognitive models." In Chapter 4,

Lakoff insists that one or more such models lies behind every cultural and linguistic category. He describes several different types (metonymic models, radial models), illustrating them with compelling linguistic examples. Lakoff suggests that the "graded structure" discovered by Rosch and Mervis – the fact that some members of a category are taken as prototypical while others are only marginal – appears because our models do not quite fit the world as it really is. The less typical exemplars of a category are those where we sense that the idealized model does not fit as well as it should, and hence are less comfortable about applying it.

Lakoff is certainly not a traditional realist; he explicitly discounts the importance of any "objectively-existing properties of objects completely external to human beings." Nevertheless, the effect of his argument is to remind us not only of the wealth of existing cognitive models but also of the richness of the real world to which they refer. It seems to me that a complete understanding of categories and concepts may be impossible without an equally complete understanding of that world itself. That would mean, of course, that it is a goal which can never be fully achieved. This limitation gives us a further reason to distinguish between the study of perception on the one hand and of categorization on the other: the aims of the former study may be more attainable than those of the latter. Perceptual systems are tuned to certain definite forms of information, which in turn specify relatively definite, local, and ecologically relevant state of affairs. Those states are complex, but perhaps they are not complex without limit; some day we may really understand how they are specified to perceivers. But our conceptual systems have a far wider scope; for all we know, there may be no limit to what forms they can take and what domains they can encompass.

The brain is wider than the sky,
For – put them side by side –
The one the other will contain
With ease – and you beside.[4]

In Chapter 5, Lawrence Barsalou reports surprising new findings about "typicality" ratings like those reported by Rosch and her collaborators. Typicality, it seems, is typically quite variable. Subjects' judgments of the degree to which a given object is typical of a category are not very stable, and intersubject agreement on typicality is much lower than earlier findings had suggested. Slight changes of task or instruction – requiring subjects to adopt different points of view, or even just asking them to justify their responses – can produce major changes in the ratings. Given this degree of variability, it is hard to imagine that typicality ratings reflect important properties of fixed mental representations. Barsalou believes that there are no such fixed representations at all. Instead, new representations are constructed as the need for them arises. The omnipresent graded structure is then a by-product of that process of construction.

In Chapter 6, Lee Brooks introduces a new element into the discussion. Brooks is not so much concerned with the definitions of categories as with how we go about categorizing the particular objects that may come before us. He suggests that we often do so nonanalytically, simply by virtue of the object's resemblance to another that was seen on an earlier occasion. To determine that the creature bounding toward us is a dog, for example, we need not compare it to some canine prototype that we have accumulated over the years; neither do we have to weigh its properties against those of an idealized canine cognitive model. It is enough to see that the beast looks much like Rover, who used to live next door. Rover was certainly a dog, so this beast is very likely a dog as well.

Although the experiments Brooks cites to support this claim are largely based on artificial tasks and materials, the claim itself is by no means incompatible with an ecological approach. The mechanism he describes is primarily applicable to categories that have a perceptual basis; in everyday experience, that means to categories at the basic level. For such categories it may well be true that some single past experience – perhaps the most recent one – can affect our immediate response more than the accumulated sum of many others. Brooks takes this phenomenon to mean that individual traces of past experiences are exerting individual effects, but other interpretations are possible: one might say, for example, that the tuning of the perceptual system is affected most strongly by what it did most recently.

Frank Keil's Chapter 7 is the first of four developmentally oriented chapters. Keil begins by describing a major change that occurs in any transition from naivete to expertise, at any age: the "characteristic-to-defining shift." What shifts is the basis of categorization. Younger children (and novices in general) tend to rely on well-known characteristic features; older children (and experts in general) use more sophisticated criteria. In the case of nominal kinds like *island* or *uncle,* those criteria may actually include explicit definitions. In the case of natural kinds like *skunk* or *raccoon* they tend to be theoretical assumptions instead – assumptions often inarticulate but nevertheless firmly held. (For example, most fourth graders believe that no amount of tinkering with characteristic features could change a skunk into a raccoon.) It is intriguing to discover that the two major alternatives considered by category theorists – featural similarities and theory-based definitions – correspond to points on a developmental continuum.

Building on these now-established phenomena, Keil speculates about how the social functions of categories may partially determine the form of their definitions. Nominal kinds are usually established by convention, and they are not sharply defined unless some social purpose specifically requires it (as is the case with kinship terms, for example). We tend to credit such categories with more precise definitions than they actually have. The meanings of natural kinds, in contrast, cannot be established simply by social convention. Proper categorization of animals, plants, minerals, or heavenly bodies depends on nonobvious but real *facts* – facts that have to be discovered, or perhaps revealed. In making these and similar arguments, Keil is calling our attention to another sort of ecological constraint. The structure of cultural categories is governed not only by the domain under consideration and the cognitive models that we apply to it, but also by the requirements of communication and social life.

The subjects of Keil's experiments were children rather than infants – children old enough to express clear opinions about what is and is not possible. Carolyn Mervis' research, reported in Chapter 8, starts with much younger children. Her detailed account of her son Ari's early categories reports observations from before Ari could utter even a single word; she also reports a longitudinal study of twelve subjects (six normal children and six with Down syndrome) that began when the normals were only nine months old. The results show again that categorization begins at the basic level, but Mervis goes further to clarify the conditions under which young children's categories will differ from those of adults. Although basic-level categories are always identified by perceptual and functional features, the features that are most salient for adults may not be so obviously important to children (and vice versa).

Mervis also contributes a thoughtful discussion of the ways in which children's categories are "shaped" during development; after all, they must eventually become adult categories. What parents say is clearly important here, but not equally so at all ages. The dynamics of categories does not, by any means, depend exclusively on language. The nature and range of the exemplars to which children are exposed also matters, and so does the spontaneous intellectual activity of the children themselves. As he grew up, Ari not only changed the basis of certain categories but came to realize that everyone does not categorize in the same way: on occasion he would maintain his own label for an object even knowing that his mother used a different one. There is always room for disagreement, even at the basic level.

The claim that children begin with perceptual and functional (basic-level) categories should not be taken to mean that they have no other criteria by which to group objects. Other bases for grouping can be derived from the use of objects in standardized action sequences, or *scripts.* In Chapter 9 Robyn Fivush distinguishes two ways in which "generalized event representations" (the hypothetical mental equivalents of familiar scripted sequences) can lead to the formation of categories. *Functional* categories are based on interchangeability: for example, various food items can play equivalent roles in the "having lunch" script. *Thematic* categories are based on common membership in a scripted sequence: comb, toothbrush, toothpaste, and soap are all used in the washing routine, although no one of them can substitute for any other. Fivush presents data to show that infants as young as fourteen months already group objects together – or at least touch them in succession – on a thematic basis. They know something about the script. Perhaps we could even say that they have acquired an "idealized cognitive model" of washing up, although they certainly do not have a word for it yet.

As adults we do have words for some familiar scripts, lunch and washing up among them. The fact is, however, that most scripts and so-called thematic relations do not have single names. For example, as Ellen Markman points out in Chapter 10, English has no words for thematically related sets of objects like "a boy and his bike" or "a baby and its bottle." Nevertheless, these are just the sorts of relations that are known to dominate young children's experimental groupings. There is a kind of paradox here: a child who is asked to "put together the things that go together" will form thematic rather than taxonomic groups, but the same child has no difficulty in learning new words that usually refer to taxonomic – not thematic – categories. How can this be?

The experiments Markman reports to Chapter 10 may resolve this paradox. Children who were shown an object called a *sud* (or other nonsense name), and were asked to select another *sud* that was "just the same" as the first one, tended to choose from the same basic-level category. In contrast, children shown an object and asked to "find another one that is the same as this" (without a specific label) usually chose on a thematic basis. Markman describes this tendency as a constraint on word meanings: young children may assume that nouns refer to classes of similar objects rather than to thematic relations.

Markman also considers other assumed constraints that may facilitate the acquisition of language. In particular, children may believe that named categories are always mutually exclusive: something that is a *sud* cannot also be a *dax*. Such an assumption would indeed help clarify the meanings of many common nouns, but it must eventually create problems of its own. In class inclusion hierarchies (*plant, flower, rose*), mutual exclusivity does not hold. Markman suggests that this may be why class terms are so notoriously difficult for children: they find it difficult to comprehend how the same object can be simultaneously a flower and a rose. In contrast, "collection" terms like *army* and *forest* are much more easily mastered: no single object is ever simultaneously an army and a soldier.

Markman concludes with a discussion of paradoxical mass nouns such as *furniture* and *jewelry*. which – in contrast to regular mass nouns like *sand* and *rice* – refer to individual and distinct objects. These odd terms, which appear in many languages, stand for classes as well as for collections. Although the furniture in this room is just a collection of objects, *furniture* is a class that includes all chairs and all tables and much more besides. Familiarity with mass nouns of this sort may make it easier for children to move from knowing about collections to understanding the difficult class inclusion relation.

The final speaker at the Emory conference, Robert McCauley, was given the nearly impossible assignment of integrating and commenting on all of the preceding papers. Chapter 11 shows that he managed surprisingly well. As befits a philosopher, McCauley concentrates on the most fundamental questions. He is particularly interested in the shift from a focus on perceptible attributes to a focus on theories and models – a shift that can be found at several levels of analysis. It occurs repeatedly during the cognitive development of children: only Keil gives it a name – the "characteristic-to-defining shift" – but all the developmental chapters in this book describe related phenomena. A similar shift is apparently occurring, right now, in the study of categorization itself. Since Rosch's original discoveries, the field as a whole seems to be moving from an emphasis on objective attributes and similarity to a more recent insistence on the role of theories and idealized models. McCauley points out that several of the chapters in this book, those by Medin & Wattenmaker, Lakoff, and myself, explicitly acknowledge this shift and insist on the importance of theoretical constructs. Indeed, he is somewhat critical of Barsalou and Brooks for what he construes as their failure to do the same.

McCauley is also critical of those who have not moved far enough in this direction – specifically, of my own distinction between theory-dependent categorization and direct perception. Relying on Kant, he insists that ". . . there is no perception without categories and (as Neisser admits) there are no categories without cognitive models." To me, this argument is not compelling. There is certainly no perception without an organism, without a specifically structured nervous system, without what I have occasionally (perhaps rashly) called "perceptual anticipations" or "schemata" (Neisser 1976). But these things are not *categories*. They are not theories or models either. I cannot say what they are: we will not know how to characterize the structural prerequisites for perception until we are able to describe the information that perceivers pick up. There is little reason to believe that those "prerequisite structures" have much in common with the cognitive models on which categorization depends; there is every reason to believe that they are exquisitely tuned to the ecologically relevant properties of the real world.

NOTES

1. A volume based on the second Emory Cognition Project Symposium will soon be published by Cambridge University Press: U. Neisser & E. Winograd (Eds.), *Real Events Remembered: Ecological Approaches to the Study of Memory*.
2. In *Cognitive Psychology* (1967), I described almost all cognitive processes – including tachistoscopic perception, normal looking, remembering, and problem-solving – as "constructive." By the time I was writing *Cognition and Reality* (1976) I had come to believe that normal perception is better thought of as *selective* rather than constructive, because it is based on the pickup of objectively existing information. Nevertheless I believed that the structures responsible for picking up that information – "anticipatory schemata" – were very similar to those used in other cognitive activities; hence a unified theory of cognition was still possible. I no longer think so. The best presently available theory of perception is surely that of J. J. Gibson (1966), but for reasons presented here that theory will not do as a basis for the study of concepts, categories, and thought. Several other areas probably also require independent theories: plausible candidates include language (which is beyond my scope here) and memory (where I have recently made some new theoretical suggestions: Neisser 1986, in press).
3. The central work in that research tradition is Smith and Medin (1981).
4. From Emily Dickenson's poem "The Brain is Wider than the Sky."

REFERENCES

Bourne, L. E. (1966). *Human conceptual behavior*. Boston: Allyn & Bacon.
Gibson, J. J. (1966). *The senses considered as perceptual systems*. Boston: Houghton Mifflin.
Neisser, U. (1967). *Cognitive psychology*. New York: Appleton-Century-Crofts.
   (1976). *Cognition and reality*. New York: W. H. Freeman.
   (1986). Nested structure in autobiographical memory. In D. Rubin (Ed.), *Autobiographical memory*. New York: Cambridge University Press.
   (in press). A sense of where you are: Functions of the spatial module. In P. Ellen & C. Thinus-Blanc (Eds.), *Spatial orientation in animals and man*. Dordrecht, The Netherlands: Martinus Nijhoff.
Rosch, E. (1973). On the internal structure of perceptual and semantic categories. In T. Moore (Ed.), *Cognitive development and the acquisition of language*. New York: Academic Press.
Rosch, E., & Mervis, C. (1975). Family resemblances: Studies in the internal structure of categories. *Cognitive Psychology*, 7, 573–605.
Rosch, E., Mervis, C., Gray, W., Johnson, D., & Boyes-Braem, P. (1976). Basic objects in natural categories. *Cognitive Psychology*, 8, 382–439.
Smith, E. E., & Medin, D. L. (1981). *Categories and concepts*. Cambridge, MA: Harvard University Press.
Woodworth, R. S. (1938). *Experimental psychology*. New York: Henry Holt.

2

From direct perception to conceptual structure

ULRIC NEISSER

Although perceiving and thinking both fall within the scope of cognitive psychology, they are very different. Under normal circumstances, perception of the local environment is immediate, effortless, and veridical; in J. J. Gibson's (1979) phrase, it is "direct." Thinking, on the other hand, is indirect almost by definition. Thought may not depend on the immediate environment at all, it is often anything but effortless or immediate, and it frequently goes astray. Described in this way, perceiving and thinking seem as unlike one another as any two forms of cognition could possibly be. Nevertheless, at least one common cognitive activity – assigning objects to categories – has a foot in both camps. Most textbooks treat categorization as a complex mental process, but subjectively it is often a very immediate experience: I can see that the object over there is a *chair* as easily as I see that it is indeed over there, or that it is large and brown. The aim of this chapter is to clarify the relations between the perceptual and the intellectual aspects of categorization and, more generally, the relations between direct perception and the spontaneous use of cognitive models and hypotheses.

My treatment of perception itself will be based on Gibson's (1966, 1979) ecological theory. For Gibson, the initial step in understanding perception is not to formulate hypotheses about mental mechanisms, but to understand what kinds of things can be perceived at all. The second step is to discover the information structures (optical structures, in the case of vision) that specify those things to be perceptual systems of humans and other animals. If we do not have a good account of the information that perceivers are actually using, our hypothetical models of their "information processing" are almost sure to be wrong. If we *do* have such an account, however, such models may turn out to be almost unnecessary.

The second part of my argument will be based on the theory of categories proposed by Eleanor Rosch and her collaborators (Rosch 1978; Rosch, Mervis, Gray, Johnson, & Boyes-Braem 1976). I will pay special attention to what Rosch has called the "basic level" of categorization.

11

There is a paradox at this level: although assigning objects to basic categories seems just as direct as simply perceiving them, the real criteria of category membership are often invisible and may even be unknown. As we shall see, children's understanding of categories reflects this duality from a very early age. One might say (and I will say) that children have a kind of "model" of animals and other natural kinds in mind: that is, that they make certain implicit assumptions about how animals come into existence and what they are like inside. Such "idealized cognitive models" also play essential roles in culturally defined superordinate categories and in scientific concepts. I will conclude by arguing that categories, like Gibson's "affordances," are basically relational terms. Membership in a category is defined by a relation between a particular object on the one hand and a particular system of thought on the other.

Perception

Any ecological theory of perception should begin with an acccount of what can be perceived. Gibson's (1966, 1979) list of perceivables is a long one: it includes not only objects and their properties but events as well. We see ourselves, too, and our own actions and movements; we can even see the possibility of actions that we have not actually undertaken. Such possibilities are called "affordances": the floor over there would afford walking, my chair affords sitting. There are infinitely many objectively existing affordances of this kind, because every environment offers endless possibilities. (Only a few are ever actually perceived, but the unperceived ones are no less real on that account.) An affordance is not a property of an organism taken alone, but a relation between an organism and its environment.

We see all these things by virtue of the optical structures to which they give rise in the presence of ambient light. Among those structures are the *invariants:* aspects of stimulus information that persist despite movements of the perceiver (or are actually brought into existence by those movements), and that correspond to relatively permanent features of the objective situation. Gibson insisted that the whole visual system – head, eyes, receptors, fibers, levels of analysis, cortex, and all – should be thought of as "resonating" to the optical invariants, just as a tuning fork resonates to a particular acoustic frequency. In doing so, the system picks up structure directly from the optic array without any intermediate steps or false starts. Since the principles of optics normally guarantee a perfect correspondence between the presence of an invariant and the presence of the corresponding real state of affairs, perception is essentially of that state itself. Note that we do not become aware of the optical structure per se, but of the real environment specified by that structure.

These principles apply even to the perception of television images and movies and (recently) holograms, where optical structure is made to appear without any real environmental substrate. No objects are actually present in such displays, but in a sense perception is still "direct."

Veridical perceiving begins very early in life. Research at many developmental laboratories has now shown that three-month-olds (and probably neonates) perceive events and affordances realistically and directly. They still have a lot of perceptual learning ahead of them – they will become much more skillful and effective perceivers as they get more experience – but their world must appear real and meaningful from the beginning. This fact has an important consequence for adult beliefs about perception and knowledge. All through life – as far back as we can remember, and even farther back to the very beginnings of our awareness – we have been perceiving just as easily and accurately as we do today. That is one reason why we take perception so much for granted; why, to the despair of many philosophers, we are so sure that the way we see things is pretty much the way they are. This vote of confidence in perception is especially impressive because no one really knows how it works. Even without anything remotely like an adequate account of the invariants on which perceiving depends, we trust them implicitly.

Basic-level categories

To take the next step in understanding the relations between perception and categorization, we must turn to the modern study of conceptual structure and especially to the work of Eleanor Rosch. The research that Rosch and her collaborators undertook in the mid-1970s was not explicitly Gibsonian, but her methods and assumptions were ecological in several important respects. One of these was her interest in ecologically valid categories like "chair" and "bird" instead of artificial ones like "a stimulus card with three blue dots on it." Even more important, perhaps, was that Rosch began by exploring the actual structure of categories instead of by modeling the mental processes of category users. As a result her empirical findings have given shape to a whole new field of study.

Together with Carolyn Mervis and her other associates (Rosch & Mervis 1975; Rosch et al. 1976; Rosch 1978), Rosch explored both the horizontal and the vertical structure of natural categories. The horizontal (within-category) structure is usually "graded," in the sense that some items are obviously members of the category, while others are relatively marginal; often the outer boundary of the category is ill-defined. The vertical structure, more important to my argument here, concerns relations among the categories themselves. Those relations often take the form of nested hierarchies extending from relatively superordinate categories to more subordinate ones: *furniture, chair, armchair,* or perhaps *animal, cow, Holstein.* One particular level in these hierarchies is called the "basic level of categorization." *Chair* is a basic-level category, for example, as in *bed;* both are included in the superordinate category *furniture. Cow* and *dog* are also basic-level categories, but in a different superordinate set. Such hierarchies often have more than three levels – there may be still higher superordinates or still lower subordinates – but there is always at least one basic level near the middle.

The basic level has two unique characteristics. First, members of basic-level categories tend to *look alike.* Rosch and her associates have shown that properly scaled and oriented photographs of different chairs overlap a good deal when they are superimposed, and that the composite photographs still look rather like chairs. No such result can be obtained for superordinate categories because different items of furniture (say) simply do not resemble one another. Second, our *physical interactions* with different members of the same basic-level category are similar. In the case of nearly all chairs, for example, you first turn your back and then lower your rump to meet the seat. There is no such similarity in our interactions with the various members of a superordinate category like *furniture;* chairs, tables, and beds afford different activities.

Rosch and her associates also reported a third characteristic of the basic level: each such category has many describable *attributes.* Cows give milk, have horns, and say "moo"; chairs have legs, backs, and seats, were made to be sat on, and are about so big. In contrast, it is surprisingly difficult to find any distinctive attributes at all for superordinates like *furniture.* But while the third criterion certainly distinguishes the basic level of categorization, it actually adds very little information to the other two: most of the attributes in question are just aspects of the appearances of objects or of their uses. (Tversky and Hemenway's [1984] observation that many of the "attributes" reported by subjects are actually physical parts – legs, horns – is not inconsistent with this analysis. Physical parts tend to be both visibly and functionally salient.) At the basic level, then, objects are categorized by their looks and by their affordances.[1] Because affordances can be perceived directly (we can see how an object might be used just about as easily as we see what it looks like), both of these criteria are essentially perceptual. Categorization at the basic level is categorization by appearances.[2]

There are both advantages and disadvantages to judging by appearances. The principal advantage is such category systems are easy to use: if a new object resembles an old one (or an old prototype), we can immediately assign it to the same category. Children learn basic-level terms readily and early because they can just see what things are: this is a dog, that's a cow; this is a chair, that thing over there is a bed. Although early "child-basic" categories differ from the corresponding basic-level categories of adults (see Mervis, Chapter 8, this volume), they are governed by the same principles. This is not surprising: we rather expect young children to judge by appearances. As if to confirm this expectation, children often respond with superficial features or affordances when they are asked to give definitions of categories. Vygotsky (1962) reports many such examples: a cow is said to be a cow "because it has horns" or "because it gives milk." These childish responses are mistaken, of course; the factors that really make a cow a cow are by no means as obviously visible as having horns or giving milk. Indeed, we shall see in the next section that young children are well aware of the inadequacy of such superficial criteria. Perhaps they only give "childish" definitions when adults ask them unanswerable questions.

Underlying structure and ontological knowledge

Judging by appearances may be good enough to begin with because so much objective information is available to perceivers, but it is not good enough in the long run. Cows are not cows just because they give milk (even camels give milk, and some cows are "dry"), nor just because they overtly resemble other cows, nor for any other perceptually available reason. There could easily be an animal that looked rather like a cow but was really some other kind of ungulate; on the other hand, there may well be cows that look a lot like goats. Although Rosch occasionally seems to suggest that categories just reflect correlations among visible attributes, this is not the case for natural kinds like *cow*. But if being a cow is not a matter of appearances or affordances, what can it be a matter of? Before turning to that question directly, we must take a more careful look at the development of concepts in young children.

Contrary to what is suggested by Vygotsky's examples, children's thinking is not driven only by appearances: they have rudimentary theories as well. Frank Keil (1983; see also Chapter 7, this volume) has shown that those theories can support a surprising amount of inference. On being told that "hyraxes" are "sometimes sleepy," for example, kindergarten children who have never heard of hyraxes before will correctly conclude that a hyrax could also sometimes be hungry. If they are told that "throstles" often "have to be fixed," they infer that a throstle could not be hungry under any circumstances. Throstles, however, might be made out of metal, whereas hyraxes could not be. These examples from Keil's experiments demonstrate that children make rather deep ontological assumptions: here, about the distinction between living things and artifacts. This distinction appears very early. Even very young children seem to know that the critical properties of living things are not all visible on the surface. In a recent study, Susan Carey (1982) told four-year-olds that people have a greenish internal organ called a "spleen." She then confronted them with a toy mechanical monkey and a real earthworm: which one was more likely to have a spleen? Toy monkeys look much more like people than earthworms do, but superficial similarity was not enough to override the children's ontological assumptions: they voted for the worm.

In another series of studies, Keil (1986) asked kindergarten through fourth-grade children about the possibility that "scientists" could shift objects from one category to another by making changes in their visible properties. Some of the objects were animals, while others were manufactured artifacts. Could a raccoon be changed into a skunk just by suitably altering its features and its behavior? Can a coffeepot be changed into a birdfeeder? All the subjects agreed that artifacts could be made into other artifacts (a coffeepot into a birdfeeder), but the older children denied that one could change the identity of an animal in the same way. Although the kindergartners were willing to judge "raccoonhood" by appearances, they used deeper criteria for ontological categories: they denied that any operation could change a toy dog into a real dog, or a porcupine into a cactus. Even for children, the proper categorization of natural kinds depends on criteria that are more than skin deep.

In light of these results, the suggestion that natural categories are defined primarily by appearances and similarities – which I once found plausible myself (Neisser 1979) – must be rejected. Although people can always judge the typicality of an item in a category, even in unfamiliar "ad hoc" categories (Barsalou 1983) and in categories like "odd number" where typicality is completely irrelevant (Armstrong, Gleitman, & Gleitman 1983), such judgments do not necessarily reflect the real criteria of category membership. In any case, they would not be stable enough to reflect those criteria (Barsalou, Chapter 5, this volume). But then what defines a category?

In the case of animals, there seem to be two possibilities. First, category membership may depend on characteristics that are perfectly real but happen to be unperceivable: they are inside the animal, or too small to be seen, or at present unknown. For example, we might argue that a given animal is a raccoon if and only if the nuclei of its cells contain raccoon DNA. The children in Keil's experiments could not have made that argument explicitly, but they may nevertheless have believed that *something* inside the raccoon defined its identity – that each type of animal has some internal "essence" that cannot be changed. One can hold such a belief without any clear idea of what the "essence" is actually like; it is enough to assume that there must be one.

The second possibility is quite different. Perhaps the identity of this animal as a raccoon depends not on its present state, but on its personal history: for example, on the fact that it was born of raccoon parents. (One school of thought in theoretical biology holds that *species* are defined in a similar way, by the evolutionary history of animals rather than by their present features.) On this view, "raccoonhood" would be an objective aspect of a very long-lasting, but entirely real event: the conception, birth, and life of the raccoon itself. If the subjects of Keil's experiments had some such idea in mind, even vaguely, their responses need not have reflected any assumptions about internal properties at all. The conceptual impossibility of changing a raccoon into a skunk may not result so much from the technical impossibility of altering its DNA as from the logical impossibility of altering its past.

These two interpretations are by no means mutually exclusive. It is perfectly possible to believe (and I do, in fact, believe) that being a racoon involves *both* having a particular inner nature and having come into existence in a particular way. Both of these criteria go beyond appearances to imply that the identity of animals depends on things that cannot be perceived, either because they are unknown and inaccessible or because they happened in the past. This twofold "cognitive model" governs my concept of *raccoon* and of all other animals, whether familiar or unfamiliar. Keil's work shows that grammar-school children have such models too. Indeed, it seems likely that children of every age have some "theory" about the nature of animals that goes beyond what they can see. Both kinds of cognition – direct perception and the use of cognitive models – are probably present from the first, and both of them undergo development. Even while children take it for granted that chair-ness and cow-ness are directly perceptible (and while they are becoming increasingly skillful at making the corresponding perceptual judgments), they are simultaneously developing a rich network of beliefs about the deeper criteria by which such things are really defined.

Why don't the children notice the inconsistency between these two ways of thinking? Because there *is* no inconsistency, if the real world is genuinely coherent. All of us take some such degree of coherence for granted. We are sure that both the life histories of cows and their intrinsic properties are causally linked to how they look and act. There is only one environment, although it is partly visible and partly not. That is why adults, as well as children, are content to classify by appearances – to call an animal a cow because it looks like other cows – even though they know that nonperceptual criteria are really at stake. The fact that we cannot easily say what those criteria may be – that our cognitive models are unclear, incomplete, and perhaps inconsistent – is of little importance. We respect what Putnam (1977) has called the "linguistic division of labor," which means that it is some expert's job to know what really makes a cow a cow. But we also know that there can be no analogous perceptual division of labor that we can and must see for ourselves.

Superordinate categories

So far I have considered only basic-level categories, but there are many other kinds. New categories are continually being produced by developments in science and culture: such exotica as *electron shell, stable nuclear deterrent, media event,* and *formless invariant* have come into existence in my lifetime. It would be rash to generalize about all of them, and I will focus on only two kinds here: the categories defined by culturally given cognitive models on the one hand and by scientific theories on the other.

Rosch and her associates (1976) have shown very clearly that members of superordinate artifact categories (*tool, furniture*) do not share appearances or affordances as the members of basic categories do. Typical items of furniture – a bed and a table, for example – need not look the least bit alike or be used in anything like the same way. What is it, then, that makes something *furniture?* There must be a cognitive model involved, but it cannot be one that deals with intrinsic characteristics.

The answer involves linguistics as well as psychology. Not all languages have words like "furniture"; they appear only when particular cultural or historical circumstances require them. There may have been an old custom of "furnishing" a new home with domestic objects, for example; certainly there is a contemporary business practice of establishing stores that sell furniture. People who use the word need not be aware of all these etymological ramifications, but they must believe that there is *something* about furniture. Like young children (Markman, Chapter 10, this volume), we are very ready to believe that nouns refer to taxonomic categories. Following Lakoff (Chapter 4, this volume), I will refer to the cultural assumptions that establish the real meanings of such words as *idealized cognitive models.*

A useful example of an idealized cognitive model is the one that underlies the word "bachelor." A bachelor is often defined simply as an "unmarried man," but there is more to it than that. Fillmore (cited in Lakoff 1982) has pointed out that the definition of that category actually depends on a rather general model of social life. Those assumptions include the existence of a primarily monogamous social system in which most young men get married, and the few who do not are thereby freed to adopt a slightly different lifestyle. "Bachelor" becomes almost vacuous where that model does not fit: that is why we do not readily apply it to homosexuals or to the Pope. (See Lakoff, Chapter 4, this volume, for further discussion of this example.) The concept *furniture* depends on an idealized cognitive model in the same way: it assumes that people live in houses or apartments, and that these are regularly "furnished" with a variety of substantial but portable objects. It would not work nearly as well for people who live nomadically on the backs of camels or dwell in orbiting space capsules.

These "idealized cognitive models" (ICMs) are what Medin and Wattenmaker (Chapter 3, this volume) and McCauley (Chapter 11, this volume) call "theories" about the world. They should not be confused with the hypothetical models of information processing that are presently popular in cognitive psychology. An ICM is not something that a few psychologists believe about cognition, it is something that everyone is likely to believe as a member of a given culture. Thus, it can give meaning to the concepts we use every day. In contrast, a theory of information processing is a scientific hypothesis. What is important about such a theory, or "model," is not how widely it is believed, but whether it is true or false. The distinction is an important one.[3]

Cultural categories take many different forms. Some are quite vague, while others have relatively sharp definitions; some are at the basic level, some are superordinates, some have still other characteristics. One type of idealized cognitive model that has recently attracted the attention of developmental psychologists is the *script*. Even very young children know the regularly scripted sequence of events that occur "when you have dinner" or "when you go to school," and find it easy to describe them (Nelson & Gruendel 1981). A child who knows a script soon acquires many special categories that depend on it: "dessert" depends on the dinner script and "teacher" on the school script. These are not basic-level categories: it would be a mistake to look for perceptual attributes that define something as a dessert or somebody as a teacher. It would be even more of a mistake to look for the critical internal structures of desserts and teachers, or for their definitive histories. The only important criterion for such categories is the fit between the object and the script: desserts appear at the ends of meals, teachers play certain roles at school. Fivush (Chapter 9, this volume) discusses script-based categories in some detail.

How do children discover the models that prevail in their culture? Generally speaking, they learn about them as part of learning about the culture itself. As they do so, they begin to use criteria of categorization that go beyond the basic level. This is the trend illustrated in the work of Keil and Batterman (1984; see Chapter 7, this volume) who call it the "characteristic-to-defining shift." While young children will use the word "island" for any place that resembles islands they have heard about already (i.e., for any vacation resort with beaches), older children know that an island must be surrounded by water. Similarly, young children often use the word "uncle" for any adult male friend of the family; older ones know that an uncle must be the brother of a parent. Domain by domain, children learn what they may have suspected from the first: appearances are often not enough to establish categories. No experts are needed in most of these cases. The proper cognitive model for "island" involves criteria that everyone can understand; it is only necessary to learn them.

The characteristic-to-defining shift does not appear all at once. It may take place earlier or later in different domains, depending on the child's individual experience and on the domain itself. Its occurrence does not mean that children stop seeing things as they really are, of course; neither does it mean that they are only now starting to see what things really are. Nor does it occur only in children: something similar occurs when we move from ignorance to expertise in any new domain. Novices have no choice but to judge by appearance, sticking as close to the basic level as they can. Experts categorize more adequately because they have better cognitive models. The use of those models does not mean that the experts have given up seeing for themselves; on the contrary, perceptual learning may enable them to perceive even more effectively.

Scientific concepts

Scientific concepts depend on cognitive models too, but scientific models are usually more explicit and more factually based than the scripts and categories of everyday experience. Science has a special responsibility to the truth, and its practices are designed in part to meet that responsibility. These practices seem to produce a high degree of certainty, comparable to the certainty of direct perception, although very differently achieved. This is not the place to consider how that certainty is actually attained (I am happy to leave that difficult question to philosophers), but there is no doubt that the concepts of science are theory-dependent. The meaning of *force* in mechanics, for example, depends entirely on Newton's laws of motion. Similarly, astronomical terms like *star* depend on the presently accepted cosmology, in which the sun counts as a star and Mars does not. In biology, animals are classified by criteria that laymen find esoteric indeed: by their teeth or their bones, their DNA, or their evolutionary history. (There is currently some disagreement about the proper criteria for biological classification, but all the candidates are supported by a good deal of theory.) Such categories change as the theories that support them change; the distinctive thing about scientific categories is not their permanence, but the sense of responsibility that lies behind them. Scientists have a particular obligation to take the real world carefully into account.

I have been distinguishing between scientific categories and those of everyday cultural usage, but there is a considerable region of overlap between them. In our own culture, the child's early conviction that the identity of animals is not just a matter of appearances soon gets translated into an appeal to official science. This particular linguistic division of labor is well established: biologists are supposed to know all about animals, and their authority outweighs all other bases of classification. Penguins and ostriches might never make it as birds if we went by basic-level appearances, but we go by conventions that follow science instead. Roger Tory Peterson (1947) will do for today, but next year if biologists announce that penguins are not birds after all we will probably go along with them. Their categories are better than ours because they have a better theory than we do, and we know it.

If there should really be a new line on penguins next month, one of our options would be to accept it in principle and yet resist its application to everyday language: to keep on speaking of penguins as birds, although we know they are not. Old categories are not always abandoned when science prescribes new ones. Sometimes both cognitive models continue to exist side by side. Astronomers may insist that the sun is a star and Mars is not, but most of us use a different semantics when we are gazing at the night sky. Physicists may have defined force very carefully, but we still speak of "forces" in everyday contexts where that definition does not apply. Ecological psychologists may know what they mean by "perception," but they must reckon with the fact that other people use the word quite differently.

There is nothing illogical about having several different sets of categories in the same domain. The real world is rich enough in structure to support any number of cognitive models. People who point to Mars and say "look at that reddish star" would be wrong if they were trying to use the categories of astronomy, but they are right with respect to the folk concept of star. Both concepts are based on cognitive models, both models are consistent with a subset of objective facts, and both have their uses. To be sure, the two models are not equally good as descriptions of the universe. The astronomers (like the biologists) have a better theory – one that is consistent with a wider range of systematic observations.

The relation between cognitive models and the real world that they attempt to describe is analogous to another, more concrete kind of relationship. *Affordances,* as J. J. Gibson (1979) defined them, are relations of possibility between animals and their environments. A particular environment has a given affordance if and only if it makes a given kind of action possible, whether that action is actually executed or not. The claim that a given affordance exists is an objective claim, always either true or false: I may or may not be able to walk on that surface, for example. But human beings are thinkers as well as doers, and every environment offers intellectual opportunities as well as affordances for action. Again there are infinitely many, of which only a few can ever be realized; again, claims about them can be either true or false. That object in the sky may or may not fit the astronomical definition of star; this animal may or may not be a cow in terms of modern biological theory. Categories are relations between particular objects and cognitive models; to assign an object to a category is to claim that such a relationship exists.

Note that the *reality* of cows and stars and other things is not at issue. The cow is really there, with its mass and momentum and some of its affordances clearly visible to anyone who looks. The cow is there whether or not anybody sees it, and whether or not anybody knows what it is. But it couldn't be a *cow,* I submit, unless there were cognitive models or theories or at least linguistic conventions about cows to which it could be related. Of course there really are such models – indeed, several of them – so it really is a cow.

In summary, categorization is somewhat less "direct" than perception. The perceptible properties of things are specified by invariants to which the perceptual systems need only resonate, but a category is always defined by reference to a cognitive model. Categorization begins at the basic level, where categories are so closely tied to looks and affordances that they seem at first to be perceptually given. The course of development soon moves beyond appearances, however: in some domains to the scripts and superordinates defined by culture, in others to an acceptance of internal or historical criteria that lie beyond immediate experience, in still others to scientific exploration or an appeal to scientific authority. In all this we are driven by a conviction that there is something coherent beneath the surface and beyond the present, and that it is knowable. That conviction is not misplaced. There is indeed much to know: we can see some of it directly, but we have to figure out the rest.

NOTES

An earlier version of this chapter was delivered as the fourth James J. Gibson Memorial Lecture at Cornell University on October 26, 1984. I am especially grateful to Edward Reed for his thoughtful critique of a draft of the Gibson lecture.

1. This principle holds even when the basic level changes, as it may during learning; the new basic level is simply defined by new perceptible characteristics. Rosch et al. (1976) give the example of an experienced airplane mechanic for whom individual types of planes (rather than simply *airplanes*) had become basic-level categories: he made use of visible differences that less-experienced viewers would miss entirely. When experts have a different basic

level of categorization than novices, it is usually because they see more real details and notice more real affordances.

2. How appearances themselves are perceived is not critical here. Some have suggested that new objects are systematically compared to stored category prototypes; in Chapter 6, Lee Brooks insists that they are compared to specific previous instances instead. For my part, I suspect that no comparisons with stored representations are necessary at all. Previous experiences may simply have tuned the perceptual systems so that a new object can be directly seen as a member of the appropriate category. Unfortunately, these processes are not yet well understood.

3. Of course there are idealized models of cognition itself, and these models can be studied in their own right. (Such studies are sometimes said to deal with "metacognition.") I have been especially interested in everyday conceptions of *intelligence* because of their influence on the theoretical aspirations of psychologists: for example, in legitimizing an intention to find out "what intelligence really is." In an earlier paper (Neisser 1979), I suggested that the concept *intelligent person* (like *honest person* and many others) was based primarily on similarity to prototypes. I would now give a larger role to idealized cognitive models in analyzing the structure of such concepts.

REFERENCES

Armstrong, S. L., Gleitman, L. R., & Gleitman, H. (1983). What some concepts might not be. *Cognition, 13,* 263–308.

Barsalou, L. W. (1983). Ad hoc categories. *Memory and Cognition, 11,* 211–227.

Carey, S. (1982). Semantic development: The state of the art. In E. Wanner & L. R. Gleitman (Eds.), *Language acquisition: The state of the art.* New York: Cambridge University Press.

Gibson, J. J. (1966). *The senses considered as perceptual systems.* Boston: Houghton Mifflin.

  (1979). *The ecological approach to visual perception.* Boston: Houghton Mifflin.

Keil. F. C. (1983). Semantic inferences and the acquisition of word meaning. In T. B. Seiler & W. Wannemacher (Eds.), *Concept development and the development of word meaning.* Berlin: Springer-Verlag.

  (1986). The acquisition of natural kind and artifact terms. In W. Demopolous & A. Marras (Eds.), *Language learning and concept acquisition.* Norwood, NJ: Ablex.

Keil, F. C., & Batterman, N. (1984). A characteristic-to-defining shift in the development of word meaning. *Journal of Verbal Learning and Verbal Behavior, 23,* 221–236.

Lakoff, G. (1982), Categories: An essay in cognitive linguistics. In Linguistic Society of Korea (Eds.), *Linguistics in the morning calm.* Seoul: Hanshin.

Neisser, U. (1979). The concept of intelligence. *Intelligence, 3,* 217–227.

Nelson, K., & Gruendel, J. (1981). Generalized event representations: Basic building blocks of cognitive development. In M. E. Lamb & A. L. Brown (Eds.), *Advances in developmental psychology* (Vol. 1). Hillsdale, NJ: Erlbaum.

Peterson, R. T. (1947). *A field guide to the birds.* Boston: Houghton Mifflin.

Putnam, H. (1977). Meaning and reference. In S. P. Schwartz (Ed.), *Naming, necessity, and natural kinds.* Ithaca, NY: Cornell University Press.

Rosch, E. (1978). Principles of categorization. In E. Rosch & B. B. Lloyd (Eds.), *Cognition and categorization*. Hillsdale, NJ: Erlbaum.

Rosch, E., & Mervis, C. B. (1975). Family resemblances: Studies in the internal structure of categories. *Cognitive Psychology, 7*, 573–605.

Rosch, E., Mervis, C. B., Gray, W. D., Johnson, D. M., & Boyes-Braem, P. (1976). Basic objects in natural categories. *Cognitive Psychology, 8*, 382–439.

Tversky, B., & Hemenway, K. (1984). Objects, parts and categories. *Journal of Experimental Psychology: General, 113*, 169–193.

Vygotsky, L. S. (1962). *Thought and language*. Cambridge, MA: MIT Press.

3

Category cohesiveness, theories, and cognitive archeology

DOUGLAS L. MEDIN and
WILLIAM D. WATTENMAKER

Why do we have the categories we have and not others? The set of entities comprising our world could be partitioned in a virtually limitless variety of ways, but most of these partitionings prove to be vague, absurd, or useless, and only a tiny minority are informative, useful, and efficient. This chapter is concerned with the question of what makes categories psychologically cohesive.

The question of what makes a concept coherent has received a variety of answers, almost all of which rely directly or indirectly on the notion of similarity (similar entities appear in the same class, dissimilar entities belong to different classes). In the first part of this chapter we will argue that similarity-based approaches are inadequate, in part because the notion of similarity is too unconstrained and in part because these approaches fail to represent intra- and interconcept relations and more general world knowledge. Following Murphy and Medin (1985) we suggest, as an alternative approach, that concepts are coherent to the extent that they fit people's background knowledge or naive theories of the world.

The second part of our chapter is concerned with constraints on theories. If anything can qualify as a theory and all theories are equally good, then the problem of coherence simply has been shifted to a different level without being addressed. An obvious alternative to the idea that all theories are equally good is the idea that people prefer simple theories to more complex ones. We shall argue, however, that the notion of simplicity with respect to theories has many of the same limitations as the notion of similarity with respect to category structures. We then outline an alternative approach to constraints on theories that relies heavily on ecological considerations. The main idea is that the interaction of organisms with their environment provides a source of constraints that may become embodied in organisms. We refer to the search for such constraints as cognitive archeology. Although many of these constraints concern perceptual processing, they may be paralleled by analogous

25

constraints in conceptual processing (e.g., theory construction). Although our particular line of argument is speculative, we believe that progress in analyzing constraints on both categories and the theories that are intertwined with them will necessarily reflect a sensitivity to the interaction of organisms and their environment.

Traditional approaches to conceptual coherence

For our present purposes it will prove convenient to work with a very informal definition of conceptual coherence. We use the term to describe groupings of entities that "make sense" to the observer as might be reflected in various measures such as ease of learning or even direct ratings of coherence. Coherence is not to be confused with the notion of naturalness as used by Keil (1981) or natural kinds as used by others because very unnatural concepts may also prove to be coherent in circumstances where the members of the category are coordinated through some theoretical frameworks. For example, consider the category comprised of the following objects: children, jewelry, portable television sets, photograph albums, manuscripts, oil paintings. Out of context such a category may not make much sense, but it becomes coherent in the context *things to take out of one's home during a fire.* Barsalou (1984; Chapter 5, this volume) has shown that these goal-derived categories behave very much like standard lexical concepts. Certainly these "ad hoc" categories are not "natural" by Keil's (1981) criteria, but they do seem to hang together in their own context. This example illustrates that coherence can be context-dependent. It is not even the case that taxonomic sorting is a cross-cultural universal. For example, Lancy (1983) has found that the Melpa of New Guinea use a pairing principle to create categories. That is, they attempt to specify a pair that, by way of contrast or complementarity between members of the two halves, forms a totality or whole. Melpa cosmology is not compatible with taxonomic categories.

The insufficiency of similarity

Perhaps the most intuitively plausible explanation of conceptual coherence is that objects, events, or entities form a concept because they are similar to each other. The basic idea is that similarity relations partition entities into natural clusters and that our concepts map onto these clusters. An immediate problem with this view is that entities may *seem* to be similar precisely because they are members of the same category. What is needed is some independent method of measuring similarity uncontaminated by people's knowledge about category memberships.

The predominant (and almost the sole) approach to being specific about similarity is to analyze concepts into constituent properties or attributes and to define similarity in terms of matching and mismatching properties. Thus, *robins* are more similar to *squirrels* than to *diamonds* because robins and squirrels share properties such as *living, mobile,* and *found in trees,* which are not possessed by diamonds.

Can the notion of similarity defined in terms of matching and mismatching properties explain why a category is formed (instead of some other) or its ease of use? As a paradigmatic case, consider Amos Tversky's (1977) theory of similarity, which defines it as a function of common and distinctive features weighted for salience or importance. An immediate problem with using Tversky's model to define category structure is that the similarity relationships among a set of entities will depend heavily on the particular weights given to individual properties or features. For example, a skunk and a zebra would be more similar than a horse and a zebra if the feature "striped" had sufficient weight. In some approaches to numerical taxonomy this issue is resolved by (somewhat arbitrarily) requiring that each feature be weighted equally. But Tversky (1977) has convincingly shown that the relative weighting of a feature (as well as the relative importance of common and distinctive features) varies with the stimulus context and experimental task, so that there is no unique answer to the question of how similar one entity is to another (see also Gati & Tversky 1984). If this were not already a serious problem, Ortony, Vondruska, Jones, and Foss (1985) have argued that Tversky's model is too constrained in that it assumes that a given feature has the same salience regardless of the entity in which it inheres. If one is forced to the further concession that the salience of a particular feature can vary across entities (e.g., *stripes* for *barber poles* may be more salient than *stripes* for *bass* or some other species of fish), then it seems that there are too many free parameters and the notion of similarity becomes too flexible to explain coherence.

But perhaps the most serious problem with defining similarity in terms of common and distinctive attributes is that no constraints have been provided on what is to count as a feature or attribute. To illustrate this point Murphy and Medin (1985) argue that the number of attributes that *plums* and *lawnmowers* have in common could be infinite: both weigh less than 1,000 kilograms (and less than 1,001 kg), both are found in our solar system (on the earth, etc.), both cannot hear well, both have a smell, both can be dropped, both take up space, and so on. The list can be infinite. Any two entities can be arbitrarily similar or dissimilar depending on the criterion of what is to count as a relevant attribute.

At best, the notion of common and distinctive attributes provides a language for talking about similarity and representing conceptual coherence. To use a rough analogy, winning basketball teams have in common scoring more points than their opponents, but one must turn to more basic principles to explain why they score more points. In the same way, similarity may be a by-product of conceptual coherence rather than its determinant – having a theory that relates objects may constrain which properties seem relevant and may make them seem similar.

It may seem that we are being a little harsh on such an important principle as similarity. We are not arguing that theories directly or dramatically alter appearances. Rather our claim is that the notion of similarity is too flexible to provide an account of conceptual coherence. The general form of argument we are advancing is that attempts to describe category coherence in terms of similarity will prove useful only to the extent that principles determining what is to count as a relevant property and determining the importance of particular properties are specified. In this case, however, it is important to realize that the explanatory work is being done by the principles that specify these constraints rather than the general notion of similarity. In many cases perceptual experience may seem to naturally partition entities into categories. One can think of the perceptual system as embodying a theory about what is important in the world. That is, the perceptual system has some built-in constraints on what will count as an attribute and what attribute relations are salient (see Ullman, 1979, for elegant work that gets at some of these constraints). The problem with the abstract notion of similarity is that it ignores both the perceptual and theory-related constraints on concepts.

Even if one were to succeed in specifying perceptual constraints, the problem of conceptual coherence would not disappear. Some categorizations blantantly contradict perceptual similarity (e.g., categorizing whales as mammals) and the question of how much of our conceptual system is based on perceptually determined features has yet to be determined. In general, people seem to be flexible about similarity (even perceptual similarity), and we know relatively little about nonperceptual constraints. We think that theories play a significant role in determining which properties are relevant but that the role of theories goes far beyond that. The notion that coherence derives from theories leads one to deemphasize individual attributes in favor of a focus on relational properties and the interaction of concepts in theorylike mental structures.

The insufficiency of correlated attributes

Although we have already argued that similarity does not sufficiently constrain concepts, it may be that some general processing principles that are based on similarity have greater explanatory power. One such principle is correlated attributes. Rosch and her associates (Rosch, Mervis, Gray, Johnson, & Boyes-Braem 1976; Rosch 1978) have proposed that natural categories divide the world up into clusters of correlated attributes that "cut the world at its joints." This clustering principle is in contrast to the idea that attributes occur in all possible combinations and are thereby uncorrelated. Natural object categories at the "basic level" (e.g., birds), which is neither the most specific nor most abstract level, are said to maximize the correlational structure of the environment by preserving these attribute clusters. In this view it is not undifferentiated "similarity" that makes concepts cohesive, but some more elaborated structure of correlations. An organism prepared to take advantage of attribute correlations will tend to form categories that have high within-category and low between-category similarity as a *consequence* of detecting correlations.

Although the correlated attribute principle is attractive, it has several limitations. One minor problem is that a cause and an effect may be highly correlated, but they would probably be placed in different categories. A more serious problem is that, even with some predetermined set of properties, there are so many possible correlations that it is not clear how the correct ones get picked out (see Keil, 1981, for an extended discussion of this problem). It would seem that some additional principles are needed to further constrain category cohesion, such as the notion that correlations may be made more or less salient by people's theories. This latter point of view leads to a further concession, namely, that categories consistent with a theory, but violating correlational structure, may nonetheless be cohesive (Barsalou 1983, 1985).

The insufficiency of categorization theories

One might think that categorization theories might constrain similarity in such a way as to give an account of category cohesiveness. The major points of view concerning concepts, however, either say nothing about structure or take a syntactic approach that is so impoverished it ignores interproperty and interconcept relations.

Smith and Medin (1981) divide theories of category representation into three basic approaches: the classical view, the probabilistic view, and the examplar view. The classical view holds that all instances of a concept share common properties that are necessary and sufficient conditions for defining the concept. The probabilistic view denies that there necessarily are defining properties and instead argues that concepts are represented in terms of properties that are only characteristic or probable of class members. Membership in a category can thus be graded rather than all-or-none, where the better members have more characteristic properties than the poorer ones. The exemplar view agrees with the claim that concepts need not contain defining properties, but further claims that categories may be represented by their individual exemplars, and that assignment of a new instance to a category is determined by whether the instance is sufficiently similar to one or more of the category's known exemplars.

The classical view implies that the defining properties provide the structure that holds a category together. But this may not be enough. For example, a category consisting of purple things bigger than a basketball and weighing between 1.65 and 9.82 kilograms satisfies a classical view definition but does not seem sensible or cohesive. Osherson (1978) and Keil (1979) have worried about this problem and suggested that some of the needed constraints result from the hierarchical structure of ontological concepts that represent the basic categories of existence, such as *thing, physical object, event, solid,* and *fluid.* Although the status of ontological concepts is a matter under debate (e.g., Carey 1985; Gerard & Mandler 1983; Keil, Chapter 7, this volume), we think reinforcing the classical view with an ontological tree will represent a positive step toward developing constraints, at least to the extent that ontological concepts embody people's world knowledge. Of course, the remaining problem with the classical view as a structural principle is that many categories may not conform to the classical view (see Medin & Smith 1981; Mervis & Rosch 1981; Smith & Medin 1981, for reviews).

The probabilistic view is constrained primarily in that it implies that categories be partitionable on the basis of summing of evidence, that is, that the categories be perfectly separable on the basis of a weighted, additive combination of component information (this is called "linear separability" by Sebestyen [1962]). The probabilistic view has looser constraints in that categories conforming to the classical view are a proper subset of categories conforming to the property of linear separability.

The constraint of linear separability is important in certain algorithms for machine pattern recognition, but it does not seem to hold for people. One way of evaluating the importance of linear separability is to set up two categorization tasks that are similar in major respects, except that in one the categories are linearly separable, whereas in the other they are not. Using this strategy in a series of four experiments varying stimulus type, category size, and instructions, Medin and Schwanenflugel (1981) found no evidence that linearly separable categories were easier to learn than categories that were not linearly separable. Kemler-Nelson (1984) ran adults and children under conditions designed to induce either analytical or nonanalytical learning and also did not find that linear separability acted as a constraint.

The probabilistic view also inherits the problems associated with a simple syntactic approach – it provides no guidelines concerning which combinations of features form possible concepts and which form coherent ones. Thus, it would not rule out the following combination of typical features: bright red, flammable, eats mealworms, found in Lapland, and used for cleaning furniture. Clearly, the mere fact that this combination is probabilistic does not mean it is coherent.

Finally, the exemplar view provides no principled account of conceptual structure, since it does not constrain what exemplars are concept members. Although most exemplar theories assume that membership is based on similarity, we have already argued that this alone is not a satisfactory explanation of coherence.

The general insufficiency of attribute matching and similarity

We started this essay by noting that, without some constraints on what is to count as an attribute, similarity-based approaches to coherence relying directly or indirectly on attribute matching will not get off the ground. Actually, we believe that the problems with this approach go deeper, and that, in principle, they will prove to be insufficient. Some of the problems derive from the idea that conceptual structure can be understood in terms of a focus on constituent attributes, whereas others seem to follow from that more abstract principle that category membership is determined by a similarity-based matching process.

Focus on attributes. The practice of breaking concepts into constituent attributes engenders a tendency to view concepts as little more than the sum of their components. As Armstrong, Gleitman, and Gleitman (1983) noted, however, the simple fact is that most concepts are not a simple sum of independent features, whatever that be. For example, all the features that are characteristic of a bird do not make it a bird – unless these properties are held together in a "bird structure." This bird structure certainly consists of a large set of relational properties and not simply attributes.

One defense of the attribute-matching perspective is that relationships and operations might be treated as attributes. To take this step, however, is to concede that attributes may have a complex internal structure. Relations need arguments, and arguments and relationships mutually constrain one another. Consequently, whenever relational properties are present, attempts to represent component properties as independent will prove very awkward. Consider some artificial stimulus that contains a triangle inside a circle. One would need to present the presence of the triangle, the circle, and the *inside* relation the triangle bears to the circle. It will not work to represent the situation as a simple list (triangle, circle, inside) because that would not distinguish between a triangle inside a circle and a circle inside a triangle. Rather, one needs an internal structure that is more than a simple list and both structural constraints and explanatory power will derive from this richer structure. One might attempt to represent this complex internal structure in terms of a (higher-level) holistic attribute. To take this step, however, is to concede the inadequacy of the notion of independent properties and to abandon the goal of explaining similarity in terms of matching and mismatching attributes.

Categorization as attribute matching. A major respect in which attribute matching may be too limited is that our representations may include information concerning operations, transformation, and (indirectly) relations among properties. Consider the following example taken from Rips and Handle (1984). The participants in their experiment were asked whether an object 5 inches in diameter was more likely to be a coin or a pizza. Although the object's size was roughly midway between large coins and small pizzas (as determined by prior norms), participants tended to categorize it as a pizza. One reason for this judgment might be that pizzas are more variable in size and though the probability of a 5-inch pizza is low, it is higher than that of a 5-inch coin. As Rips and Handle (1984) point out, however, there may be more involved here than brute knowledge about variability. We know that coins may have a size mandated by law and this and related knowledge about the nature of coins supplies information about potential size and variability.

Again one might attempt to represent this knowledge in terms of complex attributes involving higher order properties. Although this may be technically correct, it misses the important point that the explanatory work is again being done by the theory – constrained processes that generate these complex attributes – rather than by attribute matching per se. Thus, although attribute matching could be made consistent with these facts, it does not by itself explain or predict them.

Categorization as a matching process. Even if one could appropriately constrain attributes, relations, and the internal structure of attributes and relations, it still might prove misleading to think of categorization as involving a matching process establishing some form of identity between concept and exemplar. For example, the attributes and relations associated with higher level concepts and relations may be more abstract than those associated with lower level concepts or exemplars. Instead of matching of identities, categorization may be based on an inference process (see Collins 1978). For example, jumping into a swimming pool with one's clothes on is in all probability not directly associated with the concept *intoxicated,* yet that information might well be used to decide that a person is drunk. Categorizing the person as intoxicated may "explain" his or her behavior even though the specific behavior was not previously a component of the concept. Concepts may represent a form of "shorthand" for a more elaborate theory, and a concept may be invoked when it has sufficient explanatory relationship to an object rather than when it matches an object's attributes. That is, the relationship between a concept and examples may be closely analogous to the relationship between theory and data. If this is so, then it is misleading to represent categorization solely in terms of some form of matching.

Summary

We think that similarity-based approaches to category goodness are insufficient to explain conceptual coherence and the richness of conceptual structure. We choose the word *insufficient* because we do not wish to imply that this approach is completely wrong or misleading. Similarity, in an appropriately constrained form, may provide a natural explanation for at least some cases of conceptual coherence. One key to progress might rest with analyses of relational properties rather than a focus on attributes (we argue in the section on Theories, Relational Coding, and Linear Separability [below] that this is part of the solution). If one makes the plausible assumption that our perceptual apparatus becomes attuned (either ontogenetically or phylogenetically) to informative aspects of our environment, then an ecological approach to perception may provide some ways to pin down the notion of similarity. Even in this case it may prove useful to think of perceptual processes as embodying a theory about the world. At the same time it does not seem likely that one can draw a sharp distinction between perceptual and conceptual categories, and categories that seem grounded in perception may be significantly influenced by the sorts of conceptual structures developed on the basis of interaction with the associated entities. One can view our approach as supplying constraints missing from the (perceptual) similarity explanation, rather than simply contradicting it.

Table 3.1, taken from Murphy and Medin (1985), summarizes the differences between the similarity-based approach and the theory-based approach on a number of dimensions. We use "attribute" as a generic term for features, properties, propositions, and other independent chunks of knowledge, and "underlying principle" to refer to causal connects or explanatory relations that we have been describing as parts of theories.

One general way to characterize the difference between the two approaches is to say that the theory-based approach expands the bound-

Table 3.1. *Comparison of two approaches to concepts*

	Similarity-based approach	Theory-based approach
1. Concept representation	Similarity structure; attribute lists; correlated attributes	Correlated attributes plus underlying principles that determine which correlations are noticed
2. Category definition	Various similarity metrics; summation of attributes	An explanatory principle common to category members
3. Units of analysis	Attributes	Attributes plus explicitly represented relations of attributes and concepts
4. Categorization basis	Attribute matching	Matching plus inferential processes supplied by underlying principles
5. Weighting of attributes	Cue validity; salience	Determined in part by importance in the underlying principles
6. Interconceptual structure	Hierarchy based on shared attributes	Network formed by casual and explanatory links, as well as sharing properties picked out as relevant
7. Conceptual development	Feature accretion	Changing organization and explanations of concepts as a result of world knowledge

From Murphy, G. L., & Medin, D. L. (1985). The role of theories in conceptual coherence. *Psychological Review, 92,* 289–316, with permission.

aries of conceptual representation. The theory-based approach implies that to characterize knowledge about a concept we must include a complex web of relations involving that concept and the other concepts that depend on it. At the very least, similarity-based approaches are going to need a much richer view of intra- and interconcept relationships than so far has been advanced, and the explanatory work is going to be done by a theorylike process that provides appropriate constraints.

The next section of this essay shifts focus from similarity-based to theory-based approaches to conceptual coherence. We review evidence that suggests concepts should be viewed as embedded in theories. This evidence will also serve to underline the limitations of similarity-based approaches to conceptual coherence.

The role of theories in conceptual coherence

Theories and attribute selection

For all we have said about the issue of what is to count as an attribute, it may be surprising that attempts to elicit attributes of concepts from experimental subjects have proven quite successful. The basic approach is quite simple: Ask participants to list properties of concepts and if several subjects list some attribute then that attribute is included in the concept. Rosch and Mervis (1975) have shown that these listed attributes can be used to predict goodness of example ratings and times to verify that an exemplar is a member of a category (see Mervis & Rosch, 1981, for a review).

This attribute-listing technique has generated important data for categorization theories, but it raises the question of what determines which attributes are listed. Barsalou and Bower (1983) have made some progress on this issue in that they have shown that two types of properties are likely to be activated during processing. First, properties having high diagnosticity may be active because they are useful in distinguishing instances of a concept from instances of other concepts. Second, properties relevant to how people typically interact with instances of a concept are likely to be frequently active. These two principles do not exhaust people's conceptual knowledge. Thus properties that are necessary for category membership (e.g., for *birds*, having a heart, kidney, and lungs) might never be listed because they might not be discriminative properties in typical context and are only indirectly relevant to how people interact with them. These observations suggest that conceptual representations are not static entities and that attribute listing does not consist of some simple "readout" of attributes from some fixed structure. Rather, access is at least partially determined by typical forms of interaction, which may vary with context. In fact, Roth and Shoben (1983) have shown that typicality judgments vary as a function of particular contexts. For example, tea is a more typical beverage than milk in the context of librarians taking a break, but this ordering reverses in the context of truck drivers taking a break.

Actually, most of the research involving attribute listing employs judge-amended tallies. The reason for this is that participants may list attributes at one level of abstraction and fail to include them at a lower level of abstraction. For example, they may list "two-legged" for *bird* but not for robin, eagle, or other specific birds. B. Tversky and Hemenway (1984) analyze this behavior in terms of cooperative rules of communication (Grice 1975) and implicit contrast sets (the diagnosticity principle – "two legged" does not distinguish robins from eagles). It appears then that attribute listings are constrained by a variety of factors other than simple truth conditions. People are unlikely to list *flammable* as a property of money, not because it does not burn but because flammability is not central to the role money plays in our theories of economic and social interaction. Therefore, attribute listing may predict goodness-of-example ratings because both attribute listings and goodness-of-example ratings are constrained by the same theories and systems of knowledge.

Theories and correlated attributes

We earlier considered the idea that coherent concepts are structured in terms of correlated attributes, but we expressed reservations because of computational problems associated with the many possible correlations. Theories may constrain correlated attributes in at least two distinct ways. First of all, theories may influence the salience of individual attributes and pairs of attributes. More fundamental, however, is the potential role of theories in linking properties in an explanatory system. For example, within the category bird, there is probably a correlation between the type of feather and whether or not the feet are webbed. But this is not a raw correlation that just happens to emerge, but rather a matter of logical and biological necessity. Adjusting to an aquatic environment may bring about a number of adaptations (e.g., webbed feet, water-repellent feathers) that would manifest themselves as correlated attributes. That is, people not only notice feature correlations, but they can deduce *reasons* for them based on their knowledge of the way the world works.

Not only is it the case that people can develop explanations for correlations, but also the availability of such explanations plays a causal role in the development of categories. We have recently completed a set of studies in which people were asked to sort descriptions into categories. In one case, for example, the descriptions were sets of symptoms and the categories were hypothetical diseases. The task was set up so that people could sort on the basis of a single property, or on the basis of two different sets of correlated attributes. The two sets of correlated attributes differed in terms of how readily people might think of a causal association between them. Pilot work had suggested that some pairs of symptoms (e.g., dizziness and earaches, weight gain and high blood pressure) were easier to link than others (e.g., earaches to high blood pressure, dizziness to weight gain). People showed a strong tendency to cluster on the basis of correlated attributes for which a causal link could be easily made. They also justified their sortings in terms of specific causal linkages explaining dizziness and earaches in terms of an ear infection that could disturb the vestibular organ. Thus feature correlations may be important in conceptual representations primarily when they can be represented as theoretical knowledge. The focus on correlated attributes underlines the importance of relational properties, and the study just described shows that theoretical considerations determine which relational properties are used to develop categories.

There is even evidence that theoretical expectations can dominate data in the perception of correlations. Chapman and Chapman (1967, 1969) presented evidence that therapists and undergraduate subjects using certain diagnostic tests perceived correlations between test results and psychological disorders when in fact there were none – or even when the opposite correlation occurred. For example, in the draw-a-person test, observers have the expectation that paranoia or suspiciousness of others will be revealed by how the eyes are drawn and these expectancies prevent observers from objectively evaluating this relationship. On the positive side, there is evidence that in processing numerical information involving possible correlations, performance may be improved dramatically simply by the addition of meaningful labels for the variables that suggest their theoretical significance (e.g., Adelman 1981; Muchinsky & Dudycha 1974; Wright & Murphy 1984).

Theories, relational coding, and linear separability

Earlier we mentioned observations suggesting that linear separability is not a natural constraint on human categorization. Current categorization models implicitly assume that abstract structural constraints on categories hold across all realizations of that structure. We argue, however, that abstract category structures and knowledge structures interact to determine ease of learning. Linearly separable categories, for example, may be easier to learn than categories that are not linearly separable only in a limited number of contexts. The relative difficulty of the two structures may interact with the knowledge structures that are brought to bear on the task. Linear separability may not be an invariant or natural constraint because people's theories, and hence their categories, typically have more internal structure than can be captured by an independent summing of evidence or by similarity to a prototype. If this is true, then if a prior theory suggests that summing or similarity matching is important, linear separability would become important.

Some recent work by Wattenmaker, Dewey, T. Murphy, and Medin (1986) demonstrates this interaction of knowledge structures and abstract category structures. The motivation for this research derives from the argument that properties do not have the status of independent, irreducible primitives and consequently that the structure of interproperty relationships determines concept cohesiveness. For example, it is common practice to assume that the category *bird* is represented in terms of properties such as laying eggs, flying, having wings, building nests in trees, having feathers, and singing. Each of these components itself represents a complex concept with both internal structure and external structure based on interproperty relationships. Building nests is linked to laying eggs, and building them in trees poses logistic problems whose solution involves other properties (e.g., wings, hollow bones, flying). Given these complex relationships it is easy to see that there may be more to birdness than is captured by adding up a bunch of birdlike properties.

What type of interproperty encoding is compatible with using a summing strategy to learn linearly separable categories? Presumably, it is important that all features must be perceived to be related to some common theme. For example, consider apples, oranges, and pears as being analogous to component properties of an example. When the distinguishing characteristics of the components are salient, it makes little sense to sum the entities. If some superordinate concept becomes activated, however, that leads apples, oranges, and pears to be integrated (by being tied to the concept of fruit), then the notion of summing components may become sensible and linear separability may act as a constraint.

Exactly this logic was employed in the Wattenmaker et al. (1986) studies. In one experiment the examples used in learning consisted of sets of descriptions of objects and the categories were structured such that the typical attributes for one category would all be desirable properties if one were searching for a substitute for a hammer (e.g., made of metal, flat surface). The categories either were or were not linearly separable, and in one condition subjects were given the notion of hammer substitutes and in another condition they were not. The idea was that providing a theme would lead subjects to encode properties in terms of the superordinate theme – suitability as a hammer. If all the properties are encoded in relation to the hammer theme then a summing strategy should become natural and linearly separable categories will be easy to learn. The results showed a strong interaction of category structure with the presence or absence of the hammer theme. With the hammer theme the linearly separable categories were much easier to learn but in the absence of the theme the linearly separable categories actually proved harder to learn.

Other experiments by Wattenmaker et al. show that it is not the case that linear separability becomes important whenever the categories are meaningful. For example, in another study the examples were descriptions involving typical features of the occupational categories, *construction worker* and *house painter*. Here the additional clue was that the painter category consisted of both interior and exterior house painters. The categories which were not linearly separable contained correlated properties (e.g., between "works inside" and "works year round" and between "works outside" and "doesn't work in the winter"). The results of this experiment indicated that the additional theme facilitated the learning of the nonlinearly separable categories and impaired the learning of linearly separable categories.

These studies suggest that knowledge structures have systematic effects in terms of the forms of relational coding induced. The idea that linear separability is an important constraint can be thought of as holding for the special case where properties are encoded relative to an integrated category theme. One cannot describe some abstract category structure (e.g., the presence or absence of linear separability) as simple or complex, sensible or bizarre, independent of the form or theory and associated knowledge structure brought to bear on it. When theory and structure match, the task becomes simple; when there is a mismatch between theory and structure, the task becomes difficult.

This work on theories and linear separability makes two major points. First of all, ease of learning or naturalness cannot be described simply in terms of matching and mismatching properties; rather, one needs to consider relational properties. Second, the salience of these relational properties is heavily constrained by the theory or theme intertwined with them.

Theories and prototype structure

The consensus view of the structure of natural object categories is that the overwhelming evidence showing typicality effects and the absence of evidence for defining features leads inevitably to the conclusion that categories are organized around characteristic or typical features. A popular theory of learning growing out of this view is that as a result of experience with examples of a category, people form an impression of the central tendency of a category and categorical judgments come to be based on this central tendency or prototype. Prototype theory, as an instance of the probabilistic view, shares all the limitations of the probabilistic view in terms of an account of category cohesiveness. This raises the question of how one might reconcile the ubiquitous typicality effects with concept naturalness. Again, we think the answer lies in viewing concepts as embedded in theories.

First of all, Barsalou (1985) has shown that typicality effects in goal-derived categories correlate highly with the degree to which examples satisfy the relevant goal or approximate the ideal value. He also performed similar analyses on common categories such as fruit and tools. Although the underlying goal or dimension for natural categories was speculative (e.g., for *fruit*, how much people like it), they proved to be significantly correlated with exemplar goodness even after the effects of frequency and family resemblance were partialed out. This suggests that natural concepts are at least partially organized in terms of underlying dimensions that reflect how the concept normally is involved with people's goals and activities.

Fillmore (1982) has made a related suggestion about the source of typicality structure. He argued that concepts are represented in terms of "idealized cognitive models." For example, the concept *bachelor* can be defined as an unmarried adult male in the context of a society in which certain (idealized) expectations about marriage and marriageable age are realized. The existence of "poor examples" of this concept – Catholic priests, homosexual men, men cohabiting with women friends, etc. – does not mean, Fillmore argues, that the concept itself is ill-defined. Rather, the claim is that the idealized cognitive model does not fit the actual world very well. Clearly, such a model is an example of what we have been calling "theories," since it provides a means of connecting many concepts to explain diverse facts. Mohr (1977) has argued that this is the correct way to view platonic universals, and Lakoff (1982; Chapter 4, this volume) has developed this notion of idealized mental models in some detail. For example, he has shown that typicality effects arise in part from interactions associated with multiple, overlapping cognitive models.

Fixed semantic structures and dynamic theories

Our focus on similarity and categorization theories may be a little misleading with respect to the arguments we have been making concerning interproperty and interconcept relations. Much of the research on semantic memory based on networks or sets of features can be viewed as attempts to represent just these relationships. Although attempts to represent these relationships in semantic structures allow for greater richness in conceptual representations, we see two fundamental problems with current approaches.

Johnson-Laird, Herrmann, and Chaffin (1984) argue that fixed semantic structures do not adequately capture people's knowledge about the world. To borrow one of their examples, people know that a tomato is more "squishable" than a potato, although it would seem implausible that this fact is directly represented in semantic memory. Furthermore, relational properties like "squishable" are highly dependent on context and the operations of freezing the tomato and boiling the potato would reverse the observations. It is very difficult to represent this flexibility of relationships in a fixed structure. The problem is not that relational properties are unconstrained but rather that much of our knowledge is computed rather than prestored. Network models do allow computation (e.g., inheritance links may allow one to infer that Helen of Troy had both arteries and veins), but it seems from examples like the operation of freezing that not all computations are wired into a network structure. It would seem that network models must be flexible enough to allow experiments to be run and evaluated "mentally" where the results of such experiments are constrained by world knowledge and people's theories about the world.

To us it seems that this pattern of flexibility and need for concern about extension to examples in the world leads naturally to viewing concepts as embedded in theories. Theories are dynamic and represent "mental models" of the world based on perception, memory, and imagination (see Johnson-Laird, 1983, for further arguments along these lines). Note that we are arguing for an ecological approach because the notion of mental models is almost vacuous without their extension to the world.

Ziff (1972) provides some delightful examples illustrating the role of mental models or conceptual schemes in understanding. For example, it seems sensible to say "a cheetah can outrun a man," but what about a one-day-old cheetah, or an aged cheetah with arthritis, or a healthy cheetah with a 100-pound weight on its back? What we mean when we say that a cheetah can outrun a man is that under some tantalizingly difficult-to-specify circumstances, a cheetah would outrun a man. Ziff refers to this set of conditions as a conceptual scheme and makes the point that two people understand each other to the extent to which these conceptual schemes are shared. These implicit theories, which are likely quite flexible (imagine two veterinarians running a home for aged cheetahs) constrain our understanding of relationships among concepts.

Summary

We have been arguing that concepts should be viewed as embedded in theories. The idea is that coherence derives from both the internal structure of a conceptual domain and the position of the concept in the complete knowledge base (the external structure). Properties such as high within-category similarity and low between-category similarity may be by-products of internal structure as well as the rest of the knowledge base. The tendency to relate concepts and theories appears to be such that people impose more structure on concepts than simple similarity (if that can be defined) would seem to license.

Constraining theories

The arguments so far advanced do not constitute anything like a complete solution to the problem of conceptual coherence. Unless one can specify constraints on what a (good) theory is, it may not help to claim that conceptual coherence derives from having a theory. That is, the problem of category coherence may simply have been banished from the level of attributes and similarity only to reappear intact as the problem of theory coherence. This cannot be entirely true in that theories are characterized by an internal and external structure of causal linkages so that there is no clear analog to attribute matching. Still, one does not have to think this argument is devastating in order to take it seriously, and the remainder of this essay is directed toward attempts to specify constraints on theories.

The organization of this section is as follows. We begin with the notion that the principle of parsimony – the idea that simple theories are preferable to complex ones – is the only constraint needed. We contend that this approach is inadequate. We then turn to some of our recent work on rule induction, which further undermines simplicity as the sole constraint needed and which offers some guidelines for developing constraints on theories. This work is limited by exactly those factors that differentiate rules from theories, and we then return to a more ecological approach to constraints on theories. We conclude this section with a set of arguments that are responsible for the term *cognitive archeology* appearing in the title of this essay. The general need for an ecologically motivated approach to constraints on theories does not, of course, depend on the merits of these particular speculations.

Simplicity

The notion of simplicity or parsimony is so well engrained in the scientific community that one might wonder if other constraints are needed. Simplicity, however, is much like the concept of similarity in its elusiveness.

First of all, one needs to keep in mind that theories are related to data and the background for the argument about favoring the simpler of two theories is that they give an equally accurate account of the data. If the more complicated theory fits the data better, then already one is faced with the issue of trading accuracy for parsimony.

A second problem with the notion of simplicity is that it ignores the issue of the scope or domain of a theory. Both concepts and theories have an external structure defined in terms of a body of knowledge. Suppose one is comparing a theory that explains some observation in a simple way with an alternative theory that gives a more complicated account but which fits better with one's knowledge base more broadly construed. One might well prefer the latter theory. For example, one might, with some justification, opt for a very elaborate explanation of some experiment on extrasensory perception, because the alternative theory based on psychic powers does not fit in with a large body of other scientific theories and associated observations.

Perhaps the most serious problem with the notion of simplicity is that it depends upon the language of description employed. Consequently, simplicity can only be evaluated within a theoretical framework that is specified about what constitutes a basic operation and what is an elementary concept. Figure 3.1 illustrates this issue using a sequential induction problem. The task is to determine what the next figure (2 × 2 matrix) in the sequence ought to be. Presumably, the answer is that the most simple continuation is the one desired. The best continuation, however, depends on what is taken as basic. If one focuses on individual cells in the matrices and writes transition rules for successive figures (e.g., B − R, R − B for the top left cell, etc.), then the top fifth figure is clearly the most appropriate. If, instead, the complex 2 × 2 matrix is taken as basic, then one can write transition rules involving figure rotation (figures 3 and 4 are 90-degree counterclockwise rotations of figures 1 and 2, respectively) that lead one to the conclusion that the bottom fifth figure is the correct choice. If either choice were constrained to be described by a rule formulated in terms of the alternative basic operations, then the resulting rules would be very complex and unnatural. Again the point is that simplicity is not independent of the language of description.

A related problem with the notion of simplicity is that it is a product constraint (a simple theory) rather than a process constraint (theory generation). That is, it is consistent with the idea that people generate all sorts of theories varying in complexity and then select from those the

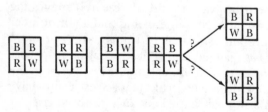

Figure 3.1. Which best fills in the fifth figure in the sequence?

most simple. Consequently, simplicity as a product constraint says little about how people come up with theories or how or why they might consider alternative descriptive languages. Although it is conceivable that simplicity constrains theories in just this way, we shall argue that it is more fruitful to look for constraints in terms of processes.

Rule induction and product versus processing constraints

There is a considerable literature on rule learning and much of it has been devoted to the relative difficulty of different types of rules (e.g., Haygood & Bourne 1965). This literature presents a mixed picture in that, for example, the greater ease of conjunctive than disjunctive rules may not be consistent over stimulus types (e.g., Reznick & Richman 1976). For our present purposes, we wish to emphasize that to the extent that research focuses on the relative difficulty of different types of rules at the expense of search for processing mechanisms, constraints will tend to be stated in terms of products rather than processes. Almost all of the work on rule learning has used experimenter-defined rules. In contrast to this approach, we have been evaluating candidate constraints using a rule-induction paradigm where subjects are presented with categories and asked to come up with a rule that not only will work for the set of examples but also could be used to classify new instances (Medin, Wattenmaker, & Michalski 1986). An example of this task is shown in Figure 3.2 where the requirement is to state a rule that could be used to decide if a train is East- or Westbound. The reader may wish to undertake this task before reading further.

It should be obvious that there is a large set of potential rules. Our goal is to develop principles that determine which subsets of these potential rules people find natural.

The task shown in Figure 3.2 is fairly difficult. Only a few people discovered the classifier using a simple property (East trains have three or more different loads). From a sample of 60 participants, we obtained 19 conjunctive rules (e.g., East trains have a triangle load and 3 or more loaded cars) and 32 disjunctive rules (e.g., West trains have two cars or a car with a jagged top). Given the background of research suggesting people have difficulty with negations, it is interesting that a fair number of rules involved negative properties (e.g., East trains have 3 or more cars and a triangle load and *not* a jagged top). These negative properties were almost exclusively associated with either conjunctive rules or the conjunctive part of a complex disjunctive rule (e.g., West trains have white engine wheels and not an oval-shaped car or else three circular

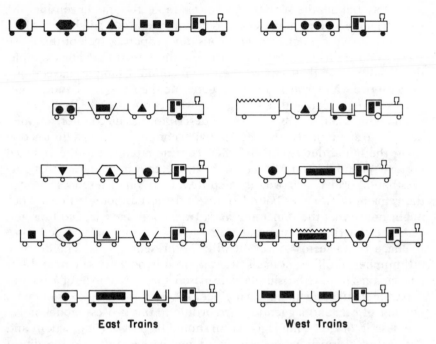

Figure 3.2. What separates the Eastbound trains from the Westbound trains?

loads). Therefore, it does not seem feasible to develop constraints at the level of products such as conjunctive versus disjunctive rules.

What happens when one attempts to develop constraints in terms of processes? Without any pretense of doing more than providing an illustration, consider the following process model for the rule-induction task: People focus on one category and begin by looking for a descriptor that holds for all members of the positive (focus) set and does not apply to any counterexample. If one is found, then a simple rule can be generated. If no single descriptor works, because there are counterexamples, then one of two strategies may be applied. If there are numerous counterexamples, then people may look for combinations of properties (e.g., "X and Y") that span the set but do not generate counterexamples. If there are only a few counterexamples, then people may attempt to eliminate them by negating properties of the counterexamples not present in the positive set. For example, for the problem in Figure 3.2, a person may notice that all Eastbound trains have a triangle load but that two Westbound trains do also. This description is complete but not consistent. They might then look for combinations of properties that apply to the East but not the West trains. For example, they might consider the rule "triangle load in nonlast car," but that rule would still have a counterexample. Next a person might consider properties true of these two Westbound trains that are not shared by the East trains. For example, they might notice that the two West train counterexamples have a long car with two white wheels and then generate the rule "Eastbound trains have a triangle load and not long cars with two white wheels."

The other main possibility is that a descriptor has no counterexamples but fails to span the positive set. In that event people form a disjunction using the initial descriptor and then confine attention to the reduced positive set and the contrast set. For example, they might notice that only Westbound trains have two cars, and then focus on differences between the remaining two Westbound trains and the Eastbound trains. They might notice that the remaining West trains both have jagged tops and generate the rule "Westbound trains have two cars or a jagged top."

This account seems consistent with the present results. The descriptor, number of different loads, was apparently not very salient and few participants found the simple rule based on it. Number of cars was apparently quite salient and many people found the simple disjunction, number of cars and jagged top. According to this process model, negative descriptors (e.g., not jagged top) should be part of conjunctions and not part of disjunctions. As was mentioned earlier, this held for almost all cases where negative descriptors were used.

In this model the relative number of disjunctive and conjunctive rules would depend on the exact structure of the trains and the salience of the associated descriptors. In general, however, because people are assumed to focus initially on properties that members of the positive set have in common, conjunctive rules are likely to result. For the trains in Figure 3.3, the conjunction of two descriptors (e.g., dark wheels and closed top) has no counterexamples, and a simple conjunctive rule could be discovered. Exactly this preference for conjunctive rules was observed.

What about the results when the trains in Figure 3.3 were presented one at a time? In terms of our descriptive model the learning procedure should make it more difficult to discover properties that hold for all examples (i.e., are complete) or which do not have counterexamples (i.e., are consistent). If a person finds a property that is consistent but not complete (e.g., *short* for Westbound trains), the remaining train might be described in detail and one might see a rule like "West trains are *short* or *long with a circular load*." Note that such a rule is different from the rule "West trains are *short or have a circular load*" because it specifically combines circular load with long car. The disjunctive rules given in the sequential presentation condition conformed to the predicted pattern.

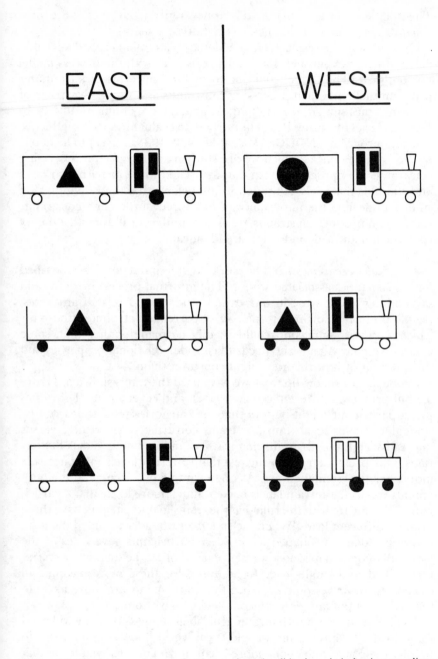

Figure 3.3. The less complex set of trains used as stimuli in the rule-induction paradigm.

The rule "short or a circular load" was never given, but rules of the form "*short* or *long with a circular load*" were fairly frequent.

Overall then, the results from the Medin, Wattenmaker, and Michalski rule-induction experiments are fairly consistent with the process model just outlined. The model could be formalized in terms of a computer program that embodied processing constraints and would be capable of inducing rules similar in form to those generated by human subjects. In fact, this series of studies had as its purpose to evaluate a specific inductive learning program, INDUCE (Michalski 1980, 1983a,b). Yet to be determined is the extent to which we are studying fairly general processing constraints as opposed to constraints associated with our particular tasks and stimulus materials. Although we do believe that the rule-induction studies underline the importance of developing processing constraints rather than product constraints, we are not under the illusion that theory construction and rule-induction are identical.

Rules versus theories. The work on rule induction just described has no semantics associated with it. The informal process model would say nothing about why, in our earlier study on correlated attributes, people preferred sorting by one pair of correlated attributes (those for which a causal connection could readily be made) rather than some alternative pair. Again, one needs to consider relational properties and the question of how theories might constrain them.

In one line of follow-up work we have used the trains shown in Figure 3.2 but presented different category labels and cover stories. For example, a participant might be told that the categories were trains run by smugglers versus legal trains, or trains constructed by creative versus uncreative children, or trains that travel in mountainous versus flat terrains. Our preliminary data suggest that different labels influence rule inductions in systematic ways. As one example of a change, the mountainous versus flat terrain labels make it much more likely that a participant will come up with the rule that the trains in one category have three or more different loads. When the smuggler category included the train carrying a diamond-shaped load, a few participants gave rules of the form "diamond-shaped load or . . ." even though the diamond descriptor applied to a single load. In addition, for these more meaningful categories, we have some evidence that participants are more likely to tolerate rules that are either incomplete or have counterexamples.

The follow-up work with meaningful labels suggests that one will need some form of representing people's real world knowledge in order to predict their rule inductions more accurately. The idea would be that this knowledge might make certain properties and combinations of properties more salient and thereby influence the particular rule inductions that people develop.

Actually, we think this example is quite deceptive in that it overlooks a crucial component of theory construction – the development of a descriptive language and basic operations associated with it. It simply is not the case that the world provides the basic units of analysis nor that competing theories necessarily subscribe to a common set of descriptive components. An illustration of this point is provided by a more recent rule-induction study (conducted in collaboration with Glenn Nakamura) using a richer set of stimulus materials. The category examples were children's drawings associated with the draw-a-person test used in clinical assessment. For a fixed set of drawings, we varied the category labels. For example, one set of participants might be told the drawings were done by mentally healthy versus disturbed children, another set told the drawings were done by creative versus noncreative children, and still another set told the drawings were done by farm versus city children. The results cannot be described simply in terms of the relative salience of a fixed set of properties, because category labels and descriptive units were not independent. For example, participants in one condition might note that the humans drawn by farm children all had at least some animal parts in them (e.g., a piglike nose), but when the same drawings were labeled as creative or mentally disturbed no participant mentioned the presence of animal parts.

One might be tempted to describe these results in terms of property salience changing across conditions, but we believe that to do so is to miss a very important point. This point is based on Kant's difference between the productive use of imagination (embodying innate perceptual constraints) and the reproductive use of imagination (involving relating particular experiences). Kant's terms (Kant 1933) correspond closely to Wittgenstein's distinction between "seeing the object" and "seeing the object as." The same object (e.g., a triangle) can be *seen as* a geometric drawing, a wedge, a mountain, a triangular hole, a threat, an arrow, and so on (see also Barresi 1981). We think this distinction is also important for the draw-a-person stimuli. Actually, in each of the different labeling conditions people stated rules at an abstract level and used the inferred properties of the drawings as support. For example, in the case of drawings supposedly done by farm children the rule might be that "each drawing reflects some aspect of farm life." One drawing might be seen to have a piglike nose, another to have a farmer's work clothes, and so on. These observations suggest that the drawings do not manifest some fixed set of properties that vary in salience so much as they "support" a limitless set of properties that derive from the interaction of the drawings with particular observers (Neisser develops this argument in Chapter 2, this volume).

Once one concedes that some set of stimuli or data "support" properties that hold only for the *interaction* of intelligent systems with aspects of their perceptual world, one must recognize that descriptive languages and basic operations may be different for different intelligent systems and may be different for the same individual at different points in time. In that sense, theory construction may represent a basic reorganization of knowledge rather than an increase or decrease in the salience of a set of prescribed properties. Susan Carey's (1985) studies of children's biological theories provide an elegant demonstration of a fundamental shift from a human-centered to a less egocentric organization of biological knowledge. Likewise, ether and phlogiston play no role in modern theories of physics. An adequate approach to constraints on theories cannot be forced to work with a fixed descriptive language because theories and descriptive languages are themselves mutually constraining. This is yet another reason why we do not see any hope for the idea that constraints can be developed in terms of products.

Naive theories

One straightforward approach to developing constraints on theories is to study people's theories about the world. There has been a recent upsurge of interest in people's mental models or naive theories (e.g., Gentner & Stevens 1983) of various physical phenomena. Many of these naive theories embody incorrect assumptions about the world and they often persist in the face of formal education. Consider the case of momentum. Suppose we have an airplane moving toward a target site to drop some cargo. Many people who are asked when the cargo should be released in order to land on the site say when the plane is directly above the site, failing to take the momentum of the cargo into account. From the point of view of looking for constraints on theories, these results are potentially of great interest in that they suggest that constraints associated with the learner lead to systematic inaccuracies.

So far, however, the work on naive theories has not led to major insights into constraints on theories. Perhaps one reason for this is that insufficient attention has been paid to an analysis of the structure of the environment in which naive theories are formulated. That is, we do not know the extent to which these naive theories are contradicted in experience. Few of us have the opportunity to drop things out of airplanes. A more typical circumstance involving momentum may be the situation of a person dropping something while in motion. But in this case, in trying to figure out when to release something, a person would also have to take into consideration their reaction time. The reaction time factor would lead them to initiate dropping of the object before they were directly over the target site. Appropriate calibration might come through experience, but because of the correlation between momentum and other factors (e.g., reaction time) there may be little in this experience that would lead a person to develop the notion of momentum for dropped objects. This line of reasoning is entirely speculative, but without an analysis of the environment in which naive theories are developed it hardly seems fair to call them naive, and at the very least it is difficult to use these observations to develop constraints on theories.

A closely related point is that insights into constraints on theories have been slow to come because greatest attention (perhaps quite appropriately, for many purposes) has been directed at the contents of naive theories rather than their structure. Typically, the naive theory is compared with the (more nearly) correct theory rather than the naive theory being compared with the environment in which the (naive) theory is formulated. It is possible that the structure of information in the environment is insufficient to allow one to converge on the correct theory (see Einhorn & Hogarth 1979). For example, psychiatrists do not see a random sample of the population and they frequently do not find out the fate of patients who do not return; anyone familiar with the principles of experimental design will recognize that these circumstances are far from optimal with respect to converging on an accurate impression of populations and treatments.

There is, of course, some work looking at the structure of naive theories. For example, the analysis of cultural belief systems in *The New Golden Bough* led to the principles of homeopathy (cause and effects tend to be similar) and contagion (a cause must have some form of contact to transmit its effect). Homeopathic medicine is based on the idea that a treatment must have physical resemblance to the symptoms associated with a disease. Despite the reservations we have expressed about the concept of similarity, some restricted form of similarity may act as a constraint or bias in theory formation. Incidentally, there is evidence that classical conditioning is more rapid if both the conditioned and unconditioned stimulus have a rapid onset or if both have a gradual onset than if one has a gradual and the other an abrupt onset (Testa 1974). Again however, we add that, without further analyses, it is difficult to know the extent to which homeopathy is supported by the environment.

There is also evidence that analogies and metaphors rather than just literal similarity serve to structure theories. In an analysis that parallels our reservations about attribute matching, Gentner (1983) has argued that analogies and metaphors involve a translation of relational structures rather than a mapping of attributes or properties. This line of work makes the important point that theories often are constrained by the fact that theories in one domain often are exported to another domain (for some interesting examples taken from psychology, see Gentner & Grudin 1985). Consider, for example, theories about extroversion and introversion. Based on a reservoir metaphor, one views extroverts as having excess energy that is often expressed socially. On the other hand, if one takes homeostasis as the appropriate metaphor, then one might think of extroverts as being chronically underaroused and seeking social stimulation. This analysis of analogy and metaphor strikes us as a very promising approach to constraints, and it should pay off to the extent that principles associated with mapping from one domain into others can be developed (see Gentner 1983). Of course, this transference from domain to domain will need to be traced back to some original theory or set of theories.

Cognitive archeology

By now it should be clear, if not by elegance of presentation then certainly by repetition, that we think that constraints on theories should be developed in terms of a process model growing out of an analysis of the relationship between people and their environment. But one needs a strategy for going about this. In this section we describe a strategy based on the work of Gibson, Neisser, and Shepard, which we refer to as cognitive archeology, and then suggest a heuristic device derived from this strategy for identifying constraints on theories.

Relationships between organisms and the environment. One of Gibson's major contributions was to argue that perception is active rather than contemplative and passive, and that the perceptual system represents an adaptation of organisms to their environment (e.g., Gibson 1979). The environment provides an anchor and perceptual systems are constrained to respond to the information embodied in that environment. For example, according to Gibson, *constancy* is not a mental construct but rather an objective property of the environment.

In his recent discussion of Gibson's work, Russell (1984) focuses on the adaptive function of perception. In his words, "So one way of describing the message of TDP [Theory of Direct Perception] is that we should not be overimpressed by the analogy between a perceptual system and a cognitive system, but should bear in mind that in the other direction there is an analogy with a respiratory system" (Russell 1984:167). One could conceive of breathing as the perception of oxygen but that would probably yield few insights into the process of respiration. Analyzing perception in terms of cognitive operations, Russell argues, may be similarly unilluminating.

Gibson recognized that there was more to perception than knowledge of properties of objects. There are also *affordances* which are based on *relationships* between objects and particular organisms. Every object is involved in infinitely many objective affordances, only some of which are specified unambiguously by optical information. Neisser (Chapter 2, this volume) extends this view by including the notion of conceptual properties, which are defined by the relationship between objects and certain systems of cultural or scientific beliefs. Thus perception is direct, whereas categorization is not, because categorization depends on the fit between objects and the theories we make about them.

Aside from the general point that theories are about the world, Neisser's view links theories to the perception of the properties of objects and affordances associated with the interaction of organisms and their environment. One might wonder whether these linkages or moorings are sufficient to keep the ship of conceptual properties and theories from going adrift. The main point we wish to make, however, is that organisms reflect the (evolutionary) history of their interaction with their environment in terms of adaptive specializations, and this is as true for the cognitive system as it is for the respiratory system.

Adaptive specializations can take a variety of forms. Consider, for example, the case of nest building in the long-tailed tailorbird, which actually sews leaves together to provide a superstructure for its nest. Conceivably, tailorbirds are very intelligent and nest building reflects just one instance of elaborate forms of learning that take place in each generation. Another possibility is that tailorbirds have a specialized ability to learn how to build nests that does not extend to other domains. Of course, the entire pattern of behavior could be innate and, in fact, for nest building in tailorbirds, that is the case. Since adaptive specializations that attune organisms with the demands of their environment can be expressed in varied forms, it may take experimental intervention to determine the particular form of adaptation that is present. For example, many organisms display day – night cycles or biological (circadian) rhythms in their behavior. These cycles could be totally driven by the presence or absence of light. When rats are placed in continuous darkness, however, they continue to manifest cycles of activity that closely mirror day and night. This result suggests that rats have some form of "internal clock." Although this clock is not accurate to the second and exposure to prolonged periods of darkness can lead to asynchrony with day and night, these clocks quickly become calibrated when rats are reexposed to a normal pattern of day and night. In brief, the form of adaptation associated with circadian rhythms in rats was discovered by breaking the normal correlation between the environment and the organism.

The above example is the key to a research strategy outlined by Roger Shepard in a recent essay (Shepard 1984). Shepard argues that an eco- logical approach to perception does not imply that one should only study perception in ecologically valid contexts. To do so would raise the prob- lem of separating constraints associated with the environment itself from those embodied in the organism. To discover which constraints are em- bodied, Shepard suggests that one needs to provide an ambiguous or neutral context and see what comes out of this decoupling of organism and typical environment. Note that this is not a license to use any experi- mental situation; rather the situation has to be carefully structured to break this organism by environment correlation. The benefits of this strategy are nicely documented by Shepard's (1984) review of his pro- gram of research on perception.

At this point the reader may be wondering what this work on percep- tion has to do with constraints on theories. In the second half of this essay we have been arguing that an ecological approach to constraints on theories is appropriate. We now wish to suggest, as a heuristic device, that constraints on theories may show strong parallels to embodied con- straints associated with perception as well as with learning and memory. Before elaborating on this idea we note that it is not particularly novel – Lakoff and others have noted, for example, that many of our most important metaphors are based on our understanding of space and spatial relationships (Lakoff & Johnson 1980).

Cognitive archeology. The notion of cognitive archeology is di- rectly based on Shepard's research strategy and the idea that constraints associated with the environment are embodied or reflected in orga- nisms. Just as one might reason from properties in some world what types of organisms could live in it, so also one might reason from proper- ties of some organism something about the world (environmental de- mands) they were part of. Decoupling provides an opportunity to evalu- ate the form in which constraints or biases have been embodied as opposed to being supported by the environment alone (see Birnbaum, 1975, for an interesting methodological approach to decoupling). The Chapmans' work on illusory correlation is an example of this strategy in that it shows that people develop theories about relationships between responses on projective tests and diagnostic categories that are not objec- tively supportable (Chapman & Chapman 1967, 1969). Since these in- correct theories tend to be shared theories (observers agree with each other), it seems likely that some basic constraints on theory formation are reflected in this phenomenon.

Consistent with the notion that constraints on theories may show strong parallels to embodied constraints associated with more basic processes. Rozin (1976) has argued that evolution involves a freeing up of special purpose mechanisms and that systems which are initially "tightly wired" and unconscious may ultimately give rise to consciousness and flexibility. As one example of special purpose mechanisms, many of the inferential systems involved in visual perception are tightly wired into the visual system and inaccessible to consciousness (see Ullman, 1979, for unconscious computational processes associated with the perception of motion). The essence of Rozin's argument is that evolutionary mechanisms result in the application of adaptive specialization from one domain to other domains. Thus, special purpose mechanisms originally tightly wired into basic processes (e.g., visual perception) may gradually become accessible to other systems (e.g., cognitive processes) and, in the extreme, may give rise to consciousness and flexibility.

If the evolution of cognitive systems is associated with a gradual increase in consciousness and flexibility, then there may be some close relationships among the mechanisms associated with basic learning, memorial, and perceptual processes and higher cognitive processes such as theory building. That is, we are suggesting that conceptually based theories may preserve some of the constraints or biases associated with more basic (less flexible) cognitive systems. Although we think that Rozin's ideas on conscious access are intriguing, our suggestion does not hinge on the issue of consciousness. Whether or not there is a close connection between perceptual and conceptual constraints is completely independent of the awareness question.

Our suggestion, then, is that constraints associated with what we normally think of as more basic (and less accessible) cognitive processes may carry over into higher-level cognitive processes. That is, a process model for theory construction may embody many of the same constraints as embodied in process models for learning, memory, and perception. It is not easy to come up with illustrations of this point, but we shall offer an example. In the section on Naive Theories we did not cite any of the vast literature on people's ordinary explanations and causal attributions associated with observing themselves and other people. We find it intriguing, however, that the principles being developed to understand people's causal attributions show some striking similarities to principles embodied in modern theories of animal conditioning (for examples of the former see chapters by Fincham and by Kelley in the volume edited by Jaspars, Fincham, & Hewstone 1983; for examples of the latter, see Rescorla & Wagner 1977, and Rescorla & Durlach 1981). For example, both domains rely on a principle of informativenss (e.g., in conditioning, learning is thought to occur only to the extent that the unconditioned stimulus is not expected) and both assume that temporal contiguity, spatial proximity, and similarity of magnitudes (of cause and effect or of conditioned and unconditioned stimulus) influence performance (attribution and conditioning, respectively). The parallels are close enough that people in animal conditioning are taking attribution theory seriously (e.g., Bolles 1976; Dickinson, Shanks, & Evenden 1984) and examination of the literature on animal conditioning might prove to be a useful source for identifying candidate constraints on causal attributions.

There may be even closer ties between perception and causal attribution. Michotte's (1963) classic work on the perception of causality still makes fascinating reading, and he himself was well aware of the potential link between causal perception and thought. In his words, "There are some cases, viz. launching and entraining, in which a causal impression arises, clear, genuine, and unmistakable and the idea of cause can be derived from it by simple abstraction in the same way as the idea of shape or movement can be derived from the perception of shape or movement" (Michotte 1963:270–271).

For a second example of our point, we turn once again to correlated attributes. Rosch, Mervis, and their associates (see Mervis & Rosch, 1981, for a review) have argued that the world is structured in terms of clusters of correlated attributes. Sensitivity to correlated attributes might be embodied in a (large) computational device that stores information about pairs of attributes, triples, and so on (see Hayes-Roth & Hayes-Roth 1977). Aside from the problem mentioned in the first section of this paper concerning the many possible correlations, we think something as important as sensitivity to correlated attributes would likely not be manifest in a general purpose computational device. As one alternative, the Medin and Schaffer (1978) context model assumes that people store examples of concepts and that categorization decisions are based on reasoning by analogy from examples that are retrieved by the probe. For instance, some novel four-legged creature might be classified as a mammal because it is quite similar to an elephant (or in another case to a mouse) and the categorizer may know that elephants (or mice) are mammals. The context model constrains similarity to be an interactive function of matching and mismatching properties. Although the model is noncomputational and makes no direct assumptions about the encoding of attribute correlations, it nonetheless behaves in a manner that is sensitive to correlated attributes (e.g., Medin, Altom, Edelson, & Freko 1982). Incidentally, there is evidence that people's categorization decisions reflect a sensitivity to correlated attributes even when they are totally unable to verbalize the basis of their decisions (Lewicki 1985;

Wattenmaker 1986). People's sensitivity to correlated attributes appears to have both analytic and nonanalytic components.

The general point is that there may be interesting linkages among structural constraints in the environment, nonconscious and relatively inflexible perceptual and memorial mechanisms, and more flexible theories. As an aside, the context model evolved out of analyses of animal learning and memory (see Medin & Reynolds, 1985, for a review). Regardless of whether the context model is otherwise a good or bad model, it seems likely that we will need categorization models that can achieve sensitivity to correlated attributes without conscious computations. Furthermore, it seems possible that more conscious, flexible theorizing may inherit or not deviate substantially from these constraints. For example, Medin and Smith (1981) asked different groups of subjects to employ different strategies in the same categorization task. These instructions produced large phenotypic differences in performance, but in each case the context model was able to provide an accurate fit to the data by the assumption that strategies worked to change the salience of different properties comprising the examples.

To extend this example a bit, we have also recently examined a modified version of the context model where it is assumed that if responding by analogy with retrieved information is successful, then similarities between the current material and what was retrieved are made more salient, whereas if the analogy fails differences between the current material and what was retrieved are made more salient. These assumptions lead the model to behave in a rulelike way without directly incorporating rules, just as earlier versions of the model led to sensitivity to correlated attributes without computing correlations. We refer to the representations that give rise to rulelike performance as rule precursors. What is interesting about these rule precursors is that they can be used to predict the explicit rules that people give in our rule-induction task. For example, for the trains shown in Figure 3.3, simulations of this modified context model lead to precursors that behave like a conjunctive rule or like a rule plus exception strategy, but we do not observe precursors that behave like a simple disjunction. In other words, the constraints associated with these precursors may tend to be paralleled by corresponding constraints on the explicit rules that people give us.

It may be that the above parallels between noncomputational processes and rules or strategies either are accidental or occur for some trivial reason. We have only begun to study nonanalytic learning to see if people's rulelike behavior conforms to predictions of the context model, and it should be clear that our example is intended to be only illustrative. We do think it is important to realize that the mere fact that theories are (usually) about the world may not sufficiently constrain them. Our speculation is that flexible, conscious (and computational) theorizing is constrained in terms of processing principles which may not stray too far from less flexible processing mechanisms that embody constraints associated with the interaction of intelligent organisms with their world. The apple may not fall far from the tree.

Summary

In this chapter we have argued that similarity-based approaches to conceptual coherence are insufficient to explain the richness of conceptual structure, and opt instead for a theory-based approach to conceptual coherence. A theory-based approach emphasizes that coherence derives from both the internal structure of a conceptual domain and the position of the concept in the complete knowledge base. Concepts are viewed as embedded in theories and are coherent to the extent that they fit people's background knowledge or naive theories about the world.

The second half of the chapter discussed possible strategies for identifying constraints on theory formation. Theories were viewed as being extensionally anchored by the interaction of people with their world both in terms of the structure manifest in the world and in terms of the structure embodied in the human organism. It was emphasized that the search for constraints should be governed by an attempt to develop process models of the interaction between people and their environment. We speculatively suggested that a useful strategy for developing such models might be to examine the possibility that constraints on theories show strong parallels to embodied constraints associated with basic perceptual, learning, and memorial processes. Adaptive specializations to the environment that are initially tightly wired into a particular system and accomplish specific purposes may eventually be incorporated into other systems, and may ultimately give rise to consciousness and flexibility. If the evolution of cognitive systems is associated with a gradual increase in accessibility, then there may be some close relationships among the mechanisms associated with basic perceptual and cognitive processes and higher cognitive processes such as theory construction. Conceptually based theories may preserve some of the constraints or biases associated with more basic and less flexible cognitive systems.

NOTE

Preparation of this paper was supported by National Institute of Mental Health grant MH32370 to Douglas L. Medin. We would like to thank Dedre Getner, David Green, and Sarah Hampson for their helpful comments on an earlier draft of this manuscript.

REFERENCES

Adelman, L. (1981). The influence of formal, substantive, and contextual task properties on the relative effectiveness of different forms of feedback in multiple-cue probability learning tasks. *Organizational Behavior and Human Performance, 27*, 423–442.

Armstrong, S. L., Gleitman, L. R., & Gleitman, H. (1983). What some concepts might not be. *Cognition, 13*, 263–308.

Baressi, J. (1981). *Perception and imagination.* Paper presented at the Conference on the Philosophy of Perception and Psychology, Montreal, Canada.

Barsalou, L. W. (1983). Ad hoc categories. *Memory & Cognition, 11*, 211–227.

(1984). *Determinants of graded structure in categories.* Unpublished manuscript, Emory University Psychology Department, Atlanta, GA.

(1985). Ideals, central tendency, and freqeuncy of instantiation. *Journal of Experimental Psychology: Learning, Memory, and Cognition, 11*, 629–654.

Barsalou, L. W., & Bowers, G. H. (1983). *A priori determinants of a concept's highly accessible information.* Unpublished manuscript, Emory University, Atlanta, GA.

Birnbaum, M. H. (1975). Expectancy and judgment. In F. Restle, R. Shiffrin, W. G. Castellan, H. Lindman, & D. Pisoni (Eds.), *Cognitive theory* (Vol. 1). Hillsdale, NJ: Erlbaum.

Bolles, R. C. (1976). Animal learning and memory. In D. L. Medin, T. J. Roberts, & R. M. Davis (Eds.), *Animal memory.* Hillsdale, NJ: Erlbaum.

Carey, S. (1985). *Conceptual change in childhood.* Cambridge, MA: M.I.T. Press.

Chapman, L. J., & Chapman, J. P. (1967). Genesis of popular but erroneous psychodiagnostic observations. *Journal of Abnormal Psychology, 72*, 193–204.

(1969). Illusory correlation as an obstacle to the use of valid psychodiagnostic signs. *Journal of Abnormal Psychology, 74*, 272–280.

Collins, A. (1978). Fragments of a theory of human plausible reasoning. In D. Waltz (Ed.), *Proceedings of the conference on theoretical issues in natural language processing II* (pp. 194–201). Urbana, IL: University of Illinois Press.

Dickinson, A., Shanks, D., & Evenden, J. (1984). Judgment of act-outcome contingency: The role of selective attribution. *Quarterly Journal of Experimental Psychology, 36A*(1), 29–50.

Einhorn, H. J., & Hogarth, R. M. (1979). Confidence in judgment: Persistence of the illusion of validity. *Psychological Review, 85*, 395–416.

Fillmore, C. (1982). Towards a descriptive framework for spatial deixis. In R. J. Jarvella & W. Klein (Eds.), *Speech, place and action: Studies in deixis and related topics* (pp. 31–59). Chichester, England: Wiley.

Gati, I., & Tversky, A. (1984). Weighting common and distinctive features in perceptual and conceptual judgments. *Cognitive Psychology, 16*, 341–370.

Gentner, D. (1983). Structure-mapping: A theoretical framework for analogy. *Cognitive Science, 7*, 115–170.

Gentner, D., & Grudin, G. (1985). The evolution of mental metaphors in psychology: A ninety-year retrospective. *American Psychologist, 40*(2), 181–192.

Gentner, D., & Stevens, A. L. (Eds.) (1983). *Mental models.* Hillsdale, NJ: Erlbaum.

Gerard, A. B., & Mandler, J. M. (1983). Ontological knowledge and sentence anomaly. *Journal of Verbal Learning and Verbal Behavior, 22*, 105–120.

Gibson, J. J. (1979). *The ecological approach to visual perception.* Boston: Houghton Mifflin.

Grice, H. P. (1975). Logic and conversation. In P. Cole & J. L. Morgan (Eds.), *Syntax and semantics*, Vol. 3: *Speech acts* (pp. 41–58). New York: Academic Press.

Hayes-Roth, B., & Hayes-Roth, F. (1977). Concept learning and the recognition and classification of exemplars. *Journal of Verbal Learning and Verbal Behavior, 16,* 321–338.

Haygood, R. C., & Bourne, L. E., Jr. (1965). Attribute and rule-learning aspects of conceptual behavior. *Psychological Review, 72,* 175–195.

Jaspars, J., Fincham, F., & Hewstone, M. (Eds.) (1983). *Attribution theory and research: Conceptual, developmental and social dimensions.* London: Academic Press.

Johnson-Laird, P. N. (1983). *Mental models: Towards a cognitive science of language, inference, and consciousness.* Cambridge, England: Cambridge University Press.

Johnson-Laird, P. N., Herrmann, D. J., & Chaffin, R. (1984). Only connections: A critique of semantic networks. *Psychological Bulletin, 96*(2), 292–315.

Kant, I. (1788/1933). *Critique of Pure Reason.* Translated by Norman Kemp Smith. London: Macmillan.

Keil, F. C. (1979). *Semantic and conceptual development: An ontological perspective.* Cambridge, MA: Harvard University Press.

  (1981). Constraints on knowledge and cognitive development. *Psychological Review, 88,* 197–227.

Kemler-Nelson, D. G. (1984). The effect of intention on what concepts are acquired. *Journal of Verbal Learning and Verbal Behavior, 23,* 734–759.

Lakoff, G. (1982). *Categories and cognitive models* (Cognitive Science Report No. 2). Berkeley: University of California, Cognitive Science Program.

Lakoff, G., & Johnson, M. (1980). *Metaphors we live by.* Chicago: University of Chicago Press.

Lancy, D. C. (1983). *Cross-cultural studies in cognition and mathematics.* New York: Academic Press.

Lewicki, P. (1985). Processing covariations among features. *Journal of Experimental Psychology: Learning, Memory, and Cognition, 12,* 135–146.

Medin, D. L., & Reynolds, T. J. (1985). Cue-context interactions in discrimination, categorization, and memory. In P. Balsam & A. Tomie (Eds.), *Context in learning and memory,* Hillsdale, NJ: Erlbaum.

Medin, D. L., & Schaffer, M. M. (1978). Context theory of classification learning. *Psychological Review, 85,* 207–238.

Medin, D. L., & Schwanenflugel, P. L. (1981). Linear separability in classification learning. *Journal of Experimental Psychology: Human Learning and Memory, 7,* 355–368.

Medin, D. L., & Smith, E. E. (1981). Strategies in classification learning. *Journal of Experimental Psychology: Human Learning and Memory, 7,* 241–253.

Medin, D. L., Altom, M. W., Edelson, S. M., & Freko, D. (1982). Correlated symptoms and simulated medical classification. *Journal of Experimental Psychology: Learning, Memory, and Cognition, 8,* 37–50.

Medin, D. L., Wattenmaker, W. D., & Michalski, R. S. (1986). *Constraints in inductive learning: An experimental study comparing human and machine performance.* Manuscript submitted for publication.

Mervis, C. B., & Rosch, E. (1981). Categorization of natural objects. *Annual Review of Psychology, 32,* 89–115.

Michalski, R. B. (1980). Pattern recognition as rule-guided induction. *IEEE Transactions on Pattern Analysis and Machine Intelligence, 2*(4), 349–361.

Michalski, R. S. (1983a). A theory and methodology of inductive learning. *Artificial Intelligence, 20*, 111–161.
   (1983b). A theory and methodology of inductive learning. In R. S. Michalski, J. G. Carbonell, & T. M. Mitchell (Eds.), *Machine learning* (pp. 83–134). Palo Alto, CA: Tioga Publishing.
Michotte, A. (1963). *Perception of Causality.* London, Methuen.
Mohr, R. D. (1977). Family resemblance, platonism, universals. *Canadian Journal of Philosophy, 7*, 593–600.
Muchinsky, P. M., & Dudycha, A. L. (1974). The influence of a suppressor variable and labeled stimuli on multiple cue probability learning. *Organizational Behavior and Human Performance, 12*, 429–444.
Murphy, G. L., & Medin, D. L. (1985). The role of theories in conceptual coherence. *Psychological Review, 92*, 289–316.
Ortony, A., Vondruska, R. J., Jones, L. E., & Foss, M. A. (1985). Salience, similes, and the asymmetry of similarity. *Journal of Memory and Language, 24*, 569–594.
Osherson, D. N. (1978). Three conditions on conceptual naturalness. *Cognition, 6*, 263–289.
Rescorla, R. A., & Durlach, P. J. (1981). Within event learning in Pavlovian conditioning. In N. E. Spear & R. R. Miller (Eds.), *Information processing in animals: Memory mechanisms* (pp. 81–112). Hillsdale, NJ: Erlbaum.
Rescorla, R. A., & Wagner, A. R. (1977). A theory of Pavlovian conditioning: Variations in the effectiveness of reinforcement and nonreinforcement. In A. H. Black & W. F. Prokasy (Eds.), *Classical conditioning II* (pp. 64–99). New York: Appleton-Century-Crofts.
Reznick, J. S., & Richman, C. L. (1976). Effects of class complexity, class frequency, and pre-experimental bias on rule learning. *Journal of Experimental Psychology: Human Learning and Memory, 2*, 774–782.
Rips, L. J., & Handle, J. (1984). *Classification without similarity.* Unpublished manuscript, University of Chicago.
Rosch, E. (1978). Principles of categorization. In E. Rosch & B. B. Lloyd (Eds.), *Cognition and categorization* (pp. 27–48). Hillsdale, NJ: Erlbaum.
Rosch, E., & Mervis, C. G. (1975). Family resemblances: Studies in the internal structure of categories. *Cognitive Psychology, 7*, 573–605.
Rosch, E., Mervis, C. G., Gray, W. D., Johnson, D. M., & Boyes-Braem, P. (1976). Basic objects in natural categories. *Cognitive Psychology, 8*, 382–439.
Roth, E. M., & Shoben, E. J. (1983). The effect of context on the structure of categories. *Cognitive Psychology, 15*, 346–378.
Rozin, P. (1976). The evolution of intelligence and access to the cognitive unconscious. In J. M. Sprague & A. N. Epstein (Eds.), *Progress in psychobiology and physiological psychology* (pp. 245–280). New York: Academic Press.
Russell, J. (1984). *Explaining mental life.* London: Macmillan Press.
Sebestyen, G. S. (1962). *Decision-making processes in pattern recognition.* New York: Macmillan.
Shepard, R. N. (1984). Ecological constraints on internal representation: Resonant kinematics of perceiving, imagining, thinking, and dreaming. *Psychological Review, 91*(4), 417–447.
Smith, E. E., & Medin, D. L. (1981). *Categories and concepts.* Cambridge, MA: Harvard University Press.
Testa, T. J. (1974). Causal relationships and the acquisition of avoidance responses. *Psychological Review, 81*(6), 491–505.
Tversky, A. (1977). Features of similarity. *Psychological Review, 84*, 327–352.

Tversky, B., & Hemenway, K. (1984). Objects, parts, and categories. *Journal of Experimental Psychology: General, 113,* 169–193.

Ullman, S. (1979). *The interpretation of visual motion.* Cambridge, MA: MIT Press.

Wattenmaker, W. D. (1986). Nonanalytic concept formation and sensitivity to correlated attributes. Manuscript in preparation, University of Illinois at Champaign-Urbana.

Wattenmaker, W. D., Dewey, G. I., Murphy, T. D., & Medin, D. L. (1986). Linear separability and concept learning: Context, relational properties, and concept naturalness. *Cognitive Psychology, 18,* 158–194.

Wright, J. C., & Murphy, G. L. (1984). The utility of theories in intuitive statistics: The robustness of theory-based judgments. *Journal of Experimental Psychology: General, 113,* 301–322.

Ziff, P. (1972). *Understanding understanding.* Ithaca, NY: Cornell University Press.

4

Cognitive models and prototype theory

GEORGE LAKOFF

My purpose in this paper is to point out what I think is a deep misunder-
standing of the nature of prototype theory. In well-replicated experiments, Eleanor Rosch and her coworkers have demonstrated the
existence of *prototype effects:* scalar goodness-of-example judgments for
categories. Thus, for a category like *bird,* subjects will consistently rate
some kinds of birds as better examples than others. The best examples
are referred to as *prototypes.* Such effects are superficial. They show
nothing *direct* about the nature of categorization. As Rosch (1978) has
observed,

> The pervasiveness of prototypes in real-world categories and of prototypicality
> as a variable indicates that prototypes must have some place in psychological
> theories of representation, processing, and learning. However, prototypes them-
> selves do not constitute any particular model of processes, representations, or
> learning. This point is so often misunderstood that it requires discussion . . . to
> speak of a *prototype* at all is simply a convenient grammatical fiction; what is really
> referred to are judgments of degree of prototypicality. . . . Prototypes do not
> constitute a theory of representation for categories. . . .

Despite Rosch's admonitions to the contrary, prototype effects have
often been interpreted as showing something *direct* about the nature of
human categorization. There are two common interpretations of prototype effects:

> *The Effects = Structure Interpretation:* Goodness-of-example ratings are a
> direct reflection of degree of category membership.

According to the Effects = Structure interpretation, scalar goodness-of-
example ratings occur if and only if category membership is not all-or-
none, but a matter of degree. The Effects = Structure interpretation
thus makes a claim that Rosch has explicitly denied – that category
membership is scalar whenever goodness-of-example ratings are scalar.

> *The Prototype = Representation Interpretation:* Categories are represented
> in the mind in terms of prototypes (that is, best examples). Degrees of
> category membership for other entities are determined by their degree
> of similarity to the prototype.

There are at least two variations on the Prototype = Representation interpretation: one in which the prototype is an abstraction, say a schema or a feature bundle, and another in which the prototype is an exemplar, that is, a particular example.

Despite the fact that Rosch has specifically disavowed both of these interpretations, and despite the fact that they are incompatible with much of what is known about prototype effects, they have remained popular. In fact, a whole school of research has developed within cognitive psychology that takes these interpretations as defining prototype theory. Smith and Medin (1981) is a survey of research based on these interpretations.

The purpose of this chapter is to suggest a different interpretation of prototype effects: Prototype effects result from the fact that knowledge is organized in terms of what I will call *cognitive models*. There are various kinds of cognitive models, and hence prototype effects come from a variety of sources.

Interactional properties

Before we proceed, there is one more common misconception about prototype theory that ought to be cleared up. In her early work, Rosch claimed that prototypes could be characterized by clusters of real-world attributes. She later recanted (Rosch 1978:29, 41–42):

When research on basic objects and their prototypes was initially conceived (Rosch et al. 1976), I thought of such attributes as inherent in the real world. . . . On contemplation of the nature of many of our attributes listed by our subjects, however, it appeared that three types of attributes presented a problem for such a realistic view. (1) some attributes, such as "seat," for the object "chair," appear to have names which showed them not to be meaningful prior to the knowledge of the object as chair; (2) some attributes, such as "large" for the object "piano" seem to have meaning only in relation to categorization of the object in terms of a superordinate category – piano is large for furniture, but small for other kinds of objects such as buildings; (3) some attributes, such as "you eat on it" for the object "table" were functional attributes that seemed to require knowledge about humans, their activities, and the real world in order to be understood.

As I have argued elsewhere (Lakoff 1986), the properties that are relevant for the characterization of human categories are not objectively existing properties that are "out there" in the world. Rather they are "interactional properties," what *we* understand as properties by virtue of our interactive functioning in our environment. The properties mentioned in cognitive models are properties of this sort, not objectively existing properties of objects completely external to human beings.

This view is in keeping with results on basic-level categorization. The determinants of basic-level categorization are all interactional in this respect: perception of overall shape, motor movements relative to objects, mental images. Each of these is a matter of interaction between people and objects. They are neither wholly objective nor wholly subjective.

With this in mind, we can turn to the role of cognitive models in prototype theory.

Cognitive models

The study of cognitive models of a certain sort has been fashionable in cognitive science for some years now. Rumelhart's "schemas," Minsky's "frames," and Schank and Abelson's "scripts" are tools for representing knowledge that are used by a wide range of cognitive scientists. To my knowledge, all of these developed out of Fillmore's earlier concept of a "case frame," which has been superseded by his frame semantics. Cognitive models of this sort are all roughly equivalent and I will refer to them as *propositional models*. Four other types of cognitive models are now being investigated within cognitive linguistics. These are: image-schematic, metaphoric, metonymic, and symbolic models (for detailed discussion, see Lakoff 1986). Cognitive models in general are used to structure and make sense of our experience, and each element in such a model can correspond to a category of mind.

Graded models

A cognitive model characterizing a concept may be either graded or ungraded. A concept such as *rich* is characterized in part by a scale with gradations; individuals are rich to some degree, and not all individuals are clearly rich or not rich. This is the sort of category described by Zadeh (1965), and fuzzy-set theory has been set up to deal with such graded categories. I find them relatively uninteresting and will not discuss them any further. Prototype effects of the sort discovered by Rosch can occur in the case of such graded categories. They can also occur in a wide variety of other cases, and it is those cases that I will primarily be addressing.

The idealized character of cognitive models

Fillmore has observed that prototype effects can occur even when a cognitive model fits the classical definition of a category – that is, when the model is defined as having clear boundaries and necessary-and-sufficient conditions. Such prototype effects arise because cognitive models are *idealized* – that is, they may be defined relative to idealized circumstances rather than circumstances as they are known to exist. Fillmore (1982a) gives the example of the concept *bachelor:*

The noun *bachelor* can be defined as an unmarried adult man, but the noun clearly exists as a motivated device for categorizing people only in the context of a human society in which certain expectations about marriage and marriageable age obtain. Male participants in long-term unmarried couplings would not ordinarily be described as bachelors; a boy abandoned in the jungle and grown to maturity away from contact with human society would not be called a bachelor: John Paul II is not properly thought of as a bachelor.

As a result of the background conditions with respect to which a bachelor is defined, certain fuzzy cases arise: homosexuals, Moslems who are permitted four wives but only have three, and so on. The fuzziness is not due to any gradience in the model of the concept *bachelor*. It is instead due to the inexactness of fit between the background conditions of that model and other knowledge that we have about the world. Thus, we can find cases where an individual might appropriately be described as "sort of a bachelor," "a bachelor to a degree." These are prototype effects, but they are not due to any graded category. In such cases, even classically defined models may give rise to prototype effects.

The moral is clear: Prototype effects are real, but superficial. They may arise from a variety of sources. It is important not to confuse prototype effects with the structure of the category as given by cognitive models.

Cognitive models versus feature bundles

One of the most common versions of the P = R interpretation is the theory of weighted feature bundles. According to this theory, the prototype can be represented by a collection of features with associated weights indicating their importance. An example of such an analysis of prototype effects is the classic study by Coleman and Kay (1981), of the use of the verb *lie*. Coleman and Kay found that their informants did not appear to have necessary-and-sufficient conditions for characterizing the meaning of *lie*. Instead they found a cluster of three conditions, not one of which was necessary, and which varied in relative importance:

a consistent pattern was found: falsity of belief is the most important element of the prototype of *lie*, intended deception the next most important element, and factual falsity is the least important. Information fairly easily and reliably assigned the word *lie* to reported speech acts in a more-or-less, rather than all-or-none, fashion, . . . [and] . . . informants agree fairly generally on the relative weights of the elements in the semantic prototype of *lie*.

Thus, there is agreement that if you, say, steal something and then say you didn't, that's a good example of a lie. A less representative example of a lie is when you compliment a hostess when you hated her dinner, or if you say something true but irrelevant, like "I'm going to the candy store, Ma," when you're really going to the poolhall but will be stopping by the candy store on the way.

An important anomaly, however, turned up in the Coleman-Kay study. When informants were asked to define a lie, they consistently said it was a false statement, even though actual falsity turned out consistently to be the least important element by far in the cluster of conditions. Sweetser (1986) provides an important argument against the feature-bundles model and in favor of a cognitive-models account of lying. What she shows is that there are independently needed cognitive models of communication and belief that are used in understanding what a lie is. Sweetser shows that these cognitive models automatically predict the weightings found in the Coleman-Kay study and, moreover, permit one to define a lie as a false statement relative to these models, and still get the correct results. For details, see Sweetser (1984, 1986) or Lakoff (1986). Sweetser's study shows that it is the structure of the cognitive models that permits an adequate explanation of the Coleman-Kay findings, and that weighted feature bundles do not even constitute an adequate description, much less an explanation. As we will see below, feature bundles cannot account for most of the prototype phenomena discussed by cognitive linguists.

Mother

Some categories are characterized by *clusters* of cognitive models. There is an all-important difference between clusters of models and clusters of features: models have an internal structure that features do not have. An example of a concept characterized by a cognitive model cluster is the concept *mother*. According to the classical theory of categorization, it should be possible to give clear necessary-and-sufficient conditions for *mother* that will fit all the cases and apply equally to all of them. Such a definition might be something like: *a woman who has given birth to a child*. But as we will see, no such definition will cover the full range of cases. *Mother* is a concept that is based on a complex model in which a number of individual cognitive models converge, forming an experiential cluster. The models in the cluster are as follows.

> The birth model: the person giving birth is the *mother*.

The birth model is usually accompanied by a genetic model, although, since the development of egg and embryo implants, they do not always coincide.

> The genetic model: the female who contributed the genetic material is the *mother*.

> The nurturance model: the female adult who nurtures and raises a child is the *mother* of that child.
>
> The marital model: the wife of the father is the *mother*.
>
> The genealogical model: the closest female ancestor is the *mother*.

The concept *mother* normally involves a complex model in which all of these individual models converge to form a cluster. There have always been divergences from this cluster; stepmothers have been around for a long time. But because of the complexities of modern life, the models in the cluster have come to diverge more and more. Still, many people feel the pressure to pick one model as being the right one, the one that "really" defines what a mother is. But, although one might try to argue that only one of these characterizes the "real" concept of *mother,* the linguistic evidence does not bear this out. As the following sentences indicate, there is more than one criterion for "real" motherhood:

> I was adopted and I don't know who my real mother is.
>
> I am not a nurturant person, so I don't think I could ever be a real mother to any child.
>
> My real mother died when I was an embryo, and I was frozen and later implanted in the womb of the woman who gave birth to me.
>
> I had a genetic mother who contributed the egg that was planted in the womb of my real mother, who gave birth to me and raised me.
>
> By genetic engineering, the genes in the egg my father's sperm fertilized were spliced together from genes in the eggs of twenty different women. I wouldn't call any of them my real mother. My real mother is the woman who bore and raised me, even though I don't have any single genetic mother.

In short, more than one of these models contributes to the characterization of a *real mother,* and any one of them may be absent from such a characterization. Still, the very idea that there is such a thing as a *real mother* seems to require a choice among models where they diverge. It would be bizarre for someone to say:

> I have four real mothers: the woman who contributed my genes, the woman who gave birth to me, the woman who raised me, and my father's current wife.

When the cluster of models that jointly characterize a concept diverge, there is still a strong pull to view one as the most important. This is reflected in the institution of dictionaries. Each dictionary, by historical convention, must list a primary meaning when a word has more than one. Not surprisingly, the human beings who write dictionaries vary in their choices. Dr. Johnson chose the birth model as primary, and many of the applied linguists who work for the publishers of dictionaries, as is so often the case, have simply played it safe and copied him. But not all. Funk and Wagnall's *Standard Dictionary* chose the nurturance model as primary, while the *American College Dictionary* chose the genealogical model. Though choices made by dictionary-makers are of no scientific importance, they do reflect the fact that, even among people who construct definitions for a living, there is no single, generally accepted cognitive model for such a common concept as "mother."

When the situation is such that the models for *mother* do not pick out a single individual, we get compound expressions like *stepmother, surrogate mother, adoptive mother, foster mother, biological mother, donor mother,* and so on. Such compounds, of course, do not represent simple subcategories, that is, kinds of ordinary mothers. Rather, they describe cases where there is a lack of convergence of the various models.

Not surprisingly, different models are used as the basis of different extended senses of *mother*. For example, the birth model is the basis of the metaphorical sense in

Necessity is the mother of invention.

whereas the nurturance model is the basis for the derived verb in

He wants his girlfriend to mother him.

The genealogical model is the basis for the metaphorical extension of *mother* and *daughter* used in the description of the tree diagrams that linguists use to describe sentence structure. If node A is immediately above node B in a tree, A is called the *mother* and B, the *daughter*. Even in the case of metaphorical extensions, there is no single privileged model for *mother* on which the extensions are based. This accords with the evidence cited above, which indicates that the concept *mother* is defined by a cluster of converging models.

This phenomenon is beyond the scope of the classical theory. The concept *mother* is not clearly defined, once and for all, in terms of common necessary-and-sufficient conditions. There need be no necessary-and-sufficient conditions for motherhood shared by normal biological mothers, donor mothers (who donate an egg), surrogate mothers (who bear the child, but may not have donated the egg), adoptive mothers, unwed mothers who give their children up for adoption, and stepmothers. They are all mothers by virtue of their relation to the ideal case, where the models converge. That ideal case is one of the many kinds of cases that give rise to prototype effects.

So far we have seen three sources of prototype effects: models with a graded scale (e.g., *rich*), classical models with background conditions (e.g., *bachelor*), and cluster models (e.g., *mother*). But there are two other types of sources of prototype effects that are even more interesting:

metonymic models and radial categories. Let us begin with metonymic models.

Metonymic models

Metonymy is one of the basic characteristics of cognition. It is extremely common for people to take one well-understood or easy-to-perceive aspect of something and use it to stand either for the thing as a whole, or for some other aspect or part of it. The best-known cases are those like the following:

> One waitress says to another: The ham sandwich just spilled beer all over himself.

Here *the ham sandwich* is standing for the person eating the sandwich. Another well-known example is the slogan:

> Don't let El Salvador become another Vietnam.

Here the place is standing for the events that occurred at that place. As Lakoff and Johnson (1980) showed, such examples are instances of general patterns; they do not just occur one-by-one. We will refer to such patterns as *metonymic models*.

A particularly interesting case of metonymy occurs in giving answers to questions. It is common to give an answer that evokes the information requested, and there seem to be language-particular metonymic models used to do so. Take, for example, the case described by Rhodes (1976). Rhodes is a linguist who does field work on Ojibwa, a Native American language of central Canada. As part of his field work, he asked speakers of Ojibwa who had come to a party how they got there. He got answers like the following (translated into English):

> I started to come.
>
> I stepped into a canoe.
>
> I got into a car.

He figured out what was going on when he read Schank and Abelson's *Scripts, Plans, Goals, and Understanding*. Going somewhere in a vehicle involves a structured scenario (or in our terms, an Idealized Cognitive Model, or ICM):

> Precondition: You have (or have access to) the vehicle.
> Embarcation: You get into the vehicle and start it up.
> Center: You drive (row, fly, etc.) to your destination,
> Finish: You park and get out.
> End Point: You are at your destination.

What Rhodes found was that in Ojibwa it is conventional to use the embarcation point of an ICM of this sort to evoke the whole ICM. That is, in answering questions, part of an ICM is used to stand for the whole. In Ojibwa, that part is the embarcation point.

Ojibwa does not look particularly strange when one considers English from the same point of view. What are possible normal answers to a question such as "How did you get to the party?"

> I drove. (Center stands for whole ICM)
> I have a car. (Precondition stands for whole ICM)
> I borrowed my brother's car. (This entails the Precondition, which in turn stands for the whole ICM)

English even has special cases that look something like Ojibwa.

> I hopped on a bus. (Embarcation stands for whole ICM)
> I just stuck out my thumb. (Embarcation stands for whole ICM)

In short, English can use the Embarcation metonymically to stand for the whole ICM, just in case there is no further effort involved, as in taking a bus or hitchhiking.

There are many metonymic models in a rich conceptual system, and they are used for a wide variety of purposes. The kind of most interest for our present purposes are those in which a member or subcategory can stand metonymically for the whole category for the purpose of making inferences or judgments.

Metonymic sources of prototype effects

As Rosch observed, prototype effects are surface phenomena. A major source of such effects is metonymy – a situation in which some subcategory or member or submodel is used (often for some limited and immediate purpose) to comprehend the category as a whole. In other words, these are cases where a part (a subcategory or member or submodel) stands for the whole category – in reasoning, recognition, and so on. Within the theory of cognitive models, such cases are represented by metonymic models.

The housewife stereotype

We have seen how the clustering of cognitive models for *mother* results in prototype effects. However, an additional level of prototype effects occurs in the *mother* category. The source of these effects is the stereotype of the mother as housewife. Social stereotypes are cases of metonymy – where a subcategory has a socially recognized status as standing for the category as a whole, usually for the purpose of making quick judgments about people. The housewife-mother subcategory, though unnamed, exists. It defines cultural expectations about what a mother is supposed to be. Because of this, it yields prototype effects. On the whole in our culture, housewife-mothers are taken as better examples of mothers than nonhousewife-mothers.

Such goodness-of-example judgments are a kind of prototype effect. But this effect is not due to the clustering of models, but rather to the case of a metonymic model in which one subcategory, the housewife-mother, stands for the whole category in defining cultural expectations of mothers. Other kinds of metonymic models will be discussed below.

Working mothers

A *working mother* is not simply a mother who happens to be working. The category *working mother* is defined in contrast to the stereotypical house-wife-mother. The housewife-mother stereotype arises from a ster-eotypical view of nurturance, which is associated with the nurturance model. According to the stereotypical view, mothers who do not stay at home all day with their children cannot properly nurture them. There is also a stereotypical view of work, according to which it is done away from the home, and housework and child-rearing do not count. This is the stereotype that the bumpersticker "Every Mother Is A Working Mother" is meant to counter.

The housewife-mother stereotype is therefore defined relative to the nurturance model of motherhood. This may be obvious, but it is not a trivial fact. It shows that metonymic models like stereotypes are not necessarily defined with respect to an entire cluster. In this case, the metonymic model is characterized relative to only one of the models in the cluster – the nurturance model. Here is some rather subtle evidence to prove the point:

> Consider an unwed mother who gives up her child for adoption and then goes out and gets a job. She is still a mother, by virtue of the birth model, and she is working – but she is not a *working mother!*

The reason is that it is the nurturance model, not the birth model, that is relevant for the interpretation of the phrase. Thus, a biological mother who is not responsible for nurturance cannot be a working mother, though an adoptive mother, of course, can be one.

This example shows the following:

> A social stereotype (e.g., the housewife-mother) may be defined with re-spect to only one of the base models of an experiential cluster (e.g., the nurturance model).

> Thus, a metonymic model where a subcategory stands for the whole cate-gory may be defined relative to only one model in a complex cluster.

> A subcategory (e.g., working mother) may be defined in contrast with a stereotype (e.g., the housewife–mother).

> When this occurs, it is only the relevant cognitive model (e.g., the nurturance model) that is used as a background for defining the subcategory (e.g., working mother).

Thus, only those mothers for whom nurturance is an issue can be so categorized. Stepmothers and adoptive mothers may also be working mothers, but biological mothers who have given up their children for adoption and surrogate mothers (who have only had a child for someone else) are not working mothers − even though they may happen to be holding down a job.

Such models of stereotypes are important for a theory of conceptual structure in a number of ways. First, as we have seen, they may be used to motivate and define a contrasting subcategory like *working mother*. This is important because, according to the classical theory, such cases should not exist. In the classical theory, social stereotypes, by definition, play no role in defining category structure because they are not part of any necessary and sufficient conditions for category membership! In the classical theory, only necessary and sufficient conditions can have a real cognitive function in defining category membership. For this reason, the classical theory permits no cognitive function at all for social stereotypes. But the fact that the conceptual category *working mother* is defined by contrast with the housewife-mother stereotype indicates that stereotypes do have a role in characterizing concepts.

Second, stereotypes define a normal expectation that is linguistically marked. For example, the word *but* in English is used to mark a situation that is in contrast to some model that serves as a norm. Stereotypic models may serve as such a norm:

> NORMAL: She is a mother, but she isn't a housewife.
> STRANGE: She is a mother, but she's a housewife.

The latter sentence could only be used if stereotypical mothers were not housewives. Conversely, a category defined in contrast to a stereotype has the opposite properties:

> NORMAL: She is a mother, but she has a job.
> STRANGE: She is a mother, but she doesn't have a job.

In summary, we have seen two kinds of models for *mother:*

> A cluster of converging cognitive models.
> A stereotypic model, which is a metonymic model in which the housewife-mother subcategory stands for the category as a whole and serves the purpose of defining cultural expectations.

Both models give rise to prototype effects, but in different ways. Together, they form a structure with a composite prototype: the best example of a mother is a biological mother who is a housewife, principally concerned with nurturance, not working at a paid position, and married to the child's father. This composite prototype imposes what is called a *representativeness structure* on the category: the closer an individual is to the prototype, the more representative a mother she is.

Representativeness structures are linear. They concern nothing but closeness to the prototypical case, and thus they hide most of the richness of structure that exists in the cognitive models that characterize the category. Representativeness structures, though real, are mere shadows of cognitive models.

It is important to bear this in mind, as prototype theory is sometimes thought of as involving only such linear representativeness structures and not cognitive models.

The study of representativeness structures has played an important role in the history of prototype theory – largely in demonstrating that prototypes do exist and in making a bare first approximation to finding out what they are and what properties they have. But a full study of category structure must go well beyond just isolating a prototype and giving a linear ranking of how close nonprototypical cases are. At the very least, it must provide an account of the details of the cognitive models that give rise to the representativeness structure.

Radial structures

Here are some kinds of mothers:

The central case, where all the models converge. This includes a mother who is and always has been female, and who gave birth to the child, supplied her half of child's genes, nurtured the child, is married to the father, is one generation older than the child, and is the child's legal guardian.

Stepmother: She didn't give birth or supply the genes, but she is currently married to the father.

Adoptive mother: She didn't give birth or supply the genes, but she is the legal guardian and has the obligation to provide nurturance.

Birth mother: This is defined in contrast to *adoptive mother:* given an adoption ICM, the woman who gives birth and puts the child up for adoption is called the *birth mother.*

Natural mother: This used to be the term used to contrast with *adoptive mother,* but it has been given up owing to the unsavory inference that adoptive mothers were, by contrast, "unnatural." This term has been replaced by *birth mother.*

Foster mother: She is being paid by the state to provide nurturance.

Biological mother: She gave birth to the child, but is not raising it, and there is someone else who is and who qualifies to be called a mother of some sort.

Surrogate mother: She has contracted to give birth and that's all. She may or may not have provided the genes, and she is not married to the father and is not obligated to provide nurturance. Also, she has contractually given up the right to be legal guardian.

Unwed mother: She is not married to the father at the time of the birth.

Genetic mother: This is a term I have seen used for a woman who supplies an egg to be planted into someone else's womb, and has nothing else whatever to do with the child. It has not yet to my knowledge become conventional.

These subcategories of mother are all understood as deviations from the central case. But not all possible variations on the central case exist as categories. There is no category of mothers who are legal guardians but do not personally supply nurturance, hiring someone else to do it. There is no category of transsexuals who gave birth but have since had a sex-change operation. Moreover, some of the above categories are products of the twentieth century, and simply did not exist earlier: The point is that the central case does not productively generate all of these subcategories. Instead, the subcategories are defined by convention as variations on the central case. There is no general rule for generating kinds of mothers. They are culturally defined and have to be learned. They are by no means the same in all cultures. In the Trobriands, a woman who gives birth often gives the child to an old woman to raise. In traditional Japanese society, it was common for a woman to give her child to her sister to raise. Both of these are cases of kinds of mothers of which we have no exact equivalent.

The category of *mother* in this culture has what we will call a *radial structure*. A radial structure is one where there is a central case and conventionalized variations on it that cannot be predicted by general rules. Categories that are generated by central cases plus general principles – say, the natural numbers – are not radial structures, as we are defining the term. We are limiting radial structures only to cases where the variations are conventionalized and have to be learned. We are also ruling out cases where the central case is just more general than the noncentral case – that is, where the noncentral cases just have more properties than the central case, but no different ones. Radial structures are extremely common, and we will discuss them in very great detail below.

Some kinds of metonymic models

So far, we have looked at one case of a metonymic model: the housewife-mother stereotype. It defines a subcategory that is used to stand for the entire category of mothers in defining social expectations. Any time a subcategory (or an individual member of a category) is used for some purpose to stand for the category as a whole, it is a potential source of prototype effects. For this reason, metonymic models play an important role in prototype theory. Let us look at them a bit more closely.

In general, a metonymic model has the following characteristics:

> There is a "target" concept A to be understood for some purpose in some context.
>
> There is a conceptual structure containing both A and another concept B.
>
> B is either part of A, or is closely associated with it in that conceptual structure. Typically, a choice of B will uniquely determine A, within that conceptual structure.
>
> Compared to A, B is either easier to understand, easier to remember, easier to recognize, or more immediately useful for the given purpose in the given context.
>
> A metonymic model is a model of how A and B are related in a conceptual structure; the relationship is specified by a function from B to A.

When such a conventional metonymic model exists as part of a conceptual system, B may be used to stand, metonymically, for A. If A is a category, the result is a metonymic model of the category, and prototype effects commonly arise.

Most metonymic models are, in fact, *not* models of categories; they are models of individuals. Lakoff and Johnson (1980:Ch. 8) have shown that there are many types of metonymic models for individuals. There are also many types of metonymic models for categories; each type is a different *kind* of source for prototype effects. There are as many types of metonymic prototype effects as there are kinds of metonymic models for categories. Following are some of the types I have come across so far.

Social stereotypes

As we saw in the case of the housewife-mother, social stereotypes can be used to stand for a category as a whole. Social stereotypes are usually conscious and are often the subject of public discussion. They are subject to change over time, and they may become public issues. Because they define cultural expectations, they are used in reasoning and especially in what is called "jumping to conclusions." However, they are usually recognized as not being accurate, and their use in reasoning may be overtly challenged.

Here are some examples of contemporary American stereotypes:

> The stereotypical politician is conniving, egotistical, and dishonest.
> The stereotypical bachelor is macho, dates a lot of different women, is interested in sexual conquest, hangs out in singles' bars, etc.
> The stereotypical Japanese is industrious, polite, and clever.

Since social stereotypes are commonly used to characterize cultural expectations, they tend to be exploited in advertising and in most forms of popular entertainment.

Incidentally, the *bachelor* stereotype provides a second level of prototype effects in addition to those that are a consequence of the *bachelor* ICM not fitting certain situations. Let us take a situation where the background conditions of the *bachelor* ICM do fit, a situation in which there are no cases that the concept was not defined to deal with: no priests, no gays, no Moslems with only three wives, no Tarzans. In these situations, there can still be prototype effects, but the effects will arise *within the clear boundaries of the category*. In such cases, the social stereotype of a *bachelor* will characterize the best examples, and those undisputed bachelors who do not fit the social stereotype will be less good examples.

A bachelor who is macho, promiscuous, and nondomestic fits the stereotype of *bachelor* better than, say, a nonmacho man who likes to take care of children, prefers stable relationships with one person, is not interested in sexual conquest, loves housework and does it well, and so on. Stereotypes are used in certain situations to define expectations, make judgments, and draw inferences. Thus, for example, if all one knew about someone was that he was a bachelor, one might be surprised to find that he loves housework and does it well, likes to care for children, and so on. Even though the *bachelor* ICM is defined within the classical theory and has clear boundaries in situations that conform to the background assumptions, prototype effects may still occur *internal* to the category boundaries because of the presence of a social stereotype.

Incidentally, we often have names for stereotypes, for example, Uncle Tom, Jewish Princess, stud. These are categories that function as stereotypes for other categories.

Typical examples

Examples of typical cases are as follows:

> Robins and sparrows are typical birds.
> Apples and oranges are typical fruits.
> Saws and hammers are typical tools.

Social stereotypes are usually conscious and subject to public discussion—and may even have names. However, the use of typical category members is usually unconscious and automatic. Typical examples are not the subject of public discussion, and they seem not to change noticeably during a person's lifetime. They are not used to define cultural expectations. They are used in reasoning, as Rips (1975) showed, in the case where subjects inferred that if the robins on a certain island got a disease, then the ducks would, but not the converse. Such examples are common. It is normal for us to make inferences from typical to non-typical examples. If a typical man has hair on his head, we infer that atypical men (all other things being equal) will have hair on their heads. Moreover, a man may be considered atypical by virtue of not having hair on his head. There is nothing mysterious about this. An enormous amount of our knowledge about categories of things is organized in terms of typical cases. We constantly draw inferences on the basis of that kind of knowledge. We do it so regularly and automatically that we are rarely aware that we are doing it.

Reasoning on the basis of typical cases is a major aspect of human reason. Our vast knowledge of typical cases leads to prototype effects. The reason is that there is an asymmetry between typical and nontypical cases. Knowledge about typical cases is generalized to nontypical cases, but not conversely.

Ideals

Many categories are understood in terms of abstract ideal cases – which may be neither typical nor stereotypical. For example:

> The ideal husband: a good provider, faithful, strong, respected, attractive.
>
> The stereotypical husband: bumbling, dull, pot-bellied, . . .

Naomi Quinn (personal communication) has observed, based on extensive research on American conceptions of marriage, that there are many kinds of ideal models for a marriage: *successful* marriages, *good* marriages, *strong* marriages, and so on. *Successful* marriages are those where the goals of the spouses are fulfilled. *Good* marriages are those where both partners find the marriage beneficial. *Strong* marriages are those likely to last. Such types of ideals seem to be of great importance in culturally significant categories – categories where making judgments of quality and making plans are important.

A lot of cultural knowledge is organized in terms of ideals. We have cultural knowledge about ideal homes, ideal families, ideal mates, ideal jobs, ideal bosses, ideal workers, and so on. Cultural knowledge about ideals leads to prototype effects. There is an asymmetry between ideal and nonideal cases: we make judgments of quality and set goals for the future in terms of ideal cases, rather than nonideal cases. This asymmetry is a consequence of a pattern of inference that we use with ideals. Ideals are assumed to have all the good qualities that nonideal cases have, but not conversely.

Paragons

We also comprehend categories in terms of individual members who represent either an ideal or its opposite. Thus, we have institutions like the ten-best and ten-worst lists, the Halls of Fame, Academy Awards, and the Guinness book of World Records. We have baseball paragons: Babe Ruth, Willie Mays, Sandy Koufax. Paragons are made use of in constructions in the language: *a regular Babe Ruth, another Willie Mays, the Cadillac of vacuum cleaners,* and so on. Scientific paradigms are also characterized by paragons. Thus, for example, The Michaelson-Morley Experiment is the paragon of physics experiments – and is used by many people to comprehend what a great experiment in physics is.

A great many of our actions have to do with paragons. We try to emulate them. We are interested in the life stories of great men and women. We use paragons as models to base our actions on. We have a great deal of interest in experiencing paragons: we watch All-Star games, go to Academy Award-winning movies, travel to the Seven Wonders of the World, and seek to own the paragons of consumer goods. We are constantly acquiring knowledge of paragons, and regularly base our actions on that knowledge. Incidentally, we also commonly base inferences on a folk theory that people who are paragons in some domain are paragons *as people.* Thus, people are shocked to find great baseball players or powerful politicians engaging in normal rotten human behavior.

Generators

There are cases where the members of a category are defined, or "generated," by the central members plus some general rules. The natural numbers are perhaps the best-known example. The natural numbers are, for most people, characterized by the integers between zero and nine, plus addition and multiplication tables and rules of arithmetic. The single-digit numbers are central members of the category *natural number;* they generate the entire category, given general arithmetic principles. In our system of numerical representation, single-digit numbers are employed in comprehending natural numbers in general. Any natural number can be written as a sequence of single-digit numbers. The properties of large numbers are understood in terms of the properties of smaller numbers, and ultimately in terms of the properties of single-digit numbers.

The single-digit numbers, together with addition and multiplication tables and rules of arithmetic, constitute a model that both generates the natural numbers and is metonymic in our sense: the category as a whole is comprehended in terms of a small subcategory.

The natural numbers, in addition, have other models that subdivide the numbers according to certain properties – odd and even, prime and nonprime, and so on. Such models are not metonymic. They work by classical Aristotelian principles. But they only define *subcategories* of the natural numbers. The category as a whole is defined metonymically and generatively by the single-digit numbers plus rules of arithmetic.

To make matters more complicated, other kinds of numbers are also defined by metonymic generative models: the rationals, the reals, the imaginaries, the transfinite cardinals, and so on. Thus rational numbers are understood as ratios of natural numbers, and real numbers are understood as infinite sequences of natural numbers. In other words, the rationals and the reals are understood metonymically in terms of the natural numbers – a subcategory used to generate the larger categories.

Submodels

Another way to comprehend a category is via a submodel. Take the category of natural numbers again. The most common submodel used is the subcategory of powers of ten: ten, a hundred, a thousand, and so on. We use this submodel to comprehend the relative size of numbers. The members of such a submodel are among what Rosch refers to as *Cognitive Reference Points,* which have a special place in reasoning, especially in making approximations and estimating size. Cognitive reference points within a submodel show prototype effects of the following sort: Subjects will judge statements like *98 is approximately 100* as being true more readily than statements like *100 is approximately 98.*

Some submodels have a biological basis: the primary colors, the basic emotions, etc. Others are culturally stipulated, for example, the Seven Deadly Sins.

Salient Examples

It is common for people to use familiar, memorable, or otherwise salient examples to comprehend categories. For example, if your best friend is a vegetarian and you don't know any others well, you will tend to generalize from your friend to other vegetarians. After a widely publicized DC-10 crash in Chicago, many people refused to fly DC-10s, choosing other types of planes despite the fact that they had overall worse safety records than DC-10s. Such people used the salient example of the DC-10 that crashed to stand metonymically for the entire category of DC-10s with respect to safety judgments.

Similarly, California earthquakes are salient examples of natural disasters. A. Tversky and Kahneman (1983) demonstrated that people use such salient examples in making probability judgments about the category of natural disasters. The reasoning used is what Tversky and Kahneman refer to as the *conjunction fallacy*. We know from probability theory that the probability of two events, A and B, occurring is always less than the probability of just one of the events, say B. Thus the probability of coins A and B both coming down heads is less than the probability of just B coming down heads.

The theory of probability is defined for events A and B, which are not related to one another. Cognitive models may, however, relate events in our minds that are unrelated in the external world. What Tversky and Kahneman found was that when we have a salient cognitive model relating events A and B, it affects our judgments of the probability of A and B both occurring.

The following is a typical example of the kind Tversky and Kahneman used. One group of subjects was asked to rate the probability of

> A massive flood somewhere in North America in 1983, in which more than 1000 people drown.

A second group was asked to rate the probability of

> An earthquake in California sometime in 1983, causing a flood in which more than 1000 people drown.

The estimates of the conjunction of earthquake and flood were considerably higher than the estimates of the flood. Tversky and Kahneman conclude:

> The attempts to predict the uncertain future, like the attempts to reconstruct the uncertain past, which is the domain of history and criminal law, are commonly based on the construction of hypothetical scenarios, These scenarios, or "best guesses," tend to be specific, coherent, and representative of our mental model of the relevant worlds.

In short, a cognitive model may function to allow a salient example to stand metonymically for a whole category. In such cases, our probability judgments about the category are affected.

To summarize, we have seen the following kinds of metonymic models: social stereotypes, typical examples, ideal cases, paragons, generators, submodels, and salient examples. They have a cognitive status, that is, they are used in reasoning. And they all yield prototype effects of some sort.

Radial categories

Radial categories are perhaps the most interesting source of prototype effects. Radial categories have the following properties:

1. There can be no single cognitive model that represents the entire category.
2. There is a central submodel characterizing a central subcategory.
3. Representations for noncentral subcategories cannot be predicted either by rule or by a general principle such as similarity.
4. There are nonarbitrary *links* between the central and noncentral subcategories. These links are other cognitive models existing independently in the conceptual system.
5. Though the noncentral subcategories cannot be predicted from the central subcategory, they are *motivated* by the central subcategory plus other, independently existing cognitive models.
6. Motivated subcategories can be learned, remembered, and used more efficiently than arbitrary, unmotivated subcategories.

Elsewhere I have given a number of very detailed examples of radial categories (Lakoff 1986). Although there is no room here to go through all those examples in sufficiently convincing detail, I will provide one relatively short example, using data provided by Pamela Downing (Downing 1984) and Haruo Aoki (personal communication).

Japanese *hon*

The Japanese classifier, *hon*, in its most common use, classifies long, thin, rigid objects: sticks, canes, pencils, candles, trees, and so on. Not surprisingly, it can be used to classify dead snakes and dried fish, both of which are long and rigid. But *hon* can be extended to what are presumably less representative cases:

martial arts contests, with staffs or swords (which are long and rigid)

hits (and sometimes pitches) in baseball (straight trajectories, formed by the forceful motion of a solid object, associated with baseball bat, which is long, thin, and rigid)

shots in basketball, serves in volleyball, and rallies in Ping-Pong

judo matches (a martial arts contest, but without a staff or sword)

a contest between a zen master and student, in which each attempts to stump the other with zen koans

rolls of tape (which can be unrolled into something long and thin)

telephone calls (which come over wires and which are instances of the CONDUIT metaphor as described by Reddy [1979] and Lakoff and Johnson [1980])

radio and television programs (like telephone calls, but without the wires) letters (another instance of communication; moreover, in traditional Japan, letters were scrolls and hence sticklike)

movies (like radio and television; moreover they come in reels like rolls of tape)

medical injections (done with a needle, which is long, thin, and rigid)

These cases, though not predictable, are nonetheless not arbitrary. They do not all have something in common with long, thin rigid objects, but it *makes sense* that they might be classified in the same way. Let us ask exactly what kind of sense it makes.

Let us begin with martial arts contests using staffs or swords. Staffs and swords are long, thin, rigid objects, which are classified by *hon*. They are also the principal functional objects in these matches. A win in such a match can also be classified by *hon*. That is, the principal goal in this domain of experience is in the same category as the principal functional object.

Baseball bats are central members of the *hon* category. They are one of the two most salient functional objects in the game, the other being the ball. Baseball is centered on a contest between the pitcher and the batter. The batter's principal goal is to get a hit. When a baseball is hit solidly, it forms a trajectory – that is, it traces a long, thin path along which a solid object travels quickly and with force. The image traced by the path of the ball is a *hon* image – long and thin.

The extension of the *hon* category from bats to hits is another case of an extension from a principal functional object to a principal goal. It is also an extension from one principal functional object with a *hon* shape to a *hon*-shaped path formed by the other principal functional object. Incidentally, in the small amount of research done on *hon* to date, it appears that, whereas base hits and home runs are categorized with *hon*, foul balls, pop flies, ground balls, and bunts appear not to be. This is not surprising because these are not principal goals of hitting, nor do their trajectories form a *hon* shape.

The relationship between the shape of the bat and the trajectory formed by the batted ball – between a long, thin thing and a trajectory – is a common relationship between image-schemas that forms the basis for the extension of a category from a central to a noncentral case. Let us consider three examples from English.

The man ran into the woods.
The road ran into the woods.

In the first case, *run* is used for a case where there is a (long, thin) trajectory. In the second case, *run* is used for a long, thin object, a road.

The bird flew over the yard.
The telephone line stretched over the yard.

In the first case, *over* is used for a (long, thin) trajectory. In the second case, *over* is used for a long, thin object, a telephone line.

> The rocket shot up.
> The lamp was standing up.

In the first case, *up* is used for a trajectory. In the second case, *up* is used for a long, thin object, a standing lamp.

Such relationships are common and suggest that there exists what might be called an *image-schema transformation* of the following sort:

TRAJECTORY SCHEMA ↔ LONG, THIN OBJECT SCHEMA

This image-schema transformation is one of the many kinds of cognitive relationship that can form a basis for the extension of a category.

Some speakers of Japanese extend the *hon* category to baseball pitches, as well as hits – again on the basis of such an image-schema relationship within the same domain of experience. Some speakers extend *hon* to pitches using both the trajectory and the contest-perspective, in which the hitter and pitcher are engaged in a contest. These speakers use *hon* only for pitches seen from the point of view of the hitter. There are also speakers who classify pitches with *hon* only if they achieve the principal goal of pitching. Since getting strikes is the principal goal of pitching, such speakers can classify strikes, but not balls, with *hon*. No speakers have been found who use *hon* to classify balls but not strikes. Similarly, no speakers have been found who classify bunts and foul balls with *hon*, but not home runs and base hits.

There are similar motivations behind the extensions of *hon* to other concepts in sports. Thus, *hon* can classify shots and free throws in basketball, but not passes. And it can classify serves in volleyball and rallies in Ping-Pong. These are cases where there is both a trajectory and a possibility of scoring (achieving a principal goal).

There are several morals to be drawn from these examples:

1. What are taken to be the central cases for the application of *hon* appear to be concrete basic-level objects: sticks, pencils, bamboo staffs, baseball bats, etc. The direction of extension appears to go from concrete basic-level objects to other things, like hits and pitches.
2. A theory of motivations for the extension of a category is required. Among the things we need in such a theory are image-schema transformations and conceptual metonymies – cases where a principal object like a staff or bat can stand for a principal goal like a win or hit.
3. Hits in baseball and long, thin rigid objects do not have anything objective in common. The relationship between the bat and the hit is given by an image-schema transformation and a metonymy. Hence the classical theory, which requires that categorization be based on common properties, is inadequate.
4. The application of *hon* to hits in baseball may make sense, but it is not

predictable. It is a matter of convention – not an arbitrary convention, but a *motivated* convention. Thus, the traditional view that everything must be either predictable or arbitrary is inadequate here. There is a third choice: motivation. In this case, the independently needed image-schema transformation and the object-for-goal metonymy provide the motivation.

Ideally, each instance of the use of a classifier outside the central sense should have a motivation. The motivation cannot be ad hoc – one cannot make up a metonymy or image-schema just to handle that case. It must be justified on the basis of other cases. This imposes a criterion of adequacy on the analysis of classifier languages.

Some investigators have suggested that such a criterion of adequacy is too strong; they have claimed that some classifications simply are arbitrary and that no non – ad hoc motivation exists. That is an empirical question, and the facts are by no means all in. But arbitrariness is a last resort. Even if there are some completely unmotivated cases, one can still apply a slightly weakened criterion of adequacy. Find out which extensions "make sense" to speakers and which extensions seem "senseless," and account for those that make sense. Each sensible extension of a category needs to be independently motivated. No analysis of a classifier system is complete until this is done.

So far, we have seen that metonymies and image-schema transformations can provide motivation for the extension of a category. Another important kind of motivation comes from conventional mental images. Take the example of a roll of tape, which can be classified by *hon*. We know what rolls of tape look like, both when they are rolled up and when they are being unrolled. That is, we have conventional mental images of tape, both when it is in storage form and when it is being put to use. We also know that we unroll tape when we are about to use it, and that the tape is functional when it is unrolled. A conventional image of tape being unrolled has two parts: the rolled part and the unrolled, functional part. The image of the unrolled, functional part fits the long, thin object image-schema associated with the central sense of *hon*. The image of the nonfunctional rolled part does not fit the central *hon* image-schema. Metonymy is involved here; the functional part of the conventional image is standing for the whole image, for the sake of categorization. The functional part fits the *hon* schema. This is, presumably, the motivation for the use of *hon* to classify rolls of tape. Again, we cannot predict the use of *hon* for rolls of tape; but we can do something that is extremely important. We can show why it makes sense. Making sense of categorization is no small matter. And doing so in a manner that shows in detail how basic cognitive mechanisms apply is anything but trivial. If the cognitive aspects of categorization are to be understood, it will require attention to detail at this level. For example, *hon* can be used to classify medical injections. Why does this make sense?

Medical injections are another case where the principal functional object (the needle) is long and thin; the needles can be classified with *hon* and, by metonymy, so can the injections.

So far we have seen how image-schema transformations, conventional mental images, and metonymy all enter into categorization by a classifier. Let us turn to a case that involves all of these plus metaphor. Recall that *hon* can be used to classify telephone calls. The conventional mental image of engaging in a telephone call involves using the most functional part of the telephone – the receiver, which is a long, thin, rigid object and fits the central image-schema for *hon*. The other principal conventional image related to telephone calls involves telephone wires. These are understood as playing a principal functional role in telephonic communication. These fit the long, thin object image-schema. They also fit the CONDUIT of the CONDUIT metaphor – the principal metaphor for communication. In short, there are two related but different motivations for the use of *hon* for telephone calls. That is, there are two ways in which this use of *hon* fits the conceptual system, and, where motivation is concerned, the more kinds of motivation, the better. That is, it is not a matter of finding which is right; both can be right simultaneously.

So far, we have seen that extended senses of *hon* can be based on the central sense of *hon*. But extended senses may themselves serve as the basis for further extensions via category chaining. Recall that letters are classified with *hon*. There are a number of considerations that motivate such a categorization. First, letters were originally in the form of scrolls, often wound around long, thin, wooden cylinders. They have been categorized with *hon* ever since, and that image remains very much alive in Japanese culture through paintings and the tradition of calligraphy. Second, the conventional image of writing a letter involves the use of a pen, which plays a principal functional role, and is also a long, thin object. Third, letters are a form of communication, and therefore an instance of the CONDUIT metaphor. These diverse motivations allow *hon* with all these senses to fit the ecology of the Japanese classifier system.

Letters and telephone calls are intermediate steps in a chain. Radio and television programs are also classified with *hon*. They are forms of communication at a distance, like letter-writing and telephone communication. They too are motivated by the CONDUIT metaphor for communication. Given that letters and telephone calls are classified by *hon*, radio and television programs constitute a well-motivated extension. Movies are also classified by *hon*. They are also instances of communication at a distance; in addition, one of the principal conventional images associated with movies is the movie reel, which looks like a spool of tape, which is classified with *hon*.

The phenomenon of category-chaining shows very clearly that the classical account of categorization is inadequate. Sticks and television programs are both in the *hon* category, but they share no relevant common properties. They are categorized in the same way by virtue of the chain structure of the *hon* category.

Finally, let us turn our attention to judo matches and contests between Zen masters and students. Judo matches are in the same domain of experience as martial arts contests with staffs or swords. A win in judo match can also be classified as a *hon*. Similarly, Zen contests are, in Japanese culture, in the same experiential domain as martial arts contests, and a win there also can be classified as a *hon*.

Incidentally, the noncentral cases of the *hon* category vary in some cases from speaker to speaker. Thus some speakers do not include baseball pitches and some do not include wins in Zen contests. But to my knowledge, every speaker of Japanese includes the central members – the candles, staffs, baseball bats, and so on. Moreover, many of the extensions have become conventionalized for speakers in general: letters, telephone conversations, home runs, spools of thread. The variation just displayed involves chaining that has not yet stabilized but which shows the same principles at work as in the stable conventionalized extensions.

Categories of mind, or mere words

A possible objection to the kind of analyses we have been discussing is that classifiers are mere linguistic devices and do not reflect conceptual structure. That is, one might object that, say, the things categorized by *hon* in Japanese do not form a single conceptual category. Thus, one might suggest that the analysis of *hon* may show something about rules of language, but that it shows nothing about our conceptual system.

Let us, for the sake of argument, consider such a suggestion. Whatever their precise cognitive status is, rules of language are some part or other of our cognitive apparatus. Just what would such "rules of language" involve? In particular, they would involve all the things we discussed above in the analysis of *hon*:

    Central and peripheral members
    Basic-level objects at the center
    Conventional mental images
    Knowledge about conventional mental images
    Image-schema transformations
    Metonymy applied to mental imagery

Metonymy applied to domains of experience
Metaphors (which map domains into other domains)

These mechanisms are needed, no matter whether one calls them linguistic or not. Moreover, they appear to be the kinds of things that one would tend to call conceptual – mental images and image transformations do not appear to be merely linguistic. Moreover, linguistic categories can be used in nonlinguistic tasks, as Kay and Kempton (1984) have demonstrated. But whether they are used in nonlinguistic tasks or not, linguistic categories *are* categories – and they are part of our overall cognitive apparatus. Whether one wants to dignify them with the term "conceptual" or not, linguistic categories are categories within our cognitive system and a study of *all* categories within our cognitive system will have to include them.

What is prototype theory?

From the point of view of a theory of cognitive models, prototype theory is a theory of how prototype effects arise. The claim implicit in the theory of cognitive models is that *prototype effects are a consequence of conceptual structure.* In some cases, they arise directly: when cognitive models contain scales, for example, a scale of wealth for the concept *rich.* They may also arise directly as a consequence of the radial structure of a category. On the other hand, they may arise indirectly, as in the case of metonymic and classical models that are idealized (cf. the *bachelor* example). All of these are cases where conceptual structure results in prototype effects.

The core + identification procedure proposal

Within recent years there has been a reactionary movement on the part of certain cognitive psychologists to return to the classical theory of categorization. The principal works are papers by Osherson and Smith (1981) and Armstrong, Gleitman, and Gleitman (1983). These papers purport to present arguments against prototype theory. Instead, they really present arguments – correct arguments – against two clearly incorrect interpretations of prototype effects: the Effects = Structure and Prototype = Representation interpretations.

These papers claim that prototype effects have nothing whatever to do with conceptual structure. Instead, they claim that all such effects result from procedures for *identifying* category members. They claim that the classical theory of categories can be kept if such procedures are postulated. Both papers make the following assumptions:

The classical theory is workable for all phenomena having to do with reasoning.

Prototype phenomena have nothing to do with reasoning.

Prototype effects result only from identification procedures and not from anything in conceptual structure.

Before we turn to examining these papers in detail, it would be worthwhile to recall how the core versus identification procedure idea came into cognitive psychology. Oddly enough, the source was a paper of mine.

A bit of history is in order. In my 1972 paper, "Hedges," I began by taking for granted the Effects = Structure Interpretation, and I observed that Zadeh's fuzzy-set theory could represent degrees of category membership. Later in the paper, I observed that the Effects = Structure Interpretation was inadequate to account for hedges like *strictly speaking, loosely speaking, technically,* and *regular.* To account for the use of *regular* one must distinguish *definitional* properties from *characteristic but incidental* properties. This corresponds to the semantics-pragmatics distinction in the objectivist paradigm, the distinction between what the word "really means" and encyclopedic knowledge that you happen to have about the things the word refers to.

However, my observation that the distinction is necessary was not in the service of supporting the semantics-pragmatics distinction; my purpose was to provide a counterexample. Here is the relevant passage (Lakoff 1972:197–198):

But hedges do not merely reveal distinctions of degree of category membership. They can also reveal a great deal more about meaning. Consider (6).

(6) a. Esther Williams is a fish.
b. Esther Williams is a regular fish.

(6a) is false, since Esther Williams is a human being, not a fish. (6b), on the other hand, would seem to be true, since it says that Esther Williams swims well and is at home in water. Note that (6b) does not assert that Esther Williams has gills, scales, fins, a tail, etc. In fact, (6b) presupposes that Esther Williams is not literally a fish and asserts that she has certain other characteristic properties of a fish. Bolinger (1972) has suggested that *regular* picks out certain "metaphorical" properties. We can see what this means in an example like (7).

(7) a. John is a bachelor.
b. John is a regular bachelor.

(7b) would not be said of a bachelor. It might be said of a married man who acts like a bachelor – dates a lot, feels unbound by marital responsibilities, etc. In short, *regular* seems to assert the connotations of "bachelor," while presupposing the negation of the literal meaning.

Edward Smith (personal communication) has remarked that this passage started him on a line of research that he has pursued ever since. What interested him was the distinction between definitional and incidental properties. The passage had provided counterevidence to the objectivist view of this distinction, which *absolutely requires* that "semantics" be kept independent of "pragmatics"; that is, definitional properties are completely independent of incidental properties. The use of the hedge *regular* violates this condition, since it makes use of incidental properties in *semantics*. Kay (1979, see also 1983) has argued that the definitional-incidental distinction is not objectively correct, but rather part of our folk theory of language. The hedge *regular* makes use of this folk theory. If Kay's argument is correct, then the semantics-pragmatics and definitional-incidental distinctions are invalidated in even a deeper way than I first suggested.

Smith seems not to have been aware that this example was in conflict with the theory of semantics in which the classical theory of categorization is embedded. He drew from the distinction a way to keep the classical theory of categories, while still accounting for prototype effects. His idea was that the definitional properties fit the classical theory and that the incidental properties gave rise to prototype effects. This idea is developed in Osherson and Smith's classic 1981 paper. That paper claims that the definitional properties characterize the conceptual "core" of a category, that which permits reasoning; incidental properties, on the other hand, have nothing to do with reasoning, but are used only to *identify* category members. Prototype effects, they claim, have to do with identification and not with reason or conceptual structure.

I find it ironic that a passage providing counterevidence to the classical view should provide the impetus for a defense of that view.

Osherson and Smith

Osherson and Smith begin their paper with the following definition of prototype theory:

Prototype theory construes membership in a concept's extension as graded, determined by similarity to the concept's "best" exemplar (or by some other measure of central tendency).

Here Osherson and Smith are assuming both the Effects = Structure Interpretation and the Prototype = Representation Interpretation. Their paper is an argument against these interpretations. Osherson and Smith also make additional assumptions:

They assume that fuzzy-set theory in the earliest of its many versions (Zadeh 1965) is the appropriate way of modeling the Effects = Structure Interpretation.

They assume *atomism*, that is, that the meaning of the whole is a regular compositional function of the meaning of its parts. As a consequence,

> gestalt effects in semantics (cf. Lakoff 1977) are eliminated as a possibility.

> They assume *objectivist semantics,* that is, that meaning is based on truth.

> They assume that all noun modifiers are to be treated via conjunction. This is commonly done in objectivist semantics, though as we will see it is grossly inadequate.

In the light of the previous discussion, we can see that these assumptions are not well founded. As we have pointed out, almost all prototype and basic-level effects are inconsistent with objectivist semantics. However, the Effects = Structure Interpretation is not inconsistent with objectivist semantics. The reason is that it treats all categories as graded categories, and as we have seen, graded categorization is consistent with most of the objectivist assumptions.

If we grant all of Osherson and Smith's assumptions, their argument follows. The examples they give are well worth considering. Like classical set theory, classical fuzzy-set theory has only three ways of forming complex categories: intersection, union, and complementation. Osherson and Smith take each of these and show that they lead to incorrect results. Their first counterexample involves three drawings:

a. A line drawing of a normally shaped apple with stripes superimposed on the apple.
b. A line drawing of a normally shaped apple.
c. A line drawing of an abnormally shaped apple with only a few stripes.

They now consider three concepts: *apple, striped,* and *striped apple.* They correctly observe that within classical fuzzy-set theory there is only one way to derive the complex category *striped apple* from the categories *apple* and *striped,* namely, by intersection of fuzzy sets – which is defined by taking the minimum of the membership values in the two-component fuzzy sets. They assume the following:

(a) is a good example of a striped apple.
  (a) is not a good example of an apple, since apples generally aren't striped.
  (a) is not a good example of a striped thing, since apples are not among the things that are typically striped.

It follows that:

(a) will have a high value in the category *striped apple.*
  (a) will have a low value in the category *apple.*
  (a) a will have a low value in the category *striped.*

But since the minimum of two low values is a low value, it should follow from fuzzy-set theory that (a) has a low value in the category *striped apple.* Thus fuzzy-set theory makes an incorrect prediction. It predicts that an excellent example of a striped apple will have a low value in that category because it has low values in the component categories *apple* and *striped.*

There is a general moral here:

GOOD EXAMPLES OF COMPLEX CATEGORIES ARE OFTEN BAD EXAMPLES OF COMPONENT CATEGORIES.

Osherson and Smith cite a similar example: *pet fish*. A guppy might be a good example of a pet fish, but a bad example of a pet and a bad example of a fish. Set intersection in classical fuzzy-set theory will give incorrect results in such cases.

Osherson and Smith also use some of what might be called "logicians' examples":

P AND NOT P: an apple that is not an apple

P OR NOT P: a fruit that either is, or is not, an apple

They assume the correctness of the usual logician's intuitions about such cases: There is no apple that is not an apple, and so the first category should have no members to any degree; and all fruits either are or are not apples, so the second category should contain all fruits as full-fledged members. Such intuitions have been disputed: a carved wooden apple might be considered an apple that is not an apple. And a cross between a pear and an apple might be considered a bad example of a fruit that clearly either is, or is not, an apple. Osherson and Smith do not consider such possibilities. They correctly argue that classical fuzzy-set theory cannot account for the usual logician's intuitions in such cases.

The argument goes like this. Take an apple that is not a representative example of an apple, say a crabapple. According to classical fuzzy-set theory, this would have a value in the category *apple* somewhere in between zero and 1. Call the value c. Its value in the category *not an apple* would then be $1 - c$, according to the definition of set complementation in fuzzy-set theory. If c is in between zero and 1, $1 - c$ will also be between zero and 1. And both the maximum and the minimum of c and $1 - c$ will be in between zero and 1. Thus, according to fuzzy-set theory, a nonrepresentative apple, like a crabapple, would have a value greater than zero in the category *an apple that is not an apple*, and it would have a value less than 1 in the category *a fruit that either is, or is not, an apple*. This is inconsistent with the intuitions assumed to be correct by Osherson and Smith. If we accept their intuitions, their argument against fuzzy-set theory is correct.

Osherson and Smith's last major argument depends on their assumption of the Prototype = Representation Interpretation, namely, that in prototype theory, degree of membership is determined by degree of similarity to a prototypical member. They correctly produce a counterexample to this interpretation. It is based on the following use of the Prototype = Representation Interpretation. Consider grizzly bears and squirrels. Since one can find some (possibly small) similarities between grizzly bears and squirrels, it follows on the Prototype = Representation Interpretation that squirrels are members of the category *grizzly bear* to some degree greater than zero. Now consider the statement:

All grizzly bears are inhabitants of North America.

Suppose someone were to find a squirrel on Mars. Because that squirrel is a member of the category *grizzly bear* to some extent, and because Mars is far from North America, the discovery of a squirrel on Mars would serve as disconfirmation of the claim that all grizzly bears are inhabitants of North America. But this is ridiculous. The existence of squirrels on Mars should have nothing to do with the truth or falsity of that statement. Given Osherson and Smith's assumptions, this is indeed a counterexample to the Prototype = Representation Interpretation of prototype effects.

What Osherson and Smith have correctly shown is that, given all their assumptions, the Effects = Structure and Prototype = Representation Interpretations are incorrect. Of course, each one of their assumptions is questionable. One need not use the classical version of fuzzy-set theory to mathematicize these interpretations. The assumption that noun modifiers work by conjunction is grossly incorrect. And objectivist semantics and atomism are, as we have seen above, inadequate to handle the kinds of prototype phenomena that we have discussed. But, most importantly, the Effects = Structure and Prototype = Representation Interpretations are wildly inaccurate ways of understanding prototype and basic-level effects. To show that they are wrong is to show virtually nothing about any reasonable version of prototype theory. In addition, their argument shows nothing whatever about the Cognitive Models Interpretation that we are suggesting. But Osherson and Smith seem unaware of all this, and conclude (p. 54) that they have provided arguments against *all* versions of prototype theory.

Osherson and Smith then endorse a proposal reminiscent of that suggested by Miller and Johnson-Laird (1976) for saving the classical theory while accounting for the experimental results of prototype theory. What they adopt is a hybrid theory: each concept has a *core* and an *identification procedure*. The core works according to the traditional theory; the identification procedure accounts for the prototype effects that show up in experiments. As they put it:

The core is concerned with those aspects of a concept that explicate its relation to other concepts, and to thoughts, while the identification procedure specifies the kind of information used to make rapid decisions about membership. . . . We can illustrate this with the concept *woman*. Its core might contain information about the presence of a reproductive system, while its identification procedures might contain information about body shape, hair length, and voice pitch.

The core, in other words, would be where the real work of the mind – thought – is done. The identification procedure would link the mind to the senses, but not do any real conceptual work. As they say,

> Given this distinction it is possible that some traditional theory of concepts correctly characterizes the core, whereas prototype theory characterizes an important identification procedure. This would explain why prototype theory does well in explicating the real-time process of determining category membership (a job for identification procedures), but fares badly in explicating conceptual combination and the truth conditions of thoughts (a job for concept cores).

This hybrid theory assumes that traditional theories actually work for complex concepts. The fact is that this is one of the most notorious weaknesses of traditional theories. The only traditional theories in existence are based on classical set theory. Such theories permit set-theoretical intersection, union, and complement operations, and occasionally a small number of additional operations. But on the whole they do very badly at accounting for complex categorization. We can see the problems best by looking first at the classical theory, without any additional operations. The traditional set-theoretical treatment of adjective-noun phrases is via set intersection. That is the only option the traditional theory makes available. So, in the classical theory, the complex concept *striped apple* would denote the intersection of the set of striped things and the set of apples.

The literature on linguistic semantics is replete with examples where simple set intersection will not work. Perhaps we should start with some that Osherson and Smith themselves mention (1981:43, fn 8; 50, fn 12).

> small galaxy – not the intersection of the set of small things and the set of galaxies
>
> good thief – not the intersection of the set of good things and the set of thieves
>
> imitation brass – not the intersection of the set of imitations and the set of brass things

Other classic examples abound:

> electrical engineer – not the intersection of the set of electrical things and the set of engineers
>
> mere child – not the intersection of the set of mere things and the set of children
>
> red hair – because the color is not focal red, it is not merely the intersection of the set of red things and the set of hairs
>
> happy coincidence – not the intersection of the set of happy things and the set of coincidences
>
> topless bar – not the intersection of the set of topless things and the set of bars

    heavy price – not the intersection of the set of heavy things and the set of
      prices

    past president – not the intersection of the set of past things and the set of
      presidents

Such examples can be multiplied indefinitely. There is nothing new
about them, and no serious student of linguistic semantics would claim
that such cases could be handled by intersection in traditional set theory.
At present there is no adequate account of most kinds of complex concepts within a traditional framework, though a small number of isolated
analyses using nonstandard set-theoretical apparatus have been attempted. For example, various logicians have attempted a treatment of
the "small galaxy" cases using Montague semantics, and there have been
occasional attempts to account for the "good thief" cases, and a couple of
the others. But the vast number have not even been seriously studied
within traditional approaches, and there is no reason whatever to think
that they could be ultimately accounted for by traditional set theory, or
any simple extension of it.

    Let us turn now from the adequacy of the traditional set-theoretical
core of the Osherson and Smith hybrid theory to the identification procedures. They do not give an indication as to what such identification
procedures might be like. But what is more important is that Osherson
and Smith do not consider the question of what the identification procedures for complex concepts would be like and how they would be
related to the identification procedures for component concepts. Take,
for example, Osherson and Smith's case of *pet fish*. As Osherson and
Smith correctly observe, "A guppy is more prototypical of *pet fish* than it
is of either *pet* or *fish*." In the hybrid theory, the identification procedure
for *pet* would not pick out a guppy as prototypical, nor would the identification procedure for *fish*. How does the hybrid theory come up with an
identification procedure for the complex concept *pet fish* that will pick
out a guppy as prototypical? In short, the hybrid theory has not solved
the problem of how to account for the prototypes of complex concepts.
It has just given the problem a new name.

    Perhaps the most inaccurate part of the hybrid theory is that it views
prototype phenomena as involving no more than "identification." But
metonymic cases of prototypes function to a large extent in the service of
reasoning; in general, what Rosch calls *reference-point reasoning* has to do
with drawing conclusions, and not mere identification. For example,
arithmetic submodels are used for doing computations and making approximations; social stereotypes are used to make rapid judgments
about people; familiar examples are used to make probability judgments; paragons are used to make comparisons, and ideals are used to
make plans. Moreover, generative prototypes are not used just for iden-

tification; they are necessary to define their categories. Radial structures characterize relationships among subcategories, and permit category extension, which is an extremely important rational function. Most actual cases of prototype phenomena simply are not used in "identification." They are used instead in thought – making inferences, doing calculations, making approximations, planning, comparing, making judgments, and so on – as well as in defining categories, extending them, and characterizing relations among subcategories. Prototypes do a great deal of the real work of the mind, and have a wide use in rational processes.

In short, Osherson and Smith have said nothing whatever that bears on the version of prototype theory that we have given. Nor have they provided any reason to believe that their proposal for saving the classical theory will work. Indeed, the fact that prototypes are used widely in rational processes of many kinds indicates that the classical theory will not account for all those aspects of rational thought.

Armstrong, Gleitman, and Gleitman

The hybrid theory, despite all the arguments against it, is not likely to disappear. The classical theory that it incorporates as its "core" has two thousand years of tradition behind it. Within the past hundred years, theories of the form *core + everything else* have appeared repeatedly as attempts preserve the classical theory of categories. A particularly interesting recent attempt to argue for some form of the Osherson and Smith core + identification procedure theory has been made by Armstrong, Gleitman, and Gleitman (1983). Armstrong et al. argue that the very ubiquity of prototype phenomena provides support for a classical theory over a prototype theory.

Like Osherson and Smith, Armstrong et al. equate prototype theory with the Effects = Structure Interpretation. That is, they assume that every version of prototype theory would have to claim that all categories are graded, and that goodness-of-example ratings correspond to degrees of membership. The form of their argument is roughly as follows:

(a) *Basic assumption:* Prototype theory assumes that whenever there are prototype effects for a category that category is graded. Goodness-of-example ratings correspond to degrees of membership. Conversely, it is assumed that prototype theory claims that ungraded categories would not yield prototype effects, since it is assumed that prototype effects only reflect degrees of membership.

(b) *Secondary assumption:* Concepts from formal mathematics are defined in terms of the classical theory, that is, by necessary and sufficient conditions, and therefore are not graded. By assumption (a), they should not show prototype effects. "Odd number" is an example.

(c) Armstrong et al. perform Rosch's experiments using the concept "odd number." They show that Rosch's prototype results appear, and that

subjects give graded responses when asked if some numbers are better examples of the category "odd number" than other numbers.
(d) From (a), they reason that prototype theory must interpret these results as indicating that the category "odd number" is graded. But (b) shows that it is not graded.
(e) Since we know that (b) is true, prototype effects cannot show that a category is graded. Therefore, (a) must be false, and so prototype theory does not show anything about the real structure of categories.
(f) But Rosch's results must show something. The "core + identification procedure" theory gives a plausible answer. Rosch's reproducible experiments reflect the identification procedure, but not the core, that is, the real cognitive structure of a category.

Like Osherson and Smith, Armstrong et al. assume the Effects = Structure Interpretation, and it is this interpretation that they, very reasonably, find wanting. They do not even consider the possibility of anything like the Cognitive Models Interpretation. But in the Cognitive Models Interpretation, their results make perfect sense.

To see why, let us first distinguish natural numbers as they are defined technically in formal arithmetic from natural numbers as ordinary people understand them. In formal arithmetic, the natural numbers are defined recursively. "0" is taken as a generator and "successor" as an operator. "1" is a name given to the successor of 0, "2" is a name given to the successor of the successor of 0, and so on. In mathematics, it is important to distinguish numbers from their names. We have a naming systems for numbers that takes 10 as a base; that is, we have ten single-digit number names – 0, 1, . . . , 9 – and form multiple-digit number names thereafter. There are an indefinitely large number of possible naming systems. The best-known one after the base 10 system is the binary system, which takes 2 as a base and has only two single-digit number names: 0 and 1.

Most nonmathematicians do not distinguish numbers from their names. We comprehend numbers in terms of our base 10 naming system. The single-digit numbers are all generators. Multiple-digit numbers are understood as sequences of single-digit numbers. In order to compute with numbers, we must learn the generators – 0 through 9 – plus the addition and multiplication tables, plus algorithms for adding, multiplying, dividing, and so on. Computation with large numbers is understood in terms of computation with smaller numbers – ultimately single-digit numbers. Without understanding large numbers in terms of single-digit numbers, we could not do arithmetic computations.

Thus, single-digit numbers have a privileged place among the numbers. Double-digit numbers, especially those in the multiplication and addition tables, are somewhat less privileged. Larger numbers in general are less privileged still. A model for understanding all natural numbers in terms of single-digit numbers is, by our definition, a metonymic model. We would therefore expect that all other things being equal, single-digit numbers should be judged as better examples than double-digit numbers, which should be judged as better examples than larger numbers.

However, our understanding of numbers is more complicated than that. To aid in computation, and in judging the relative size of numbers, we have learned to comprehend numbers using various submodels. The most common submodel consists of powers of ten – ten, a hundred, a thousand, and so on. Another common subsystem consists of multiples of five; the American monetary system is based on these submodels and it is helpful in doing monetary calculations. Other common submodels are multiples of two, powers of two, and so on. As we pointed out above, each such submodel produces prototype effects. Taking all such submodels together, we would expect prototype effects of complex sorts.

On the Cognitive Models Interpretation, such prototype effects for numbers would not correspond to degrees of membership. All numbers are equal with respect to membership in the category *number*. But with respect to the various models we use to comprehend numbers, certain numbers have privileged status.

Another submodel we use with numbers is one in which numbers are divided into odd numbers and even numbers; the even numbers are those divisible by 2, while the odd numbers are those of the form $2n + 1$. The odd-even submodel has no gradations; all numbers are either odd or even.

Let us now consider all the models together: the model used to generate the numbers, the powers-of-ten-model, the multiples-of-five model, the powers-of-two model, the prime number model, the odd-even model, and any others that we happen to have. Each model, by itself, produces prototype effects, except for the odd-even and prime number models. If we superimpose the all-or-none odd-even model on all the integers, we would expect to get prototype effects within the odd numbers and other prototype effects within the even numbers. We would expect these effects to be complex, since they would be the product of all the models together.

If we then asked subjects if the odd-even distinction was all-or-none or graded, we would expect them to say it was all-or-none. If we then asked them to give goodness-of-example ratings for odd numbers and for even numbers, we would expect them to be able to perform the task readily, and to give rather complex ratings. This is exactly what Armstrong et al. did, and those were the results they got. It is exactly what prototype theory would predict – under the Cognitive Models Interpretation.

Unfortunately, Armstong et al. were using the Effects = Structure

Interpretation of prototype theory, and the results they got were, not surprisingly, inconsistent with that interpretation. They assumed that, since the odd-even distinction was all-or-none, there should be no prototype effects, since there was no degree-of-membership gradation. When they found prototype effects in a nongraded category, they concluded that prototype effects occurred in all categories regardless of structure, and therefore reflected nothing about the structure of the category. Thus, the same experiment that confirms prototype theory under the Cognitive Models Interpretation disconfirms it under the Effects = Structure Interpretation.

Conclusion

Osherson and Smith, together with Armstrong, Gleitman, and Gleitman, have provided even more evidence that the incorrect Effects = Structure and Prototype = Representation interpretations of prototype theory are indeed incorrect. They have not shown that the core plus identification procedure theory *is* correct. In fact, the considerations we discussed above indicate that such a view is not viable for a number of reasons.

1. The classical theory of categories is hopelessly inadequate for complex concepts.
2. There is a correspondence between prototype effects and metonymically based reasoning. Such prototype effects can be accounted for by metonymic models, which are needed independently to account for what Rosch has called "reference point reasoning." Thus, prototype effects are not independent of reasoning.
3. There do exist direct correlations between conceptual structure and prototype effects. They are of two types: (a) cognitive models containing scales that define gradations of category membership, and (b) radial categories.

The best way to account for prototype effects in general seems to be via a theory of cognitive models.

NOTE

A fuller account of the issues discussed in this paper can be found in the author's book *Women, Fire, and Dangerous Things: What Categories Tell Us About the Nature of Thought*, University of Chicago Press, 1986.

REFERENCES

Armstrong, S. L., Gleitman, L., & Gleitman, H. (1983). What some concepts might not be. *Cognition, 13*, 263–308.

Coleman, L., & Kay, P. (1981). Prototype semantics: The English verb *lie*. *Language, 57*, 1.

Downing, P. (1984). *Japanese numerical classifiers: Syntax, semantics, and pragmatics.* Unpublished doctoral dissertation, University of California, Berkeley.

Fillmore, Charles. (1982). Towards a descriptive framework for spatial deixis. In R. Jarvella & W. Klein (Eds.), *Speech, place, and action.* London: Wiley.

Kay, P. (1979). *The role of cognitive schemata in word meaning: Hedges revisited.* Unpublished manuscript, Department of Linguistics, University of California, Berkeley.

——— (1983). Linguistic competence and folk theories of language: Two English hedges. In *Proceedings of the Ninth Annual Meeting of the Berkeley Linguistics Society* (pp. 128–137).

Kay, P., & Kempton, W. (1984). What is the Sapir-Whorf hypothesis? *American Anthropologist 86*, 1, 65–79.

Lakoff, G. (1972). Hedges: A study in meaning criteria and the logic of fuzzy concepts. In *Papers from the Eighth Regional Meeting of the Chicago Linguistic Society.* Also in *Journal of Philosophical Logic* (1973), *2*, 458–508.

——— (1977). Linguistic gestalts. In *Proceedings of the Thirteenth Regional Meeting of the Chicago Linguistic Society.*

——— (1986). *Women, fire, and dangerous things: What categories tell us about the nature of thought.* Chicago: University of Chicago Press.

Lakoff, G., & Johnson, M. (1980). *Metaphors we live by.* Chicago: University of Chicago Press.

Miller, G., & Johnson-Laird, P. (1976). *Language and perception.* Cambridge, MA: Harvard University Press.

Osherson, D., & Smith, E. (1981). On the adequacy of prototype theory as a theory of concepts. *Cognition 9*, 1, 35–58.

Reddy, M. (1979). The Conduit metaphor. In A. Ortony (Ed.), *Metaphor and thought.* Cambridge, England: Cambridge University Press.

Rhodes, R. (1976). The morphosyntax of the central Ojibwa verb. Unpublished doctoral dissertation, University of Michigan, Ann Arbor.

Rips, L. J. (1975). Inductive judgments about natural categories. *Journal of Verbal Learning and Verbal Behavior, 14*, 665–681.

Rosch, E. (1978). Principles of categorization. In E. Rosch & B. B. Lloyd (Eds.), *Cognition and categorization.* Hillsdale, NJ: Erlbaum.

Smith, E. E., & Medin, D. E. (1981). *Categories and concepts.* Cambridge, MA: Harvard University Press.

Sweetser, E. E. (1984). *Semantic structure and semantic change.* Unpublished doctoral dissertation, University of California, Berkeley.

——— (1986). The definition of *lie:* An examination of the folk theories underlying a semantic prototype. In D. Holland & N. Quinn (Eds.), *Cultural models in language and thought.* Cambridge, England: Cambridge University Press.

Tversky, A., & Kahneman, D. (1983). Probability, representativeness, and the conjunction fallacy. *Psychological Review, 90*(4), 293–315.

Zadeh, L. (1965). Fuzzy sets. *Information and Control, 8*, 338–353.

5

The instability of graded structure: implications for the nature of concepts

LAWRENCE W. BARSALOU

After a brief introduction to graded structure, this chapter reviews empirical findings showing that the graded structure of a category is unstable, varying widely across contexts. Implications of these findings for theories of categorization are discussed, and it is concluded that graded structures do not represent invariant structural characteristics of categories. Instead it is proposed that instability in graded structure occurs because different concepts temporarily represent the same category in working memory on different occasions. Rather than being retrieved as static units from memory to represent categories, concepts originate in a highly flexible process that retrieves generic and episodic information from long-term memory to construct temporary concepts in working memory. Because this concept construction process is highly constrained by goals, context, and recent experience, the same concept is rarely if ever constructed for a category. A theory of concept construction is presented, and the relations of this theory to dreaming (Foulkes 1985), conceptual combination (Hampton in press a,b; Smith & Osherson 1984), exemplar theories (Brooks 1978; Jacoby & Brooks 1984; Medin & Schaeffer 1978), norm theory (Kahneman & Miller, 1986), and parallel distributed processing (McClelland & Rumelhart 1986; Rumelhart & McClelland, 1986) are discussed.

Definition of graded structure

A central theme in categorization research for the last decade has been that categories possess graded structure. Instead of being equivalent, the members of a category vary in how good an example (or in how typical) they are of their category (Rips, Shoben, & Smith 1973; Rosch 1973). In the category of *birds,* for example, American college students generally agree that *robin* is very typical, *pigeon* is moderately typical, and *ostrich* is atypical. In addition, nonmembers of a category vary in how good a nonmember they are of the category (Barsalou 1983). With respect to *birds, chair* is a better nonmember than is *butterfly.* Typicality for nonmembers is analogous to the relatedness effect for nonmembers that has been well-documented in the category verification literature (Smith 1978).

Graded structure refers to this continuum of category representativeness, beginning with the most typical members of a category and continuing through its atypical members to those nonmembers least similar to category members. Although the focus of this chapter will be on graded structure within categories, much of what will be said may also apply to graded structure outside categories.

It should be noted that "graded structure" in this section and the following section does *not* refer to cognitive structure. Instead it simply refers to behavior, that is, to how people order exemplars in categories according to typicality. In this sense, the graded structure for *birds* is simply the rank ordering of *birds* from most to least typical and does not carry any representational assumptions. Various interpretations of these orderings will be considered later in this chapter.

Generality of graded structure

Because every category observed so far has been found to have graded structure, it appears that graded structure is a universal property of categories. Seminal work by Rosch, Smith, and their colleagues found that common taxonomic categories such as *fruit* and *furniture* all have graded structure (e.g., Rips et al. 1973; Rosch 1973, 1975, 1978; Rosch & Mervis 1975; Smith, Shoben, & Rips 1974). Subsequent studies have found graded structure in a wide range of category types. Armstrong, Gleitman, and Gleitman (1983) found graded structure in formal categories such as *odd numbers* and *squares*. Lakoff (1986) reviews evidence for there being graded structure in linguistic categories for phones, phonemes, and syntactic categories. Barsalou (1985) found graded structure in categories people construct to serve goals, what will be referred to as *goal-derived categories* (e.g., *things to eat on a diet, things to pack in a suitcase*). Barsalou (1983) found graded structure in categories people have rarely if ever thought of, what will be referred to as *ad hoc categories* (e.g., *ways to escape being killed by the Mafia, things that could fall on your head*). Ad hoc categories are goal-derived categories that are not well-established in memory but are instead created to achieve a novel goal.

Importance of graded structure

Besides appearing to be universally true of categories, graded structure appears to be the most important variable in predicting performance on a wide range of categorization tasks. Graded structure is central to predicting how long it takes someone to classify something as a category member, with typical exemplars being identified faster than atypical exemplars (e.g., McCloskey & Glucksberg 1979; Smith 1978). Graded structure is central to predicting the frequency with which people generate members of categories, with typical exemplars being generated more often than atypical exemplars (e.g., Barsalou 1983, 1985; Barsalou & Sewell 1985; Mervis, Catlin, & Rosch 1976). Graded structure is central to predicting ease of category learning, with typical exemplars being easier to acquire than atypical exemplars (e.g., Mervis & Pani 1980; Rosch, Simpson, & Miller 1976). In addition, graded structure is central to how people make decisions, with the typicality of exemplars often having substantial effects on decision making (Cherniak 1984; Rips 1975; Rosch 1983). Mervis and Rosch (1981), Medin and Smith (1984), and Smith and Medin (1981) further review the roles of graded structure in categorization tasks.

Preview

Given the ubiquity and predictive power of graded structure, it is important to identify its basic empirical properties and to understand its origins in the human cognitive system. The next section reviews research aimed at identifying basic empirical properties of graded structure. The remaining sections explore implications of these properties for cognitive interpretations of graded structure and for how the cognitive system produces concepts.

Before proceeding, however, it is first necessary to discuss common taxonomic and goal-derived categories in a little more detail, since they will be referred to frequently. Examples of common taxonomic categories are *birds, fruit, furniture,* and *vehicles.* Examples of goal-derived categories are *things to eat on a diet, places to vacation, birthday presents,* and *things to pack in a suitcase.* Although it has not been possible so far to define these two category types – and it may not ever be possible – each appears to have characteristic properties. First, common taxonomic categories are usually highly familiar biological and artifactual categories that are culturally transmitted, whereas goal-derived categories generally appear to be less familiar and to be less central to cultural knowledge. Second, common taxonomic categories generally reflect the correlational structure of the environment such that they form salient groups of entities (Rosch & Mervis 1975), whereas goal-derived categories generally form much less salient groups of entities because they do not reflect correlational structure (Barsalou, 1983, 1985). Third, common taxonomic categories often serve the purpose of representing kinds of things in the environment, whereas goal-derived categories often serve people's goals. Fourth, common taxonomic categories (especially basic-level categories) are often used for classifying entities in the environment, whereas goal-derived categories are often used for instantiating schema variables during planning. Further discussion of the differences between common taxonomic and goal-derived categories can be found in Barsalou (1983, 1985; Barsalou, Usher, & Sewell 1985).

The instability of graded structure

The empirical properties of graded structure to be discussed in this section can be viewed in two ways: Pessimistically, they can be viewed as showing that graded structure is unreliable and meaningless. Optimistically, they can be viewed as showing that graded structure is highly flexible, with this flexibility being a fundamental property of the human cognitive system.

Determinants of graded structure

As discussed earlier, graded structure appears to be a universal property of categories. Yet what determines whether exemplars are typical or atypical? Assuming that exemplars usually differ from each other in many ways (e.g., *familiarity, value, size, shape*), and assuming that people use one or more of these differences to order exemplars by typicality, which particular difference or differences do they use? For example, people could use differences between exemplars in familiarity such that exemplars become more typical as they become more familiar.

It appears that people use a variety of differences between exemplars when judging typicality. Instead of there being any single determinant or invariant set of determinants responsible for typicality, there appears to be a large class of determinants that is impossible to specify completely and that depends to some extent on the category and on the context in which it is perceived.

One factor that has been shown to play an important role in determining typicality is a category's *central tendency*, namely, information that is prototypical or representative of a category's members. Central tendency information can be construed as modal or average properties abstracted from exemplars, as one very representative exemplar, as several very representative exemplars, as modal correlations of properties, or as various other forms (see Smith & Medin 1981). It turns out that most major accounts of graded structure have proposed that an exemplar's similarity to the central tendency of its category determines its typicality. Smith et al. (1974) argued that exemplars are typical to the extent they possess the characteristic properties of their categories. Hampton (1979) made a similar proposal. Rosch and Mervis (1975), Rosch et al. (1976), and A. Tversky (1977) argued that an exemplar's family resemblance determines its typicality, where "family resemblance" is a particular form of similarity to central tendency.[1]

While there appears to be widespread acceptance that similarity to central tendency is responsible for graded structure, its importance appears to have been overestimated. As found by Hampton (1981), similarity to central tendency does not predict graded structure in some abstract categories. As found by Barsalou (1985), similarity to central tendency does not predict graded structure in goal-derived categories. Similarity to central tendency by no means determines the graded structure of every category.

A second factor that determines an exemplar's typicality is how similar it is to ideals associated with its category, where ideals are properties that exemplars should have if they are to best serve goals associated with their category. For example, *zero calories* is an ideal associated with *foods to eat on a diet*, since exemplars with decreasing numbers of calories are increasingly conducive to the goal of *losing weight*. As found by Barsalou (1985), exemplars of both common taxonomic and goal-derived categories become increasingly typical as they approximate *ideals* associated with their category.

A third factor that determines an exemplar's typicality is how frequently it is perceived as instantiating its category. As found by Barsalou (1985), exemplars become more typical in both common taxonomic and goal-derived categories as their frequency of instantiation increases. Barsalou (1985) also assessed the role of familiarity in predicting graded structure and found that it accounted for no unique typicality variance. More specifically, its weak correlations with typicality were completely the result of variance it shared with frequency of instantiation. People's perceptions of how frequently exemplars instantiate their category, rather than people's familiarity with exemplars, appears to be the measure of frequency that is most central to graded structure.

It should be noted that each of the factors discussed so far – central tendency, ideals, and frequency of instantiation – accounts for *unique* typicality variance. Each predicts typicality to a substantial extent after effects of other possible determinants have been partialed out.

Lakoff (1986, Chapter 4, this volume) reviews a number of additional factors that also determine graded structure. It is safe to say that there are many reasons why exemplars are typical and that no single factor or invariant set of factors is solely responsible. As found by Barsalou (1985), categories vary widely in the factors that determine their graded structure, with there being no invariant pattern of determinants. In addition, several factors may together determine a category's graded structure. In several of the categories studied by Barsalou (1985), central tendency, ideals, and frequency of instantiation each accounted for unique typicality variance in the same category; various pairs of these factors each accounted for unique typicality variance in a number of other categories. It appears that the determination of graded structure is a highly flexible phenomenon. There is no single determinant such as similarity to central tendency that is universally responsible for graded structure.

Effects of context

Different determinants in different contexts. Not only do categories vary in what determines their graded structure, different factors determine the graded structure of the *same* category in different contexts. In an experiment with artificial categories, Barsalou (1985: Experiment 2) found that subjects used central tendency to determine a category's graded structure in one context, but used ideals to determine its graded structure in another. This suggests that almost any difference between a category's exemplars could be used to order them by typicality, given the appropriate context.

Linguistic contexts. As shown by Roth and Shoben (1983), a category's graded structure can shift as a function of its linguistic context; that is, different linguistic contexts result in different orderings of exemplars by typicality within the same category. For example, when *animals* is processed in the context of milking, *cow* and *goat* are more typical than *horse* and *mule.* But when *animals* is processed in the context of riding, *horse* and *mule* are more typical than *cow* and *goat.* Roth and Shoben not only found that linguistic context affected typicality judgments, but also found that it affected time to access exemplars. Typicality as determined in the absence of explicit context was unrelated to performance measures in context.

Point of view. As shown by Barsalou and Sewell (1984), a category's graded structure can also shift as a function of the point of view from which it is perceived. In one set of experiments, subjects judged typicality from one of several international points of view (i.e., from the point of view of the average American, African, Chinese, or French citizen) or from one of several domestic points of view (i.e., from the point of view of the average businessman, housewife, hippie, or redneck).[2]

An average graded structure was obtained for each category from each point of view by averaging the rankings for each exemplar in each category from each point of view. Correlations were then computed between the average graded structures for the same category from different points of view. Groups of subjects taking different points of view generated substantially different graded structures for the same category. In *birds,* for example, *robin* and *eagle* were typical from the American point of view, whereas *swan* and *peacock* were typical from the Chinese point of view. In many cases, the ways in which different points of view ordered exemplars for the same category were uncorrelated or inversely related. Such effects occurred for both goal-derived and common taxonomic categories. In fact, context generally affected both category types to a large and equal extent.

In another experiment from Barsalou and Sewell (1984), Emory faculty generated graded structures from their own point of view, and Emory undergraduates generated graded structures from their own point of view. Other faculty generated graded structures from the undergraduate point of view, and other undergraduates generated graded structures from the faculty point of view. Across categories, the average correlation between faculty taking their own point of view and undergraduates taking their own point of view was .23, indicating that different populations of subjects may perceive very different graded structures in the same categories. Given this substantial difference, we were surprised to find that undergraduates generated graded structures from the faculty's point of view that were *identical* to those generated by faculty taking their own point of view. In addition, faculty taking the undergraduate point of view generated graded structures that were very close to those generated by undergraduates taking their own point of view, although faculty were off by a very small amount. Graduate students also participated in this study and were perfect at taking the points of view of both faculty and undergraduates.

It should be noted that these results do not indicate how well *specific individuals* from these different populations take each others' points of view. Instead these results only show that, *on the average,* different populations can be very accurate at taking each others' point of view. Work addressing the ability of specific individuals to take each others' points of view is discussed later.

Summary. The graded structures within categories do not remain stable across situations. Instead a category's graded structure can shift substantially with changes in context. This suggests that graded structures do not reflect invariant properties of categories but instead are highly dependent on constraints inherent in specific situations.

Between-subject reliability

How much do people agree with each other when they order exemplars by typicality? Previous attempts to address this issue have been highly misleading, primarily because of inappropriate statistical analyses. For example, Rosch (1975) and Armstrong et al. (1983) reported values over .9 for agreement, the implication being that subjects agree substantially on graded structure. Unfortunately the statistics used to obtain these estimates (measures of group reliability such as split-half correlation) are directly related to sample size. Depending on the number of subjects run, it is possible to obtain just about any level of agreement, with increasing numbers of subjects resulting in increasing levels of agreement. Instead of measuring how well subjects agree with each other, these statistics measure the stability of the *mean* typicality ratings for a sample (see Barsalou & Sewell, 1984, for further discussion).

More desirably, agreement should be measured by statistics that estimate the average correlation between all possible pairs of subjects in a sample and whose mean values are not influenced by sample size. Such measures exist (see Barsalou & Sewell 1984; Guilford & Fruchter 1973), and when they are used, values of subject agreement for typicality generally average around .45. This means that a given person's graded structure will correlate about .45 on the average with another person's graded structure. We have assessed subject agreement in over 20 groups of subjects over the last eight years, and we have always obtained average values across categories of around .50, with these averages generally ranging from around .30 to .60 (Barsalou 1983; unpublished values for Barsalou 1985; Barsalou & Sewell 1984; Barsalou, Sewell, & Ballato 1985). We have obtained average values of this magnitude for common taxonomic, goal-derived, and ad hoc categories; across a wide range of points of view that people take while judging typicality; for subjects from specific populations (e.g., Emory faculty, Emory graduate students); for categories of different sizes; for different sets of exemplars from the same category; and for ratings and rankings. In addition, Galambos and Rips (1982) obtained values of this magnitude for the centrality of actions in scripts, which is somewhat analogous to the typicality of exemplars in categories (Barsalou & Sewell 1985).

It should be noted that this level of agreement has generally been obtained with subjects from a fairly homogeneous population (i.e., American undergraduates). It would not be surprising if agreement dropped substantially when samples are more heterogeneous in their composition. Conversely, it is possible that certain conditions may result in higher levels of agreement. As discussed later, certain kinds of contexts may cause people to perceive categories more similarly. On the basis of results from Sewell (1985), however, it does not appear that agreement increases substantially as subjects within a sample become more homogeneous. For example, Sewell (1985) found between-subject agreement of .46 for Emory graduate students in psychology taking the American point of view. Sewell also found that between-subject agreement for close friends, each taking their own point of view (.47), was not significantly higher than agreement for superficial acquaintances, each taking their own point of view (.40).

Clearly this .50 level of between-subject agreement indicates that people differ substantially in how they perceive the graded structure of a given category. On the average, knowing one individual's typicality rankings for a category will predict about 25 percent of the variance in another person's typicality rankings (i.e., assuming an average correlation of .50 between individuals). Across individuals, graded structure is relatively unstable.

Taking the points of view of specific individuals

Between-subject reliability can be viewed as how well strangers agree with each other when they judge typicality. A related issue is how good people are at judging typicality from the points of view of their close acquaintances. It seems reasonable that getting to know someone may result in acquiring knowledge of how they view the world. As a result, people may be able to generate graded structures from the points of view of their close acquaintances that are very similar to the graded structures perceived by close acquaintances from their own points of view.

It was reported earlier that Emory undergraduates, graduates, and faculty were excellent at taking each others' point of view. As noted in that discussion, however, those results only demonstrate that populations *on the average* can in some cases generate graded structures that are identical to the *average* graded structures of another population. Because that experiment dealt with average graded structures, it doesn't really bear on how well a given individual can take the point of view of another individual.

In an unpublished study of people's ability to take individual points of view, 10 subjects judged typicality from the point of view of a close friend for the 20 common taxonomic categories and 20 goal-derived categories in Barsalou and Sewell (1984). Each subject also judged typicality for these categories from the point of view of a casual acquaintance. Each close friend and casual acquaintance also judged typicality while taking his or her own point of view. For each category, each subject's rankings from the point of view of his or her close friend were correlated with the rankings generated by that friend. Similarly, each subject's rankings from the point of view of a casual acquaintance were correlated with the rankings generated by that friend. Across subjects and categories, the average correlation between the rankings of a subject taking the point of view of his or her close friend and the rankings of that close friend was .45 for common taxonomic categories and .43 for goal-derived categories. The average correlation between the rankings of a subject taking the point of view of a casual acquaintance and the rankings of that acquaintance was .51 for common taxonomic categories and .43 for goal-derived categories.

These results indicate that people are not very good at taking the points of view of their close friends when judging typicality. Nor are people any better at taking the points of view of close friends than they are at taking the points of view of casual acquaintances, at least in the context of judging graded structure. It is interesting to note that the level of agreement in this study is about the same as that found for between-subject reliability.

To more carefully examine people's ability to take the point of view of specific individuals, Sewell (1985) had subjects take the points of view of close friends and casual acquaintances while making judgments for categories that friends are likely to share knowledge about. For example, subjects ranked how well they thought their friends liked various *kinds of food* (e.g., *Italian, Chinese*), how often they thought their friends performed various *entertainment activities* (e.g., *go to movies, go out to eat*), and so on. Each close friend and casual acquaintance also performed these judgments while taking his or her own point of view. Across subjects and categories, the average correlation between a subject and a close friend was .57, whereas the average correlation between a subject and a casual acquaintance was .45, this difference being significant. From these correlations, it follows that the rankings generated by someone from a friend's point of view only accounts for between 20 and 32 percent of the variance in the rankings generated by the friend himself. These results indicate that people do acquire some knowledge about close friends such that they can view categories from their points of view. Still, people are far from being able to do so perfectly.

Sewell (1985) also asked subjects to judge typicality from their own point of view and from various stereotypes that fit their friends (e.g., *adult black female, graduate student in clinical psychology*). Using regression analyses, he found that subjects' own points of view and their stereotypes were the best predictors of the rankings they generated from their friends' points of view. Most importantly, these two factors were generally better predictors of how a subject perceived a friend's point of view than the rankings generated by the friend from the friend's own point of view. When people perceive categories from the points of view of their friends, they often may not use (or have available) much objective knowledge about whom they are judging. As a result, they project their own point of view and use stereotypes when taking their friends' points of view.

In summary, people's ability to construct graded structures from the points of view of their friends is relatively poor. In fact the values obtained in these studies are not much higher than the values obtained for between-subject agreement for strangers. Even under advantageous circumstances, people do not agree substantially on graded structure.

Within-subject reliability

Given that between-subject reliability is much lower than has been previously believed, it is of interest to determine how stable graded structures are *within* particular individuals; that is, how well does a given subject agree with him- or herself over time. To explore this, Barsalou et al. (1986) had 36 subjects judge typicality for exemplars from 20 common taxonomic categories and 20 goal-derived categories twice, once on each of two days a month apart. Subjects received the same categories and the same exemplars from each category in different random orders on the two days. Half the subjects were asked to take the point of view of the average American on both days, and half were asked to take their own point of view.

Of primary interest was how well a given subject's rankings for the same category correlated across sessions. We had initially expected to observe within-subject agreement of .9 or higher. Although the graded structures of different individuals vary substantially, it seemed to us that particular individuals would be highly stable. For goal-derived categories, however, the average within-subject agreement was .75 from the American point of view and .76 from the subjects' own point of view. For common taxonomic categories, the average within-subject agreement was .82 from the American point of view and .80 from the subjects' own point of view. From these correlations, it follows that the rankings generated by someone on one day only account for between 56 and 67 percent of the variance in the rankings generated by the same subject a month later.

In another experiment, Barsalou et al. (1986) manipulated the delay between subjects' two sets of judgments from one hour to four weeks. In addition, half the subjects received exemplars in the same order on both days, whereas the other subjects received them in different orders. Within-subject reliability decreased from around .92 at a delay of one hour, to around .87 at a delay of one day, and to around .80 at delays of one, two, and four weeks, which did not differ. Order had no effect. In a third experiment, Barsalou et al. (1985) had subjects take either the redneck, the housewife, or their own point of view, while judging either typicality or exemplar goodness, on two days separated by a three-week delay. Subjects showed approximately a .80 level of agreement for all points of view and for both types of judgment.

The above experiments also observed whether highly typical, moderately typical, or atypical exemplars showed the most stability across the two days on which subjects judged typicality. All three experiments found that the rankings of highly typical exemplars and atypical exemplars were least likely (and equally likely) to change from day one to day two, whereas the rankings of moderately typical exemplars were most likely to change. All three experiments also found that when an exemplar's ranking did change from day one to day two the average distance it moved in its graded structure was lowest for highly typical and for atypical exemplars; it was highest for moderately typical exemplars (after correcting for potential amount of movement possible). Highly typical and atypical exemplars were most stable across time, whereas moderately typical exemplars were least stable.

In general these experiments show that there is substantial instability in the graded structures of particular subjects. Although subjects show reasonably high reliability after an hour, reliability drops substantially after a day and levels out at around .80 after a week. In terms of percent variance accounted for, subjects' initial judgments accounted for around 85 percent of the variance in their judgments an hour later, with this value dropping to around 75 percent after a day, and to around 65 percent after a week. Interestingly, when subjects took unusual points of view, reliability was approximately the same as when they took their own point of view, even though graded structures from the different points of view differed substantially. Finally, changes in the typicality of moderately typical exemplars played the largest role in the instability of graded structure, although there were also sizable changes in the typicality of both highly typical and atypical exemplars.

A finding from McCloskey and Glucksberg (1978) further indicates that the information used to judge category membership varies within individuals over time. McCloskey and Glucksberg found that individuals often changed their minds across a one-month period about whether an item did or did not belong to a category. For example, individuals often changed their minds about whether *yeast* belongs to *animals*. This further indicates that category representations are less stable than might be expected.

Production

So far, most of the results reported have been based on judgments of typicality. It appears, however, that production data also possess a high degree of instability. Bellezza (1984a) had subjects generate exemplars from the same common taxonomic categories in two sessions one week apart. He found that the average correlation between different subjects on a given day for the exemplars generated from a particular category was .44.[3] He also found that the average correlation within a subject for the exemplars generated on two days a week apart was .69. These values are remarkably similar to those reported earlier for the between- and within-subject reliability of typicality judgments. In a related study, Bellezza (1984c) had subjects provide definitions for various kinds of words in two sessions a week apart (i.e., concrete nouns, abstract nouns, and superordinate category names). Each definition generated by a subject was broken down into a set of propositions. The average between-subject agreement on a given day for the propositions generated for a word was .22. The average within-subject agreement across a week was .48. In a third study, Bellezza (1984b) asked subjects to produce information about famous people and about people they knew well in two sessions a week apart. The average between-subject reliability on a given day for famous people was .21 (this could not be computed for people subjects knew well because each subject knew a different person). The average within-subject reliability for famous people across a week was .55 and for people subjects knew well was .38.

These production data corroborate the typicality judgment data discussed earlier, namely, the way in which a particular category is represented varies widely both between and within individuals. It would not be surprising if production, similar to typicality, also varied substantially with changes in context.

Summary

As this review demonstrates, graded structure is a highly flexible and unstable phenomenon. A wide range of determinants is responsible for graded structure, and different determinants can be responsible for a category's graded structure in different contexts. A category's graded structure can vary substantially with changes in linguistic context and with changes in point of view. Different people do not agree very highly in the graded structures they generate for the same category. When people take the points of view of specific individuals, they are still not very accurate, even for close friends. Specific individuals are surprisingly inconsistent over time in the graded structures they generate for the same category. Furthermore, high variability occurs, both between and within subjects, when subjects produce information from conceptual representations, as well as when they judge typicality.

Implications for the nature of concepts

What conclusions should we draw from these data on graded structure? As was suggested earlier, a pessimist might conclude that graded structure is a useless phenomenon. Because it has so many determinants, because it is so easily affected by context, and because it is so unstable between and within individuals, one could argue that it is has little if any potential for informing us about people's representations of categories. This view, however, assumes that there are invariant cognitive structures associated with categories that we should be trying to discover. According to this view, people's representations of categories exist in some clear-cut way, and our job as cognitive scientists is, first, to develop empirical means for identifying these structures and, second, to develop theoretical means for discussing them. The remainder of this chapter argues that this view is fundamentally wrong. Invariant representations of categories do not exist in human cognitive systems. Instead, invariant representations of categories are analytic fictions created by those who study them.

Sources of graded structure

How then can we interpret results that show graded structure to be a highly dynamic and unstable phenomenon? What implications do these results have for theories of categorization? The following sections discuss several possibilities.

Memory. One possibility is that representations of graded structures are explicitly stored in long-term memory. According to this view (e.g., Glass and Holyoak 1975), associative strength underlies graded structure, with typical exemplars being highly associated to their category in long-term memory and atypical exemplars being weakly associated. In other words, a category's graded structure is represented by the associative strengths between the category and its exemplars in long-term memory. When judging typicality, people assess the strength of these associative relations and assign higher typicality values to higher strengths.

This view seems implausible for a number of reasons. First, it requires that there be a very large number of graded structures stored in long-term memory for each category. A category would need graded structures for all the possible points of view and contexts a person could possibly encounter. Second, people appear able to generate graded structures in novel contexts for which they do not have prestored graded structures. It is unlikely that subjects in our point-of-view experiments had previously constructed graded structures for all 40 categories from the Chinese point of view, the redneck point of view, and so on. Third, people appear able to generate graded structures for ad hoc categories such as *things that could fall on your head,* which are not well established in memory (Barsalou 1983). Fourth, this account does not explain how graded structures for well-established categories get constructed in the first place. Fifth, how readily an exemplar is generated during production – a measure of how strongly it is associated with its category – is far from being a perfect predictor of how typical it is. As found by Barsalou (1981: Experiment 1) and Barsalou and Sewell (1985), the order in which individual subjects generate exemplars only correlates .27 with their individual typicality judgments. In general, it seems implausible that the wide range of graded structures we observe in our experiments are all stored in long-term memory.

Similar problems exist for purely extensional approaches to fuzzy-set theory, which generally propose that exemplars have values between zero and 1 associated with them that indicate their degree of category membership (Zadeh 1965). It seems implausible that people store many such values for each exemplar to represent its degree of membership in every possible context. In addition, this theory does not explain how these values are obtained in the first place, how people obtain values for familiar categories in new contexts, or how people obtain values for ad hoc categories. As noted shortly, more intensional approaches to fuzzy-set theory (e.g., Zadeh 1982) are better suited to handle these problems.

The environment. A second account of graded structure is that it reflects the structure of the environment (Rosch 1978; Rosch & Mervis 1975). According to this view, categories originate in the correlational structure of the environment, and the typicality of exemplars reflects the extent to which they possess the pattern of correlations characteristic of their category. There are a number of problems with this view. First, it does not account for graded structure in categories that do not reflect correlational structure (e.g., goal-derived categories). Second, it provides no explanation of why graded structure varies so much with context. Third, it has no way of accounting for the importance of ideals in graded structure. People's goals appear extremely important to the organization of categories, and a complete theory of graded structure must account for them (cf. Murphy & Medin 1985).

Although the environment may not explain everything about graded structure, it probably plays an important role in people's knowledge and use of categories. There certainly seems to be structure in the environment, and people certainly appear sensitive to this structure (Neisser, Chapter 2, this volume; Rosch & Mervis 1975; Rosch, Mervis, Gray, Johnson, & Boyes-Braem 1976). Although people's knowledge may reflect environmental structure to some extent, it appears that their ability to manipulate knowledge allows them to construct representations that go far beyond those that reflect this structure.

Comparison of exemplar and category concepts in working memory. A third explanation of graded structure – and the one that seems best able to account for its flexibility – is that graded structure reflects a similarity comparison process that operates on exemplar and category concepts in working memory (Barsalou 1983, 1985; Hampton 1979; Smith et al. 1974; Zadeh 1982).

Before going into this account, it is first necessary to specify what will be meant by *concept* in this and the remaining sections. Although *concept* has typically been equated with the *definition* or *membership criteria* for a category (e.g., Armstrong et al. 1983), it will not be used as such here. Instead *concept* will refer to the particular information used to represent a category (or exemplar) on a particular occasion. More specifically, it will be assumed that the concept used to represent a category on a particular occasion contains (1) information that provides relevant expectations about the category in *that* context, and (2) information that provides relevant expectations when interacting with the category in *most* contexts. These two kinds of information correspond to context-dependent and context-independent information (Barsalou 1982), which are discussed later.

Barsalou and Medin (1986) review a number of arguments for viewing concepts in this way. For example, it is difficult, if not impossible, to find definitions for many categories. Even when such definitions exist, they often do not appear central to people's representations of categories. Instead prototypical, ideal, and context-relevant information (none of which may be definitional) generally appear most important, perhaps because they provide people with a rich source of expectations that facilitate successful interactions with category members. According to this argument, definitional information is only used to represent categories in contexts for which such information is relevant (e.g., when the payoffs for correct categorizations are high).

Returning to the issue of what determines graded structure, the comparison view proposes that the graded structure of a particular category in a particular context results from the following three steps: First, a concept is established in working memory to represent the category (what will be referred to as a *category concept*). Second, concepts for exemplars (*exemplar concepts*) are compared to the current category concept. Third, exemplars are judged as typical to the extent that they are similar to the current category concept. Highly similar exemplars are atypical, moderately similar exemplars are moderately typical, and weakly similar exemplars are atypical.

According to this account, graded structure changes across contexts because different category concepts are used in different contexts for the same category. Consider *animals* from the housewife and redneck points of view. When taking the housewife point of view, people might use a concept for *animals* that includes information about animals being small and domesticated; but when taking the redneck point of view, people might use a concept that includes information about animals being large and wild. Different graded structures would occur for *animals* because small and domesticated animals are similar to the housewife concept for *animals,* whereas large and wild animals are similar to the redneck concept for *animals.* According to this view, changes in graded structure for the same category reflect changes in the concept currently representing the category.

Exemplar concepts may also vary across contexts. For example, when judging how typical *dog* is in *animals,* the concept for *dog* from the housewife and redneck points of view may vary substantially. By affecting the similarity between exemplar and category concepts, changes in exemplar concepts may also play a role in causing graded structures to shift across contexts.

A third factor that may cause shifts in graded structure is frequency of instantiation. As suggested by Barsalou (1985), information about how frequently exemplars occur in various contexts may be stored with exemplars. When subjects judge an exemplar's typicality, frequency-related information relevant to the current context may be accessed as part of the exemplar concept and enter into the typicality judgment. Exemplars occurring frequently in that context are typical, whereas infrequent exemplars are atypical. To the extent that frequency of instantiation varies across contexts, it could also play a role in the instability of graded structure.[4]

It should be noted that this account of graded structure is *not* intended as an account of how people determine category membership. The substantial changes observed by McCloskey and Glucksberg (1978) in people's assignments of category membership across a one-month period suggest, however, that the information individuals use to determine membership also varies across occasions. Although the concepts people use for judging typicality and for determining membership may often be similar, it would not be surprising if the concepts used to represent a category vary somewhat as a function of the current task. Along these lines, Gluck (1985) has found that people represent categories with highly discriminative properties when classifying exemplars, but represent them with highly probable properties when drawing inferences about exemplars.

Sources of concepts

Assuming that graded structure largely results from a similarity comparison process in working memory, how do people obtain the concepts that enter into this process? To simplify matters, only category concepts will be considered in the remainder of this chapter, although what is said also applies to exemplar concepts.

Memory. One possibility is that concepts are stored in long-term memory and retrieved when needed. This account, however, runs into the same problems noted earlier for storage views of graded structure. It seems implausible that people have a category concept stored in long-term memory for every possible context in which they might use a category or for every possible ad hoc category.

Constructed in working memory. A more plausible alternative is that people have the ability to construct a wide range of concepts in working memory for the same category. Depending on the context, people incorporate different information from long-term memory into the current concept that they construct for a category.

People have in fact been shown to incorporate different information into their concept for a category on different occasions. As discussed earlier, Bellezza (1984c) found that the propositions comprising an individual's definition of a word only correlated .48 on the average with the propositions comprising their definition a week later. This suggests that the information an individual incorporates into a concept can vary substantially from occasion to occasion. Explicitly manipulating the context in which people produce definitions (e.g., changing their point of view) would probably result in even larger variability.

The conclusion that people construct different concepts for the same category on different occasions explains the various context effects discussed earlier. When people only incorporate ideals into category concepts, only ideals determine graded structure; when people only incorporate central tendency information into category concepts, only central tendency determines graded structure; and when both are incorporated, they determine graded structure together. In different linguistic contexts and for different points of view, people construct somewhat novel concepts for familiar categories that result in different graded structures. When using ad hoc categories, people construct new concepts that can be used to generate graded structures (see Barsalou 1983:225).

This account explains variability between and within subjects. Between-subject variability results from different subjects incorporating different information into the concept for the same category. Within-subject variability results from a given individual incorporating different information on different occasions. Between and within individuals, the concepts constructed for a given category may vary widely and may rarely be the same.

By assuming that concepts are constructed when needed, it is not necessary to assume that a large number of concepts are stored in long-term memory for a particular category. Instead the large number of concepts associated with a category simply reflects a process capable of constructing a wide variety of concepts in working memory from a constantly changing knowledge base in long-term memory. In this sense, people's conceptual ability is highly productive.

It should be noted that concepts constructed in working memory are probably not simple bundles or lists of independent properties. Instead, the properties that comprise concepts are probably highly integrated by various kinds of relations, such as those discussed by Medin (Chapter 3, this volume), Murphy & Medin (1985), and Lakoff (Chapter 4, this volume, 1986). Changes in concepts across contexts may reflect changes both in the properties comprising concepts and in the relations that structure them.

In addition, the kind of information retrieved from memory to construct concepts may take many forms. Such information may often be central tendency information that has been abstracted from specific episodes; it may be ideals specified by problem-solving processes; it may be specific episodes or fragments of specific episodes (Brooks 1978; Medin & Schaeffer 1978); or it may be generic properties summarized online from previous episodes (Kahneman & Miller 1986). In principle, a given concept in working memory could contain a variety of information, and the kind of information incorporated into concepts for the same category could vary widely across contexts.

Invariant concepts as analytic fictions. Many theorists seem to assume that there are invariant concepts in long-term memory that we should be trying to discover. When investigators collect property listings for concepts, they are trying to determine what information comprises these concepts in long-term memory. When investigators use linguistic analysis to determine prototypes, definitions, and idealized cognitive models, they appear to assume that there are invariant concepts in long-term memory that need to be fully characterized. We often seem to assume that people store invariant concepts, retrieve them under appropriate conditions, and apply them to current situations.

Yet, on the basis of the findings reviewed here, different people seem to have different concepts for the same category, and the same individual seems to have different concepts for the same category in different contexts. Consequently, the concepts that theorists "discover" for categories may never be identical to an actual concept that someone uses. Instead, they may be analytic fictions that are central tendencies or idealizations of actual concepts. Although such theoretical abstractions may be useful or sufficient for certain scientific purposes, it may be more fruitful and accurate to describe the variety of concepts that can be constructed for a category and to understand the process that generates them.

It should be noted that this argument is *not* meant to imply that there is *no* stable knowledge in long-term memory. Instead, the point is that the same exact representation does not appear to represent a category on every occasion in working memory. As discussed in the following section, it is entirely possible for there to be relatively stable knowledge in long-term memory, but for it rarely to be the case that the same information is retrieved from this knowledge to represent a category.

A theory of concept construction

Concepts as constructs

Instead of viewing long-term memory as being divided into invariant concepts, it may make more sense to view long-term memory as containing large amounts of highly interrelated and "continuous" knowledge that is used to construct concepts in working memory. Instead of viewing concepts as invariant structures that are retrieved intact from long-term memory when needed, it may make more sense to view concepts as temporary constructs in working memory that are tailored to current situations. According to this view, long-term memory contains the knowledge from which concepts in working memory are constructed rather than containing invariant concepts that are used to represent categories across all possible situations.

The structure of knowledge in long-term memory

Although the concepts people use to represent categories may not exist as invariant structures, it by no means follows that categories are not associated with stable and highly articulated knowledge in long-term memory. Loosely speaking, the knowledge associated with a category in long-term memory can be viewed as the union of many possible concepts that could represent the category in working memory. It follows that long-term memory contains concepts for categories, but in the sense that the knowledge for a particular category contains many, many concepts. On a given occasion, the concept that is constructed to represent a category only traces out a small subset of all the knowledge available in long-term memory for representing the category.

The following six sections each discuss a way in which knowledge in long-term memory might be structured so as to result in highly variable concepts for the same category across situations.[5]

Continuity. The knowledge in long-term memory from which concepts are constructed for a particular category may generally not have clear boundaries. Instead, knowledge for a particular category may share much structure with knowledge for other categories, and various kinds of knowledge may have dense relations with one another. This becomes evident when trying to compile property norms for categories on the basis of information provided by subjects. More specifically, it is often difficult to decide if certain information that subjects generate for a category really belongs to the category. Consider a few examples from norms collected in our laboratory. Although subjects generated *chased by cats* as a property of *birds*, it could just as easily be construed as a property of *cats*, and in some sense it does not seem to be a property of either. Although subjects generated *the reason for building scarecrows* as a property of *birds*, it seems more related to knowledge about farming and scarecrows. Although subjects generated *played while sitting, requires lessons, makes music for dancing, rewarding to learn,* and *requires care* as properties of *musical instruments,* each is highly related to another knowledge domain (i.e., performing, learning, dancing, self-satisfaction, and maintenance, respectively). These properties are not a few isolated examples, but instead represent a large proportion of those generated.

The fact that many of the properties generated for categories cannot be neatly assigned to a single knowledge domain suggests that the knowledge in long-term memory from which concepts are constructed is relatively undifferentiated or continuous − it does not appear to be divided into packets of knowledge associated with particular categories. In general, it may be extremely difficult, if not impossible, to identify where the knowledge for a particular category in long-term memory begins and ends. To the extent this is true, it is hard to imagine how there could be invariant representations for categories stored in long-term memory.

Mutual exclusivity. A common feature of nearly every theory of representation is the presence of variables that are bound with different instantiations in different contexts. Representations of *birds*, for example, contain variables for *color, size, eating habits,* and so on that are bound with different instantiations for different birds. Whereas these variables are bound with instantiations of *red, medium-sized,* and *eats seeds* for *cardinal,* they are bound with instantiations of *black, large,* and *eats carrion* for *vulture.*

Variables associated with a category often exhibit the property of *mutual exclusivity* and, as a result, insure instability of concepts. Mutual exclusivity holds for a variable when only one of its instantiations is typically incorporated into the concept for a category on a given occasion. Consider the variables of *size* and *ferocity* for *animals.* When taking the point of view of a forest ranger, a person might construct a concept for *animals* that contains instantiations of *large* and *wild* for these variables. In contrast, when taking the point of view of a pet store owner, a person might instantiate these variables with *small* and *tame.* For either variable, only one instantiation typically ever occurs in a concept at a particular time, and all others are excluded.

An implication of mutual exclusivity is that much of the knowledge for a category may not be included in a given concept because it has been precluded by mutually exclusive instantiations. Mutual exclusivity results in instability because the instantiations of variables vary widely across contexts. Most importantly, mutual exclusivity insures that there are no invariant representations of categories, since it is impossible for all of the knowledge associated with a category to represent the category on a single occasion.

It should be noted that multiple instantiations of a variable do occur under certain conditions. For example, when people construct disjunctive concepts, they may bind certain variables with multiple instantiations. In *physical events not well-described by Newtonian mechanics,* the variable, *size of the event,* is instantiated by both *very, very small* and *very, very large.* In addition, certain variables may normally be bound with multiple instantiations (e.g., the variable of *hobbies* for the concept of *person*). The point is, however, that those variables typically exhibiting mutual exclusivity insure that not all of the knowledge for a category represents the category on a given occasion. Categories are not associated with invariant concepts.

Accessibility. The knowledge associated with a category appears to vary substantially in its accessibility. One way to view accessibility is in terms of a distinction between context-independent and context-dependent information (Barsalou 1982). Context-independent information automatically comes to mind on every occasion in which a concept is constructed for a particular category. Several independent programs of research have shown that the activation of this information is *obligatory,* namely, there is no way of preventing its retrieval when a concept is constructed (Barsalou 1982; Barsalou & Ross 1986; Conrad 1978; Gildea & Glucksberg 1984; Greenspan 1984; Whitney, McKay, & Kellas 1985). For example, whenever people construct a concept for *skunk*, the activation of *smells* is obligatory; whenever people construct a concept for *diamond*, the activation of *valuable* is obligatory.

In contrast, context-dependent information only comes to mind in relevant contexts, thereby causing instability of concepts. Numerous studies (cited in Barsalou 1982) have shown that such information is typically inactive for a category, except when it is relevant to the current situation. For example, *floats* is typically inactive when people construct concepts for *basketball*, except in situations involving water. Upon hearing that someone used a *basketball* for a life preserver, *floats* becomes activated.[6]

As discussed by Barsalou (1982), the distinction between context-independent and context-dependent information is orthogonal to the distinction between generic and episodic information. For example, a generic property for *smells* may be context-independent for *skunk*, whereas a generic property for *floats* may be context-dependent for *basketball*. Similarly, an episode involving being bitten by a dog may have been rehearsed so often with *dog* that is has become context-independent, whereas other episodes that have not been rehearsed are context-dependent. As argued by Barsalou and Bower (1980), a property or episode only becomes context-independent after it has been incorporated into a concept on many occasions. It follows that what is context-independent for a concept may vary widely both between and within individuals as a function of their experience with a category.

This distinction between context-independent and context-dependent information may help account for the stability, as well as the instability, of graded structure. Although graded structure can clearly vary substantially, some agreement is generally observed both between and within subjects. Subjects from the same population generally correlate around .50 with each other; when individuals take the points of view of close friends, this correlation increases to around .6; and across situations, individuals generally correlate around .8 with themselves. Although agreement is generally low, it exists and must be accounted for.

That there is any agreement at all within and between subjects may be a consequence of context-independent information, although this remains to be shown empirically. Assuming that the same context-independent information is activated for the same person across situations, there should be some stability within individuals. Assuming that different individuals share at least some context-independent information, there should be some stability between individuals. Context-independent information shared by individuals may represent the properties and episodes most central to the conventional use of concepts. For example, most people may immediately think of *robins* as *red-breasted* and of *rattlesnakes* as *poisonous* because these properties represent widely shared beliefs about these categories. Similarly, the episode in which four people were shot on a New York subway may be context-independent for most people's concept of Bernard Goetz because it has become part of shared cultural knowledge.

In contrast, the large amount of disagreement both between and within individuals may be a consequence of context-dependent information. To the extent that much of the context-dependent information comprising concepts changes across situations — both between and within individuals — concepts should be unstable. Disagreement may also reflect differences between individuals in their context-independent information for the same category. For example, *bites* may be context-independent in *dog* for someone who has been bitten many times, whereas *bites* may not be context-independent for someone else who has had more positive experiences.

Correlated properties. Another way in which knowledge associated with categories may be structured is that properties may be integrated with one another. Instead of being represented independently in long-term memory, properties that co-occur and properties that are meaningfully related may be associated. Because correlations between properties vary between individuals, as well as within individuals over time, they provide another source of instability in the knowledge used to construct concepts.

Recent work by Medin and his colleagues provides evidence for correlated properties (e.g., Medin & Schaeffer 1978). Although this work is often interpreted as showing that people represent categories with exemplars, it does not rule out *all* prototype models (see Medin & Schaeffer 1978:231–232). Instead, this work demonstrates that *independent cue models* do not account for classification performance. Instead of accessing properties of a category independently of one another, people appear to access *correlations of properties*. Thus these findings could either indicate that people are accessing correlated properties that comprise individual exemplars, or it could indicate that people are accessing correlations of properties that have been abstracted from exemplars into prototypes (as in Reitman & Bower 1973). Both forms of correlated properties probably exist in people's knowledge (e.g., Malt & Smith 1984; Medin, Altom, Edelson, & Freko 1982).

As suggested by Medin (Chapter 3, this volume) and Murphy and Medin (1985), people may often interpret correlations between properties in terms of their theories about the world. These theories may explain correlations that actually exist between properties (e.g., why *cars* have both *gasoline* and *spark plugs*) and may cause people to perceive correlations that don't exist (Chapman & Chapman 1969).

Global organization. Similar to there being relations between properties, there are also probably higher-order relations between clusters of properties. Such organization may in some cases be metonymic or radial, as suggested by Lakoff (Chapter 4, this volume; 1986); and it may also take other forms such as schemas (e.g., Rumelhart & Ortony 1977), frames (Minsky 1975), scripts (Schank & Abelson 1977), and memory organization packets (MOPs) (Schank 1982).

Although there may be global structures in memory, it by no means follows that these structures form invariant units that are always retrieved intact into working memory when necessary. Instead, the representations of a particular global structure in working memory may vary widely across contexts. Along these lines, Barsalou, Usher, and Sewell (1985) have found that the variables active for a schema vary across contexts in which the schema is used – a schema does not appear to have an invariant set of variables relevant to every context. Similarly, the different tracks that people construct for scripts (Schank & Abelson 1977) appear to vary widely across contexts. One reason it may be so difficult to identify all the possible tracks of a script is because many of them only exist as temporary constructs in working memory rather than as invariant structures in long-term memory. In this sense, the representations of scripts are no different from the representations of categories.

Episodic organization. Representations of exemplars and episodes in long-term memory may be integrated with the generic knowledge they instantiate. A number of recent findings suggest the presence of such organization. Ross (1984) found that specific characteristics of a current learning episode function to cue previous learning episodes that share those characteristics. Kahneman and Miller (1986) review many cases of social decision making in which specific characteristics of a current experience function to cue related episodes. Schank (1982) provides many examples of how a current episode may remind someone of related episodes instantiating the same generic structure. Because episodes vary widely between individuals, as well as within individuals over time, episodic information provides another source of instability in the knowledge used to construct concepts.[7]

Summary. The knowledge from which concepts are constructed appears to exhibit the following properties: Knowledge associated with categories is continuous in the sense that it is not well-bounded; such knowledge contains variables, some of which may exhibit mutual exclusivity and thereby insure instability; information may vary substantially in accessibility, from being context-independent to context-dependent; information may be richly interrelated, typically being retrieved in meaningful clusters as opposed to being retrieved independently; clusters of information may be interrelated by various kinds of global structures; and exemplars and episodes may be organized by generic knowledge. Further characteristics of knowledge structures are discussed in Graesser and Clark (1985).

The process that constructs concepts

What is the nature of the mechanism that pieces together information from long-term memory to construct highly idiosyncratic concepts in working memory that are relevant to current situations? The following five sections suggest several possible characteristics of this process.

Incorporates context-independent properties. Because it is so accessible, the context-independent information associated with a category may automatically be incorporated into all concepts constructed for it. This would result in there being cores for concepts that lead them to be somewhat stable over time. As argued by Barsalou and Medin (1986), such cores are very different from those postulated by Armstrong et al. (1983), Osherson and Smith (1981, 1982), and others who take the core-plus-identification view of concepts. Instead of being definitional, as in the core-plus-identification view, context-independent cores are *experiential*. They do not represent necessary and sufficient conditions for category membership but instead represent information that has frequently been relevant in a person's experience with exemplars of the category. Consequently, these experiential cores may vary widely between individuals as a result of different experience and may vary within an individual over time as a result of changing experience. Such cores provide an individual with expectations that are useful for interacting with a category in most contexts.

As discussed by Barsalou (1982), if context-independent information turns out to be irrelevant in a particular situation, it may subsequently be inhibited by conscious processing. For example, although *sour* and *juicy* may be context-independent for *lemon*, these properties may eventually become inhibited for someone working on an arrangement of plastic lemons.

Incorporates correlated properties and episodes. When a given property is retrieved and incorporated into a concept, correlated properties may also be incorporated. In addition, properties incorporated into concepts may also cause fragments of associated episodes to be incorporated.

Correlated properties also appear to play an important role in variable instantiation. As found by Barsalou et al. (1985), the way in which a variable is instantiated in a particular concept affects how other variables are instantiated. Consider concepts for *vacation*. If *beach* instantiates *location* and *summer* instantiates *time*, then *swimming* is much more likely to instantiate *activities* than is *sledding*. The opposite is true, however, when *mountains* and *winter* instantiate *location* and *time*. Relations between the instantiations of different variables appear to play important roles in the construction of concepts.

Incorporates goal-related information. People are almost always in the process of achieving goals. Consequently, information about current goals may often be temporarily stored in working memory. When concepts are constructed for categories, the goal-related information currently in working memory may serve to cue related information from long-term memory that becomes incorporated into current category concepts. This enables people to construct concepts for categories that are tailored to current goals. For example, if someone needs something to stand on while changing a light bulb, and if he or she considers the possibility of using a chair, the goal of finding support may cause properties such as *sturdy, easy to move,* and *not too fancy* to be retrieved from knowledge in long-term memory and be incorporated into the current concept for *chair*.

Incorporates information relevant to current exemplars and to other aspects of the current context. Particular exemplars of a category are often present when concepts are being constructed for it. For example, when arranging furniture, particular exemplars of *furniture* are physically present. Similar to current goals, current exemplars may also cue relevant context-dependent information from long-term memory that becomes incorporated into the current concept. This enables people to construct concepts that are tailored to the exemplars with which they are currently interacting. For example, if all of the furniture being arranged is *expensive* and *fragile*, these properties may be incorporated into the current category concept.

Similar to current exemplars, other aspects of the current context may cue relevant information from memory that becomes incorporated into concepts. For example, the *current place* may retrieve information that was incorporated into concepts constructed in that place on previous occasions. So if someone once had overcooked pasta at a restaurant, the next time he or she eats there, *overcooked* may be retrieved by being in the same place, and this property may be incorporated into the concept for *pasta*. Other contextual information such as *time of day, participants, mood,* and so on may cue relevant information in a similar manner.

Incorporates recently activated information. There are obvious advantages of a system that can tailor concepts to particular situations. It may also be advantageous for concepts to be stable under certain circumstances. For example, it would be useful if the concept for a category remained fairly stable over a time period in which someone was pursuing the same goal with the same exemplars. One way this may work is that information used on recent occasions to construct a concept for a category may have a high likelihood of being accessed on subsequent occasions in which concepts are constructed. As a result, some stability can be maintained in the concepts constructed for a category over a short time period. An advantage of this recency bias is that people would not always have to use goal and exemplar information in working memory to construct a concept relevant to the current situation. By simply making recently used information highly accessible, the process of constructing concepts that are tailored to the current situation becomes temporarily automated.

Evidence that recent experience with exemplars biases people's representations of categories has been provided by a number of experiments on perceptual priming (Brooks, Chapter 6, this volume; Jacoby & Brooks 1984). Further evidence comes from Barsalou et al. (1985). As discussed earlier, they found that within-subject reliability dropped from .92 after an hour, to .87 after a day, to .80 after a week, with no further decreases occurring after two and four weeks. These results can be interpreted as a recency bias for concepts that dissipates over a day and that is gone after a week.

This recency bias may play a substantial role in the instability of graded structure. Low between-subject reliability for a category may partially reflect the fact that different people have had different recent experiences with the category (e.g., having recently pursued different goals and having recently encountered different exemplars). Similarly, low within-subject reliability for a category may partially reflect the fact that an individual's recent experience with a category may vary substantially over a given period of time. Higher agreement might be found both between and within individuals when recent experience with a category is held constant.

Finally, this recency bias may result in subjects appearing to have invariant concepts in laboratory experiments on categorization. Since subjects in such experiments typically pursue the same goal and interact with the same exemplars over a short time period, they may temporarily develop highly stable concepts for these categories. If their concepts for these categories were observed over longer periods of time with changing goals and exemplars, less stability might be observed.

Summary. The process that constructs concepts may exhibit stability for the following four reasons: First, by incorporating context-independent information, this process may generally retrieve information that provides some stability both between and within individuals. Second, when goals are the same, either between or within individuals, they may cue the same information from memory such that concepts are stable. Third, when exemplars and other aspects of the current context are the same, they may similarly result in stable concepts. Fourth, by incorporating recently activated information, this process may construct concepts that are temporarily stable.

The process that constructs concepts may exhibit instability for the following five reasons: First, different experience both between and within individuals may result in their having different generic and episodic knowledge from which concepts can be constructed. Second, correlations within this information may vary, such that the incorporation of particular information into a concept causes different information that is correlated to be included. Third, people's concepts for a category may vary with different goals. Fourth, people's concepts for a category may vary as current exemplars and other aspects of the current context vary. Fifth, people's concepts for a category may change as their recent experience changes.

The representation of properties

Implicit in this theory of concept construction has been the assumption that only concepts vary and that the generic properties partially comprising concepts (along with exemplars, episodes, and so on) are invariant representational units. Nevertheless, there is no reason to believe that properties are associated with invariant representations any more than are concepts, since many properties are concepts themselves (e.g., *wheel* for *car, wing* for *bird*). Consequently, what was said earlier about concepts being constructed in working memory probably also applies to many properties. The representation of many properties in working memory may typically vary widely as a function of goals, current context, and recent experience.

This raises an old and difficult problem: Are there any fundamental units used to build property and concept representations that remain invariant across contexts? While certain innate perceptual primitives (and possibly certain innate conceptual primitives) may have physiological bases that correspond to invariant representational units, it is also possible that there are no invariant primitives at all. Instead, instability may generally characterize the circuitry of the nervous system, with there being *no* pattern of neuronal firing that remains invariant across contexts. If this is true, then there is a substantial problem in describing the knowledge in long-term memory from which properties, concepts, and episodes are constructed. As noted by McCauley (Chapter 11, this volume), it is not clear what the basic units of knowledge in long-term memory would be. One possible solution is provided by theories of parallel distributed processing, which will be discussed in the next section. Related discussion can also be found in Bechtel (1985).

Relation to other theories

Recent work in a number of areas appears to be converging on the view that representations should not be viewed as invariant structures but should instead be viewed as dynamic structures that vary widely across contexts. The following sections briefly discuss five such areas.

Dreaming

One way to view dreams is as representations that are constructed from knowledge in memory by the same processes that construct representations during alert activity. This assumption is the basis of a cognitive theory of dreaming proposed by Foulkes (1985), who reviews a number of striking similarities among various cognitive states (e.g., alert activity, dreaming while asleep, daydreaming). For example, dreams generally appear to be structured by the kinds of rules that structure text (e.g., as in story grammars), dreams often follow the same scripts that structure everyday activities, and mental imagery plays a central role in both alert activity and dreaming.

Analogous to the thesis of this chapter, Foulkes (1985) suggests that a constructive approach to representation is a natural way to account for the creativity and unusualness of dreams. Instead of viewing dreams as invariant representations that are retrieved from memory, it makes much more sense to view them as representations that are constructed by the same processes responsible for cognition during alert activity. In fact, the extent to which dreams are unusual may represent the extent to which the human conceptual ability is constructive. Dreams may often contain unusual assemblages of information simply because the perceptual input that normally serves to constrain construction during alert activity is relatively absent during dreaming.

To the extent that the same processes are responsible for cognition during both dreaming and alert activity, we have further reason to believe that the representations people use during alert activity are not retrieved as invariant structures. The processes responsible for the creativity of dreams may also be responsible for the instability of concepts.

Conceptual combination

Much of the recent work on graded structure has addressed the determinants of graded structure for combinations of concepts (Cohen & Murphy 1984; Jones 1982; Hampton in press a, b; Osherson & Smith 1981, 1982; Smith & Osherson 1984). When the concepts for *pet* and *fish* are combined, for example, what determines graded structure in *pet fish*? Although this work generally assumes that the structures for constituent concepts such as *pet* and *fish* are invariant, it acknowledges the importance of people's ability to construct novel concepts from existing knowledge.

As shown by Osherson and Smith (1981, 1982) and Hampton (in press a,b) extensional approaches to fuzzy-set theory have difficulty in accounting for the graded structure of combined concepts. Consequently, alternative attempts to account for the graded structures of these concepts have been more intensional, proposing that the representations of new concepts are formed by integrating the representations of preexisting concepts. These new representations then become comparison standards by which typicality in their respective categories is judged (Cohen & Murphy 1984; Hampton in press a,b; Smith & Osherson 1984).

These intensional approaches can account to some extent for the instability of graded structure reviewed earlier. Context effects can be accounted for by assuming that representations of categories and contexts are combined to form new representations that are used to judge typicality. For example, Roth and Shoben's (1983) finding that typicality in *animals* depends on whether animals are processed in the context of riding or milking can be accounted for by assuming that the concept for animals is combined with the concepts for riding and milking. Similarly, Barsalou and Sewell's (1984) point-of-view effects can be accounted for by assuming that the concept for a category is combined with a concept for a point of view (e.g., *birds* with the *Chinese point of view*).[8]

Although intensional approaches to conceptual combination have not been oriented toward accounting for between- and within-subject instability in graded structure, they can easily be adapted to do so. For example, the Smith and Osherson (1984) approach basically assumes that concepts are represented by sets of values on dimensions. By assuming that the salience of dimensions and values for a category vary between individuals and within individuals over time, it becomes possible for different concepts to result in different graded structures between and within individuals. By additionally assuming that different dimensions can be active on different occasions, further flexibility becomes possible.

In general, intensional theories of conceptual combination are highly sympathetic to the view that people are constantly in the process of using old knowledge in new ways. These theories also provide an interesting way of viewing the construction and use of ad hoc categories (Barsalou, 1983; Barsalou, Sewell, & Usher 1985). As noted earlier, these theories primarily differ from the position being taken here in their assumption that invariant representations are associated with the categories used to form new categories.

Exemplar theories

Brooks (1978) and Medin and Schaeffer (1978) have proposed that people use exemplars instead of generic prototypes as the basis of classification. Although this approach has not yet been oriented toward accounting for the instability of graded structure, it has potential for doing so. For example, between-subject instability could result from different individuals experiencing different exemplars, and within-subjects instability may result from the same individual experiencing different exemplars over time. Similarly, context effects may result from different cues in different contexts retrieving different exemplars. In general, what seems typical to a particular person on a particular occasion may reflect the exemplars that are readily available.

Related work on perceptual priming has shown that people's ability to classify stimuli is biased toward exemplars similar to those that have been recently encountered (Brooks, Chapter 6, this volume; Jacoby & Brooks 1984). Consistent with the theory of concept construction presented earlier, and consistent with McCloskey and Glucksberg (1978), it appears that people's classification standards are unstable and vary as a function of recent experience.

Norm theory

Kahneman and Miller (1986) propose that a current experience recruits previous episodes stored in memory that are similar to it in specific ways. As these episodes are retrieved, they are compiled into a norm that summarizes them. The current experience is then compared to the norm just constructed in working memory, and on the basis of their similarity, various kinds of inferences and judgments are made. According to this theory, experiences typically do not retrieve precomputed norms that have been abstracted from previous experience. Instead, each experience engenders a somewhat unique norm that is used to evaluate it. Such norms are constructed in an ad hoc fashion and are highly constrained by the current situation.

This account of how episodes are compiled into summary representations is highly compatible with the theory of concept construction presented earlier. In fact, Kahneman and Miller also propose that concept norms are generally constructed in much the same way as experience norms. Norm theory goes further in making an intriguing suggestion regarding the construction of representations in working memory. Earlier, when discussing how a concept is formed in working memory, it was implicitly assumed that pieces of information are retrieved from long-term memory and then combined together as parts of the concept. More specifically, it was assumed that these parts do not receive much processing between being retrieved and being incorporated into the concept. In contrast, Kahneman and Miller assume that what is retrieved from long-term memory does not actually appear in working memory. Instead, the episodes that are retrieved from memory are summarized into a norm, which is then what appears in working memory. This suggests that there are important ways in which information from long-term memory is transformed in the process of being used to construct representations.

In taking norm theory (and exemplar theories) to the limit, one could argue that there are no generic representations at all in memory. Instead, memory only contains episodic information, and all generic representations are the products of an online summarization process that constructs generic representations as they are needed. While this is possible, there is no a priori reason why only episodes and not generic representations should become transferred into long-term memory after being processed in working memory. It is widely believed that information in working memory is transferred to long-term memory to the extent it is deeply processed and to the extent it is processed for a long time (e.g., Craik & Watkins 1973; Glenberg, Smith, & Green 1977). Therefore, to the extent a constructed representation is processed deeply for a long time in working memory, it should be transferred into long-term memory, although what is transferred may not be a perfect replica of what existed in working memory. Once such transfer of a generic representation has occurred, it may later be retrieved and be incorporated into a new concept. Only parts of it may be retrieved, however, and other information may also be incorporated into the current concept, as a result of context and recent experience. To the extent a generic representation is frequently incorporated into a particular concept, it may become highly accessible to the point of being context-independent. In addition, the degree to which such information is transformed in the process of being recruited and incorporated into concepts may decrease such that the form it takes in concepts becomes relatively invariant.

Parallel distributed processing

As reviewed in McClelland and Rumelhart (1986) and Rumelhart and McClelland (1986), many theorists have adopted an architecture for cognition that is fundamentally different from the one traditionally employed by cognitive psychologists. Traditional approaches have assumed that the representation of a specific entity (e.g., for a concept or a property) exists as an invariant component in memory that is retrieved from a specific memory location when needed (e.g., as in many network theories, feature theories, and production systems). On the other hand, parallel distributed processing (PDP) theories assume that the representation of an entity is distributed throughout the entire memory system, or at least throughout a large part of it. Instead of being represented by a unique part of memory, the representation of a specific entity exists as a particular *state* of activation defined over the entire memory system. Representations of different entities correspond to different states of activation in the same memory system. In addition, no component of the memory system corresponds to a particular property or concept. Instead, both properties and concepts are defined as states of activation over all components.

Central to PDP theories are the assumptions that a range of similar states represents the same concept and that these states vary as a function of context. More specifically, various aspects of the current context combine to drive a PDP system into a unique state each time a concept is represented. Consequently, instability of concepts is a natural consequence of the basis PDP architecture. Instability of properties falls out of the basic PDP architecture in a similar manner. Such flexibility makes PDP systems consistent with the empirical findings reported earlier for instability of graded structure. In general, these findings suggest that highly dynamic accounts such as PDP theories will be necessary to account for the full flexibility of cognition.

The theory of concept construction presented earlier appears on the surface to be quite different in architecture than PDP theories. Whereas the theory presented earlier follows traditional architecture in assuming that only a subset of information in long-term memory is ever active in working memory to represent a concept, PDP theories assume that all of long-term memory represents each concept. As discussed by McClelland and Rumelhart (1986) and Rumelhart and McClelland (1986), however, traditional theories and PDP theories are not necessarily mutually exclusive. Instead traditional theories may to *some* extent be higher-level descriptions of the behavior of PDP systems in some cases. Proposing that concepts are constructed in working memory from unique sets of information in long-term memory, for example, may be roughly iso-morphic to proposing that unique patterns of activation occur when PDP systems represent concepts. While it may ultimately be more accu-rate to view knowledge in the framework of PDP systems, highly flexible traditional approaches may capture the essence of PDP systems but be easier to work with.

Conclusion

Standard views of cognition assume that long-term memory contains invariant representations of categories. When exemplars of these cate-gories are encountered, or when it becomes necessary to think about them, invariant category concepts are retrieved from long-term memory into working memory for representational purposes. When these repre-sentations are no longer needed, they become inactive, perhaps being slightly altered by that processing experience.

In contrast, alternative views propose in various ways that knowledge in long-term memory is not clearly differentiated into invariant con-cepts. Instead, the concepts that people use are constructed in working memory from knowledge in long-term memory by a process sensitive to context and recent experience. Concepts in working memory may be stable under some conditions, however, concepts typically appear to vary widely as a function of goals, current context, and recent experience. Although theoretical abstractions that correspond to invariant concepts may serve some useful theoretical and empirical purposes, it may gener-ally be more useful and more accurate to view concepts as temporary constructs in working memory.

NOTES

I am grateful to Susan Ballato, Juliana Lancaster, Daniel Sewell, and JoNell Usher for their contributions to the work discussed herein. This chapter has benefited from the comments of James Hampton, Daniel Kahneman, James McClelland, Douglas Medin, Brian Ross, Daniel Sewell, and Edward Shoben. The work in this chapter was performed while the author was supported by research grants from Emory University and by National Science Foundation Grant IST-8308984. Reprint requests should be sent to Lawrence W. Barsalou, Department of Psychology, Emory University, Atlanta, GA 30322.

1. More specifically, an exemplar's family resemblance is a function of how similar it is to other category members on the average and of how dissimilar it

is to members of contrast categories on the average. As discussed by Barsalou (1983, 1985), how similar an exemplar is to other category members on the average is at least roughly equivalent to how similar it is to the central tendency of the category. This is analogous to the average difference between a number and several other numbers being the same as the difference between the first number and the average of the others. An analogous relationship exists between an exemplar's average dissimilarity to members of contrast categories and its dissimilarity to the central tendencies of contrast categories. Consequently, family resemblance is a measure of similarity to central tendency.

2. Although people make extensive use of stereotypes such as *hippie* and *redneck*, and even though such stereotypes may lead to accurate inferences on some occasions, they more often lead to inaccurate inferences and offer a narrow and prejudiced view of the world. The discussion of stereotypes in this chapter, therefore, is not meant to condone them. Instead we have chosen to study stereotypes because of the extensive role they appear to play in cognition (Fiske & Taylor 1984).

3. These correlations were measured using the *common element correlation* (Deese 1965; McNemar 1969:145–146). To compute the common element correlation between the items generated in two protocols, the number of items occurring in both is divided by the geometric mean of the total number of items occurring in each. This measure ranges from zero, when no item occurs in both protocols, to one, when all items occur in both protocols.

4. It should be noted that information pertaining to frequency of instantiation may take a number of forms. In some cases, people may have acquired frequency information from direct experience about how often exemplars have instantiated a category in a particular context. In many other cases, people may not have had such experience and may instead employ various inference procedures to obtain information about frequency. For example, most Americans have not visited Africa and so do not have direct experience about how often various exemplars of *animals* occur from that point of view. On the other hand, Americans readily make inferences about the frequency of animals in Africa based on their exposure to media and hearsay.

5. McCauley (Chapter 11, this volume) notes that my account of knowledge in long-term memory does not include intuitive theories. I do not consider them here because they are not directly relevant to the issues at hand. The focus on the role of goals in categorization in my previous work (Barsalou 1983, 1985) certainly reflects the importance of such theories. Murphy and Medin (1985) cite this work as evidence for the centrality of intuitive knowledge.

6. As pointed out by Barsalou (1982), context-independent and context-dependent information fall at the upper and lower ends of a continuum of accessibility. Consequently, there are other kinds of information that fall somewhere between being context-independent and context-dependent (e.g., the senses of ambiguous words). In addition, there are differences within the information that is context-independent and within the information that is context-dependent. For example, context-dependent information includes properties that are not stored in long-term memory at all but that are computed when necessary, as well as low accessibility properties that are actually stored in memory (Barsalou 1982:87–88).

7. It should be noted that episodes may not be stored with generic knowledge and may not be organized by generic knowledge, as just discussed. Instead, episodes could be stored separately from generic knowledge and could be

unorganized (or could be organized in some other way, such as by temporal sequence). A cluster of related episodes could be retrieved together when a concept is constructed simply because of there being a retrieval process capable of cuing related episodes simultaneously.

8. It is probably stretching things somewhat to assume that people have a single concept for *Chinese point of view* that can be combined with other concepts. As suggested by Barsalou and Sewell (1984), point-of-view effects may result from processing knowledge for categories in the context of a large knowledge base associated with a point of view. Instead of combining these two representations, the knowledge associated with the point of view may be used to cue and interpret relevant information from knowledge associated with the category.

REFERENCES

Armstrong, S. L., Gleitman, L. R., & Gleitman, H. (1983). On what some concepts might not be. *Cognition, 13*, 263–308.

Ashcraft, M. H. (1978). Property norms for typical and atypical items from 17 categories: A description and discussion. *Memory & Cognition, 6*, 227–232.

Barsalou, L. W. (1981). *Determinants of graded structure in categories.* Unpublished doctoral dissertation, Stanford University, Palo Alto, CA.

(1982). Context-independent and context-dependent information in concepts. *Memory & Cognition, 10*, 82–93.

(1983). Ad hoc categories. *Memory & Cognition, 11*, 211–227.

(1985). Ideals, central tendency, and frequency of instantiation. *Journal of Experimental Psychology: Learning, Memory, and Cognition, 11*, 629–654.

Barsalou, L. W., & Bower, G. H. (1980). *A priori determinants of a concept's highly accessible information.* Paper presented at the Meeting of the American Psychological Association, Montreal, September, 1980.

Barsalou, L. W., & Medin, D. L. (1986). Concepts: Fixed definitions or context-dependent representations? *Cahiers de Psychologie Cognitive, 6*, 187–202.

Barsalou, L. W., & Ross, B. H. (1986). The roles of automatic and strategic processing in sensitivity to superordinate and property frequency. *Journal of Experimental Psychology: Learning, Memory, and Cognition, 12*, 116–134.

Barsalou, L. W., & Sewell, D. R. (1984). *Constructing representations of categories from different points of view.* Emory Cognition Project Report #2, Emory University, Atlanta, GA.

(1985). Contrasting the representation of scripts and categories. *Journal of Memory and Language, 24*, 646–665.

Barsalou, L. W., Sewell, D. R., & Ballato, S. M. (1986). *The instability of categories as measured by graded structure.* Under review. Emory University, Atlanta, GA.

Barsalou, L. W., Usher, J., & Sewell, D. R. (1985). *Schema-based planning of events.* Work in progress, Emory University, Atlanta, GA.

Bechtel, W. (1985). Realism, instrumentalism, and the intentional stance. *Cognitive Science, 9*, 473–497.

Bellezza, F. S. (1984a). Reliability of retrieval from semantic memory: Common categories. *Bulletin of the Psychonomic Society, 22*, 324–326.

(1984b). Reliability of retrieval from semantic memory: Information about people. *Bulletin of the Psychonomic Society, 22*, 511–513.

(1984c). Reliability of retrieval from semantic memory: Noun meanings. *Bulletin of the Psychonomic Society, 22*, 377–380.

Brooks, L. (1978). Non-analytic concept formation and memory for instances. In E. Rosch & B. B. Lloyd (Eds.), *Cognition and categorization*. Hillsdale, NJ: Erlbaum.

Chapman, L. J., & Chapman, L. P. (1969). Illusory correlation as an obstacle to the use of valid pscyhodiagnostic signs. *Journal of Abnormal Psychology, 74*, 271–280.

Cohen, B., & Murphy, G. L. (1984). Models of concepts. *Cognitive Science, 8*, 27–58.

Cherniak, C. (1984). Prototypicality and deductive reasoning. *Journal of Verbal Learning and Verbal Behavior, 23*, 625–642.

Conrad, C. (1978). Some factors involved in the recognition of words. In J. W. Cotton & R. L. Klatzky (Eds.), *Semantic factors in cognition*. Hillsdale, NJ: Erlbaum.

Craik, F. I. M., & Watkins, M. J. (1973). The role of rehearsal in short-term memory. *Journal of Verbal Learning and Verbal Behavior, 12*, 599–607.

Deese, J. (1965). *The structure of associations in language and thought*. Baltimore: Johns Hopkins University Press.

Fiske, S. E., & Taylor, S. E. (1984). *Social cognition*. Reading, MA: Addison-Wesley.

Foulkes, D. (1985). *Dreaming: A cognitive-psychological analysis*. Hillsdale, NJ: Erlbaum.

Galambos, J. A., & Rips, L. J. (1982). Memory for routines. *Journal of Verbal Learning and Verbal Behavior, 21*, 260–281.

Gildea, P., & Glucksberg, S. (1984). *Does context constrain lexical access for ambiguous words?* Paper presented at the Meeting of the Psychonomic Society, San Antonio, TX.

Glass, A. L., & Holyoak, K. J. (1975). Alternative conceptions of semantic memory. *Cognition, 3*, 313–339.

Glenberg, A., Smith, S. M., & Green, C. (1977). Type I rehearsal: Maintenance and more. *Journal of Verbal Learning and Verbal Behavior, 16*, 339–352.

Gluck, M. A. (1985). *Category learning and judgment: Sources of variability in estimates of probabilistic association*. Work in progress, Stanford University, Palo Alto, CA.

Graesser, A. C., & Clark, L. F. (1985). *Structures and procedures of implicit knowledge*. Norwood, NJ: Ablex.

Greenspan, S. L. (1984). *Semantic flexibility and referential specificity*. Paper presented at the Meeting of the Psychonomic Society, San Antonio, TX.

Guilford, J. P., & Fruchter, B. (1973). *Fundamental statistics in psychology and education*. New York: McGraw-Hill.

Hampton, J. A. (1979). Polymorphous concepts in semantic memory. *Journal of Verbal Learning and Verbal Behavior, 18*, 441–461.

(1981). An investigation of the nature of abstract concepts. *Memory & Cognition, 9*, 149–156.

(in press a). Inheritance of features in natural concept conjunctions. *Memory & Cognition*.

(in press b). Overextension of conjunctive concepts; evidence for a unitary model of concept typicality and class inclusion. *Journal of Experimental Psychology: Learning, Memory, and Cognition*.

Jacoby, L. L., & Brooks, L. R. (1984). Nonanalytic cognition: Memory, perception, and concept learning. In G. H. Bower (Ed.), *The psychology of learning and motivation: Advances in research and theory* (Vol. 18). New York: Academic Press.

Jones, G. V. (1982). Stacks not fuzzy sets: An ordinal basis for prototype theory of concepts. *Cognition, 12,* 281–290.

Kahneman, D., & Miller, D. T. (1986). Norm theory: Comparing reality to its alternatives. *Psychological Review, 93,* 136–153.

Lakoff, G. (1986). *Women, fire and dangerous things: What categories tell us about the nature of thought.* Chicago: University of Chicago Press.

Malt, B. C., & Smith, E. E. (1984). Correlated properties in natural categories. *Journal of Verbal Learning and Verbal Behavior, 23,* 250–269.

McClelland, J. L., & Rumelhart, D. E. (1986). *Explorations in the microstructure of cognition,* Vol. 2: *Applications.* Cambridge, MA: Bradford.

McCloskey, M., & Glucksberg, S. (1978). Natural categories: Well-defined or fuzzy sets? *Memory & Cognition, 6,* 462–472.

(1979). Decision processes in verifying category membership statements: Implications for models of semantic memory. *Cognitive Psychology, 11,* 1–37.

McNemar, A. (1969). *Psychological statistics* (4th ed.). New York: Wiley.

Medin, D. L., & Schaeffer, M. M. (1978). A context theory of classification learning. *Psychological Review, 85,* 207–238.

Medin, D. L., & Smith, E. E. (1984). Concepts and concept formation. *Annual Review of Psychology, 35,* 113–138.

Medin, D. L., Altom, M. W., Edelson, S. M., & Freko, D. (1982). Correlated symptoms and simulated medical classification. *Journal of Experimental Psychology: Learning, Memory, and Cognition, 8,* 37–50.

Mervis, C. B., & Pani, J. R. (1980). Acquisition of basic object categories. *Cognitive Psychology, 12,* 496–522.

Mervis, C. B., & Rosch, E. (1981). Categorization of natural objects. *Annual Review of Psychology, 32,* 89–115.

Mervis, C. B., Catlin, J., & Rosch, E. (1976). Relationships among goodness-of-example, category norms, and word frequency. *Bulletin of the Psychonomic Society, 7,* 283–294.

Minsky, M. (1975). A framework for representing knowledge. In P. H. Winston (Ed.), *The psychology of computer vision.* New York: McGraw-Hill.

Murphy, G. L., & Medin, D. L. (1985). The role of theories in conceptual coherence. *Psychological Review, 92,* 289–316.

Osherson, D. N., & Smith, E. E. (1981). On the adequacy of prototype theory as a theory of concepts. *Cognition, 9,* 35–58.

(1982). Gradedness and conceptual combination. *Cognition, 12,* 299–318.

Reitman, J. S., & Bower, G. H. (1973). Storage and later recognition of exemplars. *Cognitive Psychology, 4,* 194–206.

Rips, L. J. (1975). Inductive judgments about natural categories. *Journal of Verbal Learning and Verbal Behavior, 14,* 665–681.

Rips, L. J., Shoben, E. J., & Smith, E. E. (1973). Semantic distance and the verification of semantic relations. *Journal of Verbal Learning and Verbal Behavior, 12,* 1–20.

Rosch, E. H. (1973). On the internal structure of perceptual and semantic categories. In T. E. Moore (Ed.), *Cognitive development and the acquisition of language.* New York: Academic Press.

(1975). Cognitive representations of semantic categories. *Journal of Experimental Psychology: General, 104,* 192–233.

(1978). Principles of categorization. In E. Rosch & B. B. Lloyd (Eds.), *Cognition and categorization.* Hillsdale, NJ: Erlbaum.

(1983). Prototype classification and logical classification: The two systems. In

140   LAWRENCE W. BARSALOU

E. Scholnick (Ed.), *New trends in conceptual representation: Challenges to Piaget's theory*. Hillsdale, NJ: Erlbaum.

Rosch, E. H., & Mervis, C. B. (1975). Family resemblances: Studies in the internal structure of categories. *Cognitive Psychology, 7,* 573–605.

Rosch, E. H., Mervis, C. B., Gray, W. D., Johnson, D. M., & Boyes-Braem, P. (1976). Basic objects in natural categories. *Cognitive Psychology, 8,* 382–439.

Rosch, E. H., Simpson, C., & Miller, R. S. (1976). Structural bases of typicality effects. *Journal of Experimental Psychology: Human Perception and Performance, 2,* 491–502.

Ross, B. H. (1984). Remindings and their effects in learning a cognitive skill. *Cognitive Psychology, 16,* 371–416.

Roth, E. M., & Shoben, E. J. (1983). The effect of context on the structure of categories. *Cognitive Psychology, 15,* 346–378.

Rumelhart, D. E., & McClelland, J. L. (1986). *Explorations in the microstructure of cognition*, Vol. 1: *Foundations*. Cambridge, MA: Bradford.

Rumelhart, D. E., & Ortony, A. (1977). The representation of knowledge in memory. In R. C. Anderson, R. J. Spiro, & W. E. Montague (Eds.), *Schooling and the acquisition of knowledge*. Hillsdale, NJ: Erlbaum.

Schank, R. (1982). *Dynamic memory*. Cambridge, England: Cambridge University Press.

Schank, R., & Abelson, R. P. (1977). *Scripts, plans, goals, and understanding*. Hillsdale, NJ: Erlbaum.

Sewell, D. R. (1985). *Constructing the points of view of specific individuals*. Unpublished doctoral dissertation, Emory University, Atlanta, GA.

Smith, E. E. (1978). Theories of semantic memory. In W. K. Estes (Ed.), *Handbook of learning and cognitive processes* (Vol. 6). Potomac, MD: Erlbaum.

Smith, E. E., & Medin, D. L. (1981). *Categories and concepts*. Cambridge, MA: Harvard University Press.

Smith, E. E., & Osherson, D. N. (1984). Conceptual combination with prototype concepts. *Cognitive Science, 8,* 337–361.

Smith, E. E., Shoben, E. J., and Rips, L. J. (1974). Structure and process in semantic memory: A featural model for semantic decisions. *Psychological Review, 81,* 214–241.

Tversky, A. (1977). Features of similarity. *Psychological Review, 84,* 327–352.

Tversky, B., & Hemenway, K. (1984). Objects, parts, and categories. *Journal of Experimental Psychology: General, 113,* 169–193.

Whitney, P., McKay, T., & Kellas, G. (1985). Semantic activation of noun concepts in context. *Journal of Experimental Psychology: Learning, Memory, and Cognition, 11,* 126–135.

Zadeh, L. A. (1965). Fuzzy sets. *Information and Control, 8,* 338–353.

(1982). A note on prototype theory and fuzzy sets. *Cognition, 12,* 291–297.

6

Decentralized control of categorization: the role of prior processing episodes

LEE R. BROOKS

Introduction: The interaction between analytic and nonanalytic knowledge

Cognitive psychology's earliest antagonist was behaviorism, as represented by the verbal learners and the field of animal learning. In the behaviorist approach, perception, memory, and classification were extremely literal affairs, driven by (what the experimenter designated as) objective physical descriptions of the stimulus. Much of the history of cognitive psychology has been dominated by the demonstration that mental models and subjective codings of the stimulus intrude into every aspect of processing. However, in winning this battle, cognition in my view (and that of several other writers: see especially Jacoby, 1983a, and Kolers & Smythe, 1984) has developed undue faith in the role of centralized, abstracted models as representations of everyday human knowledge.

When an object or event is presented to us for classification, we have been presented with retrieval cues for our knowledge about whole categories. But we also have been presented with retrieval cues for the particular processing associated with very similar prior events. If these prior events (as processed) strike us as being very similar to the object or event in front of us, then there is an excellent chance that they will be a good guide for our purposes in dealing with the current object. This is not an argument that the processing of a new event is restricted to "surface," literal stimulus elements, as the behaviorists would have insisted. The analogy to a specific prior processing episode is an analogy to an act of processing that itself was an interpretation, both in the organization of the perceptual stimulus and in more "semantic" aspects. The argument is that the meanings of complex everyday events are not perpetually synthesized anew from semantic components and cognitive models every time a minor variant is encountered. More generalized cognitive models undoubtedly exist, but there is no reason to assume that they are directly involved in every interpretive act. The position that I would like to defend, then, is that our conceptual resources are considerably more *decentralized* than is usually portrayed, consisting in routine analogy to prior interpreted episodes as well as to more abstract principles and models.

Most of the chapters in this volume have concentrated on the conceptual models that we use in our dealings with new situations in the world. The evidence that the competence represented by such models does exist is convincing. However, when exclusive attention is paid to this level of abstraction, I believe that a one-sided picture emerges, a picture that is too analytic. Clearly, we do have knowledge of prior processing episodes, just as we have more general knowledge. It would be an extreme position to claim that episodic knowledge has no role in classification of new objects; our problem rather is one of deciding what role it might play. One possibility whose sufficiency I would like to reject at the outset is that the generalized cognitive models exhaustively represent the competence of the learner, with the effect of analogy to prior episodes being restricted to the details of performance. In some circumstances this is undoubtedly true, but in other cases the collection of prior events may either *be* the categorical knowledge or at least strongly interact with the generalizations. For much of everyday processing, trying to make a performance-competence distinction is too costly: too much of our wisdom about interactions of concepts with local contexts is distributed across a wide variety of prior episodes.

In general, I will characterize reliance on close analogies as being *nonanalytic*. The first sense of this term is that when using a close analogy, when characterizing a previous instance as "nearly identical," little distinction is made between definitionally relevant, categorically characteristic, and blatantly irrelevant information. The current and the previous episodes are similar on so many characteristics that the relevant predictors must be in there somewhere. But such everyday analogizing is also nonanalytic in that a great deal of information is inherited in a flood and little effort is made in the current processing to selectively process categorically relevant information. Relative emphasis on attributes is dictated more by what had been important for accomplishing the prior purposes rather than what is important for the category as a whole. Seeing a striking similarity between a new dog and my golden retriever, I would be confident (if asked) that it was a dog, be hesitant to give it food that my dog (atypically for dogs) does not like, and slow to think of the possibility of it chasing cars, which my virtuous dog never does. Upon reflection I would acknowledge that a sample of one is a bit small, but this voice of rationality would, under many circumstances, come decidedly second. Nonanalytic processing, then, has the dual meaning of disparate characteristics being integrated in retrieval and of current processing unreflectively "going with the flow."

The justification for reliance on nonanalytic processing is that ecologically, most conceptual neighborhoods contain more friends than enemies, more useful than misleading analogies among stimuli that seem very similar. In more hostile regions, we soon learn to go slowly and carefully. Variations in the generality of information retrieved and in the degree of current analytic control are integral parts of our conceptual behavior. This paper is an attempt to establish interacting roles for abstracted cognitive models – models that are restricted to information that is relevant to categories as a whole – and the much more relaxed reliance on close analogies, reliance on supporting friends.

Examples: Influence of variations in the processing of prior episodes

In the following sections I will present evidence documenting the importance of episodic variations on a variety of different classification and identification tasks. Overall, I will argue that

1. The influence of prior processing episodes on seemingly general classification problems is common – unintuitively common. Even such overlearned tasks as the identification of familiar words or objects can be substantially affected by analogy with very similar prior episodes. Thus, we cannot routinely assume that familiar categorical tasks are "semantic," relying only on general abstracted knowledge, leaving episodic influences to unfamiliar tasks for which we lack the relevant abstractions.
2. The size of effect and range of generalization around an exemplar depends on both the way that exemplar was processed and how those conditions of processing fit with the conditions at the moment of categorization. We cannot assume just because the learner can recognize having previously seen an item, that it is now generally available to guide current categorization. The extent to which prior instances were processed as whole integrated units and the tasks in which they were embedded are important conditions for determining when they will be available for nonanalytic generalization.
3. The relations between analytic and nonanalytic knowledge are dynamic. We are constantly specializing general knowledge into situation-specific "friends" as well as noticing and codifying regularities that emerge in our behavior. Again the emphasis is on the surprising speed and ubiquity of such changes. A view that concentrates mainly on the accrual and use of our abstracted conceptual resources seems too static to capture this important aspect of conceptual behavior.

The research that supports this processing episode view looks very much like current work in the field of memory (for reviews see Craik

1979, 1981). This work in memory is characterized by very close attention to specifically what was done with a stimulus on a prior trial, the specific conditions of retrieval, and the way in which these two fit with one another; an approach referred to as encoding or processing specificity (Tulving & Thompson 1973; Kolers 1979). Such work demonstrates the importance of "microcontext," small variations in the setting and processing context of an item. It has produced powerful, counterintuitive effects and, as I hope to demonstrate, is relevant to categorization and conceptual behavior.

A variety of models have incorporated past instances as one of several resources that we use in solving categorization problems (Elio & Anderson 1981; Homa, Sterling, & Treppel 1981; Medin, Dewey, & Murphy 1983; Reber & Allen 1978). Many of these models do a good job of fitting the data to which they have been applied, but they (as well as my own prior work: Brooks 1978) give little prominence to the way an item was treated during the original learning period. The main concern in the underlying research was just to get the item learned, rather than to consider how it was organized and elaborated. Such a "get it learned" approach implies that the "strength" of the old item is the major effective parameter for instance-based generalization; but, a notion of overall strength has long proven inadequate in the field of memory. If we accept the influence of prior instances on categorical behavior, then it is reasonable to expect that the variables and designs that have proven effective in memory work will also show their value for conceptual classification.

By going through a number of experiments using different materials and designs, I run the risk of straining the patience of the reader. The point of running this risk (with readers who, in any event, are accomplished scanners) is to document that episodic effects are neither rare nor easily segregated from "pure" semantic tasks. First, experiments that used familiar material will be examined to demonstrate that specific prior episodes can affect even highly familiar tasks. Then experiments using recently learned material will be described to demonstrate that specific prior processing episodes are a resource for dealing with new, complex material. Even when an explicit, easy-to-apply rule is available, prior episodes can play an important role under certain perceptual conditions.

Coordination of prior processing episodes with well-learned skills

Word identification. Many of the points that I would like to make in this paper are well illustrated in a seminal experiment by Jacoby

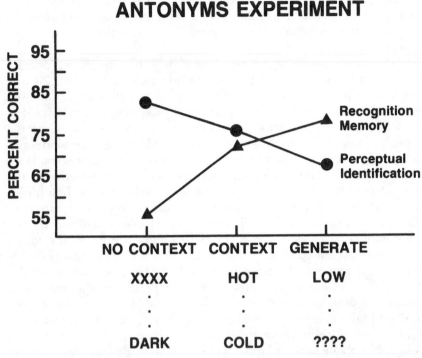

Figure 6.1. The training procedure and results of later test for Jacoby's antonym experiment. The items used for both the later perceptual identification and the recognition memory tests were always the second member of one of the training sequences. (Adapted from Experiment 2 in Jacoby, L. L. (1983a). Remembering the data: Analyzing interactive processes in reading. *Journal of Verbal Learning and Verbal Behavior, 22,* 485–508.)

(1983a). The purpose of this experiment was to show the effect of a single prior processing episode on the later perceptual identification of a word; that is, on the later identification of a word that was briefly presented and followed by a mask. The conditions in the first phase were designed to give subjects differing types of prior experience with the words that were later to be identified. In this phase, subjects were asked to do all of the three tasks illustrated in Figure 6.1, (a) *No Context:* On one third of the 60 trials, a set of four X's appeared on a video monitor. After 3 seconds, a word appeared that the subject was simply to read aloud. (b) *Context:* On another third of the trials, a word appeared, followed, after 3 seconds, by its antonym. Again the subject was simply to read the second word aloud. Because the antonyms were selected to be easily generated by the subjects, however, the word was being read in a context in which it was easily anticipated. (c) *Generate:* On the last third of the trials, a word appeared that was followed, after 3 seconds, by a set of four question marks. The subjects had been instructed to respond by generating the antonym of the first word. In this case the antonym never appeared on the screen.

In the second phase of the experiment subjects were given a perceptual identification test; that is, these 60 words, together with 20 new words, were presented one at a time for about 33 milliseconds, followed by a mask consisting of ampersands. As can be seen in Figure 6.1, variations in the way the words were processed in the first phase of the experiment made a considerable difference in later perceptual identification. The order of effectiveness of the conditions makes sense if we assume that the later perceptual identification task is sensitive to the amount and type of perceptual processing carried out in the first phase. In the Generate condition the target word was not presented visually at all, with the apparent result of little or no later facilitation of words from this condition over new words. In the Context condition, the target words were presented visually, but in the context of a cue that probably reduced the amount of perceptual processing necessary for identification. The No-Context condition probably produced the maximum amount of practice in perceptually processing the target and clearly resulted in the maximum transfer to later perceptual identification.

The order of results is very different for a later recognition memory task. Subjects (the same subjects in one variant of the experiment, independent subjects in another) were given a list consisting of the same 80 words (60 old and 20 new) and were asked to check off those words that had occurred in the first phase. In this case, as in many previous "levels-of-processing" experiments (e.g., Craik & Tulving 1975; Jacoby & Craik 1979), the best performance was obtained in the conditions that encouraged the most distinctive (usually meaning-based) elaboration. The Generate condition required the subject to work with the meaning of the word; the Context condition encouraged, but did not require, comparable meaningful elaboration; and the No-Context condition did not even encourage meaningful or distinctive processing. As with the prior levels-of-processing results, the amazing aspect of these results is that the later retrieval of familiar words is so sensitive to these minor task variations. Subjectively, one does not have the feeling of having processed the words in the "shallow" (No-Context) condition any more or less distinctively; the fact that they are all meaningful words is quite apparent at the moment. Again, one might have expected for both the perceptual identification and the recognition memory measures that the processing of these familiar words might have been so automatized that few differences would have been found.

Let us now consider several implications of these results.

Rapid specialization of a well-practiced skill. These subjects obviously had general, definitional knowledge about the words. As the words were reasonably common, the subjects would have had ample prior opportunity to have automatized a general, visual identification procedure. There evidently was still some benefit, however, from having previously seen these particular words under these circumstances, embedded in this particular list (the amount of facilitation is decreased when most of the words in the test list are new) (Jacoby 1983b). Furthermore, this specialization does not require a great many previous trials; a single prior trial was sufficient to produce a considerable benefit.

Long-lasting facilitation (not temporary priming). This perceptual facilitation has been demonstrated five days later (Jacoby 1983b) and, in the case of pseudowords, a year later (Salasoo, Shiffren, & Feustal 1985). It thus seems reasonable to describe the effect as due to episodic learning rather than to a relatively temporary priming of a stable node or identification routine. The term "priming" was originally introduced to refer to the temporary adaptation of a stable network (e.g., Collins & Loftus 1975) or decision unit (e.g., logogens in Morton 1969) to transient contextual information. Because there clearly is a temporary effect in addition to the more long-term facilitation (e.g., Ratcliff, Hackle, & McKoon 1985), it would seem advisable to save the term to refer to such phenomena, rather than to indiscriminately employ it for any facilitation at any duration.

Specialization was not occasioned by extreme difficulty. Obviously any model that stresses the importance of stable schemata provides for long-term changes of the schemata with changing circumstances. In keeping with a principle of economy, however, such changes are usually assumed to occur only when trouble is encountered. For example, Anderson's ACT* model is assumed to discriminate only on error trials (Anderson 1983). But Jacoby's subjects could hardly have had much difficulty in identifying the words in the first phase of his experiment; the words were common English words, presented in the clear for about 1 second. Under these circumstances, specialization seems to be more at the behest of availability of local precedents than of experienced difficulty. Alternatively, if difficulty is still to be cited as a necessary condition for specialization, then the necessary degree of difficulty is very much less than might have been expected.

Task specificity of transfer. Any account that relies on "the better it's learned, the better it's retrieved" cannot handle these results. For example, the notions of associative strength or of deeper or more intensive processing are by themselves insufficient. Rather, it is necessary to look more closely at how the specific requirements of the retrieval task fit the prior processing, again a theme common in the memory literature (e.g., the relations between recall and recognition). In the recognition memory task, for example, one of the learner's problems is to distinguish the occurrence of the target word in the first part of the experiment from its occurrence in (say) a previously read novel; after all, the subjects are not being asked if they have *ever* seen these common words before. For this purpose, elaborating one aspect of the meaning of the word in the experimental context might provide a more discriminable target in memory. No such discrimination between prior and experimental occurrences is necessary for performing the perceptual identification task. Instead, what seems more relevant is specific practice with the "bottom-up" processing of very similar cues in the prior episode.

Perceptual facilitation is not reliably indexed by recognition memory. There are at least two reasons why the dissociation of perceptual identification from recognition memory performance is of interest. One is that our intuitions are probably schooled mainly by the more "aware" types of memory tasks. A recognition memory task, for example, explicitly asks us to reflect on prior events, a process that, as we are all too aware, can be quite incorrect on the "unimportant surface details." As a result, it seems implausible that we could be getting much help from memory of such details in specific prior episodes. However, we get a very different view of the contribution to be made by episodic memory for perceptual features from the performance measures in which the episodic contribution is incidental. As Jacoby's experiment demonstrates, we can be quite unable to recognize such a contribution on a trial-by-trial basis (for discussion of "remembering without awareness," see Jacoby & Witherspoon, 1982). The second reason for interest in this dissociation is that it is tempting to use recognition memory as an explicit index of the potential contribution of prior episodes to a categorization process (as was done, for example, by Reber & Allen, 1978). Again, Jacoby's experiment is a demonstration of episodic effects on identification that are not well indexed by recognition memory. This is not a claim that recognition memory tasks will always be dissociated from categorization or identification tasks. For example, if subjects are trying to recognize a prior occurrence of a pseudoword, they can assume that any experienced fluency or familiarity is due to prior occurrence in the experiment. Since discrimination among prior occurrences is unimportant, the same variables that produce perceptual facilitation are positively correlated with recognition memory (e.g., Haymen 1983; Vokey, described below). Prediction is to be found in the particular problems posed by the current circumstances and their interaction with prior processing rather than in standard relations between memory tasks (see Jacoby & Brooks, 1984, for discussion of relations between various memory and judgment tasks;

also see Levy & Begin, 1984, for another task showing interactions between learned "surface" details and current performance.).

Picture classification. Another experiment by Jacoby (Jacoby, Baker, & Brooks, in press) showed the effects of variations in prior processing on later picture identification. More important for our current purposes, this experiment also showed that *processing differences affected the range of later generalization* to new drawings in the same name category. The stimuli were outline drawings presented on a video screen, sometimes presented clearly, and sometimes degraded. At the beginning of a trial using the degraded pictures, the display consisted entirely of "noise" points. By pressing a key, a subject could clarify the picture by increasing the ratio of points from the picture to noise points. With continued pressing of the key, the picture became sufficiently clear that all subjects could name the object that was pictured.

Two training conditions were run: In the Name condition, subjects simply gave basic-level names to intact outline drawings. In the Clarify&Name group, degraded drawings were presented, and subjects pressed the key, thus clarifying the picture, until they could name them. After a subject had correctly named a picture, it appeared fully clarified on the screen. The clarification procedure was expected to require subjects to deal more extensively with the visual details of the picture than would simply naming the intact picture. Due to this differential processing of detail, the Clarify&Name condition's transfer to the later test phase was expected to be more specific to the training pictures than that of the Name condition. In the test phase, both groups were shown degraded pictures and were asked to clarify them until they could identify them. The number of key presses prior to a correct response was the measure of identification performance. The test pictures were either identical to a picture that had been previously presented (Identical), belonged to the same basic-level category as a previously exposed picture but were not identical to that picture (Name Match), or were unrelated to any previously presented picture (New).

As is shown in Table 6.1, both groups showed that a single prior processing episode facilitates later identification of both identical pictures and pictures from the same category relative to pictures from a different category. But, in addition, the detail with which pictures were processed during the single presentation affected the specificity of transfer in a later naming task. For subjects who only had to name intact pictures in the first phase, there was a relatively small difference in the number of key presses required to identify Identical over Same Category pictures. The subjects who had to clarify the pictures in the first phase

Table 6.1. *Clarification study: Number of button presses before identification*

	Identical	Same name	New
Name	37.3	40.7	55.4
Clarify&Name	34.2	45.5	56.2

were able to identify the Identical pictures with many fewer clarification responses than the Same Category pictures and even with fewer responses than the Name group used for the Identical pictures. Apparently then, greater attention to detail led to a sharper generalization gradient. The role in generalization of the "surface" characteristics (emphasized by the clarification procedure) seems to depend on the prior processing conditions and their match with processing conditions at retrieval. There is no reason from this experiment to believe that the surface characteristics have any constant weight, either high or low, in an identification procedure.

Additional studies support the other themes raised in the previous section. For example, an experiment by Brooks and Whittlesea (submitted) demonstrated that for both classification of old items and generalization to new the *effects of prior episodes are long lasting.* In this experiment subjects were given one exposure to each of a series of 12 slides; four being photos of cups, four of bottles, and four of glasses. Each slide was preceded by a question for verification: "Is the object on the upcoming slide a cup (bottle, glass)?" In a subsequent test series, using the same verification task, the old items and items that were similar to them (similar, for example, in that both were children's cups, both tea cups, both coffee mugs) were verified more rapidly than items that were rated as highly typical. These Old and New Similar items were also faster than other new items from the same three categories. This facilitation of Identicals and New Similars over "Prototypes" (high typicals) and New Differents was also found when 24 hours intervened between the training and the test phase. For the current purposes, the important point is that this advantage of the old items and the new similar items was also found when 24 hours intervened between the original 12 slides and the test series.

Finally, an example of *dissociation between recognition memory and episodic facilitation of classification* of pictures has been reported recently by Carroll, Byrne, and Kirsner (1985). Subjects in one of their experiments either searched for a small but readily visible X in an outline drawing or they classified the drawing as depicting an animate or an inanimate object. The semantically "deeper" processing occasioned by the animacy judgment resulted in an improvement of 15 percent in recognition memory accuracy over that in the shallow task. In a speed of naming task, the old drawings that had been processed in either way were named faster than new drawings. However, there was no difference between the naming times for the drawings that had previously been classified in the semantically shallow or semantically deep tasks. Thus, as with Jacoby's Antonym experiment described above, increasing the semantic depth of a task had a very different effect on improving recognition memory than on a later identification task. Carroll, Byrne, and Kirsner's experiment, although it did not show a crossover interaction, did show a dissociation between the effect of a single prior processing episode on recognition memory and on an identification task.

For both word and pictures, then, single prior processing episodes have marked effects on later identification. The longevity of these effects strongly suggests that they are due to episodic learning rather than to temporary priming. In the case of pictures, the prior episodes generalize to similar items as well as to subsequent presentations of the same items. Further, since these generalization effects vary with the type of prior processing, they are not simply a function of the physical similarity between the old and the new items. Although all of these studies have restricted themselves to speed and accuracy of identification, the same retrieval processes are likely to also bring back more interpretive aspects of previous processing, a theme to be discussed later. The general point so far is that even with stimuli for which automatic identification and elaboration routines should have developed, prior specific episodes can facilitate performance. Close friends help even the experts.

Coordination of prior episodes with an explicit rule

The preceding experiments used familiar materials – materials for which the subjects were likely to have relevant analytic knowledge. This analytic knowledge, however, was unlikely to be in the form of an explicit rule. The episodic facilitation that we saw with words or pictures of familiar objects might not be present if subjects were given a simple, explicit rule that covered all cases of a set of unfamiliar material presented for categorization. As long as the rule worked unproblematically, subjects might rely solely on the rule, making the definitionally irrelevant characteristics of past instances behaviorally irrelevant as well. The issue here is whether specialization of a rule is occasioned by difficulty and error (e.g., Anderson 1983) or simply by the availability of prior instances that are retrieved by the current cues. Given the prevalence of explicit rules in formal instruction, the conditions for specialization are of interest.

Experiments relevant to this issue were carried out at McMaster by Scott Allen and me (Brooks & Allen, submitted). The stimuli to be learned were fictional animals that varied on five binary dimensions (e.g., 2 legs or 6, long neck or short), and which could be classified into one of two categories ("builders" or "diggers") by a three-dimensional additive rule: An animal was in a category if it had at least two of the three features that were predictive of that category. The animals were presented on a set of distinctive backgrounds, such as a snowy forest, by a pond, or in the desert. Each background was consistently paired with one digger and one builder, so that the backgrounds were not in themselves predictive of the category. A single training trial for one animal consisted of a set of three consecutive slides, together with redundant narration. In the first slide, the animals were shown standing in the appropriate background. In the second and third slides, they were shown either digging and then resting in a shallow hole, or building and then resting in a shelter made from local materials. These last slides, then, were a depiction of which of the two categories the animal was in: builders or diggers. Examples of the first slides for a builder and for a digger are shown at the left in Figure 6.2. The effect of this procedure was essentially to tell a ministory about each of the animals, a procedure that was performed five times for each of the eight animals. On the presentation of the first slide on each trial, the subject was required to apply the rule as rapidly as possible to predict the category; as this task was done with virtually no errors during the first trial, the subjects evidently could apply the rule. The intent of the whole training sequence was to give the subject perceptual experience with a specific set of "old" targets as well as practice with the categorization rule. As intended, the training task was quite easy, with virtually no errors being made and classification times on the initial slides getting down to the range of $\frac{1}{4}$ second.

The test sequence was designed to assess whether the subjects had specialized the rule in the sense that old stimuli and stimuli similar to them (New Similars) were treated as special cases. To do so, the New Similars were animals that differed in one *relevant* feature from old animals. In the first half of the test sequence, this change left the test animals in the same category as the most similar old animal (good analogies); in the second half of the test sequence, it changed the category of the test animal relative to the most similar old animal (bad analogies). In general, the results indicated a considerable amount of specialization of the rule. The good analogies were classified at approximately the same speed and accuracy as the old items (12 percent error), while the bad analogies were classified more slowly and with considerably more errors

RULE: AT LEAST TWO OF (LONG LEGS, ANGULAR BODY, SPOTS) ➤⎯⎯➤ BUILDER

TRAINING	TEST
KNOWN BUILDER	GOOD ANALOGY (BUILDER)
KNOWN DIGGER	BAD ANALOGY (BUILDER)

Figure 6.2. Sample material for the builders-diggers experiment. Animals could be classified by a three-feature additive rule (e.g., at least two of long legs, spots, angular bodies).
Each background was associated with one builder and one digger. After learning a set of
eight training items (such as the two shown), subjects were asked to classify test items.
Simple reliance on the rule, which the subjects knew and had practiced, would not predict
the obtained difference in speed and accuracy of classification of good and bad analogies,
since the rule applied equally well to both types of test items.

(45 percent). If classification were being done solely by a speeded application of the rule, then one would not expect more errors to the bad
analogies than to the good; in both cases the classification could have
been made perfectly by attending to the relevant features – features that
had been present in each of the eight possible combinations during
training.

We do not mean to imply, however, that the rule was having no effect
– that it was simply abandoned at an early stage. This was made clear by

the results of a control group that was not given the rule at any point during the procedure, but which was treated identically in all other respects. Subjects in this No Rule group had to rely on the last two slides in each three slide group to determine the animal's category, but they were virtually errorless by the end of the training phase. These subjects were slightly slower and less accurate than the Rule group on the good analogies (21 percent error), but made 85 percent errors on the bad analogies. This result would be expected if they were responding solely on the basis of analogy to old items, but not if they had been implicitly abstracting out a rule. The results also indicates that the subjects in the Rule group, who were correct on a majority of the bad analogies, were in fact partially relying on the rule for accuracy despite the fact that no feedback on accuracy was given during the test series. Another indication of the rule group's continued reliance on rules was that when the backgrounds on which the test animals were presented were re-paired with the animals, classification times increased, but the errors to the bad analogies went down. This suggests that the animals had been integrated with backgrounds during training, such that changing the definitionally (and in themselves predictively) irrelevant backgrounds disrupted the analogical basis of performance and encouraged more reliance on the rule.

In all, this experiment shows a case in which experience with prior instances facilitated performance on old and new similar items despite knowledge of an adequate, explicit rule. One could object that the training conditions were designed to produce perceptual specialization, but that is exactly the point. Conditions in which there is a considerable amount of distinctive item information and in which the task encourages integration between the focal object and the context are sufficiently common in the world that they should be investigated. What is unusual in the world is to have an explicit, easy-to-apply rule, but similar indications of specialization were obtained for both the group with the rule and the group without the rule. Knowledge of the rule clearly helped to maintain accuracy, but it did not prevent facilitation from instance and context-specific knowledge.

Episodic analogies in domains with no prior abstractions

In the experiments considered to this point, subjects were either given a rule or had sufficient previous experience with the material that they undoubtedly already had relevant analytic knowledge – even if that analytic knowledge was not sufficient to account for their classification performance. I would like now to consider two sets of experiments in which people were exposed to artificial domains well described by rules that were unknown to them. In neither of these two sets of experiments were the learning conditions designed to promote analytic learning; that is, in neither case were a large number of cases presented simultaneously, with adequate time for analysis or with intentional "find-the-rule" instructions. The issue is the types of learning that occur under such incidental conditions, conditions that surely occur sufficiently frequently in the world that they should be investigated. I do not mean to be claiming that the subjects in these experiments have simply abandoned any analytic abilities, nor that, if they stayed in the situation for a long time or were forced to think about it explicitly, they would not develop some analytic model. I do not believe we can find a task that completely subverts analysis anymore than I believe that the common "semantic" tasks have generally eliminated a contribution of less analytic episodic information. But there surely are situations, including natural situations, in which the subjects' analytic models and tools are at a relative disadvantage. Not surprisingly, my general conclusion is that under such conditions, generalization around prior processing episodes plays a crucial role – a role that depends on the nature of the prior processing and which can mimic the effect of learning rules.

The first set of studies, by John Vokey (reported in Vokey & Brooks, in press), used strings of consonants, such as TTXMT and VXM. The order of the letters in these strings was governed by an artificial grammar whose existence was mentioned to the subjects only after a set of the strings had already been studied. These studies were designed to reply to an interesting proposal made by Reber and Allen (1978). Reber and Allen suggested that presenting the strings as the stimuli in paired-associate learning (TTXMT-Denver, VXM-Boston), as had been done by Brooks (1978), would encourage subjects to differentiate the strings and would subsequently allow only nonanalytic transfer to new strings; that is, a new string would be categorized as having been generated by the same set of rules used for the study items only if it had close overall resemblance (differs by only one letter) to at least one of the study strings. But, if the subjects were merely to observe strings as they were being shown at a 5 second per item rate, then conditions would be so nondirective that *implicit* abstractive mechanisms would be free to operate. Under an observation condition, then, Reber and Allen expected subjects to show analytic transfer; that is, categorization based on the grammaticality of the new items rather than their overall similarity to individual old items. Their results showed that subjects in the observation condition were, if anything, more accurate than those in the paired-associate condition in judging the grammaticality of new items. This result is a surprise if one expected better nonanalytic transfer when the items were learned better, since by the criterion of poorer recognition memory the observation subjects did not know the old items as well as did the paired-associate subjects. On this better learning assumption then, Reber and Allen's results indicate that something other than non-analytic transfer was operating to produce the advantage in categorization for the observation condition.

Vokey and Brooks argued that these results did not require hypothesizing that the subjects were unconsciously abstracting the grammar. Insead, as a result of differences in item processing among the study conditions, the old items might be generalizing to different ranges of new items. The old stimuli in the paired associate conditions could be so differentiated that they would seem similar to very few of the new items. As a result, responding to the new items would show few false alarms in recognition memory and few "grammatical" responses; only a small number of the new items would be seen as similar enough to any of the old items to be judged as probably having been generated by whatever rules had generated the old items. The items studied under the observation condition would be expected to show more false alarm recognitions and more classifications as "grammatical." Because in a rule system of this sort the grammatical items might be expected to resemble one another more than they resemble the ungrammatical items, responding with the laxer criterion of similarity used by the observation subjects would be expected to produce more correct responses than would the more stringent criterion used by the paired-associate subjects. An even more stringent shift in criterion was expected in an additional condition in which subjects were given mnemonics for the study items (VXM = Virgins eXpect Miracles).

To evaluate this shift of similarity interpretation, test items were used in which grammaticality and similarity to old items were unconfounded. For example, the test item MVXRT differs in just as many letters from the old item MVXRM as does the test item MVXRV, but MVXRT violates the grammar that generated all of the study items and MVXRV does not. Using both similar and dissimilar, grammatical and ungrammatical test items made it possible to unconfound the two variables. similarity and adherence to a generative process, that are normally confounded both in these experiments and in the world at large. A majority of the variance was accounted for by the hypothesized shift in criterion of similarity to old items, leaving little reason in these data to hypothesize implicit abstraction. As in previous studies discussed in this chapter, the intent is not to claim that implicit abstractive learning never occurs, but rather that prior instances can be an important resource in unfamiliar complex domains and that variations in the processing of individual prior episodes are important for later classification.

These artificial grammar studies were designed to reply to Reber and Allen, but they have an interesting parallel with Jacoby's clarification study (Table 6.1). In both cases the major manipulation was designed to vary the specificity of processing at study. In both cases greater specificity of processing of the study items decreased the range of categorical generalization; that is, less facilitation of the perception of other pictures in the same category and fewer judgments of "grammatical" for similar items. Thus, both pictorial identification and judgments of well-formedness showed sensitivity to a processing variable that normally has been associated with explicit episodic memory tasks.

The final set of experiments to be discussed in this chapter also illustrates the importance of variations in the processing of prior instances for dealing with unfamiliar regularities. These experiments, by Bruce Whittlesea (1983, in press), dealt with both conceptual categorization and perceptual identification. Whittlesea's materials were pseudowords generated as variations from two prototypes: NOBAL and FURIG. Some of the variations on the FURIG prototype are shown in Figure 6.3. The pseudowords could vary in the number of letters in which they differed from the prototype; all of the pseudowords on the second ring, for example, differ from the prototype by two letters. They could also independently differ from a training item by various numbers of letters: if FEKIG were a training item, then FYKIG and PUKIG would differ from it by one and two letters while still being only two letters from the prototype. In Whittlesea's perceptual identification studies, training simply consisted of three trials of copying down the training items as they appeared one at a time on the screen. The perceptual identification measure was the number of letters correctly reported in position in a brief, masked presentation of the pseudoword. In the classification studies, the subjects were told that they would be shown two classes of pseudowords, some of which were nouns and some of which were verbs. Training consisted of three trials of copying down the pseudowords that were labeled as nouns, adding an -ISM affix (FEKIGISM from FEKIG) or, for those labeled as verbs, adding an -ING affix (NOTYLING from NOTYL). The dependent variables were the accuracy and confidence of classification of the same test series used in the perceptual identification studies.

Since the results were essentially the same for the studies using perceptual identification and those using confidence in classification, they will be discussed together. If training consisted of three trials apiece on a few items (five from each prototype) on the second ring, then new test items from the first ring (closer to the prototype) were classified more confidently and seen better than items on the third ring – a simulation of the usual goodness-of-exemplar gradient. The *new* items on the sec-

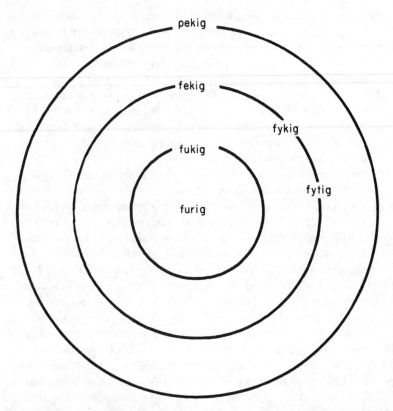

Figure 6.3. An illustration of some of the relations in the material used by Whittlesea (in press). FURIG is the prototype for this set. FEKIG, FYKIG, and FYTIG all differ from it by two letters from the prototype. If FEKIG is a training item, then FYKIG and FYTIG would be test items that differ from it by one and two letters, respectively. These stimuli were used to unconfound distance from training items and distance from the prototype for the set.

ond ring were responded to better, however, if they were one away from the nearest training item than if they were two away, suggesting that analogy to the old items was important. If the training items were moved out to the third ring, then there was little facilitation of the items on the first ring, even though the nominal prototypes, FURIG and NOBAL, were still the centers of the distributions. In this case, if closeness to training items was the most important influence on transfer, a much smaller advantage for being close to the apparent prototype would be expected, an expectation that was confirmed. For example, a one-away (from closest old) item on the fourth ring was seen better and classified more confidently than a two-away item on the third ring; in this case, closeness to the apparent prototype was outweighed by closeness to the training item. Thus, by changing the density of the training items around the nominal prototype, one could produce the usual goodness-of-exemplar gradient or its inverse; simultaneously producing closeness-to-old effects that allowed Whittlesea to fit the results with a model that depended entirely on proximity to the set of closest training items.

The primary relevance of Whittlesea's experiments for the current discussion is that this nonanalytic transfer is observed mainly when the processing of the training items is reasonably well integrated. In copying the training items from the screen, subjects were presumably using their prior experience with word pronunciation (which itself could be due at least partially to analogy: Glushko 1979; McClelland & Rumelhart 1981). However, when the training task did not encourage integrated processing of the individual training items, the advantage of the old items was dramatically decreased. This "split" training task consisted of comparing an item with its prototype, which appeared immediately above the training item, and copying the letters the two strings had in common in one place on a response sheet and (in some experiments) the differing letters in a different place. This task was designed to induce the subject to process the letters separately rather than as parts of an integrated string. When only the common letters were copied, a later perceptual identification test demonstrated an advantage for strings close to the prototype as compared to old items. When common and discrepant letters were copied into different locations during training, the differences were found between items closer to old items, and items closer to the nominal prototype disappeared. This indicates that the strong closeness-to-old effects depended on having treated the old items as whole units.

Finally, Whittlesea (manuscript in preparation) has extended these results to a word superiority paradigm. With only 30 training trials, as was used in the previous work, he has demonstrated a superiority for perceiving letters in the context of familiar strings *provided* that the original processing of those strings was integrative. No such advantage was found under the less integrative "split" training conditions.

The wide variety of conditions in both Whittlesea's and Vokey's experiments provide a rather daunting mass of detail. Their cumulative effect is to demonstrate the extreme sensitivity of recognition memory, perceptual identification, and classification to the precision and integrality of the original processing of items from an unfamiliar domain. I have emphasized Vokey's and Whittlesea's work because they are good illustrations of the importance of *variations* in the processing of prior episodes in influencing the breadth of generalization around them in dealing with unfamiliar abstractions. I do not mean to ignore the body of work that demonstrates the power of prior instances; this work provides considerable force to the necessity to take specific prior instances into account in predicting transfer. This work is thoughtfully reviewed by Medin and Smith (1984). In addition, in an article particularly relevant to the current section, Kemler-Nelson (1984) has demonstrated that an instance-based mechanism is selectively used under incidental rather than intentional learning conditions.

Summary of the influence of prior processing episodes

In general, psychology has shown considerable faith in the existence of an automatic abstraction mechanism, and more particularly in a principle of "abstractive economy": If learners know or can find a rule or schema that provides satisfactory performance, then they will rely on it for classification and identification tasks until it is proven insufficient. The preceding studies suggest that the abstraction of regularities certainly is not automatic when being exposed to novel material, and that even when regularities are known they clearly are not sufficient to explain categorical performance. Regularity in observed classification is not a sufficient condition for inferring either the existence of an underlying implicit abstraction or of reliance on abstractions, be they implicit or explicit. As mentioned in the introduction, however, this does not imply that abstractions are superfluous in conceptual classification. Rather, what I would like to argue is that analytic and nonanalytic knowledge and processing are in a dynamic relation with each other; analytic abstractions are constantly being specialized into particular processing cases, and the regularities produced in particular acts of classification are being codified into new guiding abstractions. Let us now consider some of the issues raised by the need to coordinate these two types of conceptual resources.

Implications and discussion

Processing variability and the role of similarity

The previous discussion obviously depends crucially on the notion of similarity. Because similarity-based approaches to categorization usually do not stress processing dependency, it is worth examining the relation between similarity judgments and our other conceptual resources. We need first to contrast the positivist and the processing dependent accounts of the term "similarity." The *positivist* account of similarity is that the similarity judgments of the perceiver can be fairly directly determined by the physical features and relations of the world. If an intact and responsible observer judges two objects to be physically very similar to one another, then we have reason to believe that those objects are in fact physically similar – within the competence of the sensory equipment of the perceiver. In the positivist account of science, a claim very similar to this underlies the idea of theory-independent observation: Properly conducted observation of the physical properties of the world can, in principle, be objective, can be independent of the theories and beliefs of the observer. Such a position does not have to claim that the internal representation is a literal copy of the world, that the sensory apparatus is neutral and complete, or that the observer always honors the preconditions of objectivity required for good observation. But what it does do is give special warrant to properly conducted physicalistic observations for reflecting objective properties of the world. In conceptual classification, the positivist position is consistent with the claim that some categories – those categories that are well indexed by unevenly distributed and covarying physical features[1] – are in principle independent of the rest of the conceptual and theoretical structure of the observer, and that some concepts are "natural." This construal of naturalness could underlie either a probabilistic (e.g., prototype: a term from Smith and Medin [1981]) account or an instance account of knowledge representation. In the probabilistic account, observations of the world would be abstracted into knowledge of probabilistic association or typicality for the category as a whole (by some measure, such as conditional probability or averaging, that does not depend on the perceiver's other beliefs about the object); in the instance account, the observations would be represented by a distribution of instances still acting as individuals. In either version, this account holds out the attractive possibility of culturally independent development of some concepts, given only minimal nativist constraints.

In recent, cogent papers, Murphy and Medin (1985; Medin & Wattenmaker, Chapter 3, this volume) have argued against any such attempt to treat human concepts independently of the other theoretical and conceptual knowledge of the individual. They first rejected the notion that similarity can be evaluated in a theory-neutral manner, such as the often proposed procedure of counting the number of common, "physical" attributes. They pointed out that there is no neutral way to count the number of features that are similar or dissimilar between two items because there is an infinite number of ways that any two items can be compared (e.g., a bowling ball and an aardvark both weigh less than 100 kilograms, less than 101.5 kilograms . . .). In addition, the assessed similarity of two items depends on the weighting of the features that are compared. This is not a trivial problem for a positivist account; there is considerable evidence that the weighting of a feature depends on the context, task, and item in which it occurs. Equally important, it is not clear how similarity would determine the relationships among categories, such as a hierarchy of subordinate, basic, and superordinate levels. All simple attempts to derive category structure from a theory-free measure that is dependent primarily on some distributional property of the world, such as cue or categorical validity, predicts advantage for the superordinate or subordinate level rather than the basic level. Judgments of similarity in Murphy and Medin's view do not provide a theory-free explanation of the coherence of certain categories, but rather themselves depend on prior theories or representations of the learner.

Still, we can agree with everything that Murphy and Medin claim about the theory-dependent nature of similarity and still maintain the essential claims of an instance approach. The following points are quite compatible with Murphy and Medin's position, but, because an instance-based approach has so often been associated with a positivist view of similarity, it is worth restating the arguments, assuming a processing-dependent view of similarity.[2]

1. *Some of the perceiver's similarity judgments may reflect knowledge of the world that is predictively valid for the purposes of the perceiver.* In informal observation, as in science, an observation can provide constraint on our beliefs about the world, despite the fact that it does not result in a unique description of the world. Perceived similarity, as one form of observation, may be a good predictor for the purposes of the learner without uniquely reflecting the objective state of the world. The perceiver could omit information crucial for other purposes, or have multiple ways of describing subjectively important categories, without making a judgment of close similarity useless – although such variation would provide difficulty for a positivist account of similarity. Describing the multiple similarity metrics actually used may be a depressingly difficult job for the scientist, but that does not in itself make similarity judgments problematic for prediction by the perceiver.

2. *Both similarity judgments and abstractions may be theory-dependent, but there is no reason to believe that they are dependent on the same "theories" (implicit conceptual models).* Murphy and Medin are very explicit about saying that they are only rejecting the sufficiency of a similarity-based approach, not its usefulness. However, when they state that "at its best, similarity only provides a language for talking about conceptual coherence," it would be easy to inappropriately conclude that they are also stating that similarity judgments are largely redundant with judgments of conceptual coherence. One of the points of the data described earlier is that we should not underestimate the difference between the processing influenced by similarity judgments and that influenced by unifying abstractions. Thinking of natural categories, there are some types of

decisions, such as categorical identity, for which *close* similarity provides special information that is more robust than from the analytic models available to the perceiver. At any given time some of the knowledge that will prove useful for our current objectives will be available in the form of similarity judgments, some in the form of judgments of typicality, and some in explicit analytic principles. But there is no reason to assume that the conclusions drawn from these different knowledge bases will be the same at a given time. We often search for examples of a new generalization precisely because the examples carry with them contrasting, partially independent information and frames of reference. In this case one is attempting to capitalize on the variety of examples to refine the definition of the category. But even if the result of this search is a generalization that predicts perfectly, and of course is maximally coherent, the point is that one had useful predictive knowledge in the form of exemplars prior to the formulation of the generalization. This kind of explicit search for examples is relevant to the current discussion because it is an acknowledgment of the separate, categorically useful knowledge contained in exemplars – knowledge that could also be drawn on in an unabstracted form to guide processing of a specific new stimulus.

3. *Close similarity (perceived physical near identity) is a special case that modifies the force of the weighting argument.* When we think about a problem such as "is a whale more like a bear or a shark," it is easy to be impressed with the importance and the potential variability of the exact weighting of particular features because the answer would depend on whether swimming or bearing live young was emphasized. In this example, however, one is impressed with the number of differences as well as the number of similarities among these three animals, which suggests that this is not the type of similarity judgment being discussed in the first part of this paper. In the tasks previously discussed, the test items were generally seen as nearly identical (including the highly available cues that determine judged physical identity) to previous items and the judgments of close similarity seemed quite unproblematic. This subjective ease, of course, does not mean that judgments of near identity are independent of "theory" (variable prior knowledge and judgment biases), but it does suggest that the variables affecting such perceived similarity may differ from the more problematic judgments. This is not meant to imply independence between "perceptual" and "conceptual" identity, since perceptual judgments are heavily dependent on some part of the perceiver's conceptual inventory. Rather, the distinction is made to acknowledge that the extreme of judged near identity – which includes judged physical identity – is a special case that should be respected in discussions of judged similarity. To return to the shark-bear-whale example, if a person is viewing a whale for the first time and the closest physical analogies

in memory are sharks and bears, then we could expect variable and slow classification performance. But on viewing a second whale, the person has available whatever was learned on the first encounter. On the first encounter whether a bear or a shark was retrieved as an analogy would depend critically on how the various stimulus attributes were weighted; on the second encounter the challenge would be to find circumstances – a weighting scheme – in which the processing of the first whale would not be retrieved. There are circumstances under which judgments of "near physical identity" are going to be less variable than are judgments that two items are "merely conceptually the same." To the extent that such judgments of physical near identity are strongly correlated with a combination of goals and external circumstances, then they will have some predictive privilege for the judged outcome. Under such circumstances, one would not have to subscribe to a positivist view of similarity to presume that *judgments* of physical similarity would have independent valid content for the perceiver.

Distributed knowledge and abstraction

In John Vokey's artificial grammar experiments described above, there was little sign of the subjects having either implicitly or explicitly learned the underlying grammar. Most of the variance in later classification performance could be accounted for by similarity of the test items to particular old items. In a sense, the systematic knowledge that allowed above chance performance on new, randomly selected grammatical items (i.e., items selected without a special effort to unconfound similarity-to-old from grammaticality), was *distributed* across the subjects' knowledge of the many old items that they had learned. Evidently, there was not a central criterion for grammaticality that was consistently consulted to decide whether a new item was grammatical. In these experiments there was little else the subjects could do: The grammar was deliberately selected to be complex, no mention was made of the existence of the grammar, and little time was allowed to abstract it out even if the subjects had been so inclined. However, an explicit rule *was* given in Scott Allen's experiments with the "builders" and "diggers," and there still was evidence that subjects differentiated the animals into special cases, to some extent integrating them with their backgrounds. In Jacoby's word identification experiments, there were also signs of specialization of new cases despite the subjects' already having well-practiced word identification skills. In the picture identification experiments, this differentiation was also shown to influence transfer to new members of the same category. In all of these cases then, at least some portion of the classification skill was distributed across many more special cases than would be expected if subjects only differentiated new cases in response to difficulty.

If, in fact, specialization results from processing an item interactively with a reasonably distinctive context, then decentralization of identification skill could be expected to be the norm. Many of the regularities in behavior that we observe would be statistical – of the same nature as "traffic flow," "rush hour," and "rising market." Such regularities are real, as anyone who has been stuck in rush-hour traffic can testify, but they are the product of many separate decision units rather than of a single central generator; in our case the regularities in categorization would be a result of consistency among many separate special cases, rather than resulting from a more "economical" decision rule. A manifested regularity in behavior is insufficient evidence for presuming an underlying, central abstraction, and, under many processing conditions, the abstractions that do exist are unlikely to be the operative form of knowledge for identification.

The point of stressing the distributed form of much of our knowledge is to simplify the rules and abstractions that are learned, not to deny the existence of abstracted knowledge. Distributing the complex interactions of the world across many special cases relieves abstractions from the burden of omniscience, from having to account for all of the observed accuracy and reaction speeds. Consequently, it becomes easier to understand how the abstractions that do exist would be learned. We can see a point here that is parallel to one of Gibson's points about perception: If the inferences required for normal perception seem unbelievably complex, then we may have our description of the stimulus wrong. Similarly, if the abstractions required to account for observed behavior seem too complex to learn, then a redescription of what is learned could be in order (a "taming of the clever unconscious"; Vokey & Brooks, in press). This suggestion obviously is not news in many fields, such as psycholinguistics and developmental psychology, but what I hope to have done is reinforce it with considerations based on current research in memory: special cases, of which we may not be aware, form easily and can guide the processing of new instances.

The preceding is written as if nonanalytic transfer involves only the single most similar instance or episode. In fact, the context model of Medin and his colleagues (Medin & Schaffer 1978; Medin & Smith 1981), Hintzman's Minerva II model (Hintzman 1986), and Whittlesea's high metric model (1983) all allow an influence of several similar items. This has the effect of computing a very local average at the moment of test, a local "chorus of instances." Because it is local, it would have some of the advantages of (small sample) averaging and yet still not average across the interactions in a complicated domain.

This raises the question of the relation between "distributed knowledge" in the sense discussed here and recent distributed memory models. Obviously the characteristics of interactive coding and parallel search among a large number of preserved exemplars demonstrate considerable compatibility in approach. But there is no necessary relation with the particular sense of distributed knowledge used above. Some of the distributed memory models (in general, those in Hinton & Anderson 1981) could be described as distributing items across locations; no one cell in the matrix was assigned to a particular input item. The major motivation of these models was to explain the robustness of memory across destruction of individual cells. Because many of these models did not separately code the interaction among stimulus dimensions within an item, the resulting categorical performance was linearly separable, a pattern shown by Medin and Schwanenflugel (1981) to be insufficient to explain the usual results of experiments in categorization. Other distributed models, however, such as those cited in the preceding paragraph, could be described as distributing rules across items, and these models do use the term distributed in the same sense discussed above. For example, McClelland & Rumelhart's (1981) interactive activation model demonstrates performance on pseudowords that is in accordance with the pronunciation patterns of English, despite such rules not being directly represented anywhere in the model. They accomplish this by having processing influenced by analogy to *whole* words, rather than just by separate letters in position. McClelland and Rumelhart's (1985) recent "delta rule" model accomplishes the same thing with a model that can learn the regularities that had to be built into their former model. They demonstrate that their model is able to learn the regularities in Whittlesea's materials (Figure 6.3) and simulate the results of his experiments, without the regularities being abstracted out. Again, the critical factor seems to be that the high-level interactions represented by whole past items affects current processing.[3]

Ad hoc and specialized policy

Fundamental questions about the sufficiency of generalized, acontextual conceptual resources have been raised by two recent papers (Barsalou, Chapter 5, this volume; Kahneman & Miller 1986). In a very interesting set of studies reviewed in this volume, Larry Barsalou and his colleagues demonstrated that goodness-of-exemplar ratings for a set of objects showed considerable variance depending on the concurrent task demands. For example, if subjects simultaneously had to give reasons for their rankings, then the rankings were very different than if they did not. Explicit properties given for good and bad category members tended to be ideal properties rather than the highly typical properties that might be expected from an averaged prototype interpretation of goodness-of-exemplar gradients. Furthermore, considerable variance was found both within and between subjects, again a finding that would not be expected if the ratings were mainly dependent on stable abstractions of natural structure (see also Bellezza 1984a,b,c). Collectively, these results suggest that the concept operative at any given moment is not exclusively a steady organization, but rather is strongly influenced by the particular context and the purpose for which it is being employed. If Barsalou had found dependence on context and purpose solely for ad hoc categories (such as the category of all things you would take from the house if it were on fire), then there would be little surprise; but when such effects are also found for some of the most traditional natural kinds categories (such as birds or clothing), a question is raised both about the goodness-of-exemplar rating task as a reasonably pure measure of stable prototypical structures and about the sufficiency of such structures in the first place.

However, we have no reason to assume that this degree of vulnerability to transient contextual influences will always be the case. Considering the small amount of practice Barsalou gave his subjects, a reasonable part of the variability within a given rating task probably should be attributed to transient contextual influences: to the particular thoughts that the subjects had in entering this novel rating situation and the interaction of this processing context with the particular exemplars presented and their order of presentation. Let us imagine that we repeated the same goodness-of-exemplar task several times in a row with the same subjects. The ratings probably would become more steady; the same object would be more likely to be given the same goodness-of-exemplar rating on each presentation. Some of this (imagined) consistency might be attributable to remembering the prior rating. But it is also likely that a "policy" (be it an explicit criterion or generalizing around particular old exemplars) would have developed: that transfer to new objects would also become more steady within those circumstances. This would not necessarily mean that such steadiness would be "semantic" or decontextualized. In keeping with the work reviewed earlier in this paper, it is likely that such training effects would be context-specific; that is, the training would strongly affect transfer in very similar situations and less strongly in less similar situations.

In previous sections I emphasized the role of prior processing episodes in producing different responses to different members of the same category. But against the backdrop of the variability documented by Barsalou's excellent research, we can also appreciate the potential of episodic influences in producing greater, although context-specific, stability of response. If we were to reject such practice effects as being merely episodic, we would be implying that such episodic influences were rare, that such practice distorts the task from relying on general-purpose conceptual resources that are invoked in most "normal" situations. However, given the ubiquity of effects on identification of single prior episodes, we could expect comparably widespread effects in goodness-of-exemplar ratings.

The conclusion that Barsalou takes from his data is that even the most familiar concepts are to some extent created at the moment of application, drawing on contextual and task constraints as well as semantic resources of differing degrees of stability. Kahneman and Miller (1986) have written a paper that coincidently takes such constructive, creative forces as its main theme. The importance of Barsalou's work is to show considerable variability with the very dependent variable most central to natural concept formulations. The importance of Kahneman and Miller's work is its focus on the act of constructing the norms by which we judge our ongoing activities as well as the very impressive range over which such postcomputational effects can be shown. They propose that perceived objects and events recruit representations of similar objects and events that include a considerable amount of remembered interpretation. Norms for judging the current situation are then constructed from the elements provided by these representations and from elements in the current situation. The norms that are constructed are influenced by the availability of prior instances as well as principles that dictate the relative mutability of aspects of the current situation. In their phrase, the current experience selectively recruits its own alternatives that in turn help to shape the context in which it is eventually interpreted and evaluated. This backward, postcomputational generation of norms is contrasted to the precomputation of expectations and concept norms that has been focused upon in recent cognitive psychology. This type of norm construction is used to illuminate a very wide range of phenomena, including perceptual comparisons and attributions of causality as well as affective states such as surprise, frustration, and regret.

In keeping with the stress on memory for processing episodes in this paper, I would like to emphasize the entirely compatible point that norms, once constructed, themselves become part of what could be retrieved under similar later circumstances. The immediate picture given by Barsalou's and by Kahneman and Miller's work is of much less stability of response than would be expected from the routine operation of a stable storehouse of characteristic and defining information. But the same mechanisms that have been emphasized throughout this paper would tend toward stability, albeit context-specific. One way of looking at Barsalou's work is that situations that should have been routine according to schema or prototype models appear to have been treated as if they were a bit novel; the variability found in the goodness-of-exemplar rating tasks is more like that expected in problem solving than like that expected from a simple tapping of routinely accessible knowledge. Most of Kahneman and Miller's tasks were intended to be rather novel, with the resulting creative use of item-specific information being prominent. But some future situations, such as (in the extreme) repetitions of the goodness-of-exemplar rating task, will be quite similar to the problems now being solved and could be expected to use some of the same norms and solutions; like rigid bureaucrats, we should show some aversion to thinking through the same policy twice. In less similar situations, more creative and variable responses could again be expected. We spend much of our lives in the vicinity of friends, and friends provide norms and solutions as well as names.

Varied conceptual resources: Organizations of knowledge and modes of processing

The picture suggested so far is that our processing of current episodes ordinarily relies on close analogy with very similar prior situations. This characterization of nonanalytic obviously leaves an important role for analytic knowledge and processing. There certainly are times in which it is crucial to make sure that the bases of categorization are consistent with the attributes and relations that we believe to be categorically relevant, and we do have knowledge that supports this activity. In its normal use, such knowledge may act more as a negative heuristic, as a monitor of the unrestrained use of analogy (like the conjectured role of the rule in Scott Allen's experiment on "builders" and "diggers"). In this role, analytic knowledge would not have to be sufficient to generate all of our conceptual behavior, especially the interactions with local conditions. Instead, it would only have to be sufficient to account for our spontaneous judgments of gross violation, that an essential characteristic was missing despite all the immediate signs of analogy. Combined with analytic control, analytic knowledge would be the basis of derivation, the deliberate attempt to base a decision solely on relevant characteristics. However, one of the most difficult functions that we attempt may be a clear, unbiased call for context-free information. It may, as intuition suggests, require learned, sophisticated discipline. Meaning by analogy comes in a flood and has to be eliminated by more deliberate analytic control.

Focusing, as was done in this paper, on the nonanalytic organization of knowledge was not meant to deny the judgment of the knower that some categorical knowledge is more fundamental or central than others;

after all, there is a response to the instruction "be careful." Nor does it deny the importance of a sense of coherence among the whole. However, the knowledge that holds a concept together does not have to be operational in the processing of each exemplar, and the sense of coherence does not have to come from the obligatory operation of a core. In the current view, conceptual coherence is important, but it is also a bit of an illusion. Valid, definitional knowledge can be inherited through several generations of processing episodes. As such, it is subject to a kind of "evolutionary drift." We (or at least I) often wake up to realize that we are using a term in different senses in different contexts. If the insight resulting from such self-analysis is deemed valuable enough to be the basis of action, then there follows a process of beating successive instances of behavior into line. During this process analytic control can prevent overt inconsistency, but greater care is needed each time a concept is met in a new context; the second and third times are easier, until the new insight is itself distributed across the various contexts in which it is to be used.

Both centrifugal and centripetal forces are routinely in operation in our knowledge base; we are continually specializing general principles into context-specific understandings on the one hand, and disciplining this drift into new generalities on the other. The application of the same rule on a set of similar exemplars leads to the modification of the rule, which in turn changes the way those instances are understood. Conceptual consistency may be more a result of good policing and lucky juxtaposition than of being generated from a unitary source.

Conclusions

The only positions that are clearly ruled out by the experiments reviewed in this chapter are those taking the extreme stand that episodic information is *never* used in categorical judgments. There are few advocates for such positions. However, judging by the emphasis on stable, abstracted information in the semantic memory literature, the background assumption seems to be that abstracted knowledge carries the burden of generalization and interpretation. The preceding data do speak to this presumption. More importantly, these data demonstrate the value in the memory dictum of attending to exactly what was done in a prior episode and how it fits with the conditions of application. Treating the contribution of prior processing episodes as a quantitative mixture of instance and abstracted information or as a passing phase of learning seem to me to miss important qualitative aspects of normal conceptual performance – aspects that are likely to produce crucial insights into how we cope with both familiar and new situations.

There seems to be an aesthetic preference for the possibility of simplicity and neatness in underlying conceptual knowledge. However, although conceptual elegance characterizes some of our most impressive intellectual products, it does not seem to have been the most important design consideration in the whole of our conceptual resources. Our speed of learning and prodigious memories make it possible for us to respond to the complexity of the world by learning many local variants. Scientific elegance would seem more likely to come in the principles controlling our processing than in the simplicity of the final product.

I would like to close with an analogy to the complexity of political decision making. In any large organization, decisions are rarely due solely to a single level of decision making, although only one level may have been operative for a particular decision. We would do violence to the subtlety and flexibility of a complex system to act as if any decision that is consistent with an overall policy is due to a direct invocation of that policy. To attribute all decision making to the formal statutes or directives from top management is to miss many systematicities in policy, to miss sources of change, and to miss an important element in the ability of the system to adapt to local circumstances. Similarly, to attribute all categorizations to the direct operation of a single underlying conceptual model would require more sufficiency and wisdom to the model than seems plausible, and would miss a simple mechanism for adapting to complex interactions with local contexts. The bases of decision in the republic of the mind, as in political decision making, are of different degrees of generality, function in different environments, and reflect different degrees of attempted adherence to overall policy. Sometimes we make the decisions we do because of overall policy, sometimes because of local experience, and sometimes because all our friends seem to be doing it.

NOTES

1. Whittlesea (1983) points out that in the case of graded dimensions, the nonarbitrary clustering of the world emphasized by Rosch and her associates requires a multimodal distribution of values on the dimensions as well as a correlation among the values on separate dimensions.
2. The question arises as to whether either Brooks's (1978) or Medin & Schaffer's (1978) papers can be considered to be positivist in approach. In some regards the proposition could be denied for both papers. In my paper I stated that attribute counting was just a convenience for making the argument and for crudely operationalizing similarity; further, all that is known about coding effects in memory denies the sufficiency of such a tactic. Medin and Schaffer's salience parameters are clearly a device by which theory-driven assessments of similarity could be handled. However, by an absence of any

discussion in either paper of how similarity-based knowledge was determined by, or coordinated with, the learner's other conceptual and theoretical knowledge, both papers by default implied a more positivist approach than is being advocated here. That is, all of the operational tools in both papers were more congenial to the counting of fixed, context-independent features than to a more adequate treatment of similarity.

3. This same weighting of whole-word units is accomplished in Hintzman (in press) by raising similarity measures to the third power, in Medin and Schaffer (1978) by multiplying the salience weights, and in Whittlesea (1983) by using a higher-order Minkowski metric.

REFERENCES

Anderson, J. R. (1983). *The Architecture of Cognition*. Cambridge, MA: Harvard University Press.

Bellezza, F. S. (1984a). Reliability of retrieval from semantic memory: Common categories. *Bulletin of the Psychonomic Society, 22,* 324–326.

(1984b). Reliability of retrieval from semantic memory: Noun meanings. *Bulletin of the Psychonomic Society, 22,* 377–380.

(1984c). Reliability of retrieval from semantic memory: Information about people. *Bulletin of the Psychonomic Society, 22,* 511–513.

Brooks, L. R. (1978). Non-analytic concept formation and memory for instances. In E. Rosch and B. Lloyd (Eds.), *Cognition and Categorization*. Hillsdale, NJ: Erlbaum.

Brooks, L. R., & Allen, S. (1986). Specialization of an explicit rule. Manuscript submitted for publication.

Brooks, L. R., & Whittlesea, B. A. W. (1986). Particular experiences in picture identification: Interactions with the prototypicality and basic-level advantages. Manuscript in preparation.

Carroll, M., Byrne, B., & Krisner, K. (1985). Autobiographical memory and perceptual learning: A developmental study using picture recognition, naming latency and perceptual identification. *Memory and Cognition, 13,* 273–279.

Collins, A. M., & Loftus, E. F. (1975). A spreading activation theory of semantic processing. *Psychological Review, 82,* 407–428.

Craik, F. I. M. (1979). Human memory. *Annual Review of Psychology, 30,* 63–102.

(1981). Encoding and retrieval effects in human memory: A partial review. In A. D. Baddeley & J. Long (Eds.), *Attention and performance IX*. Hillsdale, NJ: Erlbaum.

Craik, F. I. M., & Tulving, E. (1975). Depth of processing and the retention of words in episodic memory. *Journal of Experimental Psychology: General, 104,* 268–294.

Elio, R., & Anderson, J. R. (1981). Effects of category generalizations and instance similarity on schema abstraction. *Journal of Experimental Psychology: Human Learning and Memory, 7,* 397–417.

Glushko, R. J. (1979). The organization and activation of orthographic knowledge in reading aloud. *Journal of Experimental Psychology: Human perception and Performance, 5,* 674–691.

Haymen, G. (1983). *A task analysis of lexical decisions*. Unpublished doctoral dissertation, McMaster University, Hamilton, Ontario.

Hinton, G., & Anderson, J. A. (1981). *Parallel models of associative memory.* Hillsdale, NJ: Erlbaum.

Hintzman, D. L. (in press). Schema abstraction in a multiple trace memory model. *Journal of Experimental Psychology: Learning, Memory, and Cognition.*

Homa, D., Sterling, S., & Treppel, L. (1981). Limitations of exemplar-based generalization and the abstraction of categorical information. *Journal of Experimental Psychology: Human Learning and Memory, 7,* 418–439.

Jacoby, L. L. (1983a). Remembering the data: Analyzing interactive processes in reading. *Journal of Verbal Learning and Verbal Behavior, 22,* 485–508.

   (1983b). Perceptual enhancement: Persistent effects of an experience. *Journal of Experimental Psychology: Learning, Memory, and Cognition, 9,* 21–38.

Jacoby, L. L., Baker, J., & Brooks, L. R. (1986). Episodic effects in picture identification. Manuscript in preparation.

Jacoby, L. L., & Brooks, L. R. (1984). Nonanalytic congition: Memory, perception and concept learning. In G. Bower (Ed.), *The Psychology of Learning and Motivation: Advances in Research and Theory* (Vol. 18). New York: Academic Press.

Jacoby, L. L., & Craik, F. I. M. (1979). Effects of elaboration of processing at encoding and retrieval: Trace distinctiveness and recovery of initial context. In L. S. Cermak & F. I. M. Craik (Eds.), *Levels of processing and human memory.* Hillsdale, NJ: Erlbaum.

Jacoby, L. L., & Witherspoon, D. (1982). Remembering without awareness. *Canadian Journal of Psychology, 36,* 300–324.

Kahneman, D., & Miller, D. T. (1986). Norm theory: Comparing reality to its alternatives. *Psychological Review, 93,* 136–153.

Kemler-Nelson, D. G. (1984). The effect of intention on what concepts are acquired. *Journal of Verbal Learning and Verbal Behavior, 23,* 734–759.

Kolers, P. A. (1979). A pattern-analyzing basis for recognition memory. In L. S. Cermak & F. I. M. Craik (Eds.), *Levels of processing and human memory.* Hillsdale, NJ: Erlbaum.

Kolers, P. A., & Smythe, W. E. (1984). Symbol manipulation: Alteratives to the computational view of mind. *Journal of Verbal Learning and Verbal Behavior, 23,* 289–314.

Levy, B. A., & Begin, J. (1984). Proofreading familiar text: Allocating resources to perceptual and conceptual processes. *Memory & Cognition, 12,* 621–632.

McClelland, J. L., & Rumelhart, D. E. (1981). An interactive activation model of context effects in letter perception: Part 1. An account of basic findings. *Psychological Review, 88,* 375–407.

   (1985). Distributed memory and the representation of general and specific information. *Journal of Experimental Psychology: General, 114,* 159–188.

Medin, D. L., & Schaffer, M. M. (1978). Context theory of classification learning. *Psychological Review, 85,* 207–238.

Medin, D. L., & Schwanenflugel, P. (1981). Linear separability in classification learning. *Journal of Experimental Psychology: Human Learning and Memory, 7,* 355–368.

Medin, D. L., & Smith, E. E. (1981). Strategies and classification learning. *Journal of Experimental Psychology: Human Learning and Memory, 7,* 241–253.

   (1984). Concepts and concept formation. In M. R. Rozenzweig (Ed.), *Annual Review of Psychology* (Vol. 35).

Medin, D. L., Altom, M. W., Edleson, S. M., & Freko, D. (1982). Correlated symptoms and simulated medical classification. *Journal of Experimental Psychology: Human Learning and Memory, 8,* 37–50.

Medin, D. L., Dewey, G. I., & Murphy, T. D. (1983). Relationships between item and category learning: Evidence that abstraction is not automatic. *Journal of Experimental Psychology: Learning, Memory, and Cognition, 9,* 607–625.

Morton, J. (1969). Interaction of information in word recognition. *Psychological Review, 76,* 165–178.

(1979). Facilitation in word recognition: Experiments causing change in the logogen model. In P. A. Kolers, M. E. Wrolstal, & H. Bonma (Eds.), *Processing of visible language I.* New York: Plenum.

Murphy, G. L., & Medin, D. L. (1985). The role of theories in conceptual coherence. *Psychological Review, 92,* 289–316.

Ratcliff, R., Hockley, W., & McKoon, G. (1985). Components of activation: Repetition and Priming Effects in Lexical Decision and Recognition. *Journal of Experimental Psychology; General, 114,* 435–450.

Reber, A. S., & Allen, R. (1978). Analogic and abstraction strategies in synthetic grammar learning: A functionalist interpretation. *Cognition, 6,* 193–221.

Salasoo, A., Shiffrin, R. M., & Feustal, T. C. (1985). Building permanent memory codes: Codification and repetition effects in word identification. *Journal of Experimental Psychology: General, 114,* 50–78.

Tulving, E., & Thompson, D. M. (1973). Encoding specificity and retrieval processes in episodic memory. *Psychological Review, 80,* 352–373.

Smith, E. E., & Medin, D. L. (1981). *Categories and concepts.* Cambridge, MA: Harvard University Press.

Vokey, J. R., & Brooks, L. R. (in press). Taming the clever unconscious: Analogic and abstractive strategies in artificial grammar learning. *Cognition.*

Whittlesea, B. W. A. (1983). *The representation of concepts: An evaluation of the abstractive and episodic perspectives.* Unpublished doctoral dissertation, McMaster University, Hamilton, Ontario.

(in press). Preservation of particular experiences in conceptual representation. *Journal of Experimental Psychology: Learning, Memory, and Cognition.*

7

Conceptual development and category structure

FRANK C. KEIL

There has been a tendency to assume that the structure of conceptual categories is all of one sort or another. In the 1960s there was the so-called "classical view" in which conceptual categories were defined by sets of necessary and sufficient features. By contrast, in the 1970s, largely as a consequence of Rosch's work (Rosch 1975; Rosch & Mervis 1975; Rosch, Simpson, & Miller 1976), the dominant view became the probabilistic view, where concepts are viewed as having no necessary and sufficient features and instead are specified by probabilistic distributions of features and/or exemplars. The probabilistic view remains the dominant view of conceptual structure today and guides most current research on concepts. It is often referred to as the prototype view because Rosch suggested that it might be instantiated in terms of conceptual prototypes that emerge out of probabilistic distributions of features. Other nonprototype alternatives to the classical theory are also feasible (see Smith and Medin, 1981, for a summary).

Despite the widespread influence of prototype theory and other probabilistic views, several different investigators have begun to ask whether prototypelike representations are fully adequate as characterizations of conceptual structure (e.g., Osherson & Smith 1981; Armstrong, Gleitman, & Gleitman 1983; Rey 1983; Murphy & Medin 1985; Keil 1986a; Medin & Wattenmaker, Chapter 3, this volume). These investigators raise their questions for different reasons and come to different conclusions ranging from those that wish to relegate prototypes to the backroads of cognition to those who feel that prototypes need only a minor amount of supplementation. My purpose here is to consider how children acquire knowledge of categories and to see what characterizations of conceptual structure are needed for explaining that acquisition process. Since, it is obviously not possible here to give a comprehensive account of conceptual development, the focus will be on patterns of development most relevant to recent discussions of category structure in adults.

Concerns over the adequacy of prototype and other probabilistic theories have resulted in a proliferation of dichotomies that attempt to explain what else might be needed. The following dichotomies, in which the second member of each pair roughly corresponds to prototypes, are most prominent: core concept versus identification procedure, competence versus performance, belief versus use, abstract semantic model versus concrete context-specific variables, and theoretical explanatory versus phenomenological experiential. As one hears this list of dichotomies one begins to construct a "prototype" of what is meant. The prototype aspect of concepts seems to be more directly related to our immediate experience, while the other aspects of meaning are more indirectly experienced and represent a deeper, perhaps more reflective, understanding. This putative contrast leads to the question of whether developmental data support a distinction along these lines and whether any of the dichotomies listed is particularly appropriate. More generally, I will suggest that certain developmental phenomena do help us better understand these apparent dichotomies, and thereby constrain our theories of categories and concepts.

Some pervasive phenomena in conceptual development

Perhaps the simplest way in which to begin an investigation of children's concepts is to ask them for definitions of word meanings. This is hardly a novel approach, having been employed many times before in the literature (e.g., Feifel and Lorge 1950; Al-Issa 1969; Nelson 1978; Anglin 1984); but, in our own work we have placed a particular emphasis on a special class of word meanings that have not only many typical properties associated with them but also relatively clear definitions, such as "island," "uncle," and "advertisement." Informal pilot work in which we simply asked children what these words meant revealed patterns in rough accord with the past literature. There seemed to be a qualitative shift in the manner of definition, a shift that has been variously labeled: concrete to abstract, perceptual to conceptual, and holistic to analytic by earlier investigators. We interpreted it somewhat differently, however, largely as a consequence of the words that we were using. We construed it as a shift from a reliance on aspects of meaning that are typical of a category to a smaller number that seem closer to necessary and sufficient features.

This method of spontaneous definitions in its barest form is not workable, however. Many children decline to give definitions at all, or launch into tangential anecdotes triggered by the word in question. We decided to conduct more formal studies using a different paradigm and using a terminology common in the semantic memory literature: characteristic versus defining features of word meaning (Smith, Shoben, & Rips 1974).

If children were shifting in the manner suggested, this might result in a change from a reliance on characteristic features to more defining ones.

To assess our hypothesis, we gave the children two descriptions for each word studied. One of these described an object that had all the characteristic features of an object but lacked a few crucial defining features; by contrast, the other description did have the crucial defining features but also had several highly uncharacteristic ones. Thus, for the word *uncle,* one description (the high-characteristic/low-defining one) might describe a fellow who was not related to anyone in your family but was a big pal of your dad's and brought you presents on your birthday and at Christmas. The other description (the low-characteristic/high-defining one) might describe a two-year-old who was your Mom's brother. After each description we asked the children whether or not the thing described was a valid instance of the concept, and why. This technique tends to elicit more elaborate and consistent verbal responses from children, and the same developmental pattern is reliably found across a wide range of stimulus items and across studies. Children shifted in which description they regarded as describing a valid instance of the concept. Some typical crossover patterns are shown in Figure 7.1. There is a great deal more to be said about these developmental patterns, but the following points are most relevant to this chapter:

1. The shift occurs on a domain-by-domain basis.
2. It is not a shift from idiosyncratic defining features to more standard ones.
3. It does not reflect obvious changes in external input.
4. It occurs in cultures with no formal schooling and little exposure to Western thought and tradition.

Let me briefly elaborate on each of these:

1. If we take terms from different domains such as kinship terms, cooking terms, and tool terms, we find that the shifts tend to occur at roughly the same time for terms within domains and at different times for terms across domains, suggesting an important role of local knowledge in mediating the shift and arguing against the possibilities that it is either a general response strategy shift or that it reflects a general stage of cognitive development. If it was either of the emergence of a general strategy or a stage, the shift should occur at roughly similar times across all domains. (To suggest that decalage can explain the lags will not help; see Keil 1986b). These studies of domain-by-domain development also revealed something else that is important. Concepts do not develop in isolation but rather develop in a relational system with important interdependencies. These domain effects are one indication of an underlying

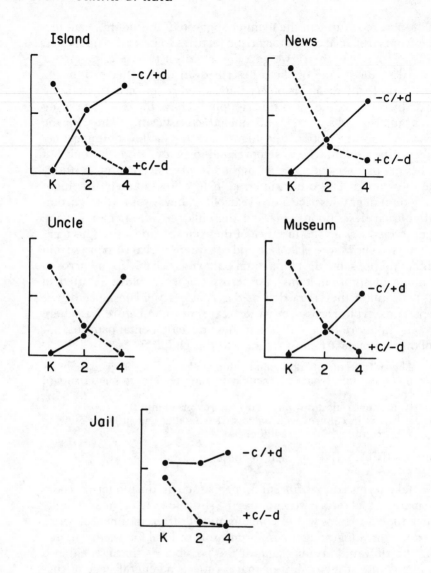

(Y-axis represents extent to which children judge story
to be valid instance of concept)

Figure 7.1. Adapted with permission of the Ablex Publishing Company.

theory or explanatory system that brings coherence to the domain, a point discussed further in a later section. In fact, a shift can conceivably occur several times at different ages for the same term, depending on which domains, or theories, are invoked either tacitly or explicitly.

2. The initial characteristic-to-defining study might be interpreted as showing that younger children simply treat different, more idiosyncratic, features as defining. Indeed, parents can tell many anecdotes to this effect, such as the child who insists that one must leave home to be on a vacation. To assess the prevalence of this alternative pattern, children were shown pictures of various situations in which the described object had three out of four highly characteristic features, but lacked the critical defining feature. Thus, we might have a pseudoisland (in fact a peninsula) with three out of the following four features: palm trees, buried treasures, sandy beach, and people in grass skirts.

For most of the items studied, younger children tend to judge such descriptions as being valid instances of the concept if any three of the four features are present, while older ones require the defining feature, in this case being surrounded by water on all four sides. Thus, the younger children usually do not differ from older ones because they have different, more idiosyncratic defining features. They do not seem to regard any single feature as essential but base their judgments on the degree to which a given instance has features typical of the category as a whole, as defined linguistically by some common label, nonlinguistically by a set of similarity relations, or both. Moreover, they usually treat the defining features, if they know them, as just more characteristic features with a status equal to other characteristic ones.

3. If one examines parental explanations of unfamiliar concepts to children their explanations do not change with the age of the child in such a way that more defining features are used with older children. The ratio of the two types of features is roughly the same throughout development as are the number of examples provided. It is equally important to note that parent's explanations change in other ways, and that judges can easily tell which ones were given to younger versus older children. Thus, it is not that the parents in our study are being excessively formal and simply treating younger and older children identically. These results suggest that the shift is not a consequence of changing patterns of input, or implicit criteria suggested by adults. It is a more endogenous process based on the child's increasing knowledge of the world.

4. It has frequently been suggested that tendencies to classify in a more analytic, defining way are a consequence of formal schooling or literacy, or of Western culture in general with its scientific/technical orientation.

However, a similar shift has been observed in at least one culture that does not have these properties. Based on work done by Sheila Jeyifous (1986) in Nigeria, we have strong indications that rural members of the Yoruba culture also show a characteristic-to-defining shift, providing that culturally appropriate stimuli are used. Nonliterate, unschooled children from highly traditional rural villages show just as strong a tendency to undergo the shift as do middle-class American children.

What do the characteristic-to-defining shift and the results of these subsequent studies mean? One clear conclusion is that as children learn more about certain categories, they change in what they emphasize as important features for specifying members of those categories. These changes do not seem explainable in terms of a simple gradual differentiation theory, in which more information of the same kind is continuously added and elaborated. Children change not only by acquiring new information but in terms of how they treat the information already at hand. They shift from a relatively even weighting of many features that co-occur frequently with a category to a heavy emphasis on just one or two primary features or fundamental organizing dimensions. At some point they seem to assume the presence of such dimensions and actively look for them.

It does not follow automatically from these developmental patterns that the shift is away from prototype-based or other probabilistic representations to a new sort of conceptual structure. For this reason, the term "characteristic-to-defining" shift is somewhat misleading. Perhaps representations at all ages never contain necessary and sufficient features, and perhaps features are always organized around prototypes. The developmental shift may simply indicate a change in the importance attached to the centrality of a feature. It is important to consider how simple probabilistic representations might model the shift because such considerations may provide some of the clearest insights into their limitations. Although there are several possible types of detailed models along these lines, only one is considered here. I suspect, however, that similar problems will arise across a broad range of such models.

Figure 7.2 shows one of the simplest ways in which this shift might be characterized. [NOTE: In this and many of the following discussions, it will seem as if it is being assumed that conceptual structures must be specified by constellations of features and certain classes of operations upon them. Closely parallel arguments can be made for exemplar-based or dimensional views (cf. Keil & Kelly in press) and the focus on features is primarily for expository reasons.] In this figure the concept, which is roughly the inner circle (whose boundaries may well be fuzzy) becomes more compact with increasing age, such that a decreasing number of

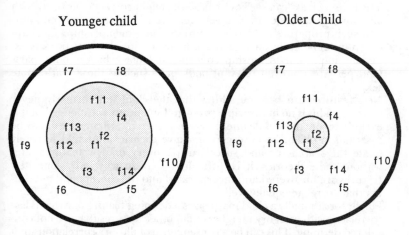

Figure 7.2. This illustration shows how prototype-based representations could be involved at all ages. The extent to which a feature is close to the center of the outer circle is the extent to which it is typical of members of the category. The inner circle represents the features that are normally used to determine category membership. The smaller the inner circle, the more important it is that only one feature be present.

features are likely to be referred to (again this may all be probabilistic); or, put differently, more importance is attached those features that are most central. The position of the features with respect to the outer circle represents the extent to which they co-occur with valid instances of the concept (i.e., labeled by adults), where those closest to the center of the circle most closely approximate a 1.0 correlation. If this characterization is accurate, the most central features (say, f1 and f2) are what are known as "defining features," while the others are characteristic. Such an account makes no reference to necessary-and-sufficient features and rigid all-or-none boundaries.

Figure 7.2 is not an adequate portrayal of the developmental phenomena for several reasons:

1. What seem to be equally typical co-occurring features are not treated as equal by older children in terms of how they influence judgments of category membership. Thus features f1 and f2 might both occur almost 100 percent of the time with known instances, yet only f1 may guide category judgments for older children. For example, both "is friends with your mom or dad" and "is your dad's or mom's brother" may correlate equally highly for many children with instances of "uncle." That is, for many children, all observed uncles might well be friends with one of the two parents. But only the younger children seem to regard the friend feature as important to deciding about category membership. A similar question arises for the younger children in that

a feature such as "can see" or "has teeth" might correlate perfectly with all known instances of uncles, yet even the youngest of children know that such properties are irrelevant to deciding membership. They apparently know early on that the domain of social interactions is especially important to kinship concepts and not arbitrary body parts (and perhaps not even relevant body parts such as those that denote sex).

2. New features can become added that the child was formerly never aware of. This is no in principle problem for a prototype model, but it is excluded from the simple one shown in Figure 7.2. In practice it may be a serious problem because certain naive theories the child has may guide the search for and successful discovery of new features, and without these theories, it is difficult to explain why only some new features are uncovered and incorporated into the concept and not others that correlate equally well.

3. Finally, occasionally a child may use as a defining feature one that is less correlated with category members than other features that are not considered defining. This can be a consequence of illusory correlations that fall out of imperfect theories about the world (Murphy & Medin 1985).

There are two ways in which one might modify the model to account for objection 1, one of which is intuitively plausible but does not seem to fit the data, the other of which could fit the data but does not make much intuitive sense. Figure 7.3 shows two variants of the first approach, which assumes that the child's intuitive typicality distributions change with increasing age. Figure 7.3a has the same overall distribution of features but shows the centrality of specific ones as changing with age. Figure 7.3b has both the centrality of specific features changing as well as the degree to which the features as a whole are clustered toward the center; in this way sampling of the feature space need not change.

The problem with both versions of this approach is that they do not seem to capture the facts. While it is occasionally true that, with more experience, the relative centrality of two features may change, this is usually not the case. An adult might easily judge it to be highly typical of uncles that they are friends of one of the two parents or that they can see and have teeth, but would nonetheless not weigh such features much in deciding who was an uncle.

Alternatively, one could have roughly the same typicality distributions at all ages, but different ways in which the distributions are sampled, where the change is not the sensible symmetrically shrinking circle, but rather a movement to a seemingly aribitrary and unmotivated sampling, as shown in Figure 7.4a. To be more accurate, one should also model the addition of new features, as shown in Figure 7.4b, which occurs in conjunction with the change in sampling pattern. This model would of course work, but it seems unmotivated, and provides a rather bizarre version of the prototype model for adult concepts wherein only some of

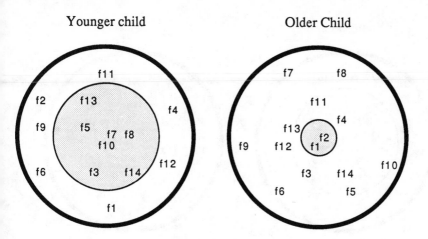

Figure 3a

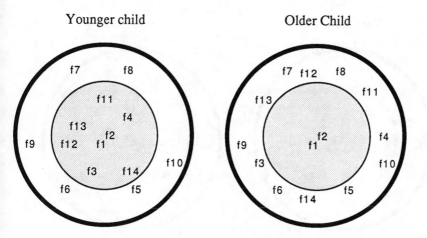

Figure 3b

Figure 7.3. In Figure 3a note how the centrality of the features changes as well as the degree to which centrality is important to judgments of category membership. In Figure 3b the importance of centrality does not change, but rather the typicality distribution of features becomes less centralized.

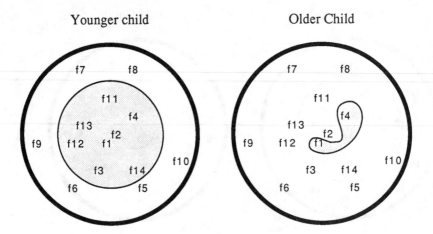

Figure 4a

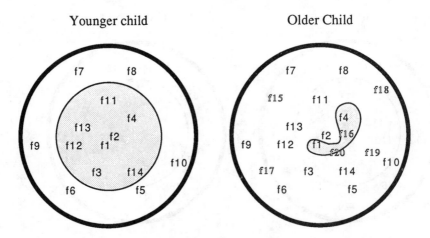

Figure 4b

Figure 7.4. In Figure 4a the typicality distribution of features stays much the same; the change is from a symmetrical assessment of the more central features to a seemingly arbitrary one. In Figure 4b the developmental change to a seemingly arbitrary sampling of the most central features is supplemented by the addition of new features.

the most typical features are involved in determining membership, and there is no principled, objective way of telling which ones.

The point of all this is rather simple. The developmental patterns of the characteristic-to-defining shift do not require abandonment of category fuzziness or probabilistic representations. It is also likely that prototype abstraction is one of the most pervasive general learning procedures and methods of representation available to us. Such representations in themselves, however, cannot explain the details of the shift in any but the most arbitrary ad hoc fashion. Typicality, or patterns of correlation among features, or similarity between exemplars, cannot be used to predict which features will become the "defining" ones. It might be argued that prototype theory never pretended to say which features would be incorporated into a concept, but only that, given the appropriate set of features and their typicality distributions, one could then describe the resulting concept. Setting aside the issue of whether the initial feature selection is not doing most of the interesting work, this approach still cannot explain illusory correlations or why, for the same given set of features and typicality distributions, differing conceptual structures are extracted by younger and older children.

Extending the examples: natural kinds and artifacts

The studies on the characteristic-to-defining shift suggest that there are at least some cases where the developmental patterns are not easily captured by an account that is merely based on typicality distributions of features without also having an ad hoc account of how features are selected and represented. This account seems to fare better with younger children, but becomes less adequate as the child learns more about each conceptual domain. It might be argued, however, that such problems are relatively unusual and pertain only to terms that have definitionlike components agreed upon by a language community. The terms in the characteristic/defining studies were carefully selected to be of this sort. They had both relatively clean definitions and clusters of highly salient characteristic features; in general, they belonged to a special subclass of the lexicon sometimes known as "nominal kinds." It is therefore important to see what happens in the acquisition of terms for which there are no simple approximations of necessary-and-sufficient features, the so-called "natural kinds."

One of the major contributions of philosophers of language in the last fifteen or so years, most notably from Putnam (1975) and Kripke (1972), has been the demonstration that no simple definitions are possible for picking out most natural kinds. Take any animal concept, for example, and try to give a list of necessary-and-sufficient conditions for determining membership, and almost invariably you will fail. These philosophical demonstrations have been widely interpreted in the psychological literature as demonstrating the prototype-based nature of natural-kind concepts, and indeed Putnam has frequently talked about the stereotypes associated with concepts in a way that sounds like prototypes. If prototypes were fully adequate for natural kinds, there could be nothing like the characteristic-to-defining shift because even adult representations would consist solely of characteristic features.

In fact, however, neither Putnam nor Kripke believes that prototypes exhaust the meaning of natural-kind concepts; they argue that a causal chain is also crucial to the fixation of reference. It is not necessary here to go into the details of their accounts. It suffices that there may be something besides prototypes at work. In our own studies we have looked for an underlying causal structure in natural kinds, and have uncovered a shift analogous to the one that occurs for terms with clear definitions. An important part of our research program has been to contrast natural kinds with artifacts, since they appear to have rather different underlying structures.

Schwartz (1977) discusses some differences in the sorts of natural changes that artifacts and natural kinds are likely to undergo. We have focused instead on the different ways in which discoveries and transformations are deemed relevant to the identities of artifacts versus natural kinds. Thus, when a scientist discovers something about the molecular structure of a plant, we are usually willing to agree that it might not be the sort of plant it appears to be, but rather is a member of a different category because of something that has been discovered about its molecular structure. For artifacts, however, discoveries about molecular or chemical structure are mostly considered irrelevant. We would not be convinced that a chair is not really a chair but a Windsurfer because it is made not out of wood as it appears to be but out of the same plastic as Windsurfers are made of. Generally such things do not matter much to the identities of artifacts, but they may be crucial for natural kinds. We tend to assume that most artifacts do not have a rich underlying structure that is closer to their "essence." If the discovery was about the function intended by the artifact's creator, we might be more inclined to reevaluate the identity. Thus, if we are told that some eccentric naval architect had designed this object to be a very special-purpose Windsurfer, we might (given appropriate degrees of confidence in the veracity of such information) be convinced that it really is a Windsurfer and only seems to be a chair.

Similarly, the ways in which transformations do and do not change identity differs for natural kinds and artifacts. In general, if one changes the salient functional and perceptual features of an object into those of another category, if it is an artifact, it will be judged to have changed identity, whereas if it is a natural kind, it will not. Thus if one takes a chair and carefully glues on leg extensions and saws off the back, most adults say that you have now turned it into a stool. By contrast, if one takes a raccoon, dyes its fur appropriately, fluffs up its tail, sews a smelly sack inside, and even trains it to secrete the contents when alarmed, most adults will say that you still have a raccoon, albeit a strange one that looks and acts just like a skunk.

We have conducted developmental studies that exploit both of these ways of contrasting artifacts and natural kinds. The artifact/natural-kind contrast is a central part of these studies because it allows us to tell whether any shifts are merely general strategy shifts or reflections of something specific to the child's changing concepts of natural kinds. Our findings are quite consistent across both methods and different subject groups, and are illustrated in Figure 7.5.

There clearly is a developmental shift for natural kinds and not for artifacts. (There is an analogous shift for artifacts involving functions and intentions; but in this study the artifacts serve only as controls against a general strategy explanation of the results.) We have found a similar shift with the Yoruba, although what they shift to may be some-what different in the details, as we shall see.

What is changing here developmentally, and what relevance does it have for understanding the nature of categorical structure in both adults and children? As in the case for the characteristic/defining (c/d) studies it is useful to start by assuming that at all ages the concepts are repre-sented by constellations of features arranged in a typicality space and to explore how such a model would attempt to describe the developmental patterns.

One might again posit the model in Figure 7.2, the first one proposed for the characteristic-to-defining data, wherein development consists of a gradually shrinking internal circle of features that are considered important in judgments of identity. Under this account, the older chil-dren and adults, while using fewer features, should still be basing their judgments on the most typical features. They are not doing so, however. For example, with many of the operations stories virtually every salient typical feature (i.e., all those features that would be listed by an adult who was asked to supply all the typical distinguishing properties of an animal) is changed, and yet the identity is judged to remain constant. Moreover, when the subjects are asked to justify their responses, they usually do not refer to another typical feature, but instead state that such things do not really matter because something more fundamental is preserved. When asked what this preserved element is, subjects give a variety of responses, ranging from internal organs to DNA. It might well

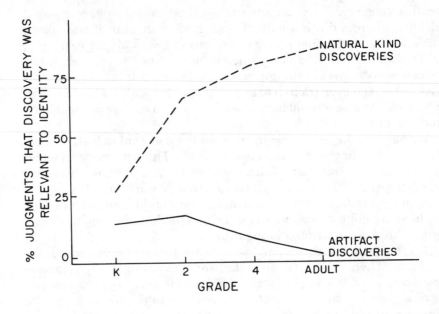

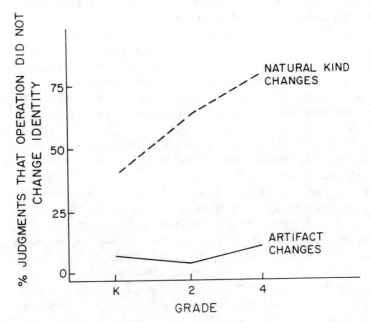

Figure 7.5. Adapted with permission of the Ablex Publishing Company.

be that their theories of internal structure, for example, about internal organs and DNA are prototypelike or probabilistic in structure; but such things are not mentioned if adults are asked to list typical properties of various animals. In fact, many subjects will confess to not having any idea what internal factors would differentiate a skunk from a raccoon, or a horse from a zebra, but will nonetheless insist that there are such factors and that members of the relevant scientific community would know them or could know them.

It is difficult to describe this pattern of responses in terms of sets of discrete features, as many subjects may not have any specific ones in mind. Rather it is a belief in biological essence that seems to grow out of a naive theory of natural kinds that is driving their intuitions. It seems as if there is a shift from younger children being phenomenologists to older ones and adults being essentialists.

One can modify the prototype models, as was done for the characteristic-to-defining studies, to include the addition of new features and the increasingly arbitrary sampling of those features, as was shown in Figure 7.4b; but, again, such a move seems arbitrary and unmotivated. An additional difficulty with natural kinds is in specifying what those new features are no matter how they are represented, when frequently all that is stated is a belief that they exist.

One common thread across most of our studies, including those in Nigeria, is that this underlying essence frequently involves theories about the origins of the natural kind. The most immediate origin for an animal is who its parents are, and this was often asked for as additional information. More elaborate origins information make reference to how the species as a whole came into being, be it either through evolution, the creationism of Western religion, or the elaborate mythologies of the Yoruba. This causal path, leading back to origin, was often invoked as the reason why identity was preserved across the various transformations we employed.

All cultures, in their attempts to explain the physical world, develop theories about where natural things come from. (They do not do this so much for artifacts because it is usually clear that they came from some person's idea and intention.) These theories do more than explain origins, however. They provide some feeling about the essence of a natural kind – a feeling that is strong enough to override many highly salient characteristic features. Incidentally, these beliefs about essence may well be erroneous or illusory. Mayr (1982) and others have noted that a kind of irrational essentialism has often impeded the growth of biological thought, in particular, evolutionary theory.

Why do the younger children fail to refer to origins or other essentialist aspects when asked about the transformed objects? Are they unrepenting phenomenologists hopelessly bound to simply compute the most typical properties that cluster about a class of things? As was the case for the characteristic-to-defining shift, there is good reason to believe that even young children will go beyond such completely domain-general forms of representation. Presumably they fail to see identity preserved in the tasks described because they have not yet learned enough about biological kinds, for example, to know what things are important for distinguishing one animal or plant from another. But if an even grosser distinction is tested, say, not that between two animals, but between an animal and a plant or an animal and an artifact, then perhaps even younger children have primitive theories that they can use to override characteristic features. To test this we had operations that changed all the characteristic features of a porcupine, for example, into those of a cactus, and then asked the children about the resulting product. Similarly, a toy bird might acquire all the characteristic features of a real bird.

While almost all kindergartners in our earlier studies judged animal/animal or plant/plant transformations to have changed identity, a majority of them claimed that identity was preserved for these broader categorical changes, thus demonstrating that they are not hopelessly bound to characteristic features and will use theories to guide their judgments.

The crucial point to keep in mind in these studies is that in all cases we transformed virtually all the distinguishing typical features of one category into those of another. The transformed chair, raccoon, and porcupine have all the normally listed characteristic features of stools, skunks, and cacti, respectively, so that the end-state description corresponds to the supposed prototype for each category. But children come to defy such information for all the natural-kind transformations, and do so from an early age for those that cross ontological categories. Thus, by merely looking at the information captured in typicality distributions, we are unable to explain the shifts that occur.

In follow-up work we have discovered that the distinctions between broad categories such as plants, animals, and artifacts depend heavily on knowledge of origins, and even preschoolers know that there are different types of typical origins for artifacts and natural kinds. These differences in origins for artifacts and natural kinds, however, are vastly more apparent than those that distinguish two kinds of animals, for example.

Although the studies on natural kinds and the c/d shift suggest the limits of looking only at typicality distributions, they still leave us with the question of what the children do come to learn and how this knowledge influences their representations. In the case of natural kinds, is our concept of "bird" the entire body of scientific knowledge that can ever be gathered about birds? If not, where do we draw the line in deciding what is part of the concept? Equally important is the question of whether the end-state representations are all of the same type for all conceptual domains, or whether there is a gradual divergence in representational types with increasing knowledge and expertise. In the next section I will show how consideration of the social context in which concepts are used, or their ecology, gives us some idea of where the lines might be drawn and why different sorts of concepts might have different types of internal structures for adults.

The social and ecological nature of categories and concepts

Discussions of categories and concepts often fail to consider what we do with them. The social aspects of these uses, that is, how concepts and categories are used in successful interaction between individuals, suggest ways in which concepts can go beyond simple prototype formats and why different category types, such as nominal and natural kinds, might have different structures.

Both nominal and natural-kind terms have their meanings strongly influenced by the social contexts in which they are involved: although in quite different ways. For nominal kinds, such as those terms used in the characteristic-to-defining shift studies, their meanings are often related to social conventions or other forms of consensual agreement between individuals. For example, those terms that tend to have the clearest definitions are usually those that have evolved in response to some frequent mode of human interaction where precision is important, be it financial terms (such as "tax," "interest," "mortgage"), kinship terms, or terms referring to rules of a game (e.g., "foul ball"). Terms that arise out of social conventions generally have the clearest definitions, whereas those that arise out of moral laws can be more fuzzy. This may be because moral laws share more properties with natural kinds, as we shall see.

Artifacts are a related case. If we look at objects themselves, and only the objects, our understanding of their meaning is incomplete and must rely on the information in their characteristic features. If, however, we are privy to information about who built them and why, our understanding may change considerably. Knowing the social context, in particular the intentions of the builder, is a crucial aspect of knowing what an artifact is. Artifacts and nominal-kind terms are similar types of concepts in that both must be created deliberately by their users. An anthill would not be an artifact by this account, but rather a natural kind, because intentions of the sort that we have been talking about are not involved when ants build a hill. This holds for humans as well. If I had randomly tossed garbage out my window for a year, and by some chance it had piled into a beautiful structure without my knowing it, one would be reluctant to call it a sculpture no matter how aesthetically beautiful or moving. Nominal kinds share this property with artifacts of being intentionally created; they tend, however, to be more abstract social creations designed to facilitate some mode of interaction.

There are unclear cases with all of these distinctions such as hunting dogs that are bred intentionally (like artifacts) but which are clearly natural kinds, at least as far as they are dogs. To a certain extent this hybrid nature exists for all artifacts because ultimately they must be made out of natural kinds, be they minerals, plants, or animals; it is just more blatant with genetic engineering. Other unclear cases involve semi-intentional animals and their "artifacts" (holes dug by dogs for bones, and so on). A different sort of peculiar case is natural metamorphoses such as caterpillar into butterfly. Why is it no longer a caterpillar if transformations supposedly do not change the identity of natural kinds? It may be because the transformation itself is governed by various natural laws and forces that then set up the new natural kind. Natural transformations are in fact very common, but are not so immediately obvious (e.g., plants are transformed via digestion into animal tissue). These unclear cases, among many others, point out the subtleties that underlie the artifact/natural-kind distinction; but they should not be construed as casting doubt on the usefulness of the distinction for a great many salient cases.

Human intentions often provide definitionlike qualities to terms. Conventions require intentional components to be considered as such. Lewis (1970) suggests that conventions arise when a group of people are confronted with coordination problems, that is, situations in which they need to coordinate activity with each other (e.g., how to drive about on the roads without crashing into everyone else). They decide to adopt a convention to solve the problem (e.g., everyone drives on the right). Moral laws are somewhat fuzzier just because people frequently do not decide to create them but rather to codify preexisting ones. As Lockhart (1980) points out, conventions are arbitrary, whereas moral laws are not; there are not equally good alternatives that people merely need to agree upon. Presumably this is because moral laws reflect something about universal nonconsensual patterns of human behavior, which are more like natural kinds. But even for moral terms such as "lie" there can be a developmental shift toward emphasizing the role of intention.

Why should intentions make meanings more definitionlike? One possibility is that people tend to talk and think about intentions in an all-or-none way. Either you intended x or you didn't. People's real intentions may well be much less clear, but they may tend to simplify them and remember them in a black-and-white manner. If so, then to the extent that a term makes use of intentions in its meaning, it will be more definitionlike. Thus, our understanding of nominal-kind terms is inescapably linked to our knowledge of the greater social context in which those terms are used, in particular our knowledge of people's intentions in creating and using them.

The need to share conceptual knowledge in communication also places constraints on concepts, constraints that will often push the conceptual structure toward a more analytic form that defies typicality distributions. People attempt to reach a common ground or consensus by tacitly agreeing on certain common values or dimensions for organizing the concepts involved. In doing so, they construct and emphasize aspects of meaning as more defining. Tarr (1984; see also Freyd, 1983) has obtained some preliminary data supporting this notion. Subjects involved in a communicative task involving integral and separable dimensions of a perceptual array tended to treat the stimuli more separably than those who did not have the communicative demand put upon them. (For links between the integral/separable distinction and the c/d shift, see Keil and Kelly, in press.) Freyd (1983) calls this a shareability constraint. This effect is compatible with other research in developmental and social psychology, showing that the appropriate communicative demands can shift a subject's concepts toward a more analytic structure (e.g., Krauss, ViveKanthan, & Weinheimer 1968).

In short, with nominal kinds and artifacts, knowledge of the social context in which they are embedded helps us to understand why there is a tendency to emphasize just a few dimensions or features to a greater extent than is warranted by consideration of factors such as typicality and similarity. This is especially true in those cases where the young children seem to know all the features that adults know (e.g., "island"), but use them differently. This is not the only reason why children might come to focus on just a few dimensions as organizing the domain. A second equally, if not more, important reason has to do with the child's increasing understanding of a set of theoretically meaningful principles for organizing that domain.

With natural-kind terms, the role of the social context is quite different. Few natural-kind terms rely on reference to human intentions, conventions, and the like. We do not create their meanings in the ways that we do for the nominal kinds as much as we discover them. Nonetheless, the philosophical literature and the studies described above both suggest an important social role having to do with division of linguistic labor. Putnam suggested that users of many natural-kind terms usually do not personally have much of the scientific knowledge that goes beyond the

publicly available stereotype. They do, however, rely upon the posses-
sion of that knowledge by a group of experts. Their knowledge of terms
and their beliefs in essence and so on rely on assumptions about the
social infrastructure they inhabit and use, that is, people have tacitly
agreed to divide up bodies of expertise, and the nonexperts need know
only ways of access to that knowledge (i.e., what domain to access and
when that access is needed).

The division of linguistic labor notion put forth by philosophers corresponds to a phenomenon known in the anthropological literature as
"ownership of knowledge" (cf. Giles 1977), which is the idea that members of a culture tend to parcel out the various domains of technical
knowledge to subgroups who become the recognized proprietors of that
knowledge. Consequently, one's concept is not just what one knows and
can immediately perceive but is also the network of relations one has to
the various groups of experts.

The different relations of natural and nominal-kind terms to the social context result in different end-state representations. The intentional
component in nominal kinds, the influence of conventions, and the communicative demands all push the end-state structure toward one that has
a definitionlike structure. For natural kinds, such a pressure is much less
strong, partly because people realize that such things are not created and
therefore are not modifiable by convention or fiat. Here the social context plays a different role, in that it provides a way of using and understanding natural-kind terms that takes into account relevant scientific
knowledge, but does not require each language user to completely know
it.

Theories, explanations, and concepts

The problem still remains of explaining the development of an uneven
sampling of the feature space shown in Figure 7.4. With increasing
knowledge people come to reject mere collections of the most typical
features as being adequate to specify a concept. I have suggested that
part of the basis for this rejection is an increasing emphasis on a special
class of features relating to the social context in which those concepts are
embedded. But while such considerations help us understand something
of what distinguishes nominal from natural kinds and why definitionlike
components may exist, they do not tell us why some features, and correlations among features, are selected over others. Above and beyond
the tendencies of social context to provide ways of going beyond pure
prototype representations, we need something else to explain the particular conceptual structures that children come to acquire.

Some predispositions to select certain constellations of features over others are undoubtedly explainable in terms of the properties of the sensory systems and what sorts of information they are able to pick up efficiently. I have argued elsewhere (Keil 1981) that a priori cognitive constraints also result in predispositions to learn certain correlations over others. But what about the developmental shifts that are observed? They are not likely to be explained in terms of changing sensory systems or changing a priori constraints, but rather by considering the knowledge and theories acquired by the child. These theories may rely on typicality structure in their own internal structure and have no necessary-and-sufficient features, but they also guide how the feature space is sampled and explored.

This idea of theories and prior knowledge guiding the acquisition of concepts is not a new one and is gaining increasing attention from both the developmental literature (Carey 1986) and adult work (Murphy & Medin 1985). At a sufficiently general level it has to be true; what you know in a particular domain will influence how you structure information in that domain and collect new information. More important, however, theories remind us of the limitations of prototypes, which are surprisingly atheoretical on their own (Keil 1986a). Prototypes merely represent correlated properties, they offer no explanation of the reasons for those correlations (e.g., why the prototypical features of birds, such as beaks, feathers, and eggs, tend to co-occur); nor do they tell us why some particular correlations and not others are important. This other information comes from our theories about how things work and about their origins. With artifacts and nominal kinds the origins involve knowledge of human intentions, with natural kinds the origins refer to knowledge of evolution or geology, or whatever.

It is clear in the transcripts from our own studies that our subjects frequently justify preservation of identity despite an operation by referring to a theory about origins and claim that origins are closer to the essence. Not surprisingly, young children's theories are vaguer and more global than those of older ones and adults, and consequently, they are not as constrained in picking out certain correlations over others. Nonetheless they are constrained to a certain extent as can be seen both from their use of simple ontological categories in the natural-kind studies and their tendency to incorrectly use theories such as that kinship terms are organized around social attributes more than biological ones. Carey (1986) specifically argues that biological theories emerge much later than social/psychological ones and thus would not be available to these children.

The influence of theories on conceptual structure need not imply anything about the degree to which those theories themselves or for that matter any part of conceptual structure requires necessary and sufficient features. While theories may tend to simplify their laws into a form that is more like defining attributes (see also Murphy & Medin 1985), much as may happen for intentions, this does not have to happen. Theories do make it impossible, however, to talk about the construction of concepts solely on the basis of probabilistic distributions of properties in the world.

The role of theories is also nicely demonstrated in the domain-by-domain examples of shifts. Thus, when children shift away from characteristic features for one kinship term, they tend to do so at the same time for all others. They have not just learned the meaning of one term, they have gained an insight into what the important principles are for organizing that domain as a whole, principles that unite the domain as a coherent whole.

It is evident that some of the most important future work on the nature of concepts and categories must focus on the sorts of theories that emerge in children and how these theories come to influence the structure of the concepts that they embrace.

Use, belief, and category structure

Surely one issue arising out of this emphasis on theories concerns what relevance they have to our daily use of concepts. I have already suggested that, for many natural kinds, any one individual's knowledge of the underlying scientific theory may be very sketchy. How much do we go beyond prototypes in talking about and thinking about our concepts? We may always go beyond them to a certain extent, but exactly how much may vary on a case-by-case basis?

There are an indefinitely large number of theoretical principles from various domains that could potentially relate to most concepts, but we surely do not access all of them with each usage. We probably do access a certain minimum in all cases to make the use of the concept comprehensible. This minimum may be the ontological type for every concept (e.g., whether it is about a plant, an animal, an event). This forms a kind of skeletal framework that influences categorization in even the youngest of children. Context will determine how much beyond that level we will want to go and are capable of going, but I suspect the ontological level represents a requisite competency required to understand and use natural language terms.

What role then do prototypes and other sorts of domain-general probabilistic representations play? None of the dichotomies listed at the beginning of this chapter may be fully appropriate in that typically effects and prototypes may not be segregable to just one level of representation or one stage in a sequence of processing. It may be just the opposite; prototypes may represent one of the most pervasive ways we have of acquiring and organizing knowledge, especially when we are relatively ignorant. Not only do you see strong typicality effects and prototypes in young children but probably also in adults whenever our theories run dry. My biological theories about birds might suggest that I use features such as carnivorous, aquatic, and nocturnal to sort them; but beyond a small set of such theoretically motivated principles I may well use just featural typicality and perceptual similarity among exemplars to segregate grouses from partridges, for example.

Theories tell us what domains of features and what relations among features are likely to be important, but if the domains are rich enough in terms of properties and relations (e.g., most natural kinds), within each domain you may see typicality effects emerging as the theory can no longer suggest principles to distinguish between finer and finer subcategories. In some cases one may believe that there are further theoretical principles that distinguish subcategories but will rely on prototypes as a kind of default option. In other cases, one may believe that the only meaningful way to further subcategorize is to use prototypes, such as sorting a group of animals that are all of the same subspecies. Prototypes are an intrinsic part of conceptual structure but are more a vehicle of representation than an explanation of conceptual structure itself. They are always constrained as to their structure by a priori perceptual and cognitive constraints as well as by acquired knowledge. They are at their purest form (i.e., require the least ad hoc accounts of how the feature space is sampled) when dealing with arbitrary meaningless information in unfamiliar contexts.

Prototype abstraction falls prey to the same problems as induction (Keil 1981) and must be supplemented by constraints for learning to succeed and for people to share similar enough concepts to be able to communicate. Its pervasiveness as a mechanism of concept formation does not entail that it will be adequate to explain conceptual structure; it is only part of the story. People do not simply record how often certain regularities occur in the world, they try to explain them by positing underlying mechanisms and theories of origins. These theories of mechanism and origin have a powerful effect on how any concepts within that theoretical domain are structured.

It may well be that we tend to access more of the sort of information that corresponds to a pure prototype in speeded identification tasks or when we know very little about a concept. But such demonstrations do not necessarily show that prototypes are only at one level of conceptual representation. Instead they may be interpreted as supporting the view that prototypes are one of the most basic and universal methods of processing and representation and are therefore frequently the first thing accessed in such tasks.

Conclusions

Even the youngest of children have primitive theories about the world and thus will be biased in terms of what regularities they focus on and learn. Nonetheless, because some of these theories are so basic and broad we may often presuppose them in observing children and thereby assume that their concepts are prototypes based purely on typicality distributions of objectively specifiable features. Although this assumption goes too far, it does seem to be true that, with increasing knowledge, children's concepts become less and less derivable from simple typicality distributions, or similarity ratings, or any other "objective" probabilistic measure of the feature space. Much of development may consist of a gradual divergence of representational types away from those that are relatively uniform and largely describable in terms of prototype structure to those that reflect more closely the various theories we have about the different patterns of regularity in the world. Thus, the laws and principles that govern entities in one domain (e.g., animals) may be very different in content and structure from those in others (e.g., metals); and as children come to better understand each set of regularities and develop theories about them, their concepts will correspondingly become more and more different not only from the early prototype-heavy formats but also from other developing concepts in different domains. Under this account much of development consists of a movement away form a homogeneous, explanatorily weak set of conceptual structures to a heterogeneous, explanatorily rich set that form better and better fits with certain parts of our world.

NOTE

The research reported herein was supported by NSF grants BNS-81-02655 and BNS-83-18076 to the author. Much of this paper was prepared while the author was a Fellow at the Center for Advanced Study in the Behavioral Sciences. I am grateful for financial support while at the Center provided by the John D. and Catherine T. MacArthur Foundation, the Alfred P. Sloan Foundation, and the Exxon Education Foundation.

REFERENCES

Al-Issa, I. (1969). The development of word definitions in children. *Journal of Genetic Psychology, 114,* 25–28.

Anglin, J. M. (1984). The child's expressible knowledge of word concepts: What preschoolers can say about the meanings of some nouns and verbs. In K. E. Nelson (Ed.), *Children's language* (Vol. 5). Hillsdale, NJ: Erlbaum.

Armstrong, S., Gleitman, L., & Gleitman, H. (1983). What some concepts might not be. *Cognition, 13,* 263–308.

Carey, S. (1986). *Conceptual change in children.* Cambridge, MA: Bradford Books.

Feifel, H., & Lorge, I. (1950). Qualitative differences in the vocabulary responses of children. *Journal of Educational Psychology, 41,* 1–18.

Freyd, J. J. (1983). Shareability: The social psychology of epistemology. *Cognitive Science, 7,* 191–210.

Giles, H. (Ed.) (1977). *Language, ethnicity, and intergroup relations.* New York: Academic Press.

Jeyifous, S. (1986). Antimodemo: Semantic and conceptual development among the Yoruba. Unpublished doctoral dissertation, Cornell University, Ithaca, NY.

Keil, F. C. (1981). Constraints on knowledge and cognitive development. *Psychological Review, 88,* 197–227.

(1986a). The acquisition of natural kind and artifact terms. In W. Demopoulos & A. Marras (Eds.), *Language learning and concept acquisition.* Norwood, NJ: Ablex.

(1986b). On the structure-dependent nature of stages of cognitive development. In I. Levin (Ed.), *Stage and structure.* Norwood, NJ: Ablex.

Keil, F. C., & Kelly, M. (in press). Developmental changes in category structure. In S. Harnad (Ed.), *Categorical perception.* New York: Cambridge University Press.

Krauss, R. M., ViveKanthan, P. S., & Weinheimer, S. (1968). "Inner speech" and "external speech." *Journal of Personality and Social Psychology, 9,* 295–300.

Kripke, S. (1972). Naming and necessity. In D. Davidson & G. Harman (Eds.), *Semantics of natural language.* Doedrecht, Holland: Reidel.

Lewis, D. (1970). *Convention.* Cambridge, MA: Harvard University Press.

Lockhart, K. (1980). *The development of knowledge about uniformities in the environment: A comparative analysis of the child's understanding of social, moral, and physical rules.* Unpublished doctoral dissertation, University of Pennsylvania, Philadelphia.

Mayr, E. (1982). *The growth of biological thought.* Cambridge, MA: Harvard University Press.

Murphy, G., & Medin, D. (1985). Conceptual coherence and category structure. *Psychological Review, 42,* 289–316.

Nelson, K. (1978). Semantic development and the development of semantic memory. In K. E. Nelson (Ed.), *Children's language* (Vol. 1). New York: Gardner Press.

Osherson, D., & Smith, E. (1981). On the adequacy of prototype theory as a theory of concepts. *Cognition, 9,* 35–68.

Putnam, H. (1975). The meaning of meaning. In K. Gunderson (Ed.), *Language, mind and knowledge. Minnesota Studies in the Philosophy of Science* (Vol. 7). Minneapolis: University of Minnesota Press.

Rey, G. (1983). Concepts and stereotypes. *Cognition, 15,* 237–262.

Rosch, E. (1975). Cognitive representations of semantic categories. *Journal of Experimental Psychology: General, 104,* 192–233.

Rosch, E., & Mervis, C. B. (1975). Family resemblance studies in the internal structure of categories. *Cognitive Psychology, 7,* 573–605.

Rosch, E. H., Simpson, C., & Miller, R. S. (1976). Structural bases of typicality effects. *Journal of Experimental Psychology: Human Perception and Performance,* 2, 491–502.

Smith, E. E., & Medin, D. L. (1981). *Categories and Concepts.* Cambridge, MA: Harvard University Press.

Smith, E. E., Shoben, E. J., & Rips, L. J. (1974). Structure and process in semantic memory: A featural model for semantic decisions. *Psychological Review,* 81, 214–241.

Schwartz, S. P. (1977). *Naming, necessity, and natural kinds.* Ithaca, NY: Cornell University Press.

Tarr, M. (1984). Shareability: Constraints on the sharing of knowledge. Unpublished Bachelor's thesis, Cornell University.

8

Child-basic object categories and early lexical development

CAROLYN B. MERVIS

When children first begin to talk, some of the names they apply to objects are not quite right. Swans may be called "duckie," tigers "kitty," vases "cup," magazines "book," boots "shoe," and so forth (e.g., Anglin 1983; Mervis & Canada 1983; Nelson, Rescorla, Gruendel, & Benedict 1978; Rescorla 1981). These are not simply production errors; in most cases, parallel errors occur in comprehension (Mervis & Canada 1983). These differences between the adult and child lexicons provide an excellent challenge for theories of lexical development. An adequate theory should be able to explain why such differences consistently occur and how these differences eventually disappear; that is, how the extension of a word for a child comes to correspond to the extension of that word for an adult. Ideally, a theory should be able to predict when these differences will appear and disappear, rather than accounting for them post hoc.

Theories of lexical development have important implications for theories of category development. Almost all concrete nouns, for example, are labels for categories of objects. Thus, measures of word comprehension and production provide a direct indication of the extension of the category corresponding to the word, as well as a basis for inferences concerning the intension of the category. In this chapter, I describe part of a new theory of lexical development. I will argue that membership in young children's categories, including deviations from adult categories, can be predicted based on the same principles that have been used to predict categorization by older children and adults. I will further argue that, in many cases, children choose to attend to or emphasize different attributes from adults, due to limited experience or lack of knowledge of culturally appropriate functions and their correlated form attributes. In such cases, children will form categories that are not isomorphic to adult categories, even though young children's beliefs concerning the basis for initial category formation are based on the same principles as adults' beliefs. I will claim that the evolution of children's early categories is dependent on the child realizing that, for particular objects, attributes

201

that he or she had not attended to previously are in fact important, and that a different categorization scheme is therefore equally or more plausible than the child's earlier scheme. My emphasis will be on the role of the child's own cognitive structures, including his or her beliefs concerning the basis for category formation, in the formation and evolution of his or her initial categories. I will also discuss the role played by adults in determining which categories the child could potentially form and in how accurate these categories will be. I will also discuss the role of adults in the evolution of a child's categories: The manner in which the adult introduces new vocabulary often determines whether or not category evolution will begin. In support of this theory, I will present data from an ongoing diary study of my son Ari's early lexical development and data from a longitudinal study of early lexical development by both normally developing children and children with Down syndrome.

Child-basic categories: Initial composition

Children's initial categories are basic-level categories. This seems reasonable, because as Rosch and I have argued previously (Rosch, Mervis, Gray, Johnson, & Boyes-Braem 1976), categories at the basic level are more fundamental psychologically than categories at other taxonomic levels. For example, *chair* (a basic-level category) is more fundamental than either *kitchen chair* (a subordinate category) or *furniture* (a superordinate category). Categories at the basic level "stand out" as categories. These categories are based on large clusters of (subjectively) correlated attributes that overlap very little from category to category. In our world, these basic-level categories are the most general categories whose members share similar overall shapes (or similar parts in particular configurations; Tversky & Hemenway 1984) and similar functions or characteristic actions. Recent research has indicated that two-year-olds can form basic-level categories easily, while formation of superordinate and subordinate categories is considerably more difficult (Daehler, Lonardo, & Bukatko 1979; Mervis & Crisafi 1982).

But children's initial basic-level categories often will not correspond to the adult-basic category labeled by the same word. Such differences are to be expected; only the principles governing the determination of basic-level categories were predicted to be universal (Dougherty, 1978; Rosch et al. 1976). The actual categories formed on the basis of these principles will vary because different groups notice or emphasize different attributes of the same object as a function of different experiences or different degrees of expertise. Very young children often do not share adults' knowledge of culturally appropriate functions of objects and the correlated form attributes, leading children to deemphasize attributes of an object that are important from an adult perspective. At the same time, children may notice a function (and its correlated form attributes) for that object that adults ignore. In such cases, children would emphasize attributes of the object that are unimportant to adults. Therefore, very young children's basic-level categories will oftentimes differ from the corresponding adult-basic categories. Mothers are often aware of these differences, and many mothers indicate this knowledge explicitly by labeling objects with the names corresponding to their child-basic category assignments, even when these names are incorrect by adult standards (Mervis & Mervis 1982; see Bowerman 1976; Mervis 1984, for parallel examples of child-adapted verb usage). Mothers tend to accept their young child's use of child-basic names for objects, although labels that mothers perceive as arbitrary are corrected (Mervis 1984; Mervis & Mervis 1984). Mothers also tend to accept their young child's use of an object in accordance with its child-basic function, even when the function is inappropriate from an adult perspective.[1] The child's categories are not derived simply from maternal input, however (see Marvis 1984; Mervis & Mervis 1984; and below).

When differences between child-basic and adult-basic categories occur, several relationships between the two types of categories may result. First, the child-basic category may be broader than the corresponding adult-basic category. These broad categories sometimes correspond to a more general level in the same taxonomy (see also Brown 1958, 1978). For example, the child-basic *kitty* category might correspond to the adult *feline* category. In other cases, the child's broad category contains exemplars from several adult taxonomies. For example, the child-basic *ball* category might include round candles, round coin banks, and multisided beads, as well as objects adults would consider balls. Second, the child's category may be narrower than the corresponding adult category. For example, the child-basic *chair* category might not include beanbag chairs. Third, the child's category may overlap the adult's category; that is, the child's category may include objects that are excluded from the adult category while at the same time excluding objects that are included in the adult category. For example, the child-basic *car* category might include trucks but exclude dune buggies.

Previous theories of early lexical development have accounted for the differences between child and adult categories by postulating that children and adults attend to different numbers of attributes when making categorization decisions. Thus, Clark (1973) has claimed that the child attends to a proper subset of the attributes relevant to an adult. Consequently, the child's categories corresponding to his or her early words are broader than the adult categories labeled by the same words. Nelson (1974) has claimed that the child attends to a superset of the attributes relevant to an adult. Consequently, the child's categories are initially narrower than the corresponding adult categories. Development consists of either adding relevant attributes (Clark 1973) or subtracting irrelevant attributes (Nelson 1974) until the appropriate adult category is acquired. In contrast, I believe (see Mervis 1982, 1984; Mervis & Canada 1983; Mervis & Mervis 1982) that, although some differences between child and adult categories may be due to variations in the number of attributes attended to, this is not the major source of difference. Instead, one of the most important causes of the differences between child and adult categories is that children are attending to or emphasizing different attributes from adults (see also Carey 1982).

For child-basic categories that are broader than the corresponding adult-basic categories, there are three reasons why a child might attend to a different set of attributes or assign a different weight to an attribute. First, the child may not know about the cultural significance of certain attributes. For example, the child may not realize that a bank is for storing money. Therefore, the slot and the keyhole of a round bank may be ignored, in favor of known attributes such as "round," "rolls," "can be thrown." The round bank accordingly will be assigned to the child's *ball* category. Second, the child may be aware of the attributes that are important to the adult category assignment, but the salience of these attributes may sometimes be less for him or her than the salience of a different set of attributes. Thus, a child may consider a round bank to be both a bank and a ball. Third, the child may include false attributes in his or her decision process. For example, the mistaken belief that a leopard says "meow" (as the child's mother may tell him or her; Mervis & Mervis 1982) may contribute to the child's decision to categorize it as a kitty.

For child-basic categories that are narrower than the corresponding adult-basic category, the child often defines the acceptable range of values for a given attribute more narrowly, for attributes that both children and adults include in their decision processes. This situation often occurs because the child is not aware of cultural conventions concerning stylized representations. For example, both children and adults expect bears to have fur. Very young children, however, may require this fur to be plush and relatively plain. Thus, a toy bear made out of a flower-print cotton fabric may be excluded from a child's *bear* category but included in an adult's *bear* category.

In many cases for which the child-basic category overlaps the corresponding adult-basic category, the factors that contribute to overly broad and overly narrow categories operate simultaneously. For example, the child may include round banks and round candles in his or her *ball* category, because he or she is unaware of the cultural significance of the slot or the wick. At the same time, the child may exclude footballs from his or her *ball* category because the shape is too deviant from round. In other cases, the factor that is primarily responsible for overgeneralization may lead to overlap: the child emphasizes attributes that are irrelevant to the adult category, while ignoring an attribute that is crucial for the adult category. For example, Keil (Chapter 7, this volume) has argued that young children emphasize such attributes as being a friend of one's father and bringing one presents in determining membership in their *uncle* category. Young children ignore the kinship criteria that adults use. Thus, young children would be expected to include not only actual adult uncles but also close male friends of the father in *uncle,* while excluding juveniles who are uncles by the kinship criterion.

Which objects, then, should be included in an initial child-basic category? The principle that basic-level categories are the most general categories whose members share similar overall shapes and similar functions or characteristic actions can be used to make predictions. An initial child-basic category should include those objects that, from a child's perspective, have similar overall shapes (or similar parts in particular configurations) and similar characteristic actions and/or can be used for similar functions.

This prediction is a general one. "Similarity" must be defined separately for each child; as Kogan (1971) has demonstrated, the breadth of any given category may vary from child to child. This variability, however, should occur only with regard to the inclusion or exclusion of borderline members/nonmembers (e.g., for the *chair* category, such items as beanbag chairs, sassy seats, and stools with backs). Thus, if the exemplars used in a study include only objects that either clearly should be included in the category being investigated (good or moderate exemplars) or clearly should not be included, then predictions across children concerning category membership can still be made.

Another factor that limits the predictability of the composition of child-basic categories concerns the initial exemplar or exemplars on which the child bases his or her category. As Pani and I have shown (Mervis & Pani 1980), when the initial exemplar is a good example of its category, a person (either child or adult) is likely to generalize appropriately to include other predicted members in his or her category. When the initial exemplar is a poor example of its category, however, the person is not likely to generalize appropriately at first. In many cases, he or she will form a category that is much narrower than the predicted category. Thus, the predictions made based on the basic-level principle will be correct when children first form a category only if the initial exemplar is a good example of its category. The predictions eventually will hold even if the initial exemplar was a poor example. The child first will have to realize, however, that the good examples are also members of the category.

In summary, very young children form basic-level categories whose composition often differs from that of adult-basic-level categories. Children's categories may be broader than, narrower than, or may overlap, the corresponding adult categories. These differences occur because the child's limited knowledge of culturally appropriate functions of objects and their correlated form attributes leads him or her to emphasize different attributes than adults do, for the same object. Because child-basic categories and adult-basic categories are formed and structured according to the same principles, it is possible to predict the composition of child-basic categories.

Evolution of initial child-basic categories

Many initial child-basic categories will not be identical to the corresponding adult-basic categories. When an adult is conversing with a child, there are four circumstances under which the adult can use the adult-basic label for an object the child does not include in its adult-basic category, thus providing the child with an opportunity to learn this label and to change his or her categorization scheme. First, the child might notice important attributes on his or her own, and then call these attributes to an adult's attention. The adult would be likely to respond by acknowledging the attribute that the child had indicated and then labeling the object with its adult-basic name. For example, the child might point out a round candle's wick to the mother, in which case she probably would respond by commenting on the wick and then labeling the object, "candle."

If the child has not noticed these important attributes on his or her own (or if the adult does not realize the child has), the adult may choose to point them out. This may be accomplished in two ways. First, the adult can show the child a critical form attribute(s) and/or demonstrate a critical function attribute(s) of an object, that serve to make it a member of its adult-basic category. Coincident with this highlighting of a critical attribute, the adult may label the object with its adult-basic name. These illustrations are often accompanied by verbal descriptions. For example, the adult might run a finger along the slot of a round bank, drop in a coin, and tell the child that this is a slot into which you put money. The adult would then label the object, "bank." Alternatively, the adult might provide a verbal description, without a concrete illustration. Both of these strategies could be used either spontaneously or in response to the child's use of a child-basic name to label the object in question.

Finally, the adult may label the object with its adult-basic name without either an implied request from the child (the first circumstance described) or some form of explanation (the second and third circumstances). The use of an adult-basic label alone constitutes an implicit statement of the existence of attributes that make the object a member of the named category. This strategy may also be used spontaneously or as a correction of the child's use of a child-basic name to label the object in question.

The four circumstances under which the adult labels an object with its adult-basic name should be differentially associated with success at leading the child to comprehend the new adult-basic label and to begin to form a new category. Success should be most likely to occur if either the child points out a relevant attribute or the adult provides a concrete illustration. In these cases, because the important attributes have been made explicit in a concrete manner, even the very young child often is able to see that they form the basis for a new category, or, in the case of an initially undergeneralized category, the basis for assignment of the object to its appropriate category. Success when the adult provides a verbal explanation without a concrete illustration is less likely. The very young child is unlikely to understand the explanation. The success of this method should increase as the child's vocabulary size increases. Success when the adult uses an adult-basic label without either a request from the child or an explanation is considerably less likely for younger children. If the labeled object already is included in a different child-basic category, success is extremely unlikely. The metacognition required to realize that categories should be altered simply because a different label is used is relatively sophisticated. If the object has not yet been assigned to any category, and the child already has the appropriate category for this object, success is more likely. Indeed, children eventually believe that all objects should belong to some category, and therefore "look" for a category to which the unassigned object could be assigned. In some cases, the child may even ask, "What's that?" in reference to an unassigned object. Success in these cases is very likely.

Comprehension of the adult-basic name for an object previously included in a different child-basic category, and formation of a new category based on that object, are the first steps in the evolution of an originally overextended category (or the overextended part of an overlapped category) to conform to the adult-basic category labeled by the same word. It often has been argued (e.g., Barrett 1978, 1982; Clark 1973, 1983) that upon learning a more appropriate name for an object, the child immediately discards the former name. That is, the old and the new categories immediately become disjunctive. This claim is based on data from either diary studies (which actually contain a few contradictions; see Lewis 1963) or observations of play rather than on systematic testing. Markman (Chapter 10, this volume) and Tversky and Hemenway (1984) have proposed that even very young children have an exclusion principle that precludes the simultaneous assignment of an object to two basic-level categories. In contrast, I would like to argue that for these children, the complete separation of the old and the new categories is gradual. The child, in considering the object that is changing category membership, at first finds two sets of attributes salient: the set that makes the object a member of the original category and the set that makes the object a member of the new category. Consequently, the child includes the object in both categories. That is, the very young child does not have a principle that precludes the simultaneous assignment of objects to two basic-level categories. For a child to decide that an object should be excluded from its old category, he or she must decide that only the set of attributes that makes the object a member of the new category is important, or in the case of previously included false attributes, that the two sets of attributes are contradictory (e.g., that a single animal does not say both "meow" and "grr"). At this point, the separation of the two categories will be complete. It is not clear what causes the child to make this decision; some possible influences are discussed in the final section of this paper.

Summary

Many child-basic categories initially are not identical to the corresponding adult-basic categories. Evolution occurs because the child realizes that the object(s) that is misassigned or unassigned has important attributes that make it a member of the adult-basic category. Successful initiation of evolution, as defined by child comprehension of the adult-basic label in reference to the relevant object, is most likely under two circumstances: Either the child has realized the importance of the relevant attributes on his or her own and has pointed them out to the adult, who responded by providing the object's adult-basic name; or the adult provided a concrete illustration of these attributes, accompanied by the object's adult-basic name. For those categories that were originally overextended, the old and the new categories initially overlap. The separation of these categories is gradual, being completed only when the child realizes that the attributes that led him or her to include the object in the initial child-basic category are either irrelevant for that object or not true of that object.

Diary study

I will begin my consideration of this theory by discussing some of the data from an ongoing study of my son Ari's early lexical development. I have been keeping records of object word comprehension and production ever since Ari first demonstrated referential comprehension. These records include the word comprehended or produced, the referent, the context, and the adult response. The production records include most instances until Ari was 16 months old. At that time, his productive vocabulary included about 80 words. Records of all new words were kept until age 21 months; at that time, Ari's productive vocabulary included over 600 root words. Records of new referents for old words and overextensions or underextensions were also kept until that time. For certain words, records are still being made. The diary records occasionally were supplemented by systematic comprehension and production testing, when the status of an object was unclear. In addition, for Ari's early object words, notes were made concerning available referents: what potential referents for a word were available to Ari the first time he comprehended or produced that word, and what labels (if any) adults had recently used for these objects. An effort was made to ensure that Ari was exposed to a wide variety of potential referents, both realistic and stylized, for each word he comprehended or produced. I believe that this exposure is critical in order to accurately infer the extension of a child's categories.

In order to discuss the initial structure and evolution of object words, I first present a detailed description of the category underlying Ari's first word (*duck*), followed by less detailed descriptions of two other categories (*mixer* and *lion*). I then make some more general statements concerning the categories underlying Ari's words.

Ari first demonstrated object word comprehension at age 10-$\frac{1}{2}$ months. The first word he comprehended was "duckie." At the time Ari first comprehended "duckie," the two exemplars of *duck* that most interested him were live mallards, which he saw several times a week at a nearby pond, and a plush mallard, which was his favorite toy. Both of these exemplars are good examples of the adult *duck* category; thus, Ari's initial *duck* category should correspond to the predicted child-basic category; objects with a ducklike shape and that either can be expected to carry out activities such as swimming and flying or represent something that can be expected to carry out such activities. A variety of other potential referents also were available. Those that often had been named for Ari included a rubber duck, a plastic duck rattle, a plush duck-head rattle, a Donald Duck head (from Disney Poppin Pals), and a variety of pictures, ranging from very realistic to somewhat stylized, in Ari's picture books. Those that were not named for Ari included a large black duck decoy, several miniature carved ducks, a miniature carved grebe, a porcelain snow goose, and several engravings of ducks. In addition, Ari had a wind-up chicken that adults consistently called "chicken," and several pictures of songbirds that adults called "birdie." There were also several porcelain songbirds available that adults had not named, as well as engravings of nonduck waterfowl and songbirds that also had not been named.

To assess comprehension of "duckie," questions of the type "Where's duckie?" or "Can Ari get the duckie?" were used. The first comprehension tests were formal: Four systematically chosen objects were placed in front of Ari, and he was asked to indicate which one was the duck. Some trials were designed to include no objects that were at all ducklike (e.g., songbird, lion, dog, kitty). On these trials, Ari consistently refused to choose an object. The formal tests were supplemented by informal questioning while Ari was playing. Examples of objects included in Ari's *duck* category are illustrated in Figure 8.1. Examples of objects excluded from *duck* are depicted in Figure 8.2. Because of the discrepancy in sizes of the objects, a constant scale across objects could not be maintained in these or subsequent figures. The results of the first set of comprehension tests, conducted immediately after Ari first demonstrated comprehension of "duckie," indicated that the following objects were included in his *duck* category: Live ducks, plush male mallard, rubber duck, black duck decoy, miniature carved ducks, miniature carved grebe, porcelain snow goose, windup chicken. These objects were all ducklike. They were three-dimensional and had duck-shaped heads and long bills. Ari believed that all of these objects represented things that were capable of swimming and flying. The following objects were excluded from Ari's *duck* category: Plastic duck rattle, plush duck-head rattle, Donald Duck head, all pictures and engravings, porcelain songbirds. The excluded objects that would have been ducks by adult standards were either stylized or two-dimensional; the songbirds did not have a ducklike shape.

For the next two weeks, efforts to find three-dimensional representations of other types of birds were not successful. Finally, however, Ari's father found a wide variety of plush birds in a store. Results of tests with these new toys (about three weeks after Ari began to comprehend "duck") fit with the previous results: A swan and a Canadian goose were included in *duck*, while an owl and a variety of songbirds were excluded. Exemplars of larger waterfowl (e.g., great blue heron) were still not available. However, data obtained once Ari did see such birds indicated that he considered the larger waterfowl to be ducks. Ostriches and ostrichlike birds were also included in *duck*.

The day after the new toys were tested, Ari produced "duck" for the

Figure 8.1. Examples of objects included in Ari's initial *duck* category. Top row: some objects that were available to be tested immediately: plush mallard, carved grebe, porcelain snow goose, wind-up chicken. Bottom row: some objects that Ari included as soon as they were available for testing: plush Canadian goose, swan, great blue heron, ostrich.

Figure 8.2. Examples of objects excluded from Ari's initial *duck* category: plastic duck rattle, Donald Duck head, porcelain songbird, plush owl.

first time. Although production testing is difficult when children first begin to talk, the results I was able to obtain suggested that Ari's *duck* category was the same, whether measured by comprehension or production.

Ari's *duck* category continued to be stable for another month and then gradually began to evolve. Initial evolution primarily consisted of reduction of undergeneralization. Thus, when Ari was 12½ months old, he began to accept pictures of ducks as ducks. A few weeks later, Ari accepted the plastic duck rattle as a duck. After another few weeks, Ari finally accepted the plush duck head rattle and the Donald Duck head as ducks. At about the time that Ari finally agreed that these two objects were ducks, he started to identify any duck or ducklike object that he saw. For example, I was leafing through a computer magazine in the grocery store when I heard Ari say his word for "duck" excitedly. I responded, "Where's the duckie? I don't see a duckie." But I started looking back through the magazine and found an advertisement that contained a picture of an extremely stylized duck inner tube. As soon as I reached the page, Ari again said his word for "duck." A few weeks later, as we were walking through a department store, I again heard Ari's word for "duck." After looking around, I finally found an extremely stylized swan soap dish. The inner tube and soap dish are illustrated in Figure 8.3.

At age 18 months, Ari began to reduce the overextension of his *duck* category. By age 18½ months, he had comprehended and produced "goose" and "swan" in reference to certain birds previously included in his *duck* category. By age 21 months, he also had comprehended and produced "ostrich" and "pelican" in reference to other birds previously included in his *duck* category. All four of these words were comprehended immediately after the first concrete illustration of characteristics that distinguished these objects from ducks, accompanied by the adult-appropriate name. In the cases of "goose" and "swan," adults often had labeled the objects correctly (but without concrete illustrations) for Ari prior to the time he first comprehended the words. In the cases of "ostrich" and "pelican," the correct name had been used only once previously. Ari clearly attended to the attributes highlighted; for the first few days after he learned "goose," when he labeled an object "goose," he also said "honk." Similarly, when Ari first learned "ostrich," he often followed the word with "fluffy." (Ari had been told that ostriches had long legs and long necks and were fluffy in the middle).

In general, by age 20 months, Ari's *goose* and *swan* categories, whether measured by comprehension or production, corresponded to the adult categories. However, geese and swans still were considered ducks occasionally. For example, the following incident occurred when Ari was 20 months old. I was rocking Ari. He was holding his plush Canadian goose. When I first started rocking him, he looked down at the goose and said "goose." About 15 minutes later, he held the goose up to me and said "duckie."

At age 19½ months, Ari formed an *ostrich* category; this category included not only ostriches but also such birds as emus and rheas. The overextension of this category clearly was based on the attributes that

Figure 8.3. Some stylized additions to Ari's *duck* category: duck inner tube and swan soap dish.

were taught to Ari in reference to ostrich: Long neck, long legs, and fluffy middle. At age 20½ months, Ari formed a *pelican* category. Overextension of this category again appears to have been based on the primary attribute that adults emphasized to Ari: the extremely long, pointed bill. Ari included not only pelicans but also larger waterfowl with long, pointed bills (e.g., great blue herons) in his *pelican* category.[2]

In summary, the initial composition and subsequent evolution of Ari's first labeled category corresponded extremely well to that predicted by the theory. The objects initially included in the category were all duck-like; in general, they were three-dimensional and had duck-shaped heads and torsos and long bills. Ari believed that all of these objects were, or represented things that were, capable of swimming and flying. The objects initially included in the category did not completely match the linguistic input Ari had received: some objects that had been called "duck" were excluded, some objects that had not been labeled at all were included, and one object that had been labeled "chicken" rather than "duck" was included. Thus, Ari's initial construction of his *duck* category clearly reflected a belief that categories should be formed on the basis of similarity of shape (parts) and predicted characteristic actions/functions, rather than on the basis of adult naming patterns. Ari's underextension, overextension, and subsequent reductions of these were principled and predictable. Adult use of the adult-appropriate label alone did not lead to comprehension of new words, but adult use of the adult-appropriate label accompanied by a concrete illustration consistently resulted in comprehension. Comprehension occurred because Ari attended to and encoded the attributes included in the illustrations. This pattern is consistent with a belief that categories should not be formed on the basis of adult labeling patterns alone. Instead, objects already assigned to a category should be assigned also to a new category only if a changed emphasis on particular attributes provided a basis for a new category based on the shape-function principle. Concrete illustrations provided a rationale for the necessary change in emphasis. The objects included in the new categories remained members of the *duck* category as well, for periods of time ranging from about a week (for later categories) to a few months (for earlier categories).

The pattern described for *duck* is generally applicable for the categories corresponding to Ari's other early words. I will describe briefly one additional example that fits this pattern, because the example illustrates an interesting methodological point concerning thinking about which objects should be included in a particular child-basic category. I will then turn to the exceptions to this pattern.

The additional example concerns the category corresponding to the word "mixer." This type of word has not been considered in the literature; generally, researchers have concentrated on animals, plants, food, and toys. Diary entries concerning "mixer" began when Ari was 15 months old. Initially, the only mixer or mixerlike object available to him was the mixer in his own home. As Ari was exposed to additional mixers or mixer-resembling objects (e.g., certain types of automatic coffee makers or sauce makers), each of these was added to his *mixer* category (whether measured by comprehension or production). The data fit the theory perfectly. Then, when Ari was 17 months old, we gave him a book that had a picture of an old-fashioned hand pump with a bucket positioned beneath. As soon as Ari saw this picture, he labeled it "mixer" excitedly. We told him that it was not a mixer, but rather a pump. Ari was equally insistent (whether measured by comprehension or production) that it was not a pump, but rather a mixer. Finally, I pretended to make the squirrel push on the pump handle. I told Ari that the squirrel pushed on the handle and that made a waterfall come out of the pump, and the duckie could drink the water. (Ari was very interested in waterfalls at the time.) Then I reiterated that the object was a pump. At this point, Ari demonstrated both comprehension and production of "pump" in reference to this object, although he still often indicated that he thought it was also a mixer. Upon closer examination of the pump, we realized why Ari had considered it a mixer: As illustrated in Figure 8.4, the combination of the pump and bucket looked very similar to a conventional mixer and bowl. In addition, the pump by itself looked very similar to a mixer without a bowl. Similar instances occurred with a picture of a jigsaw and a picture of a sewing machine, as well as with a real sewing machine. (Ari had never seen a jigsaw or a sewing machine in operation.) Again, the appearance of the items was very similar to that of a mixer without a bowl. These episodes served as a reminder that it is

 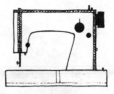

Figure 8.4. Examples of objects included in Ari's *mixer* category: mixer, hand pump, sewing machine.

important to look beyond objects included in categories in the same taxonomy as the adult-basic category, when predicting what a young child might include in his or her category. More generally, it is important to look for similarities that adults would normally ignore. If we don't remember, the child probably will remind us.

Almost all of Ari's early categories were based on good exemplars, and all of these categories fit well with the predicted categories. However, two of Ari's early categories were based initially on poor exemplars. These two exhibited a very different composition pattern at first. I will describe the development of one of these categories, in order to illustrate this pattern.

Ari first comprehended "lion" when he was 12 months old. At that time, three exemplars were available: a stylized plush lion, a picture of a somewhat stylized moderate example of a lion, and a picture of a good example of a lion cub. All three were called "lion" by the adults. The plush lion (see Figure 8.5) was such a poor example of *lion* that when I first saw it, I had to check its tag to find out what it was. This lion was one of Ari's favorite toys and the most frequent referent of "lion" in adult speech to Ari. Initial comprehension testing indicated that the plush lion and the picture of a moderate-example lion were included in Ari's *lion* category; the picture of a lion cub was not. Better examples of plush lions, brought home from the laboratory, were also excluded, as were all other types of felines. At age 13 months, when Ari first comprehended "kitty-cat," it became apparent that he considered all the good-example lions and all the other felines to belong to a single category, *kitty-cat*. When Ari was 15 months old, we took him to the zoo for the first time. He labeled the male lion with his word for "kitty." Prior to this event, we had not labeled any additional examples of lion for Ari (although we continued to label the three original exemplars) because I wanted to see if he would decide on his own that these were lions. After the episode at the zoo, however, it was clear that he would not. Therefore, we began to label lions "lion" and to tell Ari that they said "roar." Eventually, he began to include male lions in his *lion* category, although he still consid-

Figure 8.5. The prototype of Ari's *lion* category: stylized plush lion.

ered them kitty-cats as well. He did not include female lions and lion cubs in his *lion* category until about age 19 months; at age 21 months, they were still considered kitty-cats as well.

The initial composition and development of Ari's *lion* category fit the predicted pattern for a category that was based on a poor example. The category was initially extremely restricted. However, eventually it included the same exemplars as would have been expected had the category initially been based on a good exemplar. The same pattern was followed for Ari's other early category (*horsie*) that was based initially on a poor exemplar. This pattern also has been seen more recently. When Ari, at age $17\frac{1}{2}$ months, learned the word "saw" based on a chain saw, he did not realize immediately that a cross-cutting hand saw, which is generally considered the prototypical saw, was in fact a saw.

In summary, the pattern of evolution of Ari's object word categories has fit well with the theoretical predictions. When concrete illustration of crucial form and/or function attributes distinguished a named object from other members of its initial category, Ari consistently has been able to learn new names for objects previously included in categories labeled by different words, and form categories based on these new words. In contrast, when the only input was the adult-appropriate name for the object, Ari was 20 months old before he comprehended the adult-appropriate name for an object previously included in a different category. This pattern obtained even though for research purposes a new name for an object already included in a different category often was introduced first without a concrete illustration, to give Ari many opportunities to demonstrate comprehension (and new category formation) based on only the adult-appropriate word as input.

The reader might be wondering at this point just how many of Ari's object words were labels for categories that were not isomorphic to the corresponding adult categories. The great majority of his categories were at some point not perfectly matched to the adult categories. Most of Ari's early object categories were in an overlap relationship to the corresponding adult categories. The undergeneralization part of the overlap was due primarily to the exclusion of stylized exemplars and, for the earliest words, two-dimensional representations. Extremely stylized objects were still excluded from Ari's categories at age 21 months, but by then most appropriate stylized objects were included in Ari's new categories from the beginning. Both overextension and underextension still occur, but are not (and never have been) drastic. The categories underlying certain types of words (e.g., most body parts, playground equipment, and proper names) have corresponded to the predicted adult categories from the beginning.

Why did Ari's categories so often differ from the corresponding adult ones? This is a particularly relevant question since some researchers have reported relatively low incidences of differences between early child categories and adult categories (e.g., MacWhinney 1984). As I stated previously, I believe that Ari often focused on different attributes than an adult would, for a given object (as illustrated in an extreme form by the pump/mixer example). This difference in focus is understandable; Ari often was not aware of the cultural reasons for emphasizing certain attributes over others. In turn, he noticed attributes of objects that adults ignore, and based his application of the shape-function principle on these attributes. Most of the children who were reported to seldom overextend words were considerably older than Ari when they began to talk. Furthermore, these children do not appear to have been exposed to a wide variety of potential referents for their early words. In addition, their comprehension was not studied. Therefore, it is impossible to be certain that their categories initially were identical to adult categories. This problem has been overlooked when discussing the issue of the initial correspondence between child and adult categories. Recently, several researchers have reported relatively high incidences of overextension (e.g., Chapman 1983; Rescorla 1980; Poulin-Dubois & Larendeau Bendavid 1984), and Anglin (1983) had reported extremely high incidences of overextension, underextension, and overlap in an experimental study using real-world objects. I suspect that the reason relatively low estimates of the incidence of disparity between child and adult categories sometimes are reported is that the child in question was not consistently exposed to a wide variety of potential referents for each of his or her early words, and that early comprehension was not attended to.

Note also that even adults make categorization errors, particularly when they are not familiar with the items to be categorized. Two of the many domains in which I consistently have observed adult errors are construction vehicles and birds. For example, many adults include front-end loaders in their *bulldozer* category. Even more dramatic to me, 70 percent of the adults that I queried concerning the identity of a realistic plush Canadian goose confidently said that it was a duck. This was true even though the goose had a much longer neck than a duck and had all the correct markings of a Canadian goose. Similarly, such waterfowl as grebes and dovekies are consistently categorized as ducks by most adults. Many adults who consider mature robins to be robins think that juvenile robins are sparrows; according to these adults, any relatively small brown bird is a sparrow. These adult categorization errors occur for the same reason as young children's errors: Lack of knowledge concerning the object causes the adult to emphasize attributes different from those that would be emphasized by a person more expert in the relevant domain. Such errors are less common in adults because they have more extensive knowledge of culturally significant features of the world than children do.

I would like to make one final comment concerning the diary study. An important assumption underlying all theories of early lexical development is that children initially believe that when a person points at or otherwise indicates an object for which the child does not already have a name, the accompanying word refers to the whole object. That is, young children assume that a word used in reference to an object whose name is unknown refers to the object as a whole rather than to a part or attribute of that object or to an action performed by the object. Given the importance of this assumption, it is crucial that it be tested. Currently, support for this assumption is based on a single anecdote (provided by Hoffman [1968], cited in Macnamara 1982) concerning one child's assumption that "hot" meant "stove." Ari's early vocabulary development provided three additional examples in support of this assumption. Ari initially believed that "hot" meant "cuplike object," that "night-night" meant "bedlike object," and that "more" meant "juicelike beverage." Further evidence in support of the assumption comes from preliminary analyses of the early diary entries indicating that when Ari learned a verb, it was initially comprehended and produced in reference to the action of an object whose name Ari already comprehended.

Long and I are now conducting an experiment, using artificial stimuli, that addresses this assumption directly. In this study, the experimenter points directly at a part of an object at the same time as she provides a label. She then removes the original object and places three additional objects in front of the child. One object has the same overall shape as the initial object but does not have the part that was labeled, one object has a different overall shape but does have the labeled part in the same position as in the original object, and one object has a different overall shape from the original object and does not have the part that was labeled. The child is asked to show the experimenter the [label]. The data obtained from the eleven 18-month-olds who have participated so far support the position that very young children believe that words used in reference to a part of an unknown object actually refer to the whole object, rather than to the part.

Longitudinal study

The results of the diary study are valuable, in that they provide detailed information concerning the initial composition and evolution of one child's object-word categories. It is impossible to obtain such a rich description except by a diary study. At the same time, while I have argued that I expect the results to generalize beyond Ari, I have not yet presented any evidence. With this in mind, I briefly describe some of the results of a longitudinal study of the early development of the categories *ball, car,* and *kitty.* (See Mervis 1984, and Mervis & Mervis 1984, for a more detailed discussion.) The study provides a general look at a few categories, but for a number of children, including both normally developing children and children who have Down syndrome. The results provide further support for at least three important aspects of the theory described previously. First, children's initial categories are child-basic categories, formed by application of the shape-function principle to the attributes they consider important, rather than on the basis of adult labeling patterns alone. Second, for very young children, acquisition of an adult-basic name for an object previously included in a child-basic category labeled by a different name, and formation of a new category, are greatly facilitated by maternal use of concrete illustration of critical attributes that differentiate the relevant object from other members of the initial child-basic category. Third, when children first acquire a new label and form a new category, the objects included in that category almost always are still included in the old category. That is, very young children do not automatically assume, as adults do, that basic-level categories are mutually exclusive. The data supporting each of these points are summarized below, following a description of the study.

The purpose of the longitudinal study was to delineate the role of the child and the role of the mother in the child's early lexical development. Six normally developing children (three boys, three girls) and their mothers and six children with Down syndrome and their mothers participated. The normal children were matched to the children with Down syndrome for sex and birth order position. All children had vision and hearing within the normal range. All families were white and middle class, and the mother was the primary caregiver. At the start of the study, the normal children were 9 months old; the children with Down syndrome were 17 to 19 months old. None of the children was able to comprehend or produce language referentially. The mother-child dyads were visited at home every 6 weeks for between 14 and 21 months. Each session included a play period during which mother and child played together with a specially chosen set of toys, followed by systematic comprehension and production testing. The set of toys included objects that were true members of the category (by adult standards), related objects that I predicted (based on the shape-function principle) to be members of the child-basic categories, and unrelated objects from the same superordinate categories that were predicted not to be included in either the adult-basic or the child-basic categories. The toys used over the course of the study are listed in Table 8.1. With a few exceptions (see Table 8.1), all objects were realistic representations.

Both normal children and children with Down syndrome participated in the study because, based on previous research (e.g., Bell 1964; Bell & Harper 1977; Cardoso-Martins & Mervis 1985; Jones 1977, 1979, 1980), we expected the mothers of the children with Down syndrome to talk to their children differently from the way the mothers of the normal children talked to their children. Specifically, we expected the mothers of the children with Down syndrome to label objects with their adult-basic names, while mothers of normal children were expected often to label objects with their child-basic names (Cardoso-Martins & Mervis 1985; Mervis 1982). If these results were obtained, then a comparison of the initial composition of the categories of the two groups of children could yield valuable information concerning the role of the child's cognitive structures and the role of maternal labeling input in determining initial composition. The predicted results concerning maternal labeling input were in fact obtained. Mothers of children with Down syndrome consistently labeled objects with their adult-basic names, while mothers of normal children often labeled objects with their child-basic names.

To determine the initial extension of the children's *ball*, *car*, and *kitty* categories, the data from the first comprehension test on which each

Table 8.1. *Toys used in the play sessions*

Predicted membership	Category		
	Ball	Car	Kitty
Adult-basic and child-basic	Rubber ball	Sedan car	House cat
	Whiffle ball	Sports car	Sachet cat[a]
	Soccer ball	Wooden car[a]	Beanbag cat[a]
	Football[a]	Jeep[a]	Potholder cat[a]
Child-basic only	Multisided beads	Van	Panther
	Christmas ornament	Bus	Cougar
	Round candle	Moving truck	Cheetah
	Round owl bank	Fire engine	Leopard
	Round bell	Cement truck	Tiger
		Dump truck	Lion
Neither	Wooden blocks	Airplane	Dog
	Frisbee	Helicopter	Frog
	Plastic keys	Boat	Parrot
			Zebra
			Squirrel
			Rabbit
			Walrus
			Turtle
			Elephant
			Duck
			Giraffe
			Lobster
			Camel
			Dinosaur

Note. A subset of these toys was used in each of the play sessions. At the start of the study, five objects from each category were included: one predicted adult-basic and child-basic, three predicted child-basic only, and one predicted neither. By the end of the study, nine objects from each category were included: two predicted adult-basic and child-basic, five predicted child-basic only, and two predicted neither. For many of the names listed, several different exemplars of the category labeled by that name were used over the course of the study. With the exception of some of the potential undergeneralization objects, all objects were realistic representations.

[a] Potential undergeneralization object.

word was comprehended by a given child were considered. These data were compared to the predicted composition of the child-basic categories (see Table 8.1). For the normal children, 17 out of 18 initial categories corresponded exactly to the predicted child-basic categories. One child's *car* category was slightly overextended. For the children with Down syndrome, 14 out of 16 of the initial categories corresponded exactly to the predicted child-basic categories. Two children under-generalized the *ball* category slightly, by excluding the football. (One child never comprehended either "car" or "kitty.") Thus, virtually all of the categories formed by both the normal children and the children with Down syndrome corresponded exactly to the predicted child-basic categories. These results provide strong support for the position that the child's initial categories are determined by his or her cognitive structures, rather than by maternal labeling input. It appears from these data that young children believe categories should be formed by application of the shape/function principle to the attributes they consider important, rather than on the basis of adult labeling patterns alone.

To consider the predictions concerning likelihood of success in inducing the child to comprehend the adult-basic name for an object previously included in a child-basic category labeled by a different name, I have examined the transcripts of the play periods for mother-normal child interactions with the child-basic-only objects. The initial set of analyses focused on the day that the child first comprehended a relevant adult-basic label. There were 36 such cases. In 28 of them, the mother provided a concrete illustration, accompanied by the adult-basic label, during the play period immediately preceding the comprehension test. In 3 cases, the mother provided only a verbal explanation. In 4 cases, the mother only used the word, without any explanation. In the remaining 2 cases, the child produced the word before the mother did during the relevant play period; these cases are considered as missing data. Examination of the transcripts from previous play sessions, beginning when the child demonstrated referential comprehension, indicated that demonstrations during these sessions were very rare. In general, the child comprehended the adult-basic name for an object the first time that the mother provided a concrete illustration accompanied by the object's adult-basic name. The children were significantly younger at the time they comprehended the words for which concrete illustrations were provided than at the time they comprehended words that were only introduced with verbal explanations or without any explanation.

These results indicate that maternal illustrations generally are sufficient to induce the child to learn the relevant adult-basic label. However, they do not preclude the possibility that maternal use of the adult-basic label alone, as either implicit feedback (simple naming) or explicit feedback (correction of child errors), is also sufficient to account for the child's comprehension of the relevant adult-basic label. Further analyses of the data obtained from the mother-normal child dyads provided strong evidence against this counterhypothesis. First, the proportion of spontaneous maternal use of the adult-basic name for a child-basic-only toy during the play session on the day that comprehension of the word first was demonstrated was virtually identical to the proportion during the immediately previous session. Second, only two of the six mothers ever disagreed with their child's use of a child-basic label to name a toy during the play session on the day that the child first comprehended the adult-basic name of that toy. Although disagreements without concrete illustrations had occurred occasionally during previous play sessions, these disagreements had not led to the child's comprehension of the relevant adult-basic label. Furthermore, there were many instances in which a child vigorously rejected the mother's attempt to introduce (without a concrete illustration) a new name for an object the child already included in a child-basic category labeled by a different name. Thus, even when a child was aware that the mother was trying to modify the child's categorization scheme, the child often was persuaded more by the apparent soundness of his or her previously established categories than by the mother's label. The results of these additional examinations, then, suggest that maternal illustrations not only are generally sufficient for child comprehension of the relevant adult-basic label, but also are often necessary for very young children to comprehend the adult-basic name of an object previously included in a child-basic category labeled by a different name.

The results of these analyses indicate that the mother plays an important role in initiating the evolution of her child's categories. The manner in which the adult-basic label is presented is a major factor in determining if the child will comprehend this label. The child, too, plays a major role; the potential success of the presentation depends on convincing him or her that an attribute previously considered an irrelevant aspect of an object is in fact important.

To test the prediction that when children first acquire a new label for, and form a new category based on, an object previously included in a child-basic category labeled by a different name, the old and new categories overlap, each child's responses on the comprehension test for the day on which he or she first comprehended a relevant label were considered. Only categories that are mutually exclusive by adult standards were included in the analysis. The results clearly indicate that these categories are not initially mutually exclusive from the children's perspectives. For categories emerging from *ball*, membership initially was simultaneous in 95% of the test cases for the normal children and in 93% of the test cases for the children with Down syndrome. For categories emerging from *car*, membership initially was simultaneous in every case, for both groups of children. For categories emerging from *kitty*, membership initially was simultaneous in 88% of the test cases for the normal children and in 93% of the test cases for the children with Down syndrome. The period of overlap lasted from 6 weeks to several months. At the end of the study, when the normal children were at least 24 months old and the children with Down syndrome were at least 37 months old, the incidence of overlap had decreased, relative to earlier in the study. However, all children were still evidencing some cases of overlap between categories that are mutually exclusive by adult standards.

Summary and speculations

The theory that I have presented emphasizes the role of the child's cognitive structures, including beliefs about the basis on which categories should be formed, in category formation during the initial phases of lexical development. The role of the linguistic environment in conjunction with the child's cognitive structures is emphasized during later phases. The data presented support these positions. I would now like to reexamine these roles and offer some speculations.

Children do form categories without the assistance of language input. Even early in stage 5 of the sensorimotor period, when children do not evidence any language comprehension at all, they are already forming categories. The existence of these categories can be demonstrated based on measures of functional use. I used this type of measure to document one of Ari's prelinguistic categories at age 9 months (see Mervis 1985). The category studied was *horn;* the function measured was attempting to blow. Attempting to blow was the second type of functional use Ari demonstrated; the first, turning pages in a book, was not studied systematically. (For related studies see Benelli, D'Odorico, Levorato, & Simion 1977; Golinkoff & Halperin 1983.) The categories that are evidenced when comprehension of children's earliest words is tested also are very likely to be prelinguistic. That is, the categories had been formed prior to the time when the category name first was comprehended.

Prelinguistic categories are basic-level categories. The composition of these child-basic categories is predictable from the same principles as for adult-basic categories. Very young children share the adult belief that categories generally should be structured according to the shape/ function principle. Sometimes, however, the predicted composition of the child-basic category will differ from that of adult-basic category. Very young children often do not share adults' knowledge of culturally appropriate functions and their correlated form attributes, and attributes that are unimportant to an adult for a given object may be important to a child.

Child-basic categories that are not isomorphic to the corresponding adult categories must evolve, in order to become identical. The most effective method, by far, of convincing very young children of the adult-appropriate category assignment for an object is to provide a concrete illustration of these crucial attributes. If convinced, the child will begin to form a new category.

The environment plays a crucial role, beyond the effects of cognitive structures that were just described. When good examples of the categories to be formed are available to the child, he or she generally will form categories that correspond to the predicted child-basic categories. However, if only poor examples are available (or if the child strongly prefers a poor example), the child is likely initially to form severely underextended categories. The good examples provide an adequate basis for appropriate generalization, whereas poor examples do not (Mervis & Pani 1980). Thus, environmental support in the form of availability of good examples is important to the efficient formation of child-basic categories.

When a very young child forms categories, the purely linguistic input received by the child appears to have little importance either in determining that a category will be established or in determining the composition of a category. Thus, as the results of both the diary study and the longitudinal study indicate, children form prelinguistic categories before the onset of language comprehension, and once comprehension begins, the initial category composition does not correspond exactly to the linguistic input. Similarly, if an adult simply labels an object with a different name from the one the child would have considered appropriate, the very young child will not change his or her category assignment for that object. Even a verbal explanation of why the new label is appropriate seldom results in change in the child's category system. Explicit feedback indicating that the child's label is incorrect, accompanied by the adult-appropriate name alone, also is unlikely to lead to change in the young child's category system. Even after the young child acquires the sophistication necessary to realize that he or she disagrees with the adult category assignment for an object, the child often is willing for the two category systems to exist side by side. For example, consider an interchange that took place between Ari (age 20 months) and me, concerning a picture of a dik-dik partially hidden in some grass. In the four days since Ari had received the book containing this picture, Ari had consistently labeled the dik-dik, "squirrel." Adults had consistently labeled it, "deer." Now we were reading the book again. As soon as Ari saw the dik-dik, he said, "Squirrel." I responded: "Who does Mommy think that is?" Ari: "Deer." I replied: "And who does Ari think that is?" Ari: "Squirrel."

Why does purely linguistic input not play a large role in initial category formation by very young children? Very young children attend selectively to linguistic input, and are unlikely to attend to the labels for objects not of interest to them. At the same time, if a child is interested in an object, this interest probably would have already encouraged him or her to form a prelinguistic category including the object, and based on his or her shape/function principle. Thus, when a very young child attends to, and therefore eventually learns, a label, the label is most likely to be attached to an already-formed category. During the earliest phase of lexical development, adult attempts to initiate category evolution by providing verbal explanations seldom succeed, because the child is unlikely to have a large enough vocabulary and adequate syntactic knowledge to understand the explanation. If the child does not accept the explanation, then he or she will not form a new category; the child forms a new category only if a changed emphasis on particular attributes provides a basis for a new category. Adult attempts to initiate category evolution simply by labeling an object with its adult-appropriate name are even less likely to succeed. The metacognition required to realize that an object already assigned to one category should be assigned to another category – that is, that changes in attribute emphasis are justified – simply because a different label is used is quite complex. Note, too, that very young children do not understand much of the language that they hear. Therefore, when verbal input does not accord with the child's categories, it should be easy for the child to decide that he or she did not understand what was said, rather than deciding that his or her categorization scheme is incorrect. Later, even when the child understands language well enough to realize that adults consider an object to be a member of a different category from the child's choice, the child often is willing to let the two systems exist side by side.

But linguistic input does play some role. In certain cases of undergeneralization – those involving objects that the child does not consider to be members of any category, but that reasonably could be included in one of the child's already-formed categories – repeated parental labeling of the object in question may convince the child to include it in the relevant category. If the basis for exclusion is a general one, for example, that the exemplar is very stylized, once the child realizes that the object should be included in the relevant category, he or she may begin spontaneously to include other stylized objects in other child-appropriate categories. In this way, repeated adult labeling of a single exemplar excluded from an undergeneralized category, once successful in convincing the child that the object should be included in the category, may have an impact on the child's entire category system by changing the child's beliefs concerning the acceptable range of derivations (especially stylistic ones) for attributes.

The child also may rely on adult labeling to determine the category assignment of objects whose assignment the child considers ambiguous between two (or more) categories. An example of such an object for Ari was a picture of a fat yellow duck/songbird. Even adults who saw this picture had trouble deciding whether it was a duck or a songbird. These objects are poor examples that are on the border between two categories.

As children get older, the role of linguistic input in categorization should increase. I will provide several examples of this increased role. First, the child eventually acquires the metacognition necessary to realize that adult use of a different label for an object already included in another child category implies that a new category assignment would be appropriate. Inherent in this metacognition is acceptance of the expert principle, that is, a willingness to accept a category assignment made by another person because of acceptance of that person's authority on categorization issues (or particular types of categorization issues), even when the child does not understand the basis for the other person's category assignment. Older children are likely to accept the label provided by an adult as evidence of expert opinion on the category assignment of a particular object. (For a discussion of the effect of the expert principle on adjustment of categories formed by adults, see Neisser, this volume.) At this point, category evolution may be strongly influenced by linguistic input. Older children, like adults, do not always accept the expert opinion. However, in contrast to the very young child, who often is comfortable ignoring a contradictory adult label, the child who acknowledges the expert principle cannot simply ignore contradictory input. The latter child will respond to the adult when a difference in labels occurs. For example, when Ari was 17 months old, if he labeled an object, "X" and we responded, "That looks like an X," he was content. By 27 months, however, Ari knew that such a response indicated we disagreed with him. Further, it was important to him to reconcile the disagreement. Thus, one of three types of utterances consistently ensued. The first two acknowledged that the adult (expert) opinion was correct; that is, that Ari had made an error. Ari would either offer an alternative label and then wait for our response, or simply ask us what the name of the object was. The third type of utterance indicated that Ari thought we were incorrect. In these cases, Ari would insist, "That *is* an X." By 29 months, Ari was using the "looks like" construction himself, when he disagreed with a label an adult spontaneously offered.

At the same time as the child begins to accept the expert principle, he or she may also begin to assume, based on this principle, that an object should belong to only one basic-level category. Thus, once the child assigns an object to a category different from its original one, he or she may immediately delete that object from its original category. As described above, young children initially assume that an object that has been newly assigned to a different category can be simultaneously a member of the new category and the old category, even when the two categories are mutually exclusive from the adult perspective. Very young children do not automatically adhere to the principle that an object can belong to only one basic-level category (as proposed by Markman [Chapter 10, this volume] and Tversky & Hemenway [1984]). However, after children acquire the expert principle, the exclusivity principle for basic-level categories should eventually follow.

Relatively young children are able to go beyond the shape-function principle in ways other than just the expert principle. These additional principles deserve serious study (as Murphy and Medin, 1985, also have noted). I will give only one example here. When developing categories of animals, toddlers clearly begin by focusing on observable attributes, and categorize accordingly. As Neisser (Chapter 2, this volume) has pointed out, such a focus usually will yield the same category scheme as a more sophisticated approach focusing on the animals' origins or genetic makeup. Sometimes, however, the two approaches yield different category assignments. For example, baby waterfowl, regardless of species, generally are more similar in appearance to ducks than to other species. At age 18 months, Ari consistently called these babies, "duckie," even when an adult waterbird of the same species as the baby was depicted next to it. However, by age 22 months, Ari consistently labeled these babies with the same name as the adult bird. Furthermore, Ari was more accurate at labeling the baby when he could see the adult bird than when he could not. Thus, he clearly was using information not present in the physical appearance of the baby to determine its category assignment. In fact, he appeared to be generalizing the information we would give him in response to his incorrect use of "duckie." We consistently responded with utterances such as, "This is a Mommy (Daddy) X, and that is a baby X." Ari seemed to have acquired a principle of the following type: When an adult and a baby are depicted near one another, the adult is the parent of the baby, and therefore the baby is a member of the same category as the adult. This principle, of course, held only as long as the difference in shape between adult and juvenile was not extreme (e.g., a gosling next to a mare would not be considered a baby horse). This principle took precedence over the shape-function principle. At age 30 months, Ari stated this new principle more explicitly. He was looking at a picture of a baby flamingo next to a nest, with an adult flamingo nearby. I touched the picture of the baby flamingo and asked Ari what it was. He immediately responded, "Flamingo." I then asked him how he knew it was a flamingo. He replied, "Because its mommy is a flamingo." Ari's principle presumably is an early version of the origins principle used by Keil's (Chapter 7, this volume) subjects.

A second example, the case in which the child hears a word new to him or her used in reference to an object whose category assignment is unknown to the child, is similar. In fact, in this type of situation, the child should find it much easier to learn the new word. Learning a new word, and beginning to form a category based on an object not included in any of the child's previous categories, should be simpler than learning a new word and accordingly forming a category whose existence contradicts part of the child's current category system. Again, the child should realize, based on his or her emerging metacognitive abilities, that adult use of a new word implies the existence of a category previously unknown to the child.

Third, the child eventually should be able to form categories based on verbal explanation alone, without an exemplar present. The first instance of this for Ari occurred when he was 18½ months old. The word involved was "river." At this time, Ari considered rivers to be "water." One day, I explained to Ari that we were going to see a river, and that a river was "big water." This was the first time that the word "river" had been used in speech addressed to him. A few minutes later, we climbed an observation tower on a promontory and looked down at the view. Ari immediately pointed at the Connecticut River and said "River! River!" The category that Ari formed based on this verbal description was similar to the adult category. This was possible because Ari understood the constituent words, and had the constituent categories, involved in the verbal explanation.

Fourth, the child eventually should be able to form a category based on simply hearing a new word, without an explanation and without an exemplar present, combined with process of elimination. The first instance of this with Ari occurred when he was 20 months old. I told him that we were going to see a pumpkin. This is the first time that the word "pumpkin" had ever been used in speech to him, although he had heard the word in a song which provided no information about what a pumpkin might be. We went over to a display of farm produce. The only object that Ari did not already know the name for was the pumpkin. Ari looked over the display, then pointed at the pumpkin and said, "pumpkin."

Fifth, based on these or related metacognitive abilities, the child also should be able to use linguistic input as a basis for the formation of categories at other hierarchical levels, where categories do not naturally stand out. For example, adult use of subordinate-level labels in a contrastive manner should imply to the older child that more specific categories than the ones he or she had formed spontaneously also are possible. Similarly, adult use of a superordinate label in reference to objects that the child had already included in other lower-level categories should imply to the older child that more general groupings than the ones he or she had spontaneously formed are possible. Once a child understands phrases such as "is a kind of," adults can explain particular hierarchical relationships to the child even in the absence of relevant referents. Ari demonstrated appropriate comprehension and production of this phrase, in relation to both basic-superordinate and subordinate-basic hierarchies, by age 24 months. Markman, Horton, and McLanahan (1980) have demonstrated that older children consistently can learn hierarchical relationships among artifact stimuli when the only input is presentation of the stimuli, accompanied by such phrases as, "These are Xs," (while pointing at the Xs). "These are Ys," (while pointing at the Ys). "These are kinds of Zs," (while pointing at the Xs and Ys sequentially). Addition of descriptions of critical attributes should increase the effectiveness of all of these methods. The basis for the establishment of subordinate and superordinate categories is of course not entirely linguistic, but I expect language to play a major role.

Ideally, categories are based on clusters of correlated attributes that do not overlap (or overlap very little) from category to category. The categories derived from perceptual appearances (the shape-function principle) correspond to those derived from more abstract principles such as the expert principle or the origins principle. In this ideal case, which corresponds best to the basic level, categories will be based on cognition – on the shape/function principle as applied to the perceived correlated attribute structures. This is the situation for most early categories. Sometimes, however, this situation does not obtain. For example, some poor examples of a category do not obviously fit better with the correlated attribute structure of one category than that of another, related category. Some objects are stylized enough that the child does not realize that the object should be assigned to one of his or her already-established (and -named) categories. In such cases, even the very young child may believe that linguistic input can inform his or her categorization decisions. The slightly older child can use linguistic input to help derive additional principles (such as the origins principle) that take precedence over the shape-function principle. There are categories (superordinate categories) that are based on only a very small number of attributes, and there are also categories (subordinate categories) that are based on overlapping clusters of attributes. In these cases, the categories do not stand out. Under these circumstances, linguistic input can help somewhat older children, by suggesting that such categories should exist at all. Parents also can influence their child's cognition by making available clear exemplars of categories and by providing concrete illustrations of important form and/or function attributes of these exemplars. Thus, the factors of child belief concerning the shape/function principle as the initial basis for category formation, child detection of perceived correlated attribute structures, parental influence on this detection, and, later, linguistic input that suggests alternative categorization schemes, along with child discovery of such principles as the expert principle and the origins principle, combine to determine the initial structure of children's early categories and the evolution of these categories to correspond to the adult standard.

NOTES

Several people have made important contributions to the research reported in this chapter. Cindy Mervis has collaborated with me on all aspects of both the longitudinal study and the diary study. Claudia Cardoso-Martins collaborated with me on the longitudinal study. Laurel Long is collaborating with me on the part-whole study, and is also involved in reduction and analysis of the diary study data. Kathy Johnson is assisting us with the diary study data. Patricia Christensen, Kimberlee Chamberlain, and Julie Nakamura assisted us with data collection and reduction for the longitudinal study. John Pani has been involved in data collection for the diary study and has always been available for discussion of whatever aspect of the theory I am pondering. He also drew the figures for this chapter. Laurel Long, Cindy Mervis, Nancy Myers, Dick Neisser, and John Pani provided constructive comments on previous versions of this chapter. I thank the mothers and children who were involved in the longitudinal study for their enthusiastic participation. I also thank Ari for the opportunity to conduct the diary study. The research presented in this chapter and preparation of the chapter were supported by the National Science Foundation, grants #BNS 81-21169 and #BNS 84-19036. Data reduction for the diary study was also supported by an NIH BRSG grant #RR07048-18.

1. The mothers and children in the studies cited were all from white middleclass families. Unfortunately, no research relevant to this topic has been conducted with fathers and their children, with other types of American families, or cross-culturally. Claudia Cardoso-Martins (personal communication, 1983) has noted, based on informal observations, that the same patterns obtain for Portuguese-speaking middle-class mother-child dyads in Brazil.
2. Ari also formed a few additional categories (e.g., *flamingo, penguin, puffin*), which included some birds that previously had been included in *duck*. Analysis of the data from these categories is not complete, but informal examination suggests that the pattern of development was the same as for the categories just discussed.

REFERENCES

Anglin, J. M. (1983). Extensional aspects of the preschool child's word concepts. In Th. B. Seiler & W. Wannenmacher (Eds.), *Concept development and the development of word meaning* (pp. 247–266). Berlin: Springer-Verlag.

Barrett, M. D. (1978). Lexical development and overextension in child language. *Journal of Child Language, 5*, 205–219.

(1982). Distinguishing between prototypes: The early acquisition of the meaning of object names. In S. A. Kuczaj II (Ed.), *Language development* (Vol. 1: *Syntax and semantics*, pp. 313–334). Hillsdale, NJ: Erlbaum.

Bell, R. Q. (1964). The effect on the family of a limitation in coping ability in the child: A research approach and a finding. *Merrill-Palmer Quarterly, 10*, 129–142.

Bell, R. Q., & Harper, L. V. (Eds.). (1977). *Child effects on adults.* Hillsdale, NJ: Erlbaum.

Benelli, B., D'Odorico, L., Levorato, C., & Simion, F. (1977). Formation and extension of the concept of a prelinguistic child. *Italian Journal of Psychology, 3*, 429–448.

Bowerman, M. (1976). Semantic factors in the acquisition of rules for word use and sentence construction. In D. Morehead & A. Morehead (Eds.), *Directions in normal and deficient child language* (pp. 99–179). Baltimore: University Park Press.

Brown, R. (1958). How shall a thing be called? *Psychological Review, 65*, 14–21.
    (1978). A new paradigm of reference. In G. W. Miller & E. Lenneberg (Eds.), *Psychology and biology of language: Essays in honor of Eric Lenneberg.* New York: Academic Press.

Cardoso-Martins, C., & Mervis, C. B. (1985). Maternal speech to prelinguistic children with Down syndrome. *American Journal of Mental Deficiency, 89*, 451–458.

Carey, S. (1982). Semantic development: The state of the art. In E. Wanner & L. R. Gleitman (Eds.), *Language acquisition: The state of the art.* Cambridge, England: Cambridge University Press.

Chapman, K. (1983). *Inappropriate word usage in young children: A longitudinal investigation.* Doctoral dissertation, Purdue University, West Lafayette, IN.

Clark, E. V. (1973). What's in a word? On the child's acquisition of semantics in his first language. In T. E. Moore (Ed.), *Cognitive development and the acquisition of language* (pp. 65–110). New York: Academic Press.

Clark, E. V. (1983). Meanings and concepts. In P. H. Mussen (Ed.), *Handbook of Child Psychology* (Vol. 3). New York: Wiley.

Daehler, M. W., Lonardo, R., & Bukatko, D. (1979). Matching and equivalence judgments in very young children. *Child Development, 50*, 170–179.

Dougherty, J. W. D. (1978). Salience and relativity in classification. *American Ethnologist, 5*, 66–80.

Golinkoff, R. M., & Halperin, M. S. (1983). The concept of animal: One infant's view. *Infant Behavior and Development, 6*, 229–233.

Jones, O. H. M. (1977). Mother-child communication with prelinguistic Down's syndrome and normal infants. In H. R. Schaffer (Ed.), *Studies in mother-infant interaction* (pp. 379–401). New York: Academic Press.
    (1979). A comparison study of mother-child communication with Down's syndrome and normal infants. In H. R. Schaffer & J. Dunn (Eds.), *The first year of life: Psychological and medical implications of early experience* (pp. 175–195). New York: Wiley.
    (1980). Prelinguistic communication skills in Down's syndrome and normal infants. In T. M. Fields, S. Goldberg, D. Stern, & A. M. Sostek (Eds.), *High risk infants and children: Adult and peer interactions* (pp. 205–225). New York: Academic Press.

Kogan, N. (1971). Educational implications of cognitive style. In G. Lesser (Ed.), *Psychology and educational practice* (pp. 242–292). Glenview, IL: Scott Foresman.

Lewis, M. M. (1963). *Language, thought, and personality in infancy and childhood.* New York: Basic Books.

Macnamara, J. (1982). *Names for things: A study of human learning.* Cambridge, MA: MIT Press.

MacWhinney, B. (1984). Commentary: Where do categories come from? In C. Sophian (Ed.), *Origins of cognitive skills* (pp. 407–415). Hillsdale, NJ: Erlbaum.

Markman, E. M., Horton, M. S., & McLanahan, A. G. (1980). Classes and collections: Internal organization and resulting holistic properties. *Cognition, 8,* 227–241.

Mervis, C. B. (1982, May). *Mother-child interaction and early lexical development.* Paper presented at the annual meeting of the Midwestern Psychological Association, Minneapolis, MN.

(1984). Early lexical development: The contributions of mother and child. In C. Sophian (Ed.), *Origins of cognitive skills* (pp. 339–370). Hillsdale, NJ: Erlbaum.

(1985). On the existence of prelinguistic categories: A case study. *Infant Behavior and Development, 8,* 293–300.

Mervis, C. B., & Canada, K. (1983). On the existence of competence errors in comprehension: A reply to Fremgen & Fay and Chapman & Thomson. *Journal of Child Language, 10,* 431–440.

Mervis, C. B., & Crisafi, M. A. (1982). Order of acquisition of subordinate, basic, and superordinate categories. *Child Development, 53,* 258–266.

Mervis, C. B., & Mervis, C. A. (1982). Leopards are kitty-cats: Object labeling by mothers for their 13 month olds. *Child Development, 53,* 267–273.

(1984, July). *Reduction of lexical overextensions: The roles of maternal attribute illustrations and corrections.* Paper presented at the Third International Congress for the Study of Child Language, Austin, TX.

Mervis, C. B., & Pani, J. R. (1980). Acquisition of basic object categories. *Cognitive Psychology, 12,* 496–522.

Murphy, G. L., & Medin, D. L. (1985). The role of theories in conceptual coherence. *Psychological Review, 92,* 289–316.

Nelson, K. (1974). Concept, word, and sentence: Interrelations in acquisition and development. *Psychological Review, 81,* 267–285.

Nelson, K., Rescorla, L., Gruendel, J., & Benedict, H. (1978). Early lexicons: What do they mean? *Child Development, 49,* 960–968.

Poulin-Dubois, D., & Larendeau Bendavid, M. (1984, July), *Overextension of object words in production and comprehension.* Paper presented at the Third International Congress for the Study of Child Language, Austin, TX.

Rescorla, L. A. (1980). Overextension in early language development. *Journal of Child Language, 7,* 321–335.

(1981). Category development in early language. *Journal of Child Language, 8,* 225–238.

Rosch, E., Mervis, C. B., Gray, W. D., Johnson, D. M., & Boyes-Braem, P. (1976). Basic objects in natural categories. *Cognitive Psychology, 8,* 382–439.

Tversky, B., & Hemenway, K. (1984). Objects, parts, and categories. *Journal of Experimental Psychology: General, 113,* 169–193.

9

Scripts and categories: interrelationships in development

ROBYN FIVUSH

Most models of categorization converge on the idea that categories are formed by some process of analysis of the important features or dimensions of objects. Discrete objects in the world either are or are not members of a particular category based on some analysis of shared similarities between this object and other members of the category, as well as perceived differences between this object and members of other, contrasting categories. Different models emphasize different underlying components – features, dimensions, attributes, and so on – and the structure of the category may be based on a feature list, or a prototype, but the basic underlying assumption is the same. Categories are formed by analyzing the relevant attributes of objects (see Smith & Medin, 1981, for a review).

Developmentally, the process of category formation is also assumed to proceed by analysis of relevant features of objects that define category membership and much of the research has focused on children's ability to abstract features from a set of exemplars and generalize membership to new and novel exemplars (Farah & Kosslyn 1982). Recent research has demonstrated that infants as young as 10 months of age are capable of sophisticated perceptual processing of the features and dimensions of presented objects (Strauss 1979; Younger & Cohen 1983).

While these results indicate that young children are *capable* of grouping objects together based on feature analysis, twenty years of research in developmental psychology has established that young children *prefer* to group objects together on a more functional or thematic basis (Denney & Moulton 1976; Mandler 1979; Nelson 1974). Given this strong and consistent preference, we still know surprisingly little about the processes involved in the formation of functional and thematic categories, or the relationship between these kinds of categories and more traditionally defined categories. These are the issues explored in this chapter. The basic argument advanced is that functional and thematic categories emerge from children's representations of events, or scripts. Objects encountered during the same event routine come to be grouped

234

together. Rather than analysis of discrete *objects* in the world, categories are formed by analyzing the structure of *events*. Similar arguments have been advanced recently by Nelson and her colleagues (Lucariello & Nelson 1984; Lucariello & Rifkin 1985; Nelson 1983), and their research forms the groundwork for many of the ideas expressed in this chapter. If we take this idea of category formation seriously, then our task becomes, first, to examine how young children organize and represent events, and, second, to specify how event representations are related to categories of objects.

Let me stress at the outset that many of the arguments presented in this chapter are speculative. Too little research has been conducted as yet to draw any firm conclusions. My purpose here, then, is to describe a theoretical framework for studying category development and especially to argue for the fruitfulness of examining category formation in the context of children's knowledge and representations of events. The first section of the chapter gives a brief overview of how young children represent events and presents evidence for the early emergence of organized event representations, or scripts. In the second section, the structure of scripts is examined in more detail, and the relationships between functional and thematic categories and script structure are discussed.

The representation of events

Following from the work of Piaget (1954; Piaget & Inhelder 1969), much of the early research in developmental psychology focused on the limitations and incompetencies of the preschool child's thought. Across a wide variety of task domains, children younger than about age 6 or 7 demonstrated little ability to reason coherently or systematically organize information in experimental situations.

Three trends in developmental psychology called this early view of the incompetent preschooler into serious question. First, new methodologies for working with infants revealed that children in the first two years of life are capable of sophisticated processing and organization of information (Reznick & Kagan 1982). Second, findings from research on language development indicated that children in the language learning years were employing complex sets of rules for both grammar and discourse (Brown 1973; Halliday 1975). Finally, a shift toward more naturalistic, or ecologically valid, assessment of young children revealed that, with more meaningful tasks and materials, preschool children displayed surprisingly complex problem-solving abilities (Donaldson 1978; Gelman 1977). Together, these lines of evidence forced developmentalists to take a closer look at the competencies of the preschool child.

Children's scripts

It was within this framework that the investigation of young children's understanding of routine and familiar events was undertaken (Nelson 1986; Nelson, Fivush, Hudson, & Lucariello 1983; Nelson & Gruendel 1981). Rather than assessing how young children organize information in an experimental situation, the issue addressed was how children spontaneously and naturally organize and represent their real-world experiences. In the early research, children ranging in age from 3 to 8 years were asked to tell what happens when they engage in various events, such as birthday parties, or going to McDonald's. Surprisingly, children as young as 3 years of age gave general, spatially-temporally organized reports of these kinds of events.

Children's narratives conformed to a "script" framework (Schank & Abelson 1977), where a script is defined as a spatially-temporally organized body of knowledge that defines the actors, actions, and objects likely to be present in a given situation. Scripts do not specify particular occurrences of an event, but rather the range of variables and their possible instantiations that specify all occurrences. In this way, scripts are dynamic and flexible. They allow us to anticipate and predict recurring events in our world as well as providing the framework necessary for understanding new events. When asked about events with which they are familiar, children's narratives are organized as a set of expectations about what is most likely to occur during any and all instantiations of the event.

Some examples will elucidate this description; these are the reports from some of the youngest subjects, children just barely 3 years old. One child, asked "What happens when you make cookies?" responds, "Well, you bake them and you eat them." Another child, asked "What happens when you go grocery shopping?" reports, "You buy things and then you go home." Finally, another child asked "What happens when you get dressed in the morning?" says, "You put on your clothes and then you have breakfast."

Clearly these reports are very skeletal but there are a few aspects of these narratives that are important to note. First and foremost, the children are not recounting specific, autobiographical memories of what happened one time when they made cookies or went grocery shopping. The reports are general in both content and structure. Children report actions which define all occurrences of the event and they linguistically structure their reports in the third person and the timeless present tense, "You do X".[1] Moreover in virtually every event narrative analyzed, children report the component actions in their correct temporal order (Fivush 1984; French & Nelson 1982; Nelson & Gruendel 1981).

These aspects of children's reports indicate that the events are represented in a general, well-organized format.

Further each action mentioned subsumes a set of activities and objects. When you go grocery shopping, you buy "things." The child can further specify these "things" when probed – that is, the child knows that the things you buy at the grocery store are things like milk and fruit and not things like shoes and telephones. Similarly, when you get dressed, you put on clothes, and the general variable clothes can be instantiated by items such as jeans and sweaters, but not by items like blankets or lamps. Thus, the event seems to be represented as a general framework that defines the range of possible objects encountered. Notice that this sounds very much like a category definition. That is, the range of objects to be included and objects to be excluded are specified. Overall these findings demonstrate that young children have general, well-organized representations of events with which they are familiar and event representations, or scripts, provide a structure for defining a range of objects relevant to that event.

The early emergence of scripts

In the initial research the children interviewed were already 3 years old. If we want to explore the early formation of categories, we must look to a younger age group. Unfortunately, it is difficult to interview children much below the age of 3 years. Data from several sources indicate, however, that infants and very young children also have organized representations of familiar events.

First, in a study by O'Connell & Gerard (1985), children ranging in age from 20 months to 36 months were asked to imitate sequences of actions of familiar events. Sometimes actions from the same event were presented together – like getting in the tub, soaping up, and drying off – and sometimes actions from different events were presented together – like getting in the tub, eating an apple, and pulling up a blanket. In both types of sequences, the actions were familiar to the child. The only difference between the two sequence types was that one represented a coherent event and the other did not. Even at 20 months, children were aware of the differences between these types of sequences. They imitated the actions that formed a cohesive event more often than actions that did not form a cohesive event. This indicates that as young as 20 months, children know which actions belong together in familiar events.

The second piece of evidence for organized event representations in very young children comes from Nelson's (1984) analysis of one young child's bedtime conversations with herself. Like many children this age, Emily talked to herself before falling asleep at night. These monologues were tape-recorded at frequent intervals, starting when Emily was about 20 months old. Surprisingly, among the things Emily recounted to herself were routine events, such as eating breakfast and going shopping. This suggests that routine events are an important part of young children's lives, and even more, that they are actively engaged in the process of comprehending and representing such events.

Research on symbolic play provides further evidence for the early development of organized event representations. Infants as young as 13 months will spontaneously act out appropriate actions with realistic event props (Bretherton 1984; Bretherton, Bates, McNew, Shore, Williamson, & Beeghly-Smith 1981). By 15 months, infants will perform an organized sequence of actions evocative of the event in which these objects play a role (Fenson & Ramsey 1980, 1981). For example, given a cup and a spoon, virtually all infants will stir the spoon in the cup or put the spoon to their mouth. In fact, among the most common pretend-play themes acted out by young children are routine, everyday events such as cooking and serving a meal (Garvey 1977). Again, these findings indicate that infants and young children are actively engaged in representing real-world events.

The final piece of evidence for the early development of event representations really comes from the literature on language development. Many theorists, most notably Bruner (1983; Ratner & Bruner 1978), have argued that language learning occurs within the context of well-defined, joint action routines between mother and infant, and there is evidence of such routines as young as 6 months. These are simple, repetitive routines in which the mother and infant each have a role to play, such as peekaboo and give-and-take games. But the presence of these kinds of routines so early in development would seem to indicate that infants are capable of understanding actions related through time.

Taken together, these various areas of research provide overwhelming evidence that event representations are a basic, developmentally early representational system. The next question concerns the relationship between event representations, or scripts, and categories of objects.

The structure of scripts

In order to discuss the relations between scripts and categories, we need to take a closer look at the structure of scripts. As mentioned earlier, scripts are spatially-temporally organized sequences of actions. Most of these actions involve a specified type of object. Let us take the eating routine as an example. As shown in Figure 9.1, the basic script goes something like this: You get in the high chair, you put on a bib, you eat food from a plate or a bowl with a spoon, you drink from a cup or a

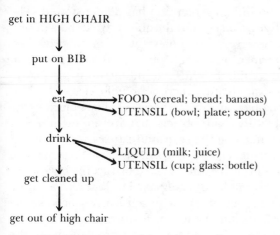

get in HIGH CHAIR

↓

put on BIB

↓

eat → FOOD (cereal; bread; bananas)
→ UTENSIL (bowl; plate; spoon)

↓

drink → LIQUID (milk; juice)
→ UTENSIL (cup; glass; bottle)

↓

get cleaned up

↓

get out of high chair

Figure 9.1. The structure of the eating routine script.

bottle, you get cleaned up, and then you get out of the high chair. When we look at this structure, it becomes apparent that objects can be specified in two different ways. First, objects that can be substituted for each other at a particular point in the routine come to be grouped together by virtue of sharing a common function. Second, objects that are encountered as the event unfolds come to be grouped together by virtue of being embedded in a common routine. The first type of category is a *functional* category, and the second is a *thematic* category. Each of these will be discussed in turn.

Functional categories

Theoretical background

Functional categories were initially posited by Nelson (1974) as an alternative to the abstraction theory of concept formation, and especially in opposition to the perceptual feature basis of categorization (Clark 1973). Although perceptual analysis of objects undoubtedly plays a role in the formation of categories, perceptual analysis alone cannot fully explain how categorization proceeds.

The basic problem facing any theory of category development is to explain how the infant knows that a newly encountered object is an instance of a particular category. If we assume that the infant is categorizing on the basis of the perceptual features that objects have in common, then we are faced with the problem of how the infant learned the relevant features in the first place. This is not to argue that infants cannot perceptually analyze features of objects. They clearly can do so, as the history of research on infant perception has demonstrated. The ability to perceptually analyze an object and the ability to extend a definition to a class of objects, however, are somewhat different processes. Perceptual analysis is performed on a single object, but a category usually includes more than one object. Thus the infant must be able to analyze and abstract the relevant features across a set of objects. But how does the infant know which objects to abstract across? Most objects in the world share overlapping features with objects that are not members of the same category. If we assume that the relevant features are defined as those features that are invariant across exemplars then we are unable to explain how the infant knows which exemplars to abstract the invariance across in the first place. This model of category development assumes that which it needs to explain: how does the infant learn which are the relevant features and which are the irrelevant features?

Nelson (1974) has argued that the solution to this problem lies in the fact that many categories are initially formed on the basis of common functions rather than on shared perceptual features. For example, the child initially defines "ball" as something to roll, and anything that fulfills this function will be categorized as a ball. Thus apples are not considered to be members of the same category as balls, even though they are perceptually quite similar, because apples are not things to roll. Rather, they are things to eat, and they will be grouped with other objects that are also eatable, such as bananas and raisins. Again, notice that the category of eatable things does not share many perceptual features in common, but is defined in terms of a common function.

According to this view, a concept is formed on the basis of the very first encounter with an object that includes both relevant and irrelevant aspects of the functional context. Children then know a second object is another example of the category because they can perform the same action on the object or the object fulfills the same function. Across repeated encounters the invariant aspects of the object and the context come to form the "functional core," which defines category membership.

Empirical evidence

In a series of studies, Nelson (1973) has demonstrated that infants between 12 and 24 months of age make use of functional attributes in categorizing objects on a variety of tasks. For example, in one task, a set of objects varying along either perceptual or functional dimensions were placed on a table in front of infants and the order of selecting the objects was recorded. (This task has been used successfully by several researchers and will be discussed in detail in the following section.) Perceptual dimensions were defined in terms of color and form (e.g., blue animals vs yellow animals or red squares vs red cylinders) and functional dimensions were defined in terms of potential action (e.g., yellow plastic cars vs yellow plastic eating utensils). Of course, the objects defined by function also have perceptual features in common, but the objects defined by form alone were not distinguished by functional features. Infants grouped objects by category under both conditions, but they were more consistent when the objects varied by function than when they varied by form alone. That is, they were more likely to put all the cars together and all the eating utensils together than to put all the square blocks together and all the cylinders together.

In another study in the series, Nelson presented infants from 12 to 24 months of age with a set of ball-like objects that varied along perceptual and functional dimensions. After infants played with the objects they were asked to hand over a "ball." Infants were much more likely to select objects which were functionally similar but perceptually different from balls (e.g., a hard plastic "whiffle" ball with holes) than objects which were perceptually similar but functionally different from balls (e.g., a spherical rattle mounted on a flat stand). The results from these studies suggest that, at least for infants, functional attributes of objects may be more salient for category definition than perceptual attributes.

Additional evidence for the early emergence of functional categories comes from a study done by Ross (1982). Using a paired-preference paradigm, she found that 12-month-old infants were sensitive to the categories of food and furniture. In this paradigm, infants are shown many exemplars from one category and are then given a choice of looking at or playing with another exemplar from the same category or an exemplar from a novel category. Since novelty is defined in terms of the previously presented exemplars, preference for the object from the novel category suggests that infants appreciated the categorical membership of the previously presented exemplars. After viewing many exemplars of a food category, infants preferred to play with a nonfood item than a food item, even though the food exemplars presented previously varied greatly in their perceptual features. Ross interpreted these results as knowledge of superordinate categories but did not discuss the basis of the relations among the category members. It seems quite likely that these categories are defined by common function. Thus, although quite limited, the research that has been done indicates that infants are making use of functional information in grouping objects together into categories.

Functional substitutability in scripts

By relating functional categories to scripts, we are able to extend our understanding of category formation in two important ways. First, scripts provide the context for defining the functions of objects by specifying the range of instantiations of a variable. In the eating routine example, you certainly must eat during the routine, but the actual food item that gets ingested is variable. You can eat bananas or cereal or bread. You can drink milk or juice. You can eat from a bowl or a plate. Those objects that can be substituted for each other at a particular point in the routine are the same kind of objects – food, or drink, or eating utensils (see Lucariello & Rifkin, 1985, and Nelson, 1983, for related discussions). Remember that in the verbal reports of events, even three-year-olds expressed their knowledge that a variety of items could serve to instantiate a particular variable at a particular point in the routine – so that you buy "food" in the supermarket and you put on "clothes" when you get dressed in the morning.

Further, although the initial basis of these categories is assumed to be functional, many of the categories based on substitutability in scripts look very much like traditional taxonomic categories. We can speculate that, developmentally, some taxonomic categories such as clothing and food may initially be based on functional substitutability. Thus, by relating functional categories to scripts, we can posit a developmental continuity between functional and taxonomic categories.

Recent research by Lucariello and Nelson (1985) supports this hypothesis. They asked preschool children to recall lists organized either by taxonomic category or categories based on substitutability. For example, for the food category, the grouping based on substitutability was food you eat for lunch – peanut butter, cheese, and bologna – and the taxonomic grouping was three types of food that could not be eaten at the same point in a routine – cheese, ice cream, and cereal. Other categories on the list were animals and clothing. Choice of exemplars was based on interviews with young children to ensure that all the items were equally familiar. But children recalled more and their recall was better organized when the categories were based on substitutability than when they were strictly taxonomic. These findings indicate that substitutability is an important dimension along which young children organize objects, and suggest that categories based on functional substitutability may be more cohesive for young children than are taxonomic categories.

Relations of substitutability

A closer examination of the relations among members of script-based functional categories suggests that there may be more than one form of substitutability. The category of "things you eat for lunch" seems to be based on a concept of *alternatives;* you eat either bologna OR peanut butter during a particular instantiation of the event, but not both during the same instantiation. The category is formed by abstracting across instantiations of the same event. Peanut butter and bologna are not spatially or temporally linked in the sense of being in the environment simultaneously. Rather, they are spatially and temporally linked in the sense of occurring at the same point in different instantiations of the event.

On the other hand, "things you wear" are not substitutable for each other in the same sense as is food. When you get dressed in the morning you don't put on pants OR a sweater. but both. But you don't put on pajamas; pajamas are not "things you wear during the day" but "things you wear to bed." These items are related by spatial-temporal *contiguity*. They occur together during the same instantiation of the event. This distinction may be a continuum. Sometimes you do eat peanut butter and cheese during the same instantiation of lunch, and you don't always wear both a shirt AND a sweater. But some functional categories seem to be based almost exclusively on a concept of alternatives. Dessert foods are a good example; it is rare to eat more than one dessert food during a given instantiation of an event. Other functional categories seem to be based much more on contiguity. For example, when you go to the zoo you rarely if ever see just one animal.

Thus we need to clarify the notion of functional substitutability. Items that serve a common function at a particular point in an event routine come to be grouped together. These items may be encountered together during the same instantiation of a routine (i.e., contiguity) or may be encountered at the same temporal point in different instantiations of the routine (i.e., alternatives). Moreover, this difference is quite variable. An item may be encountered singly during some instantiations of the routine and may be encountered with other, functionally similar items during other instantiations. The crucial distinction, however, is that ONLY those objects which are functionally similar will appear at that point in the routine. Thus foods you eat for dinner and foods you eat for dessert remain two separate functional categories; although they may be encountered during the same routine (eating dinner), they are encountered at different temporal points in the routine and serve different functions.

Future directions

Additional research is clearly needed. We simply have too little data at present to draw any firm conclusions, but what little we do have indicates that functional categories are a primary and developmentally early form of categorical organization. Future research will elucidate the structure and the development of categories based on functional substitutability. For example, categories based more on contiguity (e.g., zoo animals) may be easier to learn than categories based more on alternatives (e.g., dessert foods) because contiguity relations do not necessarily require children to abstract across different instantiations of the event. In addition, of course, the relationship between functional categories and taxonomic categories needs to be examined in more detail. Lucariello and Nelson (1984) have shown that functional categories are more salient to the young child, but it is unclear if and how taxonomic categories emerge from these early functional categories. This is not to suggest that taxonomic categories ever replace functional categories. They do not. Functional categories continue to be a salient and natural way of organizing objects in the world throughout adulthood (Barsalou & Sewell 1985). Rather, the relationship between these two forms of categorical organization needs to be examined in more detail.

Although many of the arguments concerning functional categories remain tentative for the moment, two things seem clear. First, functional similarity is an important dimension along which infants and children (as well as adults) categorize objects. Second, scripts provide a framework for defining the function of objects.

Thematic categories

The basis of thematic categories

The second type of category to emerge from scripts is based on common occurrence in an event routine. Different objects are specified at different temporal points in the routine, so first you encounter a high chair, and then a bib, and then a bowl, and so on (see Figure 9.1). Each of these objects is encountered as the event unfolds. Further, the presence of one of the objects signals the coming presence of the other objects. If you have ever left an infant waiting in a high chair, you know that this is true – the high chair is a strong signal that food is on the way. In fact, many infants will express hunger by trying to get into their high chair rather than, for example, going over to the refrigerator. Thus, objects are grouped together because they are encountered during the same routine.

A great deal of research has shown that preschool children prefer to group objects thematically rather than taxonomically on a variety of free-recall and category-sorting tasks (Denney & Moulton 1976; Worden, Mandler, & Chang 1978). Because, however, the focus of previous research has been on the development of taxonomic organization, thematic groupings were viewed as a developmentally earlier and cognitively less sophisticated type of categorization. Yet on reflection, thematic groupings are a complex cognitive accomplishment.

First of all, the objects in a thematic group are both temporally and spatially linked. That is, some objects are encountered at specific points in the routine, while others are present in the environment throughout the routine. Thus the child must be able to relate objects together along both spatial and temporal dimensions simultaneously. Second, and more important, these objects are both functionally and perceptually diverse. They neither look alike, nor are they used for the same purpose. A high chair is used for sitting and a spoon is used for scooping. Thus the child cannot rely on shared perceptual or functional features in order to form these types of groupings. Moreover, there is growing evidence that thematic organization continues to play an important role throughout development (Rabinowitz & Mandler 1983). A large literature on schemas and schematic organization clearly indicates that thematic organization is pervasive and strongly influences how adults understand and recall information about the world (Bower, Black, & Turner 1979). Yet we know virtually nothing about the early development of thematic categories. This is the issue which we addressed in some recent research (Fivush, Mandler, & Reznick 1985; Mandler, Fivush, & Reznick 1985). Specifically, we explored the development of script-based thematic categories during the second year of life.

The development of thematic categories

Demonstrating the early emergence of script-based thematic categories is important for several reasons. First, it would provide the strongest possible evidence that infants are forming categories based on scripts. That is, if infants are forming thematic groups, it would be difficult to argue that it could be on any basis other than being embedded in common spatial-temporal event routines. These objects share no other features, either perceptual or functional, in common. Although the presence of thematic categories has been amply demonstrated with older children, there is virtually no research on thematic categories with infants. As mentioned earlier, the literature on symbolic play with infants in the second year of life has shown that when presented with realistic props, infants will spontaneously perform appropriate actions. While these findings indicate that infants have organized knowledge about routine and familiar events, they do not address the issue of *categorization*. We were interested not in whether infants know the *actions* associated with particular objects, but whether they *group objects* together based on the fact that they are a part of the same routine. That is, infants may independently know that you comb your hair with a comb and wash your hands with soap, but they may not group these objects together as belonging to the same "grooming" routine.

We examined infants' categorization of objects emerging from two routines, an eating routine and a washing routine. We chose these routines because all infants are familiar with these events. Further, these events occur in a clearly defined spatial location, and other events do not occur in these same spatial locations. Eating routines occur in the kitchen and washing routines occur in the bathroom. Finally, the particular objects associated with these routines are clearly defined with these routines and only these routines. Again, high chairs are used only during eating routines, as are spoons and bibs. Bathtubs and soap are only used during washing routines, and so on. Thus, these are highly familiar, clearly defined events in infants' lives.

The object-sorting task

We used two tasks to assess 14- and 20-month-old infants' understanding of thematic, script-based categories: a preferential looking task and an object-sorting task. Only the object-sorting task will be discussed in this chapter, although the pattern of results from the two tasks was comparable (see Mandler, Fivush, & Reznick, 1985, for details). The task itself is quite simple; eight objects, four from each of the two routines are randomly placed on a table in front of the infants, with the instructions, "Here, these are for you to play with." The infants are then free to manipulate the objects in any way they desire without feedback for approximately 2 to 2½ minutes. The basic measure is whether infants sort the objects by category by successively touching members of the same category. This task successfully elicits sorting by category in infants as young as 9 months with objects varying along a few simple dimensions (Ricciuti 1965; Starkey 1981; Sugarman 1981, 1983).

Although our task was the same as that used previously, our objects were quite different. The objects we used for the eating routine were *pan, plate, cup,* and *spoon,* and for the washing routine, *comb, toothbrush, toothpaste,* and *soap.* The eight objects are perceptually and functionally quite diverse. Infants cannot group these objects together based on an analysis of similar features. The objects neither look alike nor are they used for the same purpose. If infants group these objects together by category it must be based on their occurrence in a common spatial-temporal event routine.

Another aspect of this task deserving mention is the fact that these objects are placed in front of the infant in the absence of any contextual support. That is, the assumption is that these objects are defined by their common spatial-temporal context, but when we put these objects on the table in front of the infants, they have no supporting context in which to place them. Infants are not in the spatial locations in which these objects are usually found and they are not engaged in the activities in which these objects are usually embedded. In this sense, these objects are de-contextualized. If the infants group the items together, it suggests that the grouping is no longer tied to the spatial-temporal context in which it was originally embedded.

Sequential touching. Our major focus of analysis was the order in which the infants touched the objects before them. In order to interpret these kinds of data, however, it is important to establish that infants were actively involved in this task. Involvement can be conceptualized in two ways: as the *frequency* of touching objects and as the *diversity* of objects touched. Frequency is the total number of touches the infant makes toward these objects, including repetitions, and measures how active infants were in general during the session. Diversity is the number of different objects that infants touched; that is, of the eight objects available on the table, how many did the infant actually come into contact with at some point during the session? If an infant engaged in a lot of touching behavior but only touched two or three of the objects available, the behavior could be explained in terms of saliency rather than categorization. This problem is discussed in more detail in the next section. However, the data indicate that this was not the case. Infants were actively engaged in this task – they made an average of about 15 touches during the session – and they also tended to touch most of the objects available at some point during the session – they touched an average of just over six of the eight objects available. Thus infants were clearly touching most of the objects available at some point during the session.

The primary analysis focused on sequential touching, or the number of objects from the same category touched in succession. The logic behind examining sequential touching is that if infants touch objects from one of the two categories before them at a greater than chance probability, then they must systematically be choosing objects from that category to touch. That is, they must deliberately be searching among the objects on the table to find another member of the same category, rather than simply manipulating the objects before them in a random manner. The number of objects from the same category touched in succession is a run. For example, touching the pan, and then the plate, and then the spoon is a run of three objects from the eating routine category. We calculated the mean run lengths and compared this to the run length that would be expected by chance if infants were touching objects at random. Infants at both ages showed sequential touching at greater than chance levels. Both 14- and 20-month-old infants sequentially selected objects from the same category from those objects available in the array at a greater than chance level of probability.

Single and exhaustive sorters. While the analysis of overall sequential touching indicates that infants are touching objects systematically, it does not provide any qualitative information on how infants are categorizing. Infants can show systematic touching in at least two distinct ways. First, they can sequentially touch only objects from one category and not the objects from the other category. Remember that infants did tend to touch most of the objects before them at some point during the session, and no infant touched only objects from one category during the entire session; however, there were individual differences in how many sequential touches were directed to objects from one category or the other. If infants sequentially touched objects from only one of the two available categories, they were categorized as *single* sorters. Infants can also sequentially touch first the objects from one category and then the objects from the second category. Infants who displayed this kind of behavior were categorized as *exhaustive* sorters.

In order to be considered a sorter, an infant had to touch a minimum of three different objects from the same category in succession, for example, the comb, the soap, and the toothbrush. We decided on the three-object minimum both because this is the criterion used in previous research and because the probability of touching three objects from the same category in a row by chance is relatively low. Thus infants were divided into three groups. Single sorters were those infants who touched a minimum of three different objects from the same category in succession, but who did not touch three different objects from the second category in succession. Exhaustive sorters touched a minimum of three different objects in succession from both categories. Finally, some infants did not touch a minimum of three objects from the same category in succession, and they were categorized as nonsorters.

The interpretation of single sorting. If infants sort the objects exhaustively, it is clear that they are aware of both categories before them. However, the interpretation of single sorting is a little more problematical. An argument could be made that if infants are only choosing items from one category to manipulate, then they may be selecting items based on saliency rather than category membership. That is, some objects may simply be more compelling or attractive to the infant, whether or not the infant is aware that they are members of the same category. But, if this were true, then we would expect the infant to touch *only* objects from the more attractive category, or at least to show some bias or preference toward touching only objects from the more attractive category. For example, if the infant found the objects from the washing routine more attractive, for whatever reason, then the infant should show a bias toward touching these items. This would be evidenced by a vast majority of the touches made during the entire session being directed toward the objects from the washing routine and few touches being directed toward objects from the eating routine.

Further, this kind of a bias could operate at two levels. All members of the category may be more attractive for some reason, or particular objects may be especially attractive or unattractive. If infants are attracted toward particular objects, then this could inflate their overall number of touches toward objects in that category. On the other hand, if infants tend not to touch certain objects, then this could deflate their total number of touches directed toward objects from that category. It is important to make sure that these kinds of biases are not operating in this task in order to interpret what single-sorting behavior means. Several item analyses were performed on these data and there were no preferences for particular objects, either at the category level or at the individual-object level. All infants touched items from both categories at some point during the session, and no item was consistently avoided. The fact that at some point during the session, the infant sequentially touches items from the same category indicates that at that point, the infant is deliberately choosing items from the same category. Thus, we can argue that single sorting is evidence for categorization.

The evidence for thematic categories

Infants at both ages demonstrated knowledge of thematic categories. Of the 20 infants at each age, twelve 14-month-olds (60 percent) and eighteen 20-month-olds (90 percent) sorted the objects by category. For the 14-month-olds, 10 (50 percent) exhibited single sorting and 2 (10 percent) exhibited exhaustive sorting. For the 20-month-olds, 12 (60 percent) exhibited single sorting and 6 (30 percent) exhibited exhaustive sorting. Just about half of the single sorters at each age level sorted the objects from the eating routine, and about half sorted the objects from the washing routine, again indicating that single sorting cannot be attributed to the saliency of particular category members.

Categories versus action routines. Perhaps the most convincing evidence that infants were categorizing these objects is the fact that infants were not simply relating objects through action. Not surprisingly, all infants spontaneously performed appropriate actions with many of these objects. For example, infants put the comb to their hair or the spoon to their mouth. They even performed more elaborate action routines, such as putting toothpaste on the toothbrush and then putting the toothbrush to their mouth, or tapping the spoon on the plate and then putting the spoon to their mouth. However, infants' groupings went beyond these action routines. Remember that, to be classified as a sorter, an infant must touch at least three objects from the same category in succession. Given the items used in this task, an infant must group objects together that are not directly related through action in order to be considered a sorter. Grouping the soap with the toothbrush and toothpaste, or the pan with the cup and the spoon requires the infants to go beyond simple action routines performed with these objects. Thus, infants must have been relying on more abstract, spatial-temporal relationships in grouping these objects together.

This point cannot be stressed enough. It is really the strongest evidence that infants are categorizing these objects. It is not at all surprising that infants as young as 14 months know the actions associated with particular objects, or even that they know that objects belong together by virtue of being related through action. If infants did no more than relate the toothbrush and the toothpaste or the cup and spoon, these results could not be taken as unambiguous evidence of categorization. But infants in this study demonstrated abstract categorical knowledge. Soap and toothbrush are only related to each other through a routine extended in space and time. No action unites them. The same is true for comb and toothbrush, pan and cup, and so on. In order to make these kinds of groupings infants must be relying on abstract spatial-temporal relations.

A caveat

Our results indicate that infants are forming thematic, script-based categories. The assumption is that these object groupings emerge from a common spatial-temporal event routine, but one limitation of the present findings is the confounding of spatial and temporal information. In the events studied, the objects are defined by a common spatial location as well as by a common temporal routine. In fact, most events in the real world occur in particular spatial locations. Actions are continuous in time; one of the ways we parse action streams into events may be by spatial location. A change from one spatial location to another signals that one event is ending and another event is beginning (Fivush 1984).

However, in order to study the process by which infants are forming script-based categories, it is important to try to disentangle spatial and temporal information and to examine the relative contributions of each type of information. There seem to be two ways to do this. First, there are some events that share a common spatial location but are differentiated from each other by when they occur. Getting dressed in the morning and going to bed at night are good examples. Both events occur in the bedroom but obviously occur at different times. If infants differentiate between objects associated with each of these events, then they must be relying on temporal information. Second, action routines defined either spatially or temporally can be constructed and learned in a laboratory setting. Both the process of learning the routines and the ability to categorize objects associated with the routines would provide invaluable data on infants' representations of events and the emergence of script-based categories.

Conclusions

In this chapter I have argued that functional and thematic categories emerge from the representations of events. A great deal of evidence indicates that even very young children have general, spatially-temporally organized knowledge about routine and familiar events in their world. Although more speculative, there is growing evidence that event representations, or scripts, provide a framework for two different forms of categorical organization, functional categories and thematic categories.

Functional categories are based on a principle of substitutability. Those objects that can be substituted for one another at a particular point in an event routine come to be understood as the same sort of object. Substitutability can be based on one of two relations. First, objects that serve the same function can be encountered at the same temporal point during different instantiations of an event. These objects are *alternatives* to each other. Breakfast foods is a good example; different foods are encountered at the same temporal point during different instantiations of the routine, and thus come to be grouped together as serving the same function across various occurrences of the event. Second, objects encountered at the same temporal point during the same instantiation of an event are functionally related by *contiguity*. An example of this type of category is clothes you wear to school. Although different clothing items may be worn on different days, during the same instantiation of the event, several clothing items co-occur at the same temporal point in the routine.

Developmentally, functional categories seem to emerge earlier and form more cohesive groupings than taxonomic categories. In fact, it seems quite possible that functional categories emerging from scripts provide the base from which many taxonomic categories are formed. Thematic categories are based on common occurrence in an extended-event routine. Objects encountered during the same spatially-temporally defined-event routine are grouped together. For example, bed, pillow, pajamas, and slippers belong together as part of the going-to-bed routine; high chair, bowl, spoon, and bib belong together as part of the eating routine; and so on.

Thematic categories are a developmentally early form of organization. Research on symbolic play has demonstrated that infants are aware of the actions associated with particular objects. As in that research, we also found that infants performed the appropriate actions with the objects. Given objects from an eating routine and a washing routine, virtually all the infants stirred the spoon in the cup and tried to put toothpaste on the toothbrush. However, our results further demonstrate that infants are grouping together objects that are not related through action. Toothpaste and comb cannot be related through the same actions, nor can toothbrush and soap. Yet infants grouped these objects together. These findings indicate that thematic categories are not simply based on action. Infants must be relying on more abstract spatial-temporal relations in order to form thematic categories. By analyzing the structure of event representations, or scripts, we can provide a theoretically motivated explanation of thematic categories.

Most important, functional and thematic categories emerging from scripts are not based on analysis of individual objects, but rather on analysis of the activities in which objects play a role. The infant is not abstracting a set of features or attributes of an object and then generalizing these features to new exemplars. Rather the functions of objects become apparent through active engagement with the world. In order to understand the process of category development, we cannot examine the properties of objects in isolation, but must focus our attention on the kinds of activities and routines in which objects are embedded. It is in this sense that scripts provide a fruitful framework for examining the formation and development of categorical organization.

NOTES

I am grateful to Jean Mandler for her comments on an earlier draft of this chapter, and especially to Paul Sledge for his assistance on all phases of the thematic category research. As always, I am deeply indebted to Katherine Nelson and the members of the Script Research Group at the City University of New York.

1 The linguistic structure of children's narratives cannot be attributed to the linguistic form of the question. Hudson (1983) found that children as young as 3 years structured their reports differently, both in terms of content and linguistic structure, when they were asked to report about specific occurrences of events rather than about what happens in general. Her results indicate that children were responding to the type of information being asked for and not to the form of the question.

REFERENCES

Barsalou, L. W., & Sewell, D. R. (1985). Contrasting the representation of scripts and categories. *Journal of Memory and Language, 24,* 646–665.
Bower, G. H., Black, J. B., & Turner, T. J. (1979). Scripts in memory for text. *Cognitive Psychology, 11,* 77–220.

Bretherton, I. (1984). Representing the social world in symbolic play. In I. Bretherton (Ed.), *Symbolic play* (pp. 3–41). New York: Academic Press.

Bretherton, I., Bates, E., McNew, S., Shore, C., Williamson, C., & Beeghly-Smith, M. (1981). Comprehension and production of symbols in infancy. *Developmental Psychology, 17,* 728–736.

Brown, R. (1973). *A first language: The early stages.* Cambridge, MA: Harvard University Press.

Bruner, J. (1983). *Children's talk: Learning to use language.* New York: Norton.

Clark, E. V. (1973). What's in a word? On the child's acquisition of semantics in his first language. In T. E. Moore (Ed.), *Cognitive development and the acquisition of language* (pp. 65–110). New York: Academic Press.

Denney, D. R., & Moulton, P. A. (1976). Conceptual preferences among preschool children. *Developmental Psychology, 12,* 509–513.

Donaldson, M. (1978). *Children's minds.* New York: Norton.

Farah, M. J., & Kosslyn, S. M. (1982). Concept development. In H. W. Reese & L. Lipsett (Eds.), *Advances in child development and behavior* (Vol. 16, pp. 125–167). New York: Academic Press.

Fenson, L., & Ramsey, D. (1980). Decentration and integration of the child's play in the second year. *Child Development, 51,* 171–178.

(1981). Effects of modeling action sequences on the play of twelve-, fifteen-, and nineteen-month old children. *Child Development, 52,* 1028–1036.

Fivush, R. (1984). Learning about school: The development of kindergartners' school scripts. *Child Development, 55,* 1697–1709.

Fivush, R., Mandler, J. M., & Reznick, J. S. (1985). *The development of event-related categories.* Paper presented at the meetings of the Society for Research in Child Development, Toronto, April 1985.

French, L. A., & Nelson, K. (1982). Taking away the supportive context: Preschoolers' talk about the "then and there." *Quarterly Newsletter of the Laboratory of Comparative Human Cognition, 4,* 1–6.

Garvey, C. (1977). *Play.* Cambridge, MA: Harvard University Press.

Gelman, R. (1977). Cognitive development. *Annual Review of Psychology, 29,* 297–332.

Halliday, M. A. K. (1975). *Learning how to mean: Explorations in the development of language.* London: Edward Arnold.

Hudson, J. (1983). Scripts and autobiographical memory. In K. Nelson (Chair), *Memory in the real world.* Symposium conducted at the meetings of the Society for Research in Child Development, Detroit, April 1983.

Lucariello, J., & Nelson, K. (1985). Slot-filler categories as memory organizers for young children. *Developmental Psychology, 21,* 272–282.

Lucariello, J., & Rifkin, A. (1985). Event representations as the basis for categorical knowledge. In K. Nelson (Ed.), *Event knowledge: Structure and function in development.* Hillsdale, NJ: Erlbaum.

Mandler, J. M. (1979). Categorical and schematic organization in memory. In C. R. Puff (Ed.), *Memory organization and structure* (pp. 259–299). New York: Academic Press.

Mandler, J. M., & Fivush, R., & Reznick, J. S. (1985). The development of event-related categories. Manuscript submitted for publication.

Nelson, K. (1973). Some evidence for the cognitive primacy of categorization and its functional basis. *Merrill-Palmer Quarterly, 19,* 21–39.

(1974). Concept, word and sentence: Interrelations in acquisition and development. *Psychological Review, 81,* 267–295.

(1983). The derivation of concepts and categories from event representations. In E. Scholnick (Ed.), *New trends in conceptual representation: Challenges to Piaget's theory* (pp. 129–150). Hillsdale, NJ: Erlbaum.

(1984). Memories of everyday life in infancy and early childhood. In R. Fivush (Chair), *Memory development and the development of "memory talk."* Symposium conducted at the biennial meetings of the International Conference on Infant Studies, New York, April 1984.

(1986). *Event knowledge: Structure and function in development.* Hillsdale, NJ: Erlbaum.

Nelson, K., & Gruendel, J. (1981). Generalized event representations: Basic building blocks of cognitive development. In M. E. Lamb & A. L. Brown (Eds.), *Advances in developmental psychology* (Vol. 1, pp. 131–158). New York: Academic Press.

Nelson, K., Fivush, R., Hudson, J., & Lucariello, J. (1983). Scripts and the development of memory. In M. T. H. Chi (Ed.), *Contributions to human development* Vol. 9: Trends in memory development research (pp. 52–70). New York: Kargar.

O'Connell, B. G., & Gerard, A. B. (1985). Scripts and scraps: The development of sequential understanding. *Child Development, 56,* 671–681.

Piaget, J. (1954). *The construction of reality in the child.* New York: Ballantine.

Piaget, J., & Inhelder, B. (1969). *The psychology of the child.* New York: Basic Books.

Rabinowitz, M., & Mandler, J. M. (1983). Organization and information retrieval. *Journal of Experimental Psychology: Learning, Memory, and Cognition, 9,* 430–439.

Ratner, N., & Bruner, J. (1978). Games, social exchange and the acquisition of language. *Journal of Child Language, 5,* 391–402.

Reznick, J. S., & Kagan, J. (1982). Category detection in infancy. In L. P. Lipsett & C. K. Rovee-Collier (Eds.), *Advances in infancy research* (Vol. 2, pp. 80–111). Norwood, NJ: Ablex.

Ricciuti, H. N. (1965). Object grouping and selective ordering behavior in infants 12 to 24 months old. *Merrill-Palmer Quarterly, 11,* 129–148.

Ross, G. S. (1980). Categorization in 1- to 2-year olds. *Developmental Psychology, 16,* 391–396.

Schank, R., & Abelson, R. (1977). *Scripts plans goals and understanding.* Hillsdale, NJ: Erlbaum.

Smith, E. E., & Medin, D. L. (1981). *Categories and concepts.* Cambridge, MA: Harvard University Press.

Starkey, D. (1981). The origins of concept formation: Object sorting and object preference in early infancy. *Child Development, 52,* 1172–1178.

Strauss, M. S. (1979). Abstraction of prototypical information by adults and 10-month-old infants. *Journal of Experimental Psychology: Human Learning and Memory, 5,* 618–632.

Sugarman, S. (1981). The cognitive basis of classification in very young children: An analysis of object ordering trends. *Child Development, 52,* 1172–1178.

(1983). *Children's early thought: Developments in classification.* New York: Cambridge University Press.

Worden, P. E., Mandler, J. M., & Chang, F. R. (1978). Children's free recall: An explanation of sorts. *Child Development, 49,* 836–844.

Younger, B. A., & Cohen, L. B. (1983). Infant perception of correlations among attributes. *Child Development, 54,* 858–867.

10

How children constrain the possible meanings of words

ELLEN M. MARKMAN

Children face a major problem of induction in trying to learn the conventional object categories encoded by their language. From a severely limited amount of information about how a category term is used, the child must determine what the word refers to and how it relates to other terms in the child's lexicon. According to calculations reported by Carey (1978), by age 6 children have learned 14,000 words. This works out to about 9 words a day from age 18 months on. Thus, at any given time a child might be working out the meaning of hundreds of new words simultaneously. Yet it is still largely a mystery as to how children accomplish this.

A standard explanation for how children form categories is to assume a kind of general all-purpose inductive mechanism. Inhelder and Piaget (1964) and Bruner, Olver, and Greenfield (1966), for example, all have some form of this model. From a positive exemplar of the concept or word, a tentative hypothesis is formulated and evaluated against subsequent information. New instances that are consistent with the hypothesis support it, whereas inconsistent information requires that it be revised. Reformulating the hypothesis is not a trivial matter. One must come up with a hypothesis that is consistent with all the available information to avoid repeated failures.

Children up to the age of 6 or 7 have tremendous difficulty in coping with all but the simplest hypotheses, in dealing with negative information, and in reformulating hypotheses. Yet, two- and three-year-olds excel at acquiring new terms. So something is wrong with invoking this kind of model to explain the early acquisition of word meanings.

Moreover, such models beg a fundamental question about induction raised by Quine (1960) and Peirce (1957). For any set of data there will be an indefinite number of logically possible hypotheses that are consistent with it. The data are never sufficient logically to eliminate all competing hypotheses. How is it, then, that humans so frequently converge on the same hypotheses? The answer is that humans are constrained to consider only some kinds of hypotheses, or at least to give

255

them priority over others. This is especially true, I believe, in the case of very young children first trying to learn the concepts that their language encodes. The way children succeed at acquiring these terms so rapidly probably is that they are limited in the kinds of hypotheses they consider. The few hypotheses they do consider would allow them to quickly focus in on the correct meaning. By circumventing the logical analysis of data and hypotheses that children have so much trouble with, these alternative ways of acquiring word meaning could achieve much greater success more rapidly.

Although constraints on the kinds of hypotheses children consider have been postulated to account for children's acquisition of syntax (Newport 1982; Pinker 1983), little is known about constraints for the acquisition of word meanings. In this chapter, I propose two such constraints. These constraints can help account not only for the children's success in acquiring category terms but also for children's difficulty in working out hierarchical relations among category terms.

The first constraint is the assumption of taxonomic organization. It helps explain how children acquire word meanings through ostensive definition. When someone points to an object and labels it, how does the child know that the term refers to an object category as opposed to all of the other possible things it could mean? Hutchinson and I (Markman & Hutchinson 1984) proposed that children assume first that a new word will refer to a category of objects.

Another way children may constrain the possible meanings of words is to assume that they are mutually exclusive – that each category, for example, will have one and only one label. By eliminating hypotheses, the mutual exclusivity principle can help the child successively constrain the meanings of terms.

Assumption of taxonomic organization

A common way in which children learn their first category terms is through ostensive definition. That is, a parent or other teacher points to an object and labels it. Especially in the early phases of language acquisition, when children do not know enough language that one could describe a category to them, children's learning of new category terms must depend heavily on ostensive definition. Given that an adult points to an object and labels it, how is it that the child settles on an interpretation? At first sight this would seem to be a quite simple problem, and in fact children make hundreds of such inferences correctly when acquiring new vocabulary. This apparent simplicity belies an incredibly complex inferential problem that was formulated by Quine (1960) in his well-known argument about translation. Imagine that someone points to a dog and says "chien," and our job is to figure out what "chien" means. Obviously, our first hypothesis is that it means "dog." But this is not necessary. It could mean "furry object," or "brown object," or "medium-sized object," and so on. To decide if the new term refers to dog, we might set up certain test situations where we could point to various objects and ask whether or not "chien" applies. Quine's point is that no matter how many test situations we construct, there will always be more than one hypothesis for the meaning of a new term that is consistent with the existing evidence.

Young children beginning to acquire their native language continually face this problem of narrowing down the meaning of a term from an indefinite number of possibilities. Someone points in some direction and then utters a word. On what grounds is the child to conclude that a new, unfamiliar word, for example, "dog," refers to dogs? What is to prevent a child from concluding that "dog" is a proper name for that particular dog? What prevents the child from concluding that "dog" means furry object or brown object or any number of other characteristics that dogs share? Finally, what prevents the children from concluding that "dog" means something like "the dog and his bone" or "the dog next to the tree" or "mother petting the dog"? These last examples of thematic relations pose a particular problem because children are very interested in such relations and often find them more salient than categorical relations.

Across a wide variety of tasks designed to measure children's conceptual organization, younger children have been found to prefer to organize objects according to thematic relations (cf. Markman & Callanan 1983; Gelman & Baillargeon 1983, for reviews). On sorting tasks supposed to assess how children form categories, children older than six or seven years usually sort objects on the basis of the object's taxonomic category, for example, vehicles, animals, and clothing. In contrast, younger children often represent causal, temporal, spatial, or other relations among the objects. These thematic relations emphasize events rather than taxonomic similarity. For example, children might sort a man and a car together because the man is driving the car. Or they might place a boy, a coat, and a dog together because the boy will wear his coat when he takes the dog for a walk. This attention to relations between objects rather than to how objects are alike is a common finding replicated in many studies including various studies of memory and word association (see Markman 1981). From these studies of classification, we can conclude that children are more interested in the thematic relations among objects, or that thematic relations are simpler or more readily constructed than categorical relations.

There is good reason for children to notice thematic relations – in fact, good reason for adults to notice them as well. Understanding the world cannot be achieved without attending to the ways in which objects interact. Even infants tend to place causal interpretations on events they perceive (cf. Gibson & Spelke 1983). Moreover, there seem to be fewer developmental and cross-cultural differences in understanding this type of organization (Mandler, Scribner, Cole, & DeForest 1980). This is in marked contrast to the cross-cultural and developmental differences found in studies of classification. In sum, interest in thematic relations is not limited to young children. Nor should attention to thematic relations be viewed as a useless or nonproductive bias. Noticing the way in which objects interact, attending to causal, spatial, and temporal relations between objects, is essential for understanding the world. It is the failure to notice categorical relations and not the child's attention to thematic relations that changes with development.

Although children are biased toward organizing objects thematically, single words, in particular count nouns, rarely encode thematic relations. English does not have a single noun for thematically related objects such as "a boy and his bike," "a spider and its web," or "a baby and its bottle."

Thus to return to Quine's problem of induction, we are faced with a kind of paradox here. Children seem to readily learn terms that refer to object categories. Their vocabulary is filled with words such as "ball" or "dog," simple concrete nouns referring to object categories. Yet, children tend to notice and remember thematic relations between objects more readily than the object's category. How is it that children readily learn labels for categories of objects if they are attending to these relations between objects instead? To take a concrete example, imagine a mother pointing to a baby and saying "baby." Based on the classification studies, we should assume that the child will be attending to the baby shaking a rattle, or to the baby being diapered. Why, then, doesn't the child infer that "baby" means something like "baby and its rattle" or "baby and its diaper"?

Hutchinson and I (Markman & Hutchinson 1984) have proposed that the solution to this problem is that children, even extremely young children, constrain the possible meanings of words. Regarding Quine's problem of induction, children rule out many possible meanings of a new term, in particular, many thematic meanings. That is, they do not consider thematic relations as possible meanings and focus instead on categorical relations.

We know that under simplified conditions, children are able to understand categorical organization (for reviews see Carey 1982; Gelman & Baillargeon 1983; Markman & Callanan 1983; Horton 1982), even though they prefer thematic relations. To take one example, Smiley and Brown (1979) tested whether four- and six-year-old children could understand taxonomic relations even though they prefer thematic ones. They presented children with a target picture and two choice pictures. One of the choices was thematically related to the target, and one of the choices was taxonomically related to the target. For example, children were shown a spider (target), a spider web (thematic choice), and a grasshopper (taxonomic choice). The experimenter pointed to the spider and asked for "the one that goes best with this one." As usual, these young children tended to pick the spider web, rather than the grasshopper, thereby indicating a thematic relation. Nevertheless, when they were asked about the grasshopper, all of the children except the very youngest could explain the taxonomic relation. Thus, children have a rudimentary ability to organize objects taxonomically, but it is often obscured by their attention to thematic relations.

Hutchinson and I (Markman & Hutchinson 1984) proposed that children have implicit hypotheses about the possible meaning of words that help them acquire words for categories. Children may well prefer to structure the environment in a way that conflicts with the way that language is organized. But even very young children may be aware of the constraints on word meaning so that when they believe that they are learning a new *word*, they shift their attention from thematic to categorical organization.

The first study we conducted investigated whether hearing a novel word will cause two to three-year-old children to shift their attention from thematic to categorical relations. Basic-level categories (Rosch, Mervis, Gray, Johnson, & Boyes-Braem 1976) such as "dog" or "chair," were used with these young children rather than general superordinate-level categories, such as "animal" or "furniture."

Three-year-old children participated in the study. Children were assigned to one of two conditions. In one of the conditions children were asked to find a picture that was the same as the target. The other condition was the same except that a nonsense syllable was used to label the target picture.

In both of the conditions, children were first shown the target picture. They were then shown two other pictures and had to select one of them as being the same as the target.

No-Word Condition, Study 1. To begin, children were introduced to a hand puppet and were told to put the picture they chose in the puppet's mouth. On each trial, the experimenter pointed to the target card and told the child, "Look carefully now. See this?" as she pointed to

Table 10.1. *Stimulus materials study with basic-level categories*

Standard object	Taxonomic choice	Thematic choice
Police car	Car	Policeman
Tennis shoe	High-heeled shoe	Foot
Dog	Dog	Dog food
Straightbacked chair	Easy chair	Man in sitting position
Crib	Crib	Baby
Birthday cake	Chocolate cake	Birthday present
Blue jay	Duck	Nest
Outside door	Swinging door	Key
Male football player	Man	Football
Male child in swimsuit	Female child in overalls	Swimming pool

the picture. Then the experimenter placed the two choice pictures on the table and told the child to "find another one that is the same as this," as she continued to point to the target picture.

One of the choice pictures was a member of the same basic-level category as the target: for example, the target might be a poodle and the choice a German shepherd (both dogs). We attempted to make the two category exemplars fairly dissimilar yet still readily identifiable to these young children. The other choice card was a strong thematic associate to the target, in this case, dog food. There were ten such triads in all. They are listed in Table 10.1.

Novel-Word Condition, Study 1. Everything about the Novel-Word Condition was identical to that of the No-Word Condition, with one exception. Children in this condition were told that the puppet could talk in puppet talk. They were instructed to listen carefully to find the right picture. The puppet gave the target picture an unfamiliar name and used the same name in the instructions for picking a choice picture. For example, the puppet might say, "See this? It is a sud. Find another sud that is the same as this sud."

When children in the No-Word Condition had to select between another category member and a thematically related object, they selected other category members 59 percent of the time. When the target picture was labeled with an unfamiliar word children were significantly more likely to select categorically. They now chose the other category member a mean of 83 percent of the time. This effect held up over every item. As predicted, when children think they are learning a new word they look for categorical relationships between objects and suppress the tendency to look for thematic relations. These results supported the hypothesis at least for very young children and basic-level categories.

Further studies were conducted to test the hypothesis that hearing a new word will induce older preschoolers to look for taxonomic relations rather than thematic relations at the superordinate level of categorization (see Markman & Hutchinson 1984.) One of these will be described here; it was very similar to study 1 except for the use of superordinate-level categories. In addition, the participants were four-year-old rather than three-year-old children.

No-Word Condition, Study 2. The procedure used in this condition was very similar to that used in the No-Word Condition of the first study, except that now superordinate-level categories were used. Associated with each of the target pictures were two choice pictures. One of the choice pictures was related in a thematic way to the target, for example, as milk is to cow. The other choice picture was a member of the same superordinate category as the target, for example, as pig is to cow. An attempt was made to use a variety of thematic relations rather than just one, so as not to limit the generality of the results. Examples of the materials used are shown in Table 10.2.

On each trial in the No-Word Condition, the experimenter, using a hand puppet, said, "I'm going to show you something. Then I want you to think carefully and find another one." The experimenter then placed the target picture face up on the table directly in front of the child, and said, "See this?" She placed the two choice pictures to the left and right of the target, then said, "Can you find another one?" After children made a choice, they were asked to justify their response: "How did you know it was this one?"

Table 10.2. *Stimulus materials for study with superordinate categories*

Standard object	Taxonomic choice	Thematic choice
Cow	Pig	Milk
Ring	Necklace	Hand
Door	Window	Key
Crib	Adult bed	Baby
Bee	Ant	Flower
Hanger	Book	Dress
Cup	Glass	Kettle
Car	Bicycle	Car tire
Train	Bus	Tracks
Dog	Cat	Bone

Novel-Word Condition, Study 2. Everything about the procedure for this condition was identical to that of the No-Word Condition, except that the target picture was now labeled with a novel word. Children were told that the puppet could talk in puppet talk, and that they were to listen carefully to what he said. The instructions now included an unfamiliar label for the target: "I'm going to show you a dax. Then I want you to think carefully and find another dax." "See this dax. Can you find another dax?" Children were asked to justify their choices.

We predicted that children in the Novel-Word Condition, because they were given a label, should choose the taxonomically related choice picture more often than children in the No-Word Condition. As is typical for children this age, when no word was present they did not often make categorical choices. When children in the No-Word Condition had to select between another member of the same superordinate category and a thematically related object, they chose the categorical relation only 25 percent of the time. As predicted, the presence of a new word caused children to seek taxonomic relations. When the target picture was labeled with an unfamiliar word, children were much more likely than children hearing no label to select categorically. They now chose the other category member 65 percent of the time. This effect held up over every item.

The proposal is that children focus on categorical relationships because of the sheer presence of the word, and not because of any particular knowledge about the meaning of the word. The next study was designed to provide evidence that children use abstract knowledge about words rather than specific known meanings to facilitate taxonomic responding. In this study, pictures of artificial objects were used instead of real objects. Children are not likely to translate unfamiliar names for these pictures into known words, because they do not know real word names for them. If the presence of an unfamiliar word still causes children to shift from thematic to taxonomic responding when the materials are also unfamiliar, then this would rule out translation as an explanation for the effect.

Four- and five-year-old children participated in the study. The design and procedure were essentially the same as in the previous study. The main difference was that the experimenter first taught children the taxonomic and thematic relations for the artificial objects before asking them to select the picture that was like the target.

No-Word Condition, Study 3. Children were shown eight sets of pictures. Each set included a target picture and two choice pictures, one thematically related and one taxonomically related to the target. Before children saw the target picture and the two choices, they were shown two

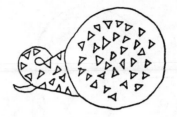

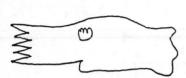

Figure 10.1. Sample taxonomic training picture.

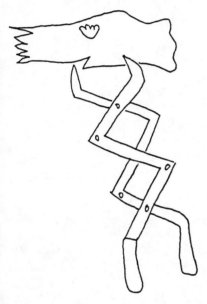

Figure 10.2. Sample thematic training picture.

training pictures that illustrated how the target picture related to each of the choice pictures. One picture showed the target object and the taxonomic choice, side by side. For these pairs, children were told a common function that the two objects shared. An example taxonomic training picture is shown in Figure 10.1. For this example, the experimenter said, "This swims in the water" (pointing to the left-hand object). "This swims in the water" (pointing to the right-hand object).

A second training picture showed the target and the thematic choice in an interactive relationship. The experimenter told the children how the two objects interacted. The thematic training picture for the set just given is shown in Figure 10.2. For this example, the experimenter said,

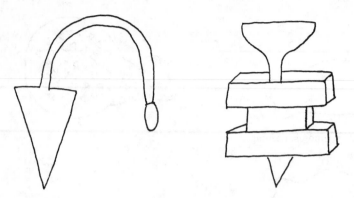

Figure 10.3. Sample taxonomic training picture.

Figure 10.4. Sample thematic training picture.

"This catches this" (pointing to the objects she was referring to as she said the sentence).

A second example taxonomic training picture is shown in Figure 10.3. For this example, the experimenter said, "This pokes holes in things" (pointing to the left-hand object). "This pokes holes in things" (pointing to the right-hand object). The thematic training picture for the same set is shown in Figure 10.4. For this picture, the spoken information was "You keep this in here."

After children saw the two training pictures in a set, the pictures were removed from the table. The procedure for the rest of the trial was identical to the procedure in the No-Word Condition of the previous experiment. The experimenter said, "I'm going to show you something. Then I want you to think carefully, and find another one." The experimenter then placed the target picture face up on the table directly in front of the child, and said, "See this?" She placed the two choice pictures to the left and right of the target, and then said, "Can you find another one?" Note that the choices were pictures of the individual objects as in the previous studies, rather than pictures of two objects together.

Novel-Word Condition, Study 3. The materials and procedure for this condition were identical to those of the No-Word Condition, except that a novel word was used to label the target picture. After children saw the training pictures, the experimenter said, "I'm going to show you a dax. Then I want you to think carefully, and find another dax. See this dax? Can you say dax? Can you find another dax?" A different unfamiliar word was used for each set.

The results for the choices were parallel to those of the previous studies. As usual, when children in the No-Word Condition had to select between another member of the same superordinate category and a thematically related object, they often chose the thematic relation. They selected the other category member a mean of only 37 percent of the time. When the target picture was labeled with an unfamiliar word children were more likely to select categorically. They now chose the other category member a mean of 63 percent of the time. Children hearing a novel word were significantly more likely to select an object from the same category than children not hearing a label. Moreover, the difference held up over every item.

The hypothesis tested by these studies is that children place an abstract constraint on what single nouns might mean. Children limit count nouns to refer mainly to objects that share some property or function rather than allowing them to refer to objects that are united by thematic relations. This would help explain how children acquire words that refer to categories, even though, in many other situations, they seem to find the thematic associations between objects to be more salient. That is, the simple presence of a noun, even an unfamiliar one such as "dax," should cause children to search for objects that share some perceptual or functional properties. Thus, labeling a picture as "dax" and asking children to find "another dax" should help override their preference for choosing thematically.

The results from several studies supported the hypothesis. Even children as young as two and three years place constraints on what an unfamiliar word might mean. When presented with two basic-level objects, such as two different kinds of dogs, and a third object that was thematically related such as dog food, very young children would often select a dog and dog food as being the same kind of thing. If, however, one of the dogs was called by an unfamiliar label such as "dax," and children were told to find another dax, they now were much more likely to select the other dog.

At four or five years old, a word induces children to search for categorical relations even among objects that can only be related at the superordinate level of categorization. For example, with no word present, children often selected a dog and dog bone as being the same kind of thing because of the strong thematic association between dog and bone. When one of the dogs was called a "dax," however, and children were asked to find another dax, they more often selected a dog and a cat as being the same because they are both in the same superordinate category, animals.

The hypothesis is that the presence of an unfamiliar word shifts children's attention to taxonomic relations because of an abstract constraint children place on possible word meanings, and not because they know the meaning of the word. Thus, we would like to rule out translation into a known word as accounting for the effect.

The most compelling evidence that translation into known terms cannot account for the results comes from the last study where unfamiliar objects were used as well as unfamiliar words. Here children were shown three novel objects. They were taught a taxonomic relation for two of the objects and a thematic relation for two. When no label was used children often selected the two objects that were related thematically as being the same. When an unfamiliar word was used to label the target picture, children now selected the two objects that were related taxonomically. Children could not have been translating in this study because they did not know what these unfamiliar objects were and had no familiar labels for them. Nevertheless, the results from this study replicated the results from the studies that used familiar objects. Again, the presence of an unfamiliar meaningless word caused children to shift from selecting objects that are thematically related to selecting objects that are taxonomically related. This suggests that children have placed an abstract constraint on what words can mean that is not mediated by the meaning of known terms.

These findings raise the question of how children come to constrain their hypotheses about what a word can mean. What leads children to assume that a word is likely to refer to objects that are similar in some way rather than to objects that participate in the same event or context? There are at least two possibilities. One is that sensitivity to the constraint is innate – from the start, children assume words will refer to categories of similar objects. Having such implicit knowledge would provide children with an entry into the formidable problem of learning language. Children would at least be able to readily acquire count nouns, and once they had a reasonable vocabulary of category terms, they could then begin to comprehend other linguistic forms. In fact, the huge majority of children's first words are count nouns (Clark 1983; Nelson 1973; Huttenlocher 1974).

Another possibility is that the constraint is induced from early language experience. Having learned many count nouns, almost all of which refer to objects that are taxonomically related, children may come to expect this to be true of subsequent terms they learn. If so, then this induction must take place fairly rapidly at an early point in language acquisition, as even two-year-olds believe that count nouns are more likely to refer to objects that belong to the same category than to objects that are thematically related.

We do not yet know whether or not very young children limit the constraint to count nouns. Particularly if children have some innate knowledge of the constraint, they may at first overextend it, indiscriminately believing that any word they hear must refer to a taxonomic category. Only somewhat later might they become sensitive to form class and expect count nouns to be more likely than other classes of words to refer to categorical relations.

Children's sensitivity to this constraint raises the possibility that language may help children acquire new categories. In contrast, it is often argued that words must map onto concepts that have already been worked out nonlinguistically (Clark 1973; Huttenlocher 1974; Macnamara 1972; Nelson 1974; Wittgenstein 1953, 1958). On this view, language plays little role in concept learning. But this view may underestimate the importance of language. Young children may create concepts to fit new words, guided by abstract constraints on word meaning. This alternative view is a mild form of linguistic determinism (Whorf 1956), in that language is believed to shape thought. It is quite different, however, from Whorf's conception that each language imposes a particular world view on its speakers, and that cognition is determined and limited by the specific language one speaks. First, all languages are likely to share similar constraints on possible meanings for count nouns. Thus the hypothesis is that, regardless of native language, children look for categories of similar objects when they hear new nouns. Second, although nouns help focus children's attention on categorical relations, we are not arguing that children would be incapable of forming categories without exposure to language.

The small amount of research that bears on this milder form of linguistic determinism suggests that children can use abstract knowledge of the semantic correlates of form class to help them discover the concept to which a word refers. Brown (1957) found that three- to five-year-old children interpreted an unfamiliar count noun ("a dax") as referring to a new concrete object, whereas they interpreted an unfamiliar mass noun ("some dax") as referring to a novel undifferentiated mass. In a study by Katz, Baker, and Macnamara (1974), children as young as 18 months interpreted an unfamiliar proper noun ("Dax") as referring to an individual. At the same time, these young children understood an unfamiliar count noun ("a dax") as referring to a category of similar objects.

The question arises as to why language is organized this way. Why don't words refer typically to objects that are thematically related? As pointed out earlier, thematic relations between objects certainly are important for adults as well as for children. In naturally occurring situations, objects are not found organized by category, but rather are embedded in spatial, temporal, and causal contexts. Such relational structures as events and themes are a common way of organizing information to make sense of what we encounter.

Given that these thematic event-like organizations are a natural way of construing the world, why should languages force a taxonomic or categorical structure rather than capturing this thematic bias? Why don't we have single words to refer to a boy or his bike, a baby or its bottle, a spider or its web?

The most important reason may be that if a language had single nouns refer exclusively to pairs of thematically related objects, it would be at great cost. The enormous expressive power of language would be lost. The expressive power of language derives from its ability to convey new relations through combinations of words. There are a potentially infinite number of thematic relations that one might want to express. The many thematic relations can easily be described through combinations of words combinations of words -- for example, sentences and phrases. If single words referred only to thematic relations, however, there would be an extraordinary proliferation of words, probably more than humans could learn. One would need separate words for a baby and its bottle, a baby and its crib, a baby and its mother, a baby and its diaper, and so on. Thus, the combinatorial power of language would be wasted. This, then, may be the major reason why nouns refer primarily to taxonomic categories rather than to thematically related objects.

In conclusion, young children possess the knowledge that single nouns are more likely to refer to objects that share perceptual or functional properties than to objects associated by their participation in a common event or theme. This knowledge helps explain how children acquire new words. By constraining the meaning of a term to categorical relations, children are able to rule out a huge number of other potential meanings for any given term. For example, suppose an adult points to a cup and says "cup." With no constraints on possible meanings, a child would have to consider that "cup" might mean "the cup is on the table," because the cup was on the table, or "coffee in the cup," because the cup was filled with coffee, or "mother lifting the cup," because mother was lifting the cup. All of these relational meanings would be eliminated from consideration by the constraint that nouns refer to object categories. By limiting the number and kind of hypotheses that children need to consider, this constraint tremendously simplifies the problem of language learning.

Assumption of mutual exclusivity

The second way children may limit possible word meanings is to assume that terms are mutually exclusive. This would be a reasonable assumption to make. If an object could be a member of just about any category, then the categories would tell us little about the objects. In contrast, to the extent categories are informative about objects, to the extent that they contain much correlated information, they tend to be mutually exclusive. For example, an object cannot be a cat *and* a dog or a bird or a horse, and so on.

Principles related to mutual exclusivity have been hypothesized as necessary to account for other aspects of language acquisition. Slobin's (1973) principle of one-to-one correspondence, Pinker's (1983) Uniqueness Principle, and Clark's (1983) contrastive organization are all related principles. Thus, the assumption of mutual exclusivity has precedence in that similar assumptions are needed to account for how children acquire language in general.

There is a fair amount of suggestive evidence for this assumption from vocabulary acquisition. Inspection of the first words in children's vocabulary (e.g., Goldin-Meadow, Seligman, & Gelman 1976; Gillham 1979) reveals that they consist of object category labels that are largely mutually exclusive with no subordinate or superordinate categories.

In an extensive review of early vocabulary development, Clark (1983) argues that several patterns of language acquisition support her lexical contrast theory. According to this view, any pair of words should contrast in meaning. Clark reinterpreted the data on overgeneralization of terms in light of this view. Her analysis revealed that children narrow down the domains of a previously overextended word by contrasting a newly acquired term with an old one. Children will not overextend a term to cover a new object when they already have a term for that object.

Clark also cites data from children's coinages of new terms to support the lexical contrast theory. Mutual exclusivity is a kind of contrast, but not all kinds of contrast are mutually exclusive. So some of the data Clark cites are directly relevant.

Thus, there is some suggestive evidence that children do try to honor the mutual exclusivity principle. One striking characteristic of human categories, however, is that they tend to be organized into systems where the categories are related to each other in various ways rather than each concept being represented in isolation. Many categories form hierarchies that consist of more and more general levels of categorization (e.g., delicious apple, apple, fruit, food; poodle, dog, mammal, animal). It is the systematic organization of categories that Callanan and I argued (Markman & Callanan 1983) to be the major intellectual achievement of human conceptualization.

Class inclusion is an asymmetric transitive relation (cf. Markman & Callanan 1983, for a discussion of what counts as evidence that someone has represented categories hierarchically). In a class-inclusion hierarchy, of course, one category is included in another, and both category names can refer to the same object. That is, the subordinate and superordinate categories are not mutually exclusive in such a hierarchy.

From the child's point of view then, class-inclusion hierarchies pose special problems. The child knows that a particular object, a doll, say, *is a* doll. Now the child hears that the object *is a* toy. The child will be puzzled, on the assumption of mutual exclusivity, as to how a given object can both be a doll and be a toy. Thus, one reason why class-inclusion relations are difficult for children may be because they violate mutual exclusivity. The mutual-exclusivity assumption may also help explain why it is that children find the part-whole hierarchies of collections easier to represent than class inclusion hierarchies.

Collections versus classes as hierarchical organization

I turn now to describe work that has contrasted the hierarchical structure of classes with a different type of hierarchical structure – the part-whole structure of collections. Collections are the referents of collective nouns, for example, forest, pile, family, army, and are structured into part-whole hierarchies, for example, a tree is part of a forest, a block is part of a pile, a child is part of a family, and so on.

In the past, I have offered several distinctions between classes and collections and argued how these distinctions contribute to the differences in children's abilities to deal with these two kinds of hierarchical organization (cf. Markman 1981, 1984). What I want to emphasize now is the possibility that collection hierarchies are easier for children because, unlike class-inclusion hierarchies, they do not violate mutual exclusivity.

In a collection structure, a particular object is not given two labels. Something *is an* oak, for example, but is *part of* a forest. So, mutual exclusivity is maintained. Moreover, because there are not two "is a" relations to cope with, the asymmetry of part-whole relations is easier to maintain than that of class inclusion. That is, the two levels of a collection hierarchy are clearly distinct, while the levels of a class-inclusion hierarchy are more similar, and thus more confusable. For class inclusion, both levels of the hierarchy involve the same *is a* relation. A poodle *is a* dog and *is an* animal. This may contribute to the child's confusion of levels and difficulty in keeping track of the asymmetry. If there were less confusion between part and whole than between subclass and superclass, then the asymmetrical relations of collections would have greater psychological stability.

Since collections are predicted to help children maintain the asymmetry of the hierarchy, one might think that collections should also help children appreciate transitivity. This does not follow, however, because the part-whole relations of collections are not transitive. A property true of the whole will not necessarily be true of the part. For example, if we know that the family is large, it does not follow that the child in the family is large. If we know that a pile of bricks is U-shaped, it does not follow that the bricks in the pile are U-shaped. Because the two levels of the collection hierarchy are defined by different relations, transitivity is violated, but the asymmetry should be simpler for children to establish and maintain.

There are several lines of evidence supporting the hypothesis that children find collection hierarchies simpler than class-inclusion hierarchies. I will give a couple of examples below, but for a more complete discussion see Markman (1981).

Some evidence for the differences in children's ability to deal with classes and collections comes from work on the Piagetian class inclusion problem (Inhelder & Piaget 1964). This task requires, among other things (see Markman & Callanan 1983) that children be able to keep both levels of a hierarchy in mind to compare them. For this problem, children are asked to make a quantitative comparison between a superordinate set and the larger of its subordinate sets. For example, a child might be shown pictures of five boys and three girls and asked: "Are there more boys or more children?" Although children are asked to make a subclass-superclass comparison (boys versus children) they make subclass (boys versus girls) comparisons instead.

In several studies, children have consistently revealed a superior ability to make part-whole comparisons with collections than with classes

(Markman 1973; Markman 1978; Markman & Seibert 1976). In each of the studies, the objects children viewed and the questions they were asked in the two conditions were identical. The only difference in the two conditions was in the description given the higher level of the hierarchy. As one example, for the "boys-children" comparison in the class condition, children were told "Here are some kindergarten children. These are the boys and these are the girls and these are the children." They were then asked "Who would have a bigger birthday party, someone who invited the boys or someone who invited the children?" As usual, young children often answered incorrectly, claiming that there were more boys. The collection version of this question was identical, except that "kindergarten children" was changed to "kindergarten class" (note that *class* is a collection term). So the question became "Who would have a bigger birthday party, someone who invited the boys or someone who invited the class?" With this change of how the higher-level category was labeled, children became better able to solve the part-whole comparison that they usually find so difficult. For further discussion of this work and some possible objections see Markman and Callanan (1983).

Children are also better able to deal with cardinal number when objects are conceptualized as belonging to collections rather than classes. The argument here is that dealing with cardinal numbers implicitly requires a hierarchical analysis and that children should be better able to solve number problems when they conceptualize the objects as organized into the part-whole structure of collections.

The cardinal number of a given set of items is not a property of the individual items themselves. Number is a property of the set taken as a whole and not a property of the elements that compose the set. To see why, consider the following syllogism: "Men are numerous. John is a man. Therefore, John is numerous." The syllogism is absurd because numerosity does not distribute over each element of a set, but is a characteristic of sets themselves. To take another example, "There are five books" does not imply that any one of the books is five. "Five" applies only to the group, not the individuals in it. Of course, one cannot ignore individual members when calculating the numerical value of a set. Individuals must be counted or otherwise enumerated – that is, the "parts" must be noticed. But it is not enough to focus on just the individuals – one must also consider the set taken as a whole. There are many well-known problems that young children have in dealing with cardinal number. Young children should be better able to solve these problems when the objects are thought of as collections rather than classes. This hypothesis was investigated in several studies (Markman 1979) that focused on different aspects of a full appreciation of cardinal number. I will describe here only the number-conservation experiment.

In the standard conservation task (Piaget 1965) two equal rows of pennies, or other items, are lined up in one-to-one correspondence. A four- to five-year-old child will judge the rows to be equal. One of the rows is spread out in front of the child who then typically judges that the lengthened row now has more pennies, though no pennies have been added or subtracted from either row. A child must correctly interpret the original judgment in terms of number and must attend to number per se throughout the physical transformation in order realize that the quantities remain the same. By making it easier to think about the hierarchical relations, collections were predicted to help children conserve.

This hypothesis was tested by having four-year-old children solve conservation problems where the objects were given either class or collection labels. Half of the children received class questions and half received collection questions. Each child was given four conservation problems. The only difference between conditions was that a collection label (e.g., *forest*) was substituted for a class label (e.g., *trees*) for the rows. For example a child in the class condition saw two rows of trees lined up in one-to-one correspondence and heard: "These are your trees and these are my trees. What are more: my trees, your trees, or are they both the same?" A child in the collection condition saw the identical two rows and heard: "This is your forest and this is my forest. What's more: my forest, your forest, or are they both the same?" Then in both conditions, the experimenter spread out one of the rows and repeated the question.

The children in the two conditions were presented with identical perceptual information and asked virtually identical questions. Yet, simply relabeling the objects as collections helped children to conserve.

Learning hierarchical relations

In the previous studies on the Piagetian class-inclusion problem and on cardinal number, the experimenter determined what type of organization the child should impose on the objects by labeling the array for the child. These studies found that the part-whole structure of collections is easier for children to represent and deal with than the class-inclusion relations. In the studies to be reported now, we did not manipulate the organization ourselves, but rather examined what kind of organization children would impose on their own. If children find the structure of collections simpler than that of class inclusion, then they might organize objects into collections rather than classes when they need to construct a hierarchy. If so, this would run counter to what one would expect, based on the familiarity or frequency of words in English. Class terms (count nouns) are far more frequent in the language and children must have encountered many more of them. Although collective nouns are scarce relative to class terms, it still could be that the collection hierarchy is easier for children to construct. When children are relatively free to impose their own structure on a novel hierarchy, they might prefer a collection to a class organization.

This hypothesis was tested by contriving a situation where children were presented with only minimal information about a hierarchical relation (Markman, Horton, & McLanahan 1980). This study was designed to see how children would spontaneously interpret the relations when given relative freedom. In actuality, the relations were novel class-inclusion hierarchies, analogous to the relations between oaks, pines, and trees. Ostensive definition (pointing and labeling) was used to achieve a minimal specification of the relationship. To illustrate, imagine that oaks and pines are lined up in a row in front of the child. As the experimenter points to the oaks, he says "These are oaks"; as he points to the pines he says "These are pines"; and as he points to the trees he says "These are trees." When one describes trees in the plural, "These are trees," it means that each individual tree is a tree. Thus the use of the plural establishes the class-inclusion relation. The singular would have to be used to establish a collection, for example, "This is a forest." Although the ostensive definition provides only minimal information, it does establish that the objects presented form a class-inclusion hierarchy.

Suppose children misinterpret the class-inclusion relation as a collection hierarchy. What errors should they make? They should erroneously believe that several of the items together form an instance of the concept at the higher level of the hierarchy (trees in the example) and should not believe that any single item is an instance. To see why, consider what the correct response would be had children actually learned a collection, for example, "forest." If asked to point to the forest, the child should point to many trees, but should deny that a pine or any other single tree is itself a forest.

Children from 6 to 17 years old participated in the study. Each child learned four novel categories, one at a time, each composed of two subcategories. All of the category exemplars were small construction paper figures of novel shapes or novel animate figures. Nonsense syllables were used as names for the novel figures.

The results of this study revealed that children, until a surprisingly late age, tend to misinterpret class-inclusion relations as collections when only minimal information is provided. When novel class-inclusion relations were taught by ostensive definition, children as old as 14 years often mistakenly interpreted the relations as collections. When asked what would be analogous to "Show me a pine," children correctly picked up a single pine. When the experimenter, while pointing to a pine, asked "Is this a pine?" children responded correctly. The errors occurred almost exclusively on the upper level of the hierarchy. When asked "Show me a tree," children scooped up a handful rather than just one. When the experimenter, while pointing to a tree asked, "Is this a tree?" children often said "No." This is exactly as one would expect if children were answering questions about a collection.

At least in the somewhat artificial conditions of the present study, children found it simpler to impose a collection structure on a novel hierarchy than to correctly interpret it as inclusion. This is true despite the fact that children must certainly have more experience learning inclusion relations because collective nouns are relatively rare. Because this was an unusual way to learn novel concepts, collection errors may be unlikely in natural situations. There is, however, some anecdotal evidence revealing that children will revise their interpretation of words in order to avoid violating mutual exclusivity. Grieve (1975) cites data from an unpublished study by Curtis (1973). A two-year-old child used the term "car" to refer to all cars. Eleven days later the child used "car" to refer to cars and used "Cadillac" to refer to Cadillacs. The child now denied that Cadillac was a car. Related anecdotes have been reported by Valentine (1942) and Macnamara (1982).

Callanan and I have provided more general evidence suggesting that collection errors are found in a naturalistic context (Callanan & Markman 1982). We questioned two- and three-year old children about five categories: toys (balls and dolls), animals (horses and cows), drinks (milk and juice), children (boys and girls), and cars (racing cars and Volkswagens). In general there was a very low error rate, in part because these category terms were pretested to ensure that children knew them (in the plural). However, there was a significant tendency for children to interpret the terms as collections. Children agree, for example, that a set of toys is toys, but deny that a single toy (a doll, for example) is itself a toy, and they pick up several toys when asked for one. These findings suggest that in first acquiring superordinate terms, young children distort some class-inclusion relations into collections. Thus, even in naturally occurring contexts, very young children may find it simpler to impose a collection structure on what are actually inclusion hierarchies they are trying to learn.

These findings suggest that if superordinate category terms were represented by collective nouns then children would find them easier to learn. But collective nouns cannot themselves serve as superordinate terms, for the very reason that they express a different relation. And this difference is extremely important when one considers the function of taxonomies. One of the main purposes of taxonomies is to support inductive and deductive inferences. For example, if I know something that is true of all mammals (e.g., that they breathe, eat, are warm-blooded), once I learn that a previously unfamiliar animal is a mammal I can transfer all of this knowledge to the newly learned animal. Collections do not support inferences in the same way. Properties true of the forest may not be true of individual trees. Nor will similarities that exist between the trees allow an inductive inference that the properties will also be true of the forest. Thus, although the part-whole organization of collections is simpler for children to learn, it is not a useful substitute for the inclusion relation that defines taxonomies. Mass nouns, however, may provide an appropriate substitute for collective nouns.

Many superordinate category terms in English are mass nouns (e.g., *furniture, jewelry, money*), though conceptually they refer to diverse, discrete, countable objects. This violates the common intuition that mass terms refer to masslike homogeneous substances, such as milk or clay, or to substances made of small virtually identical particles, such as sand or grass. That is, the homogeneity of the substance and the difficulty of individuating elements of the substance characterize the semantic basis of many typical mass terms. Yet, "furniture," for example, refers to heterogeneous readily individuated objects. I have argued (Markman in press) for a functional explanation for this violation of the semantic basis of mass terms. However, there are many other exceptions to this oversimplified semantic rule (cf. Gordon 1981) that may reflect only unprincipled vagaries of English. For example, some (but not all) abstract concepts are referred to by mass nouns (e.g., justice); some seemingly countable objects are referred to by mass nouns (e.g., toast, paper); and some substances are referred to by mass nouns (e.g., gravel), whereas some very similar substances are referred to by count nouns (e.g., pebbles). There may not be any cogent explanation for all of these idiosyncrasies. But I believe the exception for superordinate categories is a principled one.

By referring to superordinate categories as mass nouns, languages may help speakers learn hierarchical relations between the upper- and lower-level categories. Mass nouns may, like collective nouns, help keep the two levels of a hierarchy more stable and distinct but, unlike collective nouns, may be able to accomplish this while still maintaining a taxonomic organization. In a sense, mass nouns can be viewed as a compromise between collections and classes, or, to be more precise, as a compromise between "part-whole" and "is a" relations. Consider a typical mass such as clay. A piece of clay is part of the whole mass of clay. This is similar to the part-whole organization of collections where each tree, for example, is part of the forest. On the other hand, each piece of clay is itself clay. This is more like the "is a" relation of class inclusion, where each oak is a tree.

By referring to discrete objects with mass terms, a language might be able to provide some of the stability that the part-whole organization of collections would have achieved, yet remind the speaker that an inclusion relation is still involved.

This analysis predicts that this peculiarity should not be limited to English. Other languages with a count-mass distinction should also have this type of aberration. Further, if these aberrations serve the purpose of helping to give stability to hierarchically organized categories, then such "inappropriate" mass terms should occur mainly on superordinate or relatively high levels of the hierarchy, not on relatively low levels. That is, languages should contain terms that require one to say "a piece of furniture" or "a piece of vehicle" when one wants to refer to a single piece of furniture or a single vehicle. But they should not require speakers to say "a piece of chair" or "a piece of car" when one wants to refer to

Table 10.3. *Number of languages (N = 18) treating each superordinate term as a mass noun*

Term	Number of languages
Money	17
Food	16
Clothing	13
Furniture	11
Reading material	11
Sports equipment	11
Jewelry	10
Silverware	9
Fruit	9
Vegetable	9
Footwear	6
Headgear	6
Linen	5
Weapon	6
Human dwelling	6
Tools	5
People	5[a]
Toy	2[a]
Building	1
Musical instrument	2
Flowers	1
Vehicle	1[a]
Tree	0
Animal	0
Bird	0

[a]One additional language had an optional mass usage.

Table 10.4. *Number of languages (N = 18) treating each lower-level term as a mass noun*

Term	Number of languages	Term	Number of languages
Dollar	0	Towel	0
Penny	0	Gun	0
Egg	0	Sword	0
Shirt	0	House	0
Belt	0	Apartment	0
Chair	0	Hammer	0
Mirror	0	Saw	0
Book	0	Man	0
Magazine	0	Woman	0
Ball	0	Doll	0
Racquet	0	Church	0
Ring	0	School	0
Bracelet	0	Piano	0
Fork	0	Guitar	0
Spoon	0	Rose	0
Apple	1	Daisy	0
Melon	1	Car	0
Carrot	2	Airplane	0
Onion	2	Oak	1
Shoe	0	Palm	0
Skate	0	Dog	0
Hat	0	Pig	0
Scarf	0	Robin	0
Sheet	0	Eagle	0

a single chair or a single car. This hypothesis was tested in Markman (1985) by asking native speakers of various languages to judge whether terms were count nouns or mass nouns in their language.

All of the participants in this study were speakers of English as a second language. Informants were asked to translate English category terms into their native language and judge whether or not the terms could be used in a phrase where the objects were counted directly, such as "two pencils" or whether they required a quantificational phrase, as in "two cups of sugar." Informants were asked to translate terms for 25 higher-level categories that are relatively common in English. All of the object categories that appeared in Rosch et al. (1976) and Rosch (1975) that fulfilled Rosch's criteria of superordinate categories were used in this study as were some others. The left-hand column of Table 10.3 presents these categories. Forty-eight lower-level terms from the same categories were also selected to be translated. Thus, there were almost twice as many opportunities for lower-level terms to be judged as mass nouns as for superordinate terms. Table 10.4 presents the 48 lower-level categories used, arranged to correspond to the higher-level categories of Table 10.3.

Table 10.5 presents the languages that were included in this study classified according to their language family and subgroup. Eighteen languages, at least 11 different subgroups, and 7 different language families were represented (Katzner 1975; Voegelin & Voegelin 1977).

The results of this study strongly support a functional explanation for why superordinate terms are often mass nouns. As can be seen in Table 10.5, in every language family, every language subgroup, and, in fact, in every language, some superordinate categories were represented by mass nouns. In marked contrast, lower-level category terms are almost always represented by count nouns. Overall, languages represented an average of 34 percent of the superordinate categories as mass nouns. In

Table 10.5. *Percentage of superordinate and basic-level terms that are mass nouns in each language*

Family	Subgroup	Branch	Language	Higher-level category	Lower-level category
Indo-European	Germanic	Western	Afrikaans	44	0
Indo-European	Germanic	Western	Dutch	48	0
Indo-European	Germanic	Western	English	48	0
Indo-European	Germanic	Western	German	40	0
Indo-European	Romance		French	36	0
Indo-European	Hellenic		Greek	16	0
Indo-European	Slavic	Eastern	Ukranian	16	0
Indo-European	Indo-Iranian		Urdue	44	0
Uralic	Finno-Ugric	Finnic	Finnish	16	0
	Finno-Ugric	Ugric	Hungarian	24	0
Altaic	Turkic	Southwestern	Turkish	44	0
Independent			Japanese	28	0
			Korean	24	0
Afro-Asiatic	Semitic	North Arabic	Arabic	44	2
		Camanitic	Hebrew	20	0
African			Guro	32	8
			Nzema	20	0
			American Sign Language	68	4
Mean percent				34	.7

marked contrast, languages represented an average of less than 1 percent of the lower-level terms as mass nouns. Every one of the 18 languages studied had more superordinate terms as mass nouns than lower-level terms as mass nouns.

Table 10.3 presents the number of languages out of 18 that represented each of the 25 superordinate categories as a mass noun. With the exception of "tree," "animal," and "bird," every superordinate category was represented by a mass noun in at least one language. In contrast, as can be seen in Table 10.4, of the 48 lower-level category terms, only 5 were mass nouns in any language.

In summary these findings reveal a striking tendency for languages to refer to higher-level but not lower-level categories with mass nouns. Moreover, the procedure used probably underestimated the magnitude of the effect. Although the 25 category terms selected were familiar to English-speaking cultures, they were not always important in other cultures. For example, there were 13 categories with no translation into Nxema; 10 with no translation into Ukranian; 7 with no translation into Turkish. Thus the proportion of superordinate categories that were mass nouns is greater when considered as a proportion of the easily translatable categories than as a proportion of the total number of categories. If superordinate categories had been selected that were more frequent in these various cultures, even more of them may have been referred to by mass nouns.

This study established that it is not just English that refers to superordinate categories with mass nouns. There is a systematic tendency across languages to use mass nouns to refer to these categories. This finding provides indirect support for the hypothesis that having superordinate categories referred to by mass nouns should help speakers learn the categories. A second study in Markman (1985) tested the hypothesis more directly by comparing how well children learn a new category when it is labeled by a mass versus a count noun. Preschool children were taught a new superordinate category for familiar objects. For example, they were taught the new category "vehicle" for a bicycle, a boat, a plane, and a fire truck. There were two training conditions. In one, the category was referred to with a mass noun, in the other with a count noun. Otherwise the training procedures and categories taught were identical. The prediction is that children who hear, for example, "A car is a piece of vehicle," "This (a boat, a plane, a bicycle, and a fire truck) is some vehicle," and "How much vehicle is here?" should be better able to learn the category than children who hear "A car is a vehicle," "These (a boat, a plane, a bicycle, and a fire truck) are vehicles," and "How many vehicles are here?"

Three- to five-year-old children participated in this study. These children are quite young to be taught superordinate-level categories. They may be the youngest children who both understand the basic-object categories well enough to begin to learn superordinate-level categories and who could master the mass-count distinction. There is evidence that children this young can learn the mass-count distinction, even when it is taught as a syntactic distinction, that is, without semantic support (Gordon 1981).

Children were taught one of three categories: "sports equipment," "vehicles," or "bathroom supplies." Four exemplars were used to first teach the category. For example, for the category "sports equipment" children were shown a racquet, a helmet, a hockey stick, and a baseball mitt. In the subsequent tests children were shown new exemplars and distractors for each category. Some of the exemplars were very similar to the training exemplars, for example, a different helmet. Some of the exemplars were novel, for example, a soccer ball. Some of the distractors were designed to be simple to reject, that is, they were quite distinct from the category exemplars, whereas some were designed to be more difficult to distinguish from the exemplars.

Children were introduced to a puppet and told that the puppet was going to play a game with them where she would teach them a special puppet word for some of the pictures they would see. Children were given training to learn the new category, were tested on their ability to distinguish category exemplars from distractors, were retrained, and then retested. The only difference between the two conditions was that children in the mass-noun condition always heard the new term (a nonsense syllable) used as a mass noun, whereas children in the count-noun condition always heard the new word used as a count noun. To illustrate, if the new word was "veb" and the category was bathroom supplies, some of the training items for the two conditions were: (1) The puppet would point to the four exemplars (soap, shampoo, comb, and toothpaste) and say "This is veb" for children in the mass-noun condition and "These are vebs" for children in the count-noun condition. (2) The puppet would point to several of the items saying "Here are some pieces of veb" for the mass noun condition and "Here are some vebs" for the count noun condition. (3) The puppet would ask "How much veb is here?" for children in the mass-noun condition and "How many vebs are here?" for children in the count-noun condition.

In general, these four-year-old children found these superordinate categories difficult to learn. This is to be expected given the well-known difficulty that young children have with superordinate categories and that this procedure provided only minimal training. Nevertheless, having the categories encoded by mass nouns rather than count nouns helped children learn them. Although the effects were small, children who heard mass nouns were significantly better able to discriminate category exemplars from distractors, especially after the second training session. These findings were replicated in a similar study reported in Markman (1985).

To summarize, I observed that in English many superordinate categories are referred to by mass nouns although conceptually they encompass discrete countable objects. Why should we have to say "two pieces of jewelry" instead of "two jewelries" or "two pieces of furniture" instead of "two furnitures"? The argument is that this construction is not just an accident of English but instead may have evolved to help speakers learn and represent hierarchically organized category terms. This hypothesis derives from the findings with collective nouns that demonstrated that children find part-whole hierarchies of collection simpler than class-inclusion hierarchies. Collective nouns could not, however, serve as superordinate terms in a language because they form a different type of hierarchical structure. Mass nouns can be viewed as a type of compromise between collective and count nouns. A piece of clay is part of the mass of clay (as a tree is part of a forest) but a piece of clay is itself clay (as an oak is a tree). Thus mass nouns can encode superordinate categories in a way that simplifies the hierarchical representation yet remains faithful to the inclusion relation.

The hypothesis here is that children rely on the mass nouns as a way of bootstrapping a class-inclusion hierarchy from a part-whole hierarchy. Children can first work out the asymmetry of the hierarchical structure based on the simpler part-whole organization and then use the similarity of the objects at both levels to draw the relevant transitive inferences.

General discussion

In this chapter, I have considered two ways that children may constrain the meaning of words. The first way is that children first assume that a novel word will refer to a category of similar objects. In a neutral context, children find thematic relations of interest, often of greater interest than categorical similarity, focusing, for example, on relations such as a spider and its web, or a boy and his bike. Yet, they acquire many words referring to categories. Children are able to acquire category terms despite their interest in thematic relations, in part because they limit the possible meanings of nouns to refer to categorically related items (Markman & Hutchinson 1984). So when hearing a new word, a child suppresses the tendency to look for thematic relations and looks for categorical relations instead.

The second way children constrain word meanings is to assume that category terms are mutually exclusive. This helps explain both why class-inclusion hierarchies are difficult for children (they violate mutual exclusivity) and why the part-whole hierarchies of collections are not (they maintain mutual exclusivity). There is a substantial amount of evidence that children find the part-whole hierarchies of collections (e.g., a tree is part of a forest) simpler to represent and understand than the inclusion relation of classes (e.g., an oak is a tree). Very young children may even misrepresent high-level category terms as collections. Extrapolating from the work with collections, the mutual exclusivity principle suggests further that children can rely on their knowledge of mass nouns to bootstrap their way into a hierarchical relation. I argued that this is why so many superordinate-category terms are mass nouns, for example, *furniture, clothing, food,* and *fruit.* If superordinate categories could be encoded by collective nouns, children would find them easier to learn. Collective nouns could not serve as superordinate terms, however, because they do not allow for the transitive inferences important in a taxonomy. That is, something true of the whole will not necessarily be true of the parts. Yet one of the major functions of taxonomies is to support such transitive inferences so that something true of the more general class (e.g., mammals) will be true of more specific classes within it (e.g., dogs). Mass nouns would be effective superordinate terms because they are a hybrid of collective and count nouns. That is, mass nouns refer to a part-whole structure as do collective nouns (e.g., a piece of clay is part of the whole mass clay), but they also encode an "is a" relation as do count nouns (e.g., a piece of clay is itself clay). In the special case of mass nouns, therefore, properties of the whole can be transmitted to the parts. Thus, children's knowledge of the count-mass distinction helps them organize categories into hierarchies.

The assumptions of taxonomic organization and of mutual exclusivity need to be reconciled and integrated with each other. The argument about mass nouns is based on children's preference for a collectionlike organization. Collections defined by their part-whole structures are a kind of relational concept. To be sure, they are a relation defined on similar objects, for example, trees in a forest, soldiers in an army, and not objects as diverse as a baby and its bottle, or a dog and its bone. But they are relational nonetheless. By the first assumption – to look for taxonomic relations – one would expect children to avoid interpreting category labels in this way. Yet, when children work out hierarchical categories they may first consider this kind of relational concept, although it is important to keep in mind that it is a relation uniting similar objects.

We can make sense of this problem by considering a developmental progression in the kinds of problems children are trying to solve. In the first case, children are trying to acquire a single new category. In the second case, children are attempting to work out a hierarchical relation between categories, one of which they already have interpreted as having a categorical organization. To work out the hierarchy one or the other of these two constraints must be weakened. They cannot both be satisfied. The correct solution, in this case, is to weaken the mutual-exclusivity assumption in favor of the taxonomic one. Of course, the child will eventually weaken or relinquish this assumption and work out the class-inclusion relations. But as I have already argued, class inclusion is a difficult relation, in part because it violates mutual exclusivity, but also because the asymmetry of inclusion is difficult to understand and represent for children. The part-whole organization finesses the problem of two labels for the same object and maintains the exclusivity assumption. It accomplishes this, however, at the expense of the first assumption of not allowing relational organization. Thus, in some cases, children maintain mutual exclusivity instead, and weaken the constraint on taxonomic organization by representing the hierarchies as part-whole relations.

This is almost certainly not a universal solution to this problem, however. One or the other of these assumptions must be weakened to acquire hierarchically related terms, but it need not always be the mutual exclusivity assumption. Which assumption is relinquished probably depends on a number of factors. One may be how explicitly and persistently the hierarchical relation is taught. If a parent repeatedly specifies, for example, that a poodle is a kind of dog, that might help the child overcome his or her initial reluctance to map two category terms onto the same object. In older children, explicit mentioning of the relation does help (Markman et al. 1980) and parents of younger children do often try such explicit formulations in teaching children superordinate categories (Callanan 1982). A second factor likely to determine which assumption is relinquished is the relative difficulty of fulfilling each. When the similarity among the objects is great and easy to perceive then children will likely preserve the assumption of categorical relations and violate the assumption of mutual exclusivity. This would suggest that children should not be very likely to misinterpret a hierarchy of subordinate-basic level categories as having a collection structure. It also suggests that mass nouns should not be helpful for representing the higher-level category of a subordinate-basic hierarchy. Thus in relations such as poodle-dog or rocking chair-chair, it would not benefit children to have "dog" or "chair" be mass nouns. When the category similarity is difficult to discern, as in superordinate level categories, then imposing a part-whole structure would simplify the hierarchy and preserve the assumption of mutual exclusivity. It does this, however, by allowing relational meanings of the category term. Nevertheless, it still might work to the child's advantage to be able to construct a part-whole scaffolding on which to build an asymmetric hierarchical relation, which can later be transformed to support transitive inferences.

In addition to helping to explain how children deal with category terms, the assumption of mutual exclusivity may be the impetus behind children's acquisition of property terms. Suppose someone points to an object and says "red" or "round." If the child already has a category label for the term, he or she will know on the assumption of mutual exclusivity that this new description cannot be another category label. That will lead the child to look for some other property or attribute to label. Thus, children should begin learning color terms, for example, on an object that already can be labeled. Otherwise the child will erroneously assume that the term refers to the object instead of its color.

One can envision how this simple principle could be extended to help the child successively constrain the meanings of terms. Suppose the child has words for apple and for red and someone points to an apple and says "See that, it's round." Now, by mutual exclusivity, the child can eliminate red and apple for the meaning of "round" and try to analyze the apple for some other property to label. Thus, as each successive word is learned it further constrains the meanings of the yet to be learned words, thereby helping children figure out the new words.

REFERENCES

Brown, R. (1957). Linguistic determinism and the parts of speech. *The Journal of Abnormal and Social Psychology, 55,* 1–5.

Bruner, J. S., Olver, R., & Greenfield, P. (1966). *Studies in cognitive growth.* New York: Wiley.

Callanan, M. A. (1982). *Parental input and young children's acquisition of hierarchically organized concepts.* Unpublished doctoral dissertation, Stanford University, Palo Alto, CA.

Callanan, M. A., & Markman, E. M. (1982). Principles of organization in young children's natural language hierarchies. *Child Development, 53,* 1093–1101.

Carey, S. (1978). The child as word learner. In M. Halle, J. Bresnan, & G. Miller (Eds.), *Linguistic theory and psychological reality.* Cambridge, MA: MIT Press.

(1982). Semantic development: State of the art. In L. R. Gleitman & E. Wanner (Eds.), *Language acquisition: The state of the art.* Cambridge, England: Cambridge University Press.

Clark, E. V. (1973). What's in a word? On the child's acquisition of semantics in his first language. In T. E. Moore (Ed.), *Cognitive development and the acquisition of language.* New York: Academic Press.

(1983). Meanings and concepts. In P. H. Mussen (Gen. Ed.), *Handbook of child psychology,* Vol. 3: J. H. Flavell & E. M. Markman (Eds.), *Cognitive development.* New York: Wiley.

Curtis, K. A. (1973). *A study of semantic development.* Unpublished M.A. thesis, Psychological Laboratory, University of St. Andrews.

Gelman, R., & Baillargeon, R. (1983). A review of some Piagetian concepts. I. P. H. Mussen (Gen. Ed.), *Handbook of child psychology*, Vol. 3: J. H. Flavell & E. M. Markman (Eds.), *Cognitive development*. New York: Wiley.

Gibson, E. J., & Spelke, E. S. (1983). The development of perception. In P. H. Mussen (Gen. Ed.), *Handbook of child psychology*, Vol. 3: J. H. Flavell & E. M. Markman (Eds.), *Cognitive development*. New York: Wiley.

Gillham, B. (1979). *The first words language program*. London: George Allen & Unwin Ltd.

Goldin-Meadow, S., Seligman, M. E. P., & Gelman, R. (1976). Language in the two-year-old. *Cognition, 4,* 189–202.

Gordon, P. (1981). *Syntactic acquisition of the count/mass distinction*. Paper presented at the Stanford Child Language Research Forum.

Grieve, R. (1975). Problems in the study of early semantic development. In C. Drachman (Ed.), *Salzburger Beitrage zur Linguistic II*. Tübingen: Gunter Marr.

Horton, M. S. (1982). *Category familiarity and taxonomic organization in young children*. Unpublished doctoral dissertation, Stanford University, Palo Alto, CA.

Huttenlocher, J. (1974). The origins of language comprehension. In R. L. Solso (Ed.), *Theories in cognitive psychology: The Loyola symposium*. Potomac, MD: Erlbaum.

Inhelder, B., & Piaget, J. (1964). *The early growth of logic in the child*. New York: Norton.

Katz, Baker, & Macnamara. (1974). What's a name? On the child's acquisition of proper and common nouns. *Child Development, 45,* 469–473.

Katzner, K. (1975). *Languages of the world*. New York: Funk & Wagnalls.

Macnamara, J. (1972). *Names for things: A study of human learning*. Cambridge, MA: MIT Press.

Mandler, J. M., Scribner, S., Cole, M., & DeForest, M. (1980). Cross-cultural invariance in story recall. *Child Development, 51,* 19–26.

Markman, E. M. (1973). Facilitation of part-whole comparisons by use of the collective noun "family." *Child Development, 44,* 837–840.

  (1978). Empirical versus logical solutions to part-whole comparison problems concerning classes and collections. *Child Development, 49,* 168–177.

  (1979). Classes and collections: Conceptual organization and numerical abilities. *Cognitive Psychology, 11,* 395–411.

  (1981). Two different principles of conceptual organization. In M. E. Lamb & A. L. Brown (Eds.), *Advances in developmental psychology* (Vol. 1). Hillside, NJ: Erlbaum.

  (1984). The acquisition and hierarchical organization of categories by children. In C. Sophian (Ed.), *Origins of cognitive skills* (pp. 371–406). The Eighteenth Annual Carnegie Symposium on Cognition. Hillsdale, NJ: Erlbaum.

  (1985). Why superordinate category terms can be mass nouns. *Cognition, 19,* 31–53.

Markman, E. M., & Callanan, M. A. (1983). An analysis of hierarchical classification. In R. Sternberg (Ed.), *Advances in the psychology of human intelligence* (Vol. 2). Hillside, NJ: Erlbaum.

Markman, E. M., & Hutchinson, J. E. (1984). Children's sensitivity to constraints on word meaning: Taxonomic vs thematic relations. *Cognitive Psychology, 16,* 1–27.

Markman, E., & Seibert, J. (1976). Classes and collections: Internal organization and resulting holistic properties. *Cognitive Psychology, 8,* 561–577.

Markman, E. M., Horton, M. S., & McLanahan, A. G. (1980). Classes and collections: Principles of organization in the learning of hierarchical relations. *Cognition, 8,* 227–241.

Nelson, K. (1973). Structure and strategy in learning to talk. *Monographs of the Society for Research in Child Development, 38* (Serial No. 149).

(1974). Concept, word and sentence: Interrelations in acquisition and development. *Psychological Review, 81,* 267–285.

Newport, E. L. (1982). Task-specificity in language learning? Evidence from speech perception and American Sign Language. In E. Wanner & L. R. Gleitman (Eds.), *Language acquisition: The state of the art.* New York: Cambridge University Press.

Peirce, C. S. (1957). The logic of abduction. *Essays in the philosophy of science.* New York: The Liberal Arts Press.

Piaget, J. (1965). *The child's conception of number.* New York: Norton.

Pinker, S. (1983). *Language, learnability, and language development.* Cambridge, MA: Harvard University Press.

Quine, W. V. O. (1960). *Word and object.* Cambridge, MA: MIT Press.

Rosch, E. (1975). Cognitive representations of semantic categories. *Journal of Experimental Psychology: General, 104,* 192–233.

Rosch, E. H., Mervis, C. B., Gray, W., Johnson, D., & Boyes-Braem, P. (1976). Basic objects in natural categories. *Cognitive Psychology, 3,* 382–439.

Slobin, D. I. (1973). Cognitive prerequisites for the development of grammar. In G. A. Gerguson & D. I. Slobin (Eds.), *Studies of child language development.* New York: Holt, Rinehart & Winston.

Smiley, S. S., & Brown, A. L. (1979). Conceptual preference for thematic or taxonomic relations: A nonmonotonic age trend from preschool to old age. *Journal of Experimental Child Psychology, 28,* 249–257.

Valentine, C. W. (1942). *The psychology of early childhood.* London: Methuen.

Voegelin, C. F., & Voegelin, F. M. (1977). *Classification and index of the world's languages.* New York: Elsevier.

Whorf, B. L. (1956). *Language, thought and reality.* Cambridge, MA: MIT Press.

Wittgenstein, L. (1953). *Philosophical investigations.* New York: Macmillan.

(1958). *The blue and brown books.* New York: Harper & Row.

11

The role of theories in a theory of concepts

ROBERT N. McCAULEY

During the past decade in cognitive psychology, research on concepts has burgeoned in response to important work by Eleanor Rosch and her associates (see, for example, Rosch 1973, 1975; Rosch & Mervis 1975; Rosch, Mervis, Gray, Johnson, & Boyes-Braem 1976; Mervis & Rosch 1981). To a considerable extent, their work has informed most subsequent research in the area both substantively and methodologically. It has suggested a number of problems for further research, including, among other things, the extension and elaboration of the findings concerning typicality effects (or graded structure) and basic-level categories.

The chapters in this volume either present further relevant experimental results or related developmental research or they offer theoretical suggestions for organizing and explaining these phenomena. The majority of my comments will address the theoretical proposals. The following section offers a short summary of the relation of this research to traditional perspectives on concepts and categorization. The next section discusses the emphasis in a number of the papers in this volume on the importance of the role that cognitive constructs (namely, our idealized cognitive models and our theories) play in a theory of categorization. The next two sections explore two particularly important consequences of the general approach to categorization that emerges from this theoretical orientation: (1) that our cognitive constructs are, nearly always, about the world (and not about categories) and (2) that categories, therefore, are best understood as relations between objects in the world and those cognitive constructs. The final section suggests some connections between this general theoretical approach and certain philosophical problems that traditionally accompany discussions of categorization concerning the (perceptual) link between our cognitive constructs and the world.

The classical theory of categories

The findings concerning typicality effects and basic-level categories both diverge from the predictions of the classical theory of categories (and the

288

empiricist learning theory with which that theory has come to be so closely allied). The classical theory holds that something is a member of a particular category because it satisfies the set of necessary and sufficient conditions which constitute the category's defining properties. Consequently, for any particular thing it either does or does not satisfy these conditions and hence either is or is not a member of that category.

Empiricist learning theory enters in the specification of the necessary and sufficient conditions for membership in any particular category. (Necessarily, the following account is seriously oversimplified.) That peculiar collection of properties that constitutes a category's set of necessary and sufficient conditions distinguishes it uniquely. However, any particular property (some color, for example) may serve as a relevant property for membership in any number of different categories. We become acquainted with these particular properties in a general way through our experience of the individuals that instantiate them. Since Locke (1959), empiricists have assumed that certain of these features more readily lend themselves to abstraction from perceptual experience than others. Presumably, these are the simple features (such as colors, shapes, textures, etc.) that, in combination, form more complex properties. In addition, many of the more recent accounts have maintained that (1) the meaning of a term is exhausted by its reference, i.e., that cataloging the individuals which instantiate the properties named by some term exhausts that term's meaning, (2) basic-set theory (employing the functions of set union, intersection, and complementation) contains all the necessary resources for modeling the psychological processes involved in categorization, and (3) learning in general and concept learning in particular proceed from the simple to the complex according to principles of combination like that alluded to above.

Thoroughly extensional theories of meaning have suffered withering criticism in the last thirty years. However, the notions that set theory can adequately model the psychology of categorization (see, for example, Osherson & Smith 1981) and that concept learning is basically a bottom-up process of manipulating atomistic features have both displayed far greater staying power. These consequences of conjoining the classical theory of categories and empiricist learning theory have remained, until quite recently, well entrenched.

Rosch's experimental findings generate so much interest because they seem to challenge these two well-entrenched notions. Without employing some rather implausible assumptions, neither traditional set theory nor modified versions thereof seem sufficient to account for the wide range of typicality effects that Rosch and others have produced in scores of experiments. (What these typicality findings portend, though, is quite another issue.) The evidence neither suggests (1) that people acquire, employ, or represent most categories by means of a set of necessary and sufficient properties nor (2) that relevant properties are complex combinations of simple features previously acquired and abstracted. In addition, findings about basic-level categories contravene certain crucial assumptions of empiricist learning theory. It is middle-level categories, namely, those at the basic level, and not the most subordinate categories, which are, apparently, both first and most easily learned. Indeed, the vast array of experimental results indicates that it is basic-level categories that are cognitively simple, that is, are most easily acquired, manipulated, and represented.

This research challenges psychologists to develop theories of categorization that will organize and, perhaps, even unify the whole range of (apparently) relevant results. (I will take up some of these issues in the next three sections.) This theorizing, though, inevitably generates certain classical philosophical difficulties, which I will briefly address in the final section of the chapter.

Theoretical coincidence

Various chapters in this volume (especially those of Lakoff [Chapter 4], Neisser [Chapter 2], and Medin and Wattenmaker [Chapter 3]) offer theoretical suggestions that appeal to one or both of two possible sources of conceptual order. The first (which I will refer to as the *ecological*) looks to the order in the world generally and to an organism's immediate environment (and its interactions with that environment) in particular as the basis for conceptual order. In contrast, the second (the *intellectual*) looks to the order in the organism and especially to the organization of its cognitive constructs as the basis for conceptual order. (The classical theory of categories is crucially ambiguous precisely insofar as it can be taken as an account of either *or both* of these sources of order.) Although they all ultimately agree on the overriding importance of our cognitive constructs in categorization, Neisser, Lakoff, and Medin and Wattenmaker arrive at this point by somewhat different routes.

Initially, Neisser emphasizes the "resonance" of an organism's perceptual apparatus to the structure of the environment. In his view this is where an account of categorization must begin. Both he and Mervis emphasize that members of basic-level categories (especially those from nature) generally look alike and function similarly. On their account (and, presumably, in the case of appearances, on nearly anyone's account) these sorts of similarities are (in one sense or another) directly perceptible. Basic-level categorization is grounded, then, in the way things appear to perceivers of a certain sort. Hence at the basic level people can typically see what things are in virtue of the limited variation between what things typically do and the way they typically look. Neisser readily admits, though, that as a story, even about this aspect of the psychology of categorization, this account has important limitations, some of which Mervis' paper (Chapter 8) documents. Neisser soon abandons talk of direct perception and, instead, affirms the centrality of our cognitive constructs when he discusses superordinate and scientific concepts. He finally concludes that "a category is always defined by reference to a cognitive model" (p. 22).

Similarly, Lakoff emphasizes what might broadly be called the ecological foundations of basic-level categories. He highlights their perceptual, functional, and communicative salience for human beings and claims that the form of the human body sets important constraints on how we acquire, use, and represent categories generally (also see Lakoff 1986). Like Neisser, Lakoff also holds that such ecological factors are *ultimately* insufficient to account for the richness and diversity of human categorization. Both insist that membership in basic-level categories only *seems* perceptually transparent, for the world sometimes proves, upon reflection, not to always be as it appears: whales are not fish, spiders are not insects, and palm trees are grasses. (See, for example, Gould's discussion [1983] of the problems that the category "zebra" presents.) Even at the basic level, clearly cognitive factors operate in perception and categorization. Lakoff also turns to intellectual considerations as his ultimate explanatory engine. Nonetheless, neither Neisser's nor Lakoff's accounts rely exclusively on the intellectual bases of categorization because they take constraints on the most primitive interactions of organisms with their environments (such as bodily shape and orientation) and the practical, perceptual, and evolutionary effects thereof as suggesting grounds for explaining a great deal of basic-level phenomena.

At least in the first half of their chapter, Medin and Wattenmaker are the most unequivocal advocates of the role of higher-order cognitive constructs in conceptual coherence (see also Murphy & Medin 1985). They argue that "coherence derives both from the internal structure of a conceptual domain and the position of the concept in the complete knowledge base" (p. 41). They, however, return to what are, at least, less obviously intellectual considerations, not so much as the origin of specific distinctions with which we operate but rather as the basis for postulating pervasive, natural constraints on the range of our theorizing – as a means of ensuring a measure of conceptual stability.

Arguably, the developmental papers offer evidence for emphasizing the increasing influence on categorization of children's cognitive constructs. Fivush's research indicates that very young children employ event schemata as the basis for categorization. This is, however, a pattern that certainly *seems* less central at later stages in life. Keil has provided substantial evidence of what he has called "a characteristic-to-defining shift" in children across a wide range of categories. He has shown that the process of mastering a concept has a systematic effect on the cues that children attend to. Mervis construes this accomplishment as a specific consequence of the child's accepting a general "expert principle"; that is, in virtue of their superior cultural and theoretical knowledge, experts (usually adults) can overrule the child's initial judgments based on a simple shape/function principle. Markman documents a shift that seems to relate to (indeed, even presuppose) Keil's. In the course of development children also shift away from hierarchies based on part-whole relations to ones based on class inclusion as they fine-tune their categorical systems. Presumably, it is our theories that delineate these class-inclusion relationships.

All of these papers point to a developmental trend *away from* a narrative and/or directly perceptual account of categorization where there is a strong emphasis on temporal and spatial relations between things generally and on temporal and spatial proximity between features in particular. They also point *toward* a more theoretical and inferential basis for categorization where the focus is on hypothetical and logical relations between categories (*apparently*, as classically defined!). Developmental shifts in either the processes of categorization or the organization of our categories would seem to indicate that the environment uniquely determines neither a particular set of categories nor a particular categorization strategy.

Lakoff and Medin and Wattenmaker (see also Murphy & Medin 1985) offer the most extensive proposals about the cognitive devices involved. Their analyses overlap considerably, although Lakoff talks about idealized cognitive models and Medin and Wattenmaker use the term "theory." (Like Neisser, I will employ both notions, depending upon the context in question.) "Theory," in contrast to "idealized cognitive model," connotes constructs that *systematically* characterize certain aspects of the world, but also a degree of formality, which probably does not apply to all the cognitive structures in question. Presumably, many are quite informal – even intuitive. In contrast, "idealized cognitive model" includes less systematic constructs that may not adequately describe the more developed cognitive frameworks that structure large areas of human experience (the complex of theories and practices that constitute an advanced science, for example). On the other hand, the phrase "idealized cognitive model" also highlights three important aspects of these cognitive structures: they are idealized, cognitive, and models. Idealized cognitive models are simplified mental constructs that organize various domains of human experience, both practical and theoretical. Theories should, perhaps, be construed simply as the more elaborate and complex of our idealized cognitive models.

Such structures *must* be idealized. This means, among other things, that they *select* from among all the possible features of the stimuli those that are systematically efficacious (in more purely theoretical domains) or socially or instrumentally significant (in practical domains). Our idealized models simplify our world. Only idealized worlds manifest enough order to permit comprehensive categorization (see McCauley, in progress). The point is that idealizations underemphasize or ignore a huge number of possible features by means of ceteris paribus clauses that implicitly presume their relative lack of import. In making idealizations ". . . we construct a picture of the world as it is that is consciously different in several ways from the world as it is seen, touched, heard, and tasted" (Harre 1972). We bring these idealized models to bear upon the world of our experience. They specify a set of cues in the environment that serve to define the situation and therefore establish expectations about both probable changes in the environment and appropriate responses to them. (I do not presume concerning the relative complexity of the cues.) Contrary, then, to empiricist learning theory, it is not from the blooming, buzzing confusion that we induce categories, but rather from our idealizations that we impose them.

These models are also cognitive. As Lakoff and Neisser emphasize, we can and often do entertain more than one model for a particular domain. Furthermore, the use of these models seems to depend upon our imaginative abilities to take a particular point of view (see Barsalou & Sewell 1984). Lakoff holds that either a lack of coincidence between multiple models for a particular domain or a system of priorities an individual might employ when using these diverse models could explain a number of typicality effects. Various members of categories are judged better examples or not, depending upon the model or models that the subject happens to employ in a particular situation. If an example satisfies *more* than one model, it is even better. If a woman is both the biological mother and the primary caretaker of a child, then she is a better exemplar of the concept "mother" than women who meet the conditions of either the biological or the social model, but not both.

This general view has two particularly important consequences. In the following two sections I will discuss (1) what it is that idealized cognitive models and theories are about and (2) the most important implication *that* has for their role in categorization.

The cognitive precedence of our models of the world

Idealized cognitive models (and theories) are *about the world*. The sum of those models and theories constitutes the superstructure of our knowledge of the world. The crucial point is that *they are not, generally, about categories*. This point should not be confused with the fact that both I and various contributors to this volume are employing the general notion of a cognitive model (or theory) at the heart of our proposals for a psychological theory of categorization. It is necessary throughout to distinguish between theories about the world and the general theoretical approach to the psychology of categorization advanced here. This is especially important because that general theoretical perspective (endorsed directly or indirectly in all of the contributions in this volume mentioned to this point) holds that our theories about the world constitute the most important links in a satisfactory account of categorization.

The meaning of a concept is a function of a number of considerations, especially the roles the concept plays in the larger theories or models in which it appears (see Quine 1953). Concepts gain their significance in virtue of their positions and relations in the networks of claims that constitute our models. Meanings often change, therefore, as our models do (although see Putnam 1975; Rey 1983). Whether they do, in fact, depends on the extent and the localizability of the changes in our models (see Wimsatt 1981). Concepts may also appear to change, depending upon our choice of a particular model on any given occasion.

Brooks (Chapter 6) and Barsalou (Chapter 5), suggest, however, that this sort of variability within our system of categories is often more easily explained as a function of various context effects. On their views it is the peculiarities of the situations in which we find ourselves that substantially determine not only the concepts we employ and how we employ them, but their semantic contours and relations as well. (This is, perhaps, more obvious in some settings, e.g., diplomacy, than in others, e.g., science.) Consequently, both Barsalou and Brooks are ultimately rather skeptical of the importance of the often-demonstrated typicality effects in research on categorization insofar as those effects are taken to indicate relatively invariant structures in our representations of concepts. Indeed, at times it seems that neither Brooks nor Barsalou thinks either that human beings have that many stable, abstract representations of concepts or that whatever ones we do have will play a very central role in any promising theory of categorization. Although they advance these negative theses in somewhat different ways, Brooks, at least, explicitly claims that his position and these claims in particular are compatible with the approaches to the psychology of categorization outlined in the previous section.

Brooks acknowledges that approaches to categorization that focus on our cognitive constructs have some value, but he also holds that cognitive psychology "has developed undue faith in the role of centralized, abstractive models as representations of everyday human knowledge" (p. 141). He offers considerable evidence suggesting that the retention and manipulation of instances from some, perhaps even one, prior processing episode suffice to account for many aspects of our classificatory activities without appealing to complex systems of abstractions. Brooks claims that "prior instances can be an important resource in unfamiliar complex domains and that variations in the processing of individual prior episodes are important for later classification" (p. 156). He provides evidence that a wide range of categorization tasks reflects considerable sensitivity to the manipulation of episodic variables. (It would not be too misleading to describe his position as an extension of the encoding specificity hypothesis to the psychology of categorization.) Differences in subjects' aims and purposes, in their past experiences, in demand characteristics, and in the context generally have significant effects on the shape of the concepts that we employ in any particular situation. (Brooks regards the findings that Barsalou presents in this volume as only further reinforcing his position.) He emphasizes the role of "nonanalytic" considerations in knowledge organization and cognitive processing and concludes that, in the end, the conceptual coherence, which the more "analytic" cognitive approaches emphasize, proves "a bit of an illusion" (p. 170).

Analytic control of conceptual activity on Brooks' view is a conscious overlay which the reduction of the inconsistencies that arise in our rough and ready use of concepts from one context to the next periodically requires. He attempts to show that his nonanalytic account adequately handles the empirical results that he reviews, usually completely exclusive of appeals to analytic or abstractive mechanisms (see also Jacoby & Brooks 1984; Hintzman & Ludlum 1980). This account hangs on "analogies," which Brooks describes as both "routine" (p. 142) and "close" (p. 142), where "the current and previous episodes are similar on so many characteristics that the relevant predictors must be in there somewhere" (p. 142). Presumably, most of our everyday negotiations with the world do not require appeal to higher-order rules and representations. Brooks, however, carefully avoids hyperbole. He does not deny the existence of analytic or abstractive mechanisms, but simply cautions against assumptions about their explanatory hegemony.

Barsalou is even less sympathetic with approaches to categorization that focus on stable representations of concepts. On the basis of the extreme variability among typicality findings he has demonstrated here and elsewhere (see also Barsalou 1982, 1983), Barsalou rejects the view that "there are invariant cognitive structures associated with categories that we should be trying to discover" (p. 114). Instead, he proposes that "different concepts temporarily represent the same category in working memory on different occasions." These "temporary concepts," which Barsalou calls "category concepts," are constructed by means of "a highly flexible process that retrieves generic and episodic information from long-term memory." Barsalou's approach, like Brooks's, depends upon the assumption that categorization is done on the basis of a "similarity comparison process in working memory" (p. 118). Subjects' typicality judgments arise, then, as a function of comparisons of provisional category concepts (constructed on the spot from information mustered from long-term memory) with what Barsalou calls "exemplar concepts." (As to what *these* are, where they come from, and in what sense they too count as "concepts," Barsalou does not say.) Because both our interests and the contexts that we find ourselves in are constantly changing, "the same concept is rarely if ever constructed for a category" (p. 101).

On Barsalou's view our cognitive systems constantly change, but not enough to explain the degree of instability in typicality judgments that his research has uncovered. So, the source of that diversity must be primarily in changing contexts, not in the head. Thus, Barsalou proposes (along with Brooks) that the processes of categorization (or, at least, their products) are relatively peripheral phenomena cognitively.

Brooks's and Barsalou's positions do affirm a welcome corrective (well represented throughout this volume) to much current research on categories. On both their relatively "peripheralist" or, to use Brooks's term, "decentralized" views of categorization (e.g., Barsalou insists that even the *term* "graded structure" refers not to cognitive structure but rather to behavior) and Lakoff's, Neisser's, and Medin and Wattenmaker's relatively more "centralist" alternatives, particular concepts are not the primary units of either cognitive representation or processing. These two groups arrive at this conclusion, though, by different means. The centralists look to higher-order knowledge structure (viz., idealized cognitive models and theories) to explain the relevant empirical findings. Although they do not deny the importance of higher-order structures, the peripheralists, on the other hand, take those findings (and their diversity, in particular) as indications, in Brooks's case, of the explanatory priority in most contexts of prior processing episodes and the instances they involve and, in Barsalou's case, of the relative inaccessibility (*at least*) of stable conceptual representations within our cognitive systems. Both Brooks's and Barsalou's positions, however, face some potentially important difficulties.

Brooks holds that our observations (and, presumably, therefore our categorizations) "would be represented by a distribution of instances still acting as individuals." In such judgments, though, the similarity that unifies these instances *as instances of the same concept* requires some explanation. Brooks thinks that it would require "only minimal nativist constraints" (p. 161) to account for the "special case" (p. 163) that our everyday judgments of similarity constitute. In light of the diversity of the experimental materials he discusses and, simultaneously, the specificity *and* abstractness of many of our most common judgments of similarity, Brooks may have underestimated the size of the nativistic promissory note he has underwritten.

Brooks's claim that (1) "more generalized cognitive models undoubtedly exist, but there is no reason to assume that they are directly involved in every interpretive act," and (2) "the collection of prior events may . . . *be* the categorical knowledge" (p. 142) offers some evidence for this suspicion. The contents of prior processing episodes may have important effects on various aspects of human categorization, but they could *never* exhaust our "categorical knowledge." Brooks has overlooked Kant's fundamental insight (Kant 1965:182) that no (amount of) instances of, for example, a triangle

. . . could ever be adequate to the concept of a triangle in general. It would never attain the universality of the concept which renders it valid of all triangles, whether right-angled, obtuse-angled, or acute angled; it would always be limited to a part only of this sphere. The schema of the triangle can exist nowhere but in thought . . . *Still less is an object of experience or its image ever adequate to the empirical concept* . . . [emphasis mine]

It is difficult to see how this logical constraint cannot have psychological implications. If individual instances exhausted our categorical knowledge, then in virtue of what could we recognize them as instances of the *same* concept? Brooks's emphasis on the role of previously experienced individual instances in the processes of categorization can make no sense without the direct implication of stable, higher-order cognitive structures.

Barsalou's position seems even more vulnerable on this count. He repeatedly talks about the "knowledge" (e.g., p. 120) and "information" (e.g., p. 133) in long-term memory from which his category concepts are constructed in working memory. But how can we organize, sort, store, or retrieve this material in long-term memory without using concepts? Although he insists (p. 120) that his view does "*not* . . . imply that there is *no* stable knowledge in long-term memory" and that the problem may be nothing more than one concerning its relative inaccessibility, in fact Barsalou seems to end up merely kicking Brooks's problem upstairs. He says that "the knowledge associated with a category in long-term memory can be viewed as the union of many possible concepts that could represent the category in working memory" and that "long-term memory contains concepts for categories, but in the sense that the knowledge for a particular category contains many, many concepts" (p. 121). But in virtue of what are those many, many concepts concepts *for the same category*? There must be some criterion for recognizing them as concepts for *the same category*. Such judgments are impossible without presupposing either extensive innate machinery (see, for example, Fodor 1975) or some stable basis for (representing) the category's logical integrity within the cognitive system (see Note 3).

Both Brooks's and Barsalou's proposals, then, seem to put the psychological cart before the logical horse *whenever* they assume that the notion of information in the cognitive system can be explicated exclusive of some measure of stability among our conceptual structures. The need for some conceptual stability is logically inescapable. The centralists' proposals, which *focus* on our higher-order knowledge structures, can accommodate the wide range of context effects with which Brooks and Barsalou are (rightfully) concerned without completely surrendering the initiative with respect to conceptual coherence.

Categories as relations

If idealized cognitive models and theories are about the world, then, Neisser argues, categories are best understood relationally (also see Barsalou, Chapter 5, this volume, p. 116). Construing categories on an analogy with Gibsonian affordances, Neisser characterizes them as relations "between cognitive models and the real world" (p. 21). It follows that, if the relation changes, then our categories change. If either or both of the relata change, then the relation changes. Thus, it also follows that our categories can change at least as frequently and as severely as do our theories and cognitive models.

This account of categories as relations between our cognitive constructs and the world explains why the classical theory of categorization falls short. The cognitive structures in which our categories are embedded are *models* – models that, when sufficiently elaborated and developed, constitute *theories*. The point is not only that we entertain alternative models and theories depending upon our different aims and purposes, but that we can also entertain multiple (and not fully consistent) models and theories in the *same* context. Furthermore, our preferences about theories, at least in science, change. Indeed, in this century our preferred theories in physics and biology have done much to undermine our cherished intuitions about natural kinds and the metaphysical assumptions (captured in the classical theory of categories) underlying them.

Recent experimental findings generally reinforce this negative verdict. The classical theory cannot easily accommodate many of them, including Barsalou's typicality findings for goal-derived (1984) and ad hoc categories (1983), the role of context effects on all typicality findings (as Barsalou and Brooks have emphasized here and elsewhere), and the complexities of Lakoff's radial categories (also see Lakoff 1986; Lakoff & Johnson 1980). In addition, the classical theory simply seems orthogonal to many of the well-known findings concerning basic-level categories. The problem, though, is that the general constraints on category organization are so few even on the idealized cognitive model/theory approach[1] to categorization that it is not immediately obvious how it will account for the apparent systematicity and logical perspicuity that pervades many areas of our categorical system. The classical theory, by contrast, readily explains these properties, and that is, to a considerable extent, the source of its appeal.

The theoretical upheavals of science notwithstanding, the idealized cognitive model/theory account of categorization *can* explain the *apparently* classical character of certain empirical categories (for example, natural kinds) and therefore the corollary persistence of the classical theory's appeal. First of all, certain idealized cognitive models and the categories they employ have assumed central roles in our knowledge schemes – either in our own lifetimes, in that of our culture, or even, perhaps, in that of our species. The stability of these cognitive models and of the categories they contain is an important source of the classical theory's plausibility. In these domains in particular, maintaining the order that the classical theory captures is crucial to many of our practical and theoretical negotiations with the world. In addition, our idealized cognitive models (and theories) deal with *idealized* worlds. Idealizations not only free our conceptual system from exhaustively accommodating the world's myriad details and apparent anomalies, but they also simplify and order the world as well. They ensure conceptual systematicity locally, at least.

It is in order to explain the variabilities and inconsistencies in our conceptual system, which so concern Brooks and Barsalou, though, that researchers have sought alternative principles of category organization. The idealized cognitive model/theory approach to categorization suggests that most of the pertinent "principles" will concern the internal structures and the external relations of our cognitive constructs both with one another and with the world. Within the framework of this approach to categorization, we can distinguish at least two general kinds of principles, though crucially, *their implications for particular categories depend upon the substantive details of the specific theories and models in question.* (Medin and Wattenmaker's proposals [and Barsalou's, for that matter] could be taken as suggesting principles of a higher order, which operate on our representations of categories *as defined by our cognitive constructs.*) The first, which I do not intend to discuss, I will call *internal* principles of category organization. These refer to the relations *internal* to particular cognitive models. Examples include Lakoff's metaphoric (see Lakoff & Johnson 1980) and metonymic models. These principles specify structures internal to our cognitive models.

The second type are *external* principles, which, themselves, come in two varieties. Both concern cognitive models' *external relations* and questions of their fit in particular. The first variety deals with the relative *fit with one another* of two or more cognitive models for the same domain (e.g., biological and social conceptions of motherhood). Such models inevitably conflict somewhere. These conflicts lay the foundations for the variabilities in graded structure that Barsalou reports. The differences in the relative centrality of the particular instance in question to the various models involved permits alternative prototypicality judgments. Which judgment a subject, in fact, makes depends in part upon which of the contextual influences prevail, as Brooks and Barsalou emphasize. For example, it is not even completely obvious that being female is an essential property of mothers as they are socially defined. (See Lakoff, 1986, for a much more detailed discussion of both the issues and the examples.) Undoubtedly, the most interesting cases of conflict among our cognitive models are those between what Sellars (1963) has called our commonsense or "manifest image" and our "scientific image" of the world.

It is the second sort of external principle on which I intend to focus. It concerns a second sort of fit, namely, the *fit between our cognitive models and the world*. Short of radical sceptics' and idealists' worries, it remains relatively noncontroversial that our cognitive constructs constrain perception – but also that they do not determine it absolutely. The interesting problems concern making sense of these constraints and delineating their limits. The crucial point is that the way the world is influences both the directions in which our knowledge grows and (therefore) the directions in which our systems of concepts change. Even Kuhn (1970:150) argues that it is *not* the case that scientists "can see anything they please." If we assume that our cognitive constructs do not merely constrain our experience but, in fact, exhaust it, we can preserve only the lamest accounts of the growth of human knowledge. Our inability to make some sense of the possibility of the world detectably failing to fit the predictions of our theories or the forms of our models, at least some of the time, would seriously jeopardize the epistemic privileges we typically claim in science's behalf. That such failures occur in scientific inquiry, however, is undeniable. The problem is to explain how that can be so on an approach to categorization that so stresses the role of our cognitive constructs.

Any approach that countenances both ecological and intellectual bases of categorization (as Lakoff's, Neisser's, and Medin and Wattenmaker's all do), that is, one that attempts to address the effects on our categories both of the discontinuities in nature and of our cognitive constructs, inevitably raises old epistemological problems about the relation of the categories of the mind (housed in our cognitive models) and the categories of the world. In short, what reasons do we have for thinking that our idealized cognitive models and theories cut the world at its joints?

I should emphasize that I take the presence of these problems as a cardinal virtue of such approaches. All of the greatest philosophers since Aristotle have confronted them and to fail to do so is just an indication that we are on the wrong track. Furthermore, to fail to do so brings an end to cognitive psychology (at least), either by assuming that the mind does *all* of the work of categorization (see Fodor 1975) or (as the most radical of the behaviorists and certain Gibsonians do) by assuming that the environment does it all (see Dennett 1978). Either way leaves little room for a plausible account of the growth of knowledge because, among other things, neither way leaves much room for a plausible account of mistakes. On both views there would seem to be too few or far, far too many.

Theories, categories, and perceptual transparency

We have now turned toward more obviously philosophical territory. On the idealized cognitive model/theory approach to categorization there is no escaping our cognitive constructs. Consequently (as Hilary Putnam maintains), ". . . statements are not 'made true' . . . by mind-independent states of affairs, but by states of affairs *as perceived and conceptualized* . . ." (Putnam (1983:83–84).[2] Indeed, the notion of "mind-independent states of affairs" is incoherent on this view except, as Kant held, as a postulate of pure reason. The *world-in-itself* is forever inaccessible. But the problem, then, is to make sense of how that world, perceived through the filters our cognitive constructs constitute, can, nonetheless, influence not only which of those cognitive constructs we employ but also how we adjust them and, *ultimately*, whether we even accept them!

It is, of course, precisely on these sorts of decisions that our standard picture of rationality turns. Our various cognitive models offer alternative descriptions of the world. Everyone recognizes from time to time that certain of these descriptions are not only less helpful than others (given the problems at hand), but also that some are *for all intents and purposes* false. Although we permit everyone a certain amount of slack, we have a limited tolerance for failures to reject such problematic views, especially when they concern those parts of the world that seem transparent perceptually. But given the presumptive inaccessibility of uncognized reality, the question is how we justify these customs. For it is not at all clear now what perceptual transparency amounts to.

We would *apparently* need to make sense (independent of the role our theories play) of our access to the categories of the world and the basis of

the similarity judgments in virtue of which we place particular individuals in the same category. But, of course, on the approach advanced
here the influence of our cognitive constructs on categorization is pervasive and, presumably, precludes precisely the sort of perceptual transparency that the solutions to these problems would seem to require.

The convention in the psychological literature of *merely* distinguishing
between *categories* (in the world) and *concepts* (in the mind) has, generally,
not only not helped to clarify these epistemological issues, it has tended
to obscure them. If our concepts have their form as a result of the roles
they play in our models and theories, and if all observation is as theory-
laden both as the present position implies and as most contemporary
philosophers maintain (see Hanson 1969; Kuhn 1970; Brown 1979),
then this distinction simply illustrates the problem; it does not solve it.[3]

Medin's work exemplifies this tension. In both Murphy and Medin
(1985) and his and Wattenmaker's Chapter 3 in this volume, Medin
breaks with a number of his and others' earlier papers on certain counts
(see Brooks, Chapter 6, this volume, Note 2). Those earlier papers propose general principles of category acquisition and organization in terms
of increasingly refined, all-purpose, data-driven, feature-comparison
strategies. These strategies all operate on the *assumption* that the perceptual transparency of certain features of the input enables us to compare
the individuals that instantiate them straightforwardly and unreflectively with respect to their similarity. The problem is that these proposals
fail to provide any account of why some similarities matter and an indefinitely large number of others do not (as Medin and Wattenmaker show
so powerfully on pp. 26–33). What was required was not increasingly
sophisticated heuristics for feature comparison but rather an account of
those features' perceptual transparency! *Crucially,* that is exactly what
discussions of this general sort have lacked.

Medin's more recent emphasis on the role of theories in categorization, however, seems in certain respects to be at odds with both the spirit
and the letter of these proposals. If our cognitive constructs are the
engines of categorization, then the general feature-comparison strategies Medin and other researchers advanced concern second-order issues at best.

No doubt, some basic "cognitive" structures and the dispositions to
discriminate among stimuli for which they are responsible are, in a
rather strong sense, genetically predetermined features of our physiology. The assumption, however, that such general strategies of feature
comparison describe innate constraints on human categorization –
which employ, in the case of each category, a primitive notion of similarity – will not wash. As I suggested above (pp. 296–297) regarding
Brooks's nativist gambit, to claim simultaneously (1) that the applicability
of these principles is pervasive, (2) that their implications are specific,

and (3) that they are innate, involves a serious underestimate of the range, diversity, and complexity of our system of empirical categories.

On the idealized cognitive model/theory account of categorization, it is the substantive commitments of the specific models and theories with which we operate (and especially of those that we acquire) that determine our empirical distinctions. Empirical considerations support both claims. It is the logical considerations that support the weaker and more general claim, however, that I wish to discuss at some length.

On the empirical side research in human development has consistently found human beings at increasingly early ages capable of making complex discriminations about the world. We seem to be born organizers (and theorizers) ready and equipped to employ very soon after birth a host of models that are both highly constrained and strategically specific (see, e.g., Fivush [Chapter 9], Markman [Chapter 10], Mervis [Chapter 8], this volume; Churchland 1984). Proposals along these lines have been made for such diverse areas as language acquisition (e.g., Chomsky 1975), face recognition (Gibson 1969), and ontological presupposition (Keil 1979).

The logical considerations, however, overshadow the empirical ones. What categories we find most readily available, and therefore what we find perceptually transparent, must be a function of a prior model or theory that offers criteria for discriminating (and organizing) the significant from among the input. All perception is selective. The crucial point is that *any* account of category induction (including the nonanalytic variety for which Brooks argues) based on strategies of feature analysis (no matter how "close" the analogies!) already *presupposes* that we know what will count as a relevant feature. These positions, then, already presuppose some *cognitive structure* that informs all of their operations and defines the relevant similarities. Consequently, such feature-analysis strategies could never be the fundamental apparatus of categorization.

Of course, Medin and Wattenmaker and I are employing the terms "cognitive," "model," and "theory" here in wider than usual senses. I temporarily tinker with these notions *only* to emphasize the affinity of the effects on categorization and perception of our (innate) physiological biases with those of the theories and models that we consciously entertain. This is of a piece with Popper's claim (1972:71–71) that

All acquired knowledge, all learning, consists of the modification (possibly the rejection) of some form of knowledge, or disposition, which was there previously, and in the last instance of inborn dispositions . . . [which] can be described as *theory-impregnated,* assuming a sufficiently wide sense of the term "theory."

I assume that Murphy and Medin (1985), at least some of the time, expand the term "theory" in just the same way. The informal, intuitive, even unconscious character of many of our cognitive structures does not preclude their influencing perception and categorization just as profoundly as the theories and models do with which we consciously operate.

It is, then, a logical point that we cannot escape our theories (either narrowly or broadly construed). If we could, we would have no means for deciding which among the infinite features of our perceptual input were relevant to the situations at hand. (In fact, we would have no means for even distinguishing alternative situations!) What I have been broadly calling the *theory* does the work. We *are* born theorizers disposed to perceive and react to the world in certain specific ways because we *must* have theories (in the broad sense at least) in order to have any empirical knowledge at all. As our knowledge grows and changes we do not abandon all of our previous expectations (no matter what their origin). We fine-tune many[4] and generate more in the course of facing new problems. Recent research on the psychology of reasoning and problem-solving (see, e.g., Kahneman, Slovik, & Tversky 1982; Tweney, Doherty, & Mynatt 1980) consistently reveals subjects' proclivity to rush to all sorts of premature conclusions, that is, to *immediately* employ all sorts of unsupported theories. This illustrates the centrality of theorizing (no matter how unreflective) for the rest of cognition.

Not only do theories *not* preclude perceptual transparency, they are essential to it (see Heil 1983). It is *only* where we have salient cognitive constructs (again, in the broad sense at least) that the world's contents become perceptually transparent. Precisely because of dominant theories for those domains, we *know* both what to look for and what is similar to what.

Note that it does *not* follow on this account of the role of theories in perception and categorization that we cannot perceive either the novel or the unexpected. Such anomalies need not, indeed presumably cannot, violate the systems of natural constraints that operate in human perception. It only follows that we may not immediately (automatically?) know *specifically* what to make of them or what to do with them. They will not be transparent, because they violate the system of expectations the specific highest-level theory with which we are presently operating determines. No theory of perception and categorization should rule out the possibility of such anomalies. It is often because of such experiences that we choose either to employ an alternative theory at our disposal for the pertinent domain or to consider constructing wholly new ones. On the other hand, this is precisely why the basic-level findings are so interesting.

Basic-level objects, as Neisser and Mervis have emphasized, are perceptually salient objects. Basic-level categories seem to define some of the major joints of the world. That their members are perceptually transparent and that we can identify typical patterns of interaction with the objects that our basic-level categories pick out are evidence of dominant theories at work.

It should come as no surprise, though, that at least *on certain criteria* there is some evidence that the basic level for experts sometimes changes. This readily follows on the idealized cognitive model/theory account of categorization. Generally, experts have better cognitive models for the domains that they have mastered. In *practical* affairs the expert constructs increasingly detailed models of the patterns typical of the materials and the pursuit in question, presumably as a function of accumulating experience with each. Here the "new" basic level would probably be the level in the hierarchy with the next greatest amount of detail, namely, that subordinate to the original basic level. In *theoretical* pursuits the basic level should change according to the specifications of the pertinent theory[5] that the expert has mastered, presumably violating on occasion his or her original system of basic-level categories on one or more counts. The theoretically inspired adjustments may, however, neither be too severe nor have any practical implications. Also, in many of our everyday activities most of us neither acquire nor require such levels of expertise. With respect to these activities we do not typically advance much beyond childhood knowledge. These may well be contributing factors to the stability of the overwhelming majority of basic-level categories for the overwhelming majority of people.

Certainly, the situation *is* less clear-cut in areas of personal or cultural expertise (see Dougherty 1978) where the relevant basic-level distinctions seem to shift on linguistic criteria to a more subordinate level. Still, *there is no evidence* (contra Murphy & Medin 1985:305) *that subjects' basic-level distinctions change on any of the standard perceptual criteria.* The theories and models that we consciously hold (e.g., in contemporary physics) can supersede the picture of reality that some of our (apparently) innate biases suggest. However, the persisting perceptual prominence of our basic-level distinctions would indicate that there are other innate constraints that they *generally* do not supersede. Medin and Wattenmaker suggest (p. 55) that "constraints associated with what we normally think of as more basic (and less accessible) cognitive processes may carry over into higher-level cognitive processes." That so many basic-level distinctions would persist in the face of considerable contextual, theoretical, cultural, and, perhaps even, historical diversity would suggest that a relatively stable and extensive set of expectations informs (without conscious reflection) at least one aspect of human perception and categorization (see Wimsatt 1974).

By contrast, Neisser speaks (p. 12) of "invariants . . . that correspond to relatively permanent features of the objective situation." I agree with

Neisser (and Kant) that objective situations have invariant features, but (Kant and) I disagree with Neisser when he implies that we can know that they are ultimately an exclusive function of stabilities in the environment. For example, Neisser summarizes his position by claiming (p. 22) that "categorization is somewhat less 'direct' than perception. The perceptible properties of things are specified by invariants to which perceptual systems need only resonate, but a category is always defined by reference to a cognitive model." However, neither this attempt to drive a wedge between perception and categorization nor Brooks's (when he draws a distinction [p. 164] between things' "near physical identity" and when they are "merely conceptually the same") can stand, because there is no perception without categories and (as Neisser admits) there are no categories without cognitive models. (This is of a piece with Shepard's point which Medin and Wattenmaker cite [p. 54] that research on perception in ecologically valid contexts begs the question with respect to the issue of "separating constraints associated with the environment itself from those embodied in the organism.")

Even if it is true, as Neisser claims, that the visual system "resonates" to *optical* invariants, it need not follow (unless the sense of the term "resonate" employed here begs precisely the tacit epistemological question) that "the system picks up structure directly from the optic array without any intermediate steps or false starts" (in *any* of the relevant senses of the term "false"). Nor would the fact that some of the relevant invariants seem to be multimodal (see Gibson 1984) suffice to justify this sort of strong claim.

There is some evidence, though, that Neisser's confidence on this point stems from his belief that, in fact, we *can* have access to unconceptualized (external) reality after all. At one point, for example, Neisser states (p. 12) that "perception is *essentially* of . . . [the real] state [of affairs] *itself*" (emphasis mine). This position would overlook two important considerations: (1) that the objective situation *as perceived* invariably includes the embodied biases (in each perceptual modality) with which the perceiving subject operates and (2) that the theories, for example, *in optics,* which reign in contemporary science (*and which direct our understanding of situations generally*) are, indeed, just that – *theories.* They are no less immune to the possibility of future revision than any other theories in the history of science have been (see Putnam 1983:177). They guarantee nothing about the structure of the world-in-itself.

Our best accounts of reality (including its joints) are the ones that our best theories entail, and it is through scientific inquiry that we ascertain the relative value of our theories. The history of science is replete with examples of theoretical advances superseding what was, theretofore, the perceptually obvious (see Churchland 1984:44). The true source of

Copernicus' greatness, according to Galileo, was his ability to see beyond the appearances (see Galilei 1967:328; also see Popper 1963:97–119.) New theories (in science) and newly acquired theories (in development) enable us to see more and more (see Bechtel 1984). From time to time new theoretical accomplishments supply compelling reasons for rejecting what had previously been perceptually transparent. These new superior theories show anew what it is that we should look for. Their explanatory and predictive successes entitle them to define the categories in their domains.

It is when we undertake steps of increasing cognitive sophistication (all of which are akin to Keil's characteristic-to-defining-shift) that we rely increasingly on the developed, abstract theories that we consciously entertain. These cognitive constructs further structure and sometimes even amend how we have previously perceived and categorized the world. Since Thales' claim that everything is made of water, human inquirers have known that at least some things are not the way they appear. The problem ever since has been to discover which ones, in fact, are not. Hereafter in this pursuit, though, we cannot ignore the central role our theories play with respect to what we see.

NOTES

I wish to express my gratitude to Larry Barsalou, William Bechtel, Marshall Gregory, and Robert Richardson for their helpful comments on earlier drafts of this paper. I also wish to thank George Lakoff, Doug Medin, and Ulric Neisser for helpful conversations about many of the issues treated here.

1 I regret this somewhat concocted name, but it does have the virtues of remaining both faithful to all of the texts in question and transparent with respect to the position's most fundamental substantive commitments.
2 Although in this same passage Putnam refers to this account of truth as "nonrealist," and he subsequently rejects an account of truth as correspondence, these conclusions seem a bit misleading on two counts. First, this is as much realism as Putnam (or I) would ever allow. (Putnam *does* refer to the resulting position as "internal realism.") In addition, this position does not deny the possibility of claims corresponding with the world, but only the notion that particular claims could ever *uniquely* correspond to and hence delineate unconceptualized reality, i.e., the world-in-itself.
3 Thus Barsalou's references throughout his paper to the "categories," which his "category concepts" instantiate, present him with a dilemma. Either somewhere within our cognitive systems we must possess some basis for (representing) these categories' logical integrity (as I argued above [p. 297] and which Barsalou sometimes seems to deny), or Barsalou would, apparently, need to assume that we have some sort of direct (and, apparently, constant) access to unconceptualized reality – an assumption, incidentally, which I do not think that he would find congenial.

308   ROBERT N. MCCAULEY

4 I think that Keil's research on the ontological tree should be construed as filling out *some* of the details of the processes in question (see Keil 1979).
5 Distinguishing these two processes is no clearer than distinguishing theoretical and practical pursuits. Expert practitioners are typically well aware of theoretical advances relevant to their pursuits, just as theoretical experts must quite frequently acquire a great deal of practical skill in certain areas. (Consider the relationships between organic chemistry and cooking on the one hand and bird-watching and ornithology on the other.)

REFERENCES

Barsalou, L. (1982). Context-independent and context-dependent information in concepts. *Memory and Cognition, 10*, 82–93.
(1983). Ad hoc categories. *Memory and Cognition, 11*, 211–27.
(1984). *Determinants of graded structure in categories.* Emory Cognition Project Report #4.
Barsalou, L., & Sewell, D. (1984). *Constructing representations of categories from different points of view.* Emory Cognition Project Report #2.
Bechtel, W. (1984). The evolution of our understanding of the cell: A study in the dynamics of scientific progress. *Studies in History and Philosophy of Science, 15*, 309–56.
Brown, H. (1979). *Perception, theory and commitment.* Chicago: University of Chicago Press.
Chomsky, N. (1975). *Reflections on language.* New York: Random House.
Churchland, P. (1984). *Matter and consciousness.* Cambridge, MA: MIT Press.
Dennett, D. (1978). Skinner skinned. In *Brainstorms.* Cambridge, MA: Bradford/MIT Press.
Dougherty, J. (1978). Salience and relativity in classification. *American Ethnologist, 5*, 66–80.
Fodor, J. (1975). *The language of thought.* New York: Crowell.
Galilei, Galileo (1967). *Dialogue concerning the two chief world systems* (2nd ed.). Translated by Stillman Drake. Berkeley: University of California Press.
Gibson, E. (1969). *Principles of perceptual learning and development.* New York: Appleton-Century-Crofts.
(1984). Development of knowledge about intermodal unity: Two views. In *Piaget and the foundations of knowledge.* Hillsdale, NJ: Erlbaum.
Gould, S. (1983). What, if anything, is a zebra. In *Hen's teeth and horse's toes.* New York: Norton.
Hanson, N. (1969). *Patterns of discovery.* Cambridge, England: Cambridge University Press.
Harre, R. (1972). *The philosophies of science.* Oxford: Oxford University Press.
Heil, J. (1983). *Cognition and perception.* Berkeley: University of California Press.
Hintzman, D., & Ludlum, G. (1980). Differential forgetting of prototypes and old instances: Simulation by an exemplar-based classification model. *Memory and Cognition, 8*, 378–82.
Jacoby, L., & Brooks, L. (1984). Nonanalytic cognition: Memory, perception, and concept learning. In G. Bower (Ed.), *The psychology of learning and motivation: Advances in research and theory.* New York: Academic Press.
Kahneman, D., Slovic, P., & Tversky, A. (Eds.) (1982). *Judgment under uncertainty: Heuristics and biases.* New York: Cambridge University Press.

Kant, I. (1965). *Critique of pure reason.* Translated by Norman Kemp Smith. New York: St. Martin's Press.

Keil, F. (1979). *Semantic and conceptual development.* Cambridge, MA: Harvard University Press.

Kuhn, T. (1970). *The structure of scientific revolutions* (2nd ed.). Chicago: University of Chicago Press.

Lakoff, G. (1986). *Women, fire, and dangerous things.* Chicago: University of Chicago Press.

Lakoff, G., & Johnson, M. (1980). *Metaphors we live by.* Chicago: University of Chicago Press.

Locke, J. (1959). *An essay concerning human understanding.* New York: Dover.

McCauley, R. (in progress). Problem solving in science and the competence approach to theorizing in linguistics.

Mervis, C., & Rosch, E. (1981). Categorization of natural objects. *Annual Review of Psychology, 32,* 89–115.

Murphy, G., & Medin, D. (1985). The role of theories in conceptual coherence. *Psychological Review, 92,* 289–316.

Osherson, D., & Smith, E. (1981). On the adequacy of prototype theory as a theory of concepts. *Cognition, 9,* 35–58.

Popper, K. (1963). *Conjectures and refutations.* New York: Harper & Row.

(1972). *Objective knowledge.* Oxford: Oxford University Press.

Putnam, H. (1975). The meaning of "meaning." In *Mind, language and reality* (pp. 215–271). New York: Cambridge University Press.

(1983). *Realism and reason.* New York: Cambridge University Press.

Quine, W. (1953). Two dogmas of empiricism. In *From a logical point of view* (pp. 20–46). New York: Harper & Row.

Rey, G. (1983). Concepts and stereotypes. *Cognition, 15,* 237–262.

Rosch, E. (1973). On the internal structure of perceptual and semantic categories. In T. Moore (Ed.), *Cognitive development and the acquisition of language* (pp. 111–144). New York: Academic Press.

(1975). Cognitive representations of semantic categories. *Journal of Experimental Psychology: General, 104,* 192–233.

Rosch, E., & Mervis, C. (1975). Family resemblances: Studies in the internal structure of categories. *Cognitive Psychology, 7,* 573–605.

Rosch, E., Mervis, C., Gray, W., Johnson, D., & Boyes-Braem, P. (1976). Basic objects in natural categories. *Cognitive Psychology, 8,* 382–439.

Sellars, W. (1963). *Science, perception, and reality.* New York: Humanities Press.

Tweney, R., Doherty, M., & Mynatt, C. (Eds.) (1980). *On scientific thinking.* New York: Columbia University Press.

Wimsatt, W. (1974). Reductionism, levels of organization, and the mind-body problem. In G. Globus, G. Maxwell, & I. Savodnik (Eds.), *Consciousness and the brain.* New York: Plenum.

(1981). Robustness, reliability, and overdetermination. In M. Brewer & B. Collins (Eds.), *Scientific inquiry and the social sciences.* San Francisco: Jossey-Bass.

Author index

Abelson, R. P., 65, 70, 125, 236
Adelman, L., 37
Al Issa, I., 176
Allen, R., 144, 148
Allen, Scott, 152, 155, 156, 157, 164, 169
Altom, M. W., 56, 124
Anderson, J. A., 166
Anderson, J. R., 144, 147
Anglin, J. M., 176, 217–18
Aoki, Haruo, 82
Armstrong, S. L., 16, 31, 88, 96–9, 102, 108, 175

Baillargeon, R., 257, 258
Baker, J., 149
Ballato, S. M., 108, 135
Barresi, J., 49
Barrett, M. D., 207
Barsalou, L. W., 3, 5, 9, 16, 26, 29, 35, 39, 102, 104, 105–6, 107, 108, 109, 111–12, 115, 116, 117, 119, 122, 123, 125, 126, 127, 128, 131, 132, 135, 136, 137, 166, 167, 168, 244, 294, 295, 296, 297, 298, 299, 300, 307
Bates, E., 238
Batterman, N., 19
Bechtel, W., 130, 307
Beeghly-Smith, M., 238
Begin, J., 149
Bell, R. Q., 220
Bellezza, F. S., 113, 118
Benelli, B., 224
Black, J. B., 245
Bolles, R. C., 56
Bower, G. H., 35, 123, 124, 245
Bowerman, M., 203
Boyes-Braem, P., 11, 28, 116, 202, 259
Bretherton, I., 238
Brooks, L., 6, 9, 23, 101, 119, 128, 132, 144, 148, 149, 150, 152, 155, 165, 171, 294, 295, 296, 297, 298, 299, 300, 302, 303, 306

Brown, A. L., 259
Brown, R., 203, 235, 268
Bruner, J., 238, 255
Bukatko, D., 202
Byrne, B., 150, 151

Callanan, M. A., 257, 258, 270, 272, 272, 275, 284
Canada, K., 201, 204
Cardoso-Martins, C., 220, 231
Carey, Susan, 16, 30, 50, 195, 204, 255, 258
Carroll, M., 150, 151
Catlin, J., 103
Chaffin, R., 40
Chamberlain, K., 231
Chang, F. R., 244
Chapman, J. P., 37, 54, 125
Chapman, K., 217
Chapman, L. J., 37, 54, 125
Chomsky, N., 303
Christensen, P., 231
Churchland, P., 303, 306
Clark, E. V., 203, 204, 207, 239, 267, 269–70
Clark, L. F., 126
Cohen, B., 131
Cohen, L. B., 234
Cole, M., 258
Coleman, L., 66–71
Collins, A., 32, 147
Conrad, C., 123
Craik, F. I. M., 143, 146
Crisafi, M. A., 202

Dachler, M. W., 202
Deese, J., 136
DeForest, M., 258
Dennett, D., 301
Denney, D. R., 234, 244
Dewey, G. I., 37
Dickinson, A., 56

311

Subject index

ad hoc categories, 16, 26, 102, 108, 115, 119, 132, 167, 298; *see also* goal-derived categories

affordances, 4, 12–15, 21–2, 23n, 53, 298

artifacts, 16, 185–95

attributes: as listed by experimental subjects, 14, 35–6, 121; criteria for children's categorization, 203–8, 285; not adequate for defining categories, 27, 31–3; *see also* correlated attributes, features

basic-level categories, 3, 11–15, 64–5, 87, 91, 202, 259–60, 284, 288, 299; based on environmental structure, 29, 162; change with skill, 22n, 305; different for children, 7, 202–8, 224; perceptually given, 4, 14–15, 290–1, 304–5; *see also* child-basic categories

characteristic-to-defining shift, 6, 9, 19–20, 176–91, 197, 292, 307

child-basic categories, 7, 15, 203–8, 209, 214, 219–24

class inclusion hierarchies, 8, 270–6, 282–4, 292

classical theory of categories, viii, 29–30, 67, 69, 73, 89–90, 93–9, 175, 288–90, 298–9

cluster models, 67–8, 72, 73

cognitive archeology, 25, 43, 52–8

cognitive models: basis of categories, vii, 4–5, 9–10, 17–22, 66–7, 141–3, 291–306; basis of prototype effects, 64–88, 98–9; idealized, 4, 6, 8, 18–19, 40, 63, 70–1, 119, 288, 292–4, 299–301; in science, 19–20, 298–300; of animal species, 17, 187–91, 291; of "bachelor," 18, 40, 66, 77, 88–9; of cognition itself, 11, 23n, 294; of "hon," 82–7; of "mother," 67–9, 72–5, 293, 300; of superordinate categories 18, 291; *see also* cluster models, image-schematic models, metaphoric models, metonymic models, radial models, theories as bases of categorization

coherence of categories, 25, 26–35, 38–42, 179, 291, 295

collection terms 8–9, 270–6, 282–3

conservation of number, 273

constraints: cognitive and perceptual, 195, 197, 302; ecological, 7, 54–8, 291; on relevance of properties, 28, 30, 33; on theories, 25, 42–50; on word meanings, 8, 256, 258–9, 265–9, 282–5; social, 7, 191–4; *see also* mutual exclusivity

context effects: on memory, 145–6; on typicality ratings, 106–7, 115–19, 131, 299, 300

context-independent properties, 122–4, 126, 133, 136n

convention, as basis of categories, 191–4, 205

core-plus-identification-procedure hypothesis, 88–99, 126, 176

correlated attributes 28–9, 56, 124, 126–7, 202, 230; inadequate to explain category structure, 4, 15, 29, 56, 115–16, 185; relation to theories, 36–7, 124–5, 195; *see also* illusory correlation

cross-cultural findings, 177, 179–80, 189, 258

definitions, variability of, 113, 118

direct perception, 9, 11, 13, 17, 20, 52, 291

distributed knowledge, 164–6; *see also* parallel distributed processing

Down syndrome, 7, 202, 219–24

dreams, 130–1

ecological approach, vii, viii, 2–3, 4, 6, 10, 11, 25, 33, 42, 52–4, 290–1, 300; *see also* environmental factors in